COMMUNICATIVE READING

COMMUNICATIVE

Otis J. Aggertt

Professor, Department of Speech
Indiana State College

Second Edition

READING

Elbert R. Bowen

Professor, Department of Speech and Drama
Central Michigan University

New York: THE MACMILLAN COMPANY

Seventh Printing 1967

Library of Congress catalog card number: 63-14197

The Macmillan Company, New York
Collier-Macmillan Canada, Ltd., Toronto, Ontario

Printed in the United States of America

ACKNOWLEDGMENTS

■ CHAPTER 1

"An Overworked Elocutionist" by Carolyn Wells. Originally this selection appeared in *St. Nicholas.* Reprinted by permission of Maurice O'Connell, heir to the copyright.

"On the Death of a Student Hopelessly Failing My Course" by George Cuomo. Copyright, 1959, *Saturday Review.*

"Gielgud Reading Lear" by Peter Kane Dufault. Copyright, 1959, *Saturday Review.*

■ CHAPTER 2

Quotations from *The Human Comedy.* Copyright, 1943, by William Saroyan. Reprinted by permission of Harcourt, Brace & World, Inc.

Quotations from "The Green Door" and "The Cop and the Anthem" from *The Four Million,* by O. Henry. Copyright, 1906, by Doubleday & Company, Inc.

"A Christmas Carol" from the book *Christmas Songs and Easter Carols* by Phillips Brooks. Published by E. P. Dutton & Co., Inc. and reprinted with their permission.

"The Spires of Oxford" from the book *The Spires of Oxford and Other Poems* by Winifred Letts. Copyright, 1917, by E. P. Dutton & Co., Inc. Renewal, 1945, by Winifred M. Letts. Reprinted by permission of the publishers.

"The Death of the Ball Turret Gunner" from *Little Friend, Little Friend* by Randall Jarrell. Published by The Dial Press. Copyright, 1945, by Randall Jarrell. Reprinted by permission of the author.

■ CHAPTER 3

Quotation from "The Symphony" from *Poems of Sidney Lanier,* published by Charles Scribner's Sons.

Quotation from "The Highwayman" from *Collected Poems, Volume I* by Alfred Noyes. Copyright, 1913, 1941, by Alfred Noyes, published by J. B. Lippincott Company.

The selection "December 7 1924" from *The Autobiography of Will Rogers,* copyright, 1921, 1949, is reprinted by permission of and arrangement with Houghton Mifflin Company, the authorized publishers.

"Christmas Afternoon" from *Inside Benchley* by Robert Benchley. Copyright, 1921, by Harper & Brothers. Copyright, 1949, by Gertrude Benchley. Reprinted by permission of Harper & Brothers.

"The Poetry Reading" by Karl Shapiro. Copyright, 1954. The New Yorker Magazine, Inc.

"A Tonversation with Baby" by Morris Bishop. Reprinted from Spilt Milk, Morris Bishop, ed., by permission of the author.

"End of Summer" by Stanley Kunitz. Copyright, 1958, by Stanley Kunitz. From *Selected Poems, 1928–1958,* by Stanley Kunitz, by permission of Little, Brown & Company.

"The Campus on the Hill" by W. D. Snodgrass. Reprinted from *Heart's Needle* by W. D. Snodgrass, by permission of Alfred A. Knopf, Inc. Copyright, 1958, 1959, by W. D. Snodgrass.

"Loveliest of Trees" by A. E. Housman, from "A Shropshire Lad," Authorized Edition, from *Complete Poems.* Copyright © 1959 by Holt, Rinehart and Winston, Inc. Reprinted by permission of Holt, Rinehart and Winston, Inc.

■ CHAPTER 4

Quotation from "A Sense of Shelter." Reprinted from *Pigeon Feathers and Other Stories* by John Updike, by permission of Alfred A. Knopf, Inc. Copyright, 1960, 1962, by John Updike. "A Sense of Shelter" originally appeared in *The New Yorker.*

Quotation from "University Days" by James Thurber. Copyright, 1933, by James Thurber. Originally published in *The New Yorker.*

"How to Eat Watermelon" by William Allen White. Originally printed in *The New Emporia Gazette.* Reprinted by permission of W. L. White.

The excerpt from "The Baby Party" (Copyright 1925 Hearst International Magazines Company, Inc.; renewal copyright 1953 Frances S. F. Lanahan) is reprinted with the permission of Charles Scribner's Sons from *The Stories of F. Scott Fitzgerald,* edited with an Introduction and Notes by Malcolm Cowley.

■ CHAPTER 5

"The Great Lover" from *The Collected Poems of Rupert Brooke.* Copyright, 1915, by Dodd, Mead & Company. Copyright, 1943, Edward Marsh. Reprinted by permission of Dodd, Mead & Company, Inc.

Lines from "Create Great Peace" from *War and Laughter* by James Oppenheim. Copyright, 1916, by Appleton-Century-Crofts, Inc. Reprinted by permission of the publishers, Appleton-Century-Crofts, Inc.

"The Unknown Citizen" (ANOTHER TIME) W. H. Auden. Copyright, 1940, by W. H. Auden. Reprinted from *The Collected Poetry of W. H. Auden,* by permission of Random House, Inc.

Quotation from *The Forgotten Language* by Erich Fromm. Reprinted by permission of Holt, Rinehart and Winston, Inc.

"Piazza Piece" reprinted from *Selected Poems* by John Crowe Ransom, by permission of Alfred A. Knopf, Inc. Copyright, 1927, 1945, by Alfred A. Knopf, Inc.

"Journey of the Magi" from *Collected Poems 1909–1935* by T. S. Eliot. Copyright, 1936, by Harcourt, Brace and Company, Inc.

"Barter" from *The Collected Poems of Sara Teasdale.* Copyright, 1937, by The Macmillan Company. Reprinted by permission of The Macmillan Company.

Quotation from *Manhattan Transfer* by John Dos Passos. Copyright, 1925, by John Dos Passos. Published by Houghton Mifflin Company.

"Mrs. Merritt" from *Spoon River Anthology.* Copyright, 1914, 1942, 1944, by Edgar Lee Masters. Published by The Macmillan Company. Reprinted by permission of the estate of Edgar Lee Masters.

"A Glass of Beer" from *Collected Poems of James Stephens.* Copyright, 1926, by The Macmillan Company, 1954, by Cynthia Stephens. Reprinted by permission of The Macmillan Company.

Quotation from *Spark of Life* by Erich Maria Remarque. Copyright, 1952, Erich Maria Remarque. Reprinted by permission of the publishers, Appleton-Century-Crofts, Inc.

Quotation from "A Soldier Looks at the Church" by Russell C. Stroup. Copyright, 1944, by *Harper's Magazine.* Reprinted by permission of the author.

Luke 10:3–36, from The Revised Standard Version of the Bible. Copyright, 1952, by the National Council of Churches of Christ in the U. S. A. Reprinted by permission of the copyright owners and Thomas Nelson and Sons.

Psalm 148, from The Revised Standard Version of the Bible. Copyright, 1952, by the

National Council of Churches of Christ in the U. S. A. Reprinted by permission of the copyright owners and Thomas Nelson and Sons.

"The Tree" from *Duo-Tone* by Richard M. Rothman. Copyright, 1952, by The Christopher Publishing House. Reprinted by permission of Richard M. Rothman.

"Take-Off" from *North to the Orient* by Anne Morrow Lindbergh. Copyright, 1935, by Anne Morrow Lindbergh. Reprinted by permission of Harcourt, Brace and Company, Inc.

"Owners and Tenants" from *The Grapes of Wrath* by John Steinbeck. Copyright, 1939, by John Steinbeck. Reprinted by permission of The Viking Press, Inc., New York.

"Sea Chill" from the book *Gaily the Troubador* by Arthur Guiterman. Copyright, 1936, by E. P. Dutton & Co. Reprinted by permission of the publishers.

From *The Wapshot Chronicle* by John Cheever. Copyright, 1954, 1956, 1957, by John Cheever. Reprinted by permission of Harper & Row, Publishers.

The selection from *Raintree County* by Ross Lockridge, Jr., copyright, 1947, 1948, is reprinted by permission of and arrangement with Houghton Mifflin Company, the authorized publishers.

■ CHAPTER 6

"The Creation" from *God's Trombones* by James Weldon Johnson. Copyright, 1927, by The Viking Press, Inc. Reprinted by permission of The Viking Press, Inc., New York.

PP. 35–37 *Here Is New York* by E. B. White. Copyright 1949 by The Curtis Publishing Company. Reprinted by permission of Harper & Row, Publishers.

"The Mountain Whippoorwill" from *Ballads and Poems* by Stephen Vincent Benét. Copyright, 1931, by Stephen Vincent Benét. Copyright renewed ©, 1959, by Rosemary Carr Benét. Reprinted by permission of Holt, Rinehart and Winston, Inc.

"Sunrise" by Samuel Clemens. Reprinted by permission of Harper & Brothers.

From *The Circus of Dr. Lao* by Charles G. Finney. Copyright 1935 by Charles G. Finney. Reprinted by permission of The Viking Press, Inc.

"Poem" from *The Selected Poems of William Carlos Williams.* Copyright, 1949, by William Carlos Williams. Reprinted by permission of New Directions, Publishers.

■ CHAPTER 7

Quotation from "A bird came down the walk" from *Poems by Emily Dickinson* edited by Martha Dickinson Bianchi and Alfred Leete Hampson, Little, Brown & Company.

Quotation from *Van Loon's Geography.* Copyright, 1932, by Hendrik Willem Van Loon, published by Simon and Schuster, Inc.

"Silver" from *Rhymes and Verses* by Walter de la Mare. Copyright, 1947, by Henry Holt and Company, Inc. Reprinted by permission of The Literary Trustees of Walter de la Mare and The Society of Authors as their representative.

"Silence" from *Songs and Satires* by Edgar Lee Masters. Copyright, 1916, by The Macmillan Company, 1944, by Edgar Lee Masters. Reprinted by permission of the estate of Edgar Lee Masters.

Quotation from "The Man He Killed" from *Collected Poems of Thomas Hardy.* Copyright, 1925, 1953, by The Macmillan Company. Reprinted by permission of The Macmillan Company.

Quotation from "The Chromatic Family" by Philip Hamburger. Originally this selection appeared in *The New Yorker Magazine,* September, 1954. Reprinted by permission of The New Yorker Magazine, Inc.

The selection "The Man in the Onion Bed" from John Ciardi, *I Met a Man* by John Ciardi, copyright 1961, is reprinted by permission of and arrangement with Houghton Mifflin Company, the authorized publishers.

"The Red-Haired Man's Wife" by James Stephens. Reprinted with the permission of the publisher from *Collected Poems* by James Stephens. Copyright, 1909, by The Macmillan Company.

"Let Me Live Out My Years" from *Collected Poems* by John G. Neihardt. Copyright, 1926, by The Macmillan Company.

■ Chapter 8

Quotation from *The Adventures of Tom Sawyer* by Mark Twain, published by Harper & Brothers.

"A Noiseless Patient Spider" from *Leaves of Grass,* by Walt Whitman. Copyright, 1924, by Doubleday & Company, Inc.

Quotation from "The Highwayman" from *Collected Poems, Volume I,* by Alfred Noyes. Copyright, 1913, 1941, by Alfred Noyes, published by J. B. Lippincott Company.

"Death Snips Proud Men" from *Smoke and Steel* by Carl Sandburg. Copyright, 1920, by Harcourt, Brace and Company, Inc. Copyright renewed, 1948, by Carl Sandburg.

Quotation from *Guide to Mars* by Patrick Moore. Reprinted with the permission of The Macmillan Company from *Guide to Mars* by Patrick Moore. Copyright, 1956, 1958 by Patrick Moore.

The selection "A Poe-'m of Passion" from *A Bronco Pegasus* by C. F. Lummis, copyright 1928, is reprinted by permission of and arrangement with Houghton Mifflin Company, the authorized publishers.

"O what is that sound" from *The Collected Poetry of W. H. Auden.* Copyright, 1945, by W. H. Auden. Reprinted by permission of Random House, Inc.

Quotation from the book *Clea* by Lawrence Durrell. Copyright, 1960, by Lawrence Durrell. Reprinted by permission of E. P. Dutton & Co., Inc.

"Preludes" from *Collected Poems 1909–1935* by T. S. Eliot. Copyright, 1936, by Harcourt, Brace & World, Inc.

"In My Craft or Sullen Art" from *The Collected Poems of Dylan Thomas.* Copyright, 1952, 1953, by Dylan Thomas. Reprinted by permission of New Directions, Publishers.

"A Good Night" from *The Collected Earlier Poems of William Carlos Williams.* Copyright, 1938, 1951, by William Carlos Williams. Reprinted by permission of New Directions, Publishers.

■ Chapter 9

"Who Loves the Rain" by Frances Shaw. Reprinted by permission of Sylvia Shaw Judson. Copyright, 1914, by *Poetry Magazine.*

"Four Little Foxes" from *Slow Smoke* by Lew Sarett. Copyright, 1925, by Henry Holt and Company, Inc. Copyright, 1953, by Lew Sarett. Reprinted by permission of the publishers.

The selection "The Plaint of the Camel" from *Grimm Tales Made Gay* by Guy Wetmore Carryl, copyright, 1902, is reprinted by permission of and arrangement with Houghton Mifflin Company, the authorized publishers.

"The Little Turtle" from *Collected Poems* by Vachel Lindsay. Copyright, 1923, by The Macmillan Company.

Quotation from *Native Son* by Richard Wright. Copyright, 1940, by Richard Wright. Published by Harper & Brothers.

"The Laughers" from *Selected Poems and Parodies of Louis Untermeyer.* Copyright, 1935, by Harcourt, Brace, and Company, Inc.

"Portrait of a Girl with a Comic Book" from *The Love Letters of Phyllis McGinley* by Phyllis McGinley. Copyright, 1952, by Phyllis McGinley. First appeared in *The New Yorker.* Reprinted by permission of The Viking Press, Inc.

■ Chapter 10

Quotation from *The Other Wise Men* by Henry Van Dyke. Copyright, 1920, by Harper & Brothers. Reprinted by permission of the publishers.

Quotation from *Spark of Life* by Erich Maria Remarque. Copyright, 1952, by Erich Maria Remarque. Reprinted by permission of the publishers, Appleton-Century-Crofts, Inc.

Quotation from "University Days" by James Thurber. Copyright, 1933, by James Thurber. Originally published in *The New Yorker Magazine.*

"The Duck" from *The Face Is Familiar* by Ogden Nash. Copyright, 1936, by Ogden Nash. Reprinted by permission of Little, Brown and Company.

"There Was a Child Went Forth" from *Leaves of Grass* by Walt Whitman. Copyright, 1924, by Doubleday & Company.

"I Saw in Louisiana a Live-Oak Growing" from *Leaves of Grass* by Walt Whitman. Copyright, 1924, by Doubleday & Company.

"Country Club Sunday" from *A Short Walk from the Station* by Phyllis McGinley. Copyright, 1946, by Phyllis McGinley. First appeared in *The New Yorker*. Reprinted by permission of The Viking Press, Inc.

"I Hear America Singing" from *Leaves of Grass* by Walt Whitman. Copyright, 1924, by Doubleday & Company.

"Carol: New Style" from *Tiger Joy* by Stephen Vincent Benét. George H. Doran Company. Copyright, 1925, by Stephen Vincent Benét. Copyright renewed, 1953, by Rosemary Carr Benét. Reprinted by permission of Brandt and Brandt.

"History Repeats Itself" by Samuel Clemens. Reprinted by permission of Harper & Brothers.

"The Lottery" by Shirley Jackson. Copyright, 1948, The New Yorker Magazine, Inc.

■ CHAPTER 11

Lines from "The Man with the Hoe" by Edwin Markham. Copyright, 1899, by Doxey's. Reprinted by permission of Virgil Markham.

"I'm Nobody" from *The Poems of Emily Dickinson*. Copyright, 1924, by Little, Brown and Company.

Lines from *Cyrano de Bergerac* by Edmond Rostand (Brian Hooker translation). Copyright, 1923, by Holt, Rinehart and Winston, Inc. Copyright, 1951, by Doris C. Hooker. Reprinted by permission of Holt, Rinehart and Winston, Inc.

"The Clean Platter" from *Many Long Years Ago* by Ogden Nash. Copyright, 1935, by Ogden Nash. Reprinted by permission of Little, Brown and Company.

"Four Poems" reprinted from *The Collected Poems of Stephen Crane* by Stephen Crane, by permission of Alfred A. Knopf, Inc. Copyright, 1930, by Alfred A. Knopf, Inc.

"A Death in the Stadium" by Robert Nathan. Published in *Scribner's Magazine,* Sept. 1927. Copyright by Robert Nathan.

■ CHAPTER 12

Quotation from *The Caine Mutiny* by Herman Wouk. Copyright, 1951, by Herman Wouk, reprinted by permission of Doubleday & Company, Inc.

Quotation from "The Fight" from *Portrait of the Artist as a Young Dog* by Dylan Thomas. Copyright, 1940, by New Directions, Publishers. Reprinted by permission of New Directions.

"Everyone Sang" from *Collected Poems of Siegfried Sassoon*. Copyright, 1920, by E. P. Dutton & Co., 1948, by Siegfried Sassoon. Reprinted by permission of The Viking Press, Inc., New York.

"Breakfast" from *Battle and Other Poems* by Wilfrid Gibson, published by The Macmillan Company. Reprinted by permission of the author.

The selection "Epistle to Be Left in the Earth" from *Collected Poems* by Archibald Macleish copyright 1952, is reprinted by permission of and arrangement with Houghton Mifflin Company, the authorized publishers.

"hist whist" by E. E. Cummings. Copyright 1923, 1951, by E. E. Cummings. Reprinted from *Poems 1923–1954* by E. E. Cummings by permission of Harcourt, Brace & World, Inc.

"Birches" from *Complete Poems of Robert Frost*. Copyright, 1916, 1921, by Holt, Rinehart and Winston, Inc. Copyright renewed 1944 by Robert Frost. Reprinted by permission of Holt, Rinehart and Winston, Inc.

"The World" from *A Coney Island of the Mind* by Lawrence Ferlinghetti. Copyright, 1955, © 1958, by Lawrence Ferlinghetti. Reprinted by permission of New Directions, Publishers.

"The Express" from *Poems* by Stephen Spender. Copyright, 1934, by The Modern Library, Inc. Reprinted by permission of Random House, Inc.

"Nightmare at Noon" from *Selected Works of Stephen Vincent Benét,* Rinehart & Company. Copyright, 1940, by Stephen Vincent Benét.

"Girl's-Eye View of Relatives (First Lesson)" from *Times Three* by Phyllis McGinley. Copyright © 1959 by Phyllis McGinley. Originally printed in *The New Yorker*. Reprinted by permission of The Viking Press, Inc.

■ CHAPTER 13

Quotation from *Native Son* by Richard Wright. Copyright, 1940, by Richard Wright. Reprinted by permission of Harper & Brothers.

"How to Tell a Major Poet from a Minor Poet" from *Quo Vadimus?* by E. B. White. Copyright, 1930, by E. B. White. Published by Harper & Brothers.

Quotation from "In the Zoo" by Jean Stafford on pages 380–81. Copyright, 1953, The New Yorker Magazine, Inc.

"Island of Fear" by William Sambrot. Copyright © 1958, The Curtis Publishing Company. Reprinted by permission of the author. Reprinted by special permission of The Saturday Evening Post.

■ CHAPTER 14

"Poetry" from *The Collected Poems of Marianne Moore.* Copyright, 1951, by Marianne Moore. Reprinted by permission of The Macmillan Company.

"Prayers of Steel" from *Cornhuskers* by Carl Sandburg. Copyright, 1918, by Henry Holt and Company, Inc. Copyright, 1946, by Carl Sandburg. Reprinted by permission of the publishers.

"The Coin" from *The Collected Poems of Sara Teasdale.* Copyright, 1937, by The Macmillan Company.

"Grass" from *Cornhuskers* by Carl Sandburg. Copyright, 1918, by Henry Holt and Company, Inc. Copyright, 1946, by Carl Sandburg. Reprinted by permission of the publishers.

"End of the Seers' Convention" from *Afternoon of a Pawnbroker and Other Poems.* Copyright, 1943, by Kenneth Fearing. Reprinted by permission of Harcourt, Brace, and Company, Inc.

"Mother to Son" reprinted from *The Dream Keeper* by Langston Hughes, by permission of Alfred A. Knopf, Inc. Copyright, 1932, by Alfred A. Knopf, Inc.

Lines from "Leaves" from *The Collected Poems of Sara Teasdale.* Copyright, 1937, by The Macmillan Company.

Lines from "A Lady" from *Sword, Blades and Poppy Seed* by Amy Lowell. Copyright, 1914, is reprinted by permission of and arrangement with Houghton Mifflin Company, the authorized publishers.

Quotation from "Patterns" from *Men, Women, and Ghosts* by Amy Lowell. Copyright, 1944, is reprinted by permission of and arrangement with Houghton Mifflin Company, the authorized publishers.

"Chill of the Eve" from *Collected Poems* by James Stephens. Copyright, 1926, by The Macmillan Company, 1954, by Cynthia Stephens. Reprinted by permission of The Macmillan Company.

"A Word" from *The Complete Poems of Emily Dickinson.* Copyright, 1929, by Little, Brown and Company.

"Stopping by Woods on a Snowy Evening" from *Complete Poems of Robert Frost.* Copyright, 1923, by Holt, Rinehart and Winston, Inc. Copyright renewed 1951 by Robert Frost. Reprinted by permission of Holt, Rinehart and Winston, Inc.

"God's World" from *Collected Poems* by Edna St. Vincent Millay. Copyright, 1913, by Harper & Brothers, 1940, by Edna St. Vincent Millay. Reprinted by permission of Norman Millay-Ellis.

"The Secret Heart" from *Collected Poems of Robert P. Tristram Coffin.* Copyright, 1939, by The Macmillan Company.

"Deacon Taylor" from *Spoon River Anthology.* Copyright, 1914, 1942, 1944, by Edgar Lee Masters. Published by The Macmillan Company. Reprinted by permission of the estate of Edgar Lee Masters.

"Anne Rutledge" from *Spoon River Anthology.* Copyright, 1914, 1942, 1944, by Edgar Lee Masters. Published by The Macmillan Company. Reprinted by permission of the estate of Edgar Lee Masters.

"Lucinda Matlock" from *Spoon River Anthology.* Copyright, 1914, 1942, 1944, by Edgar Lee Masters. Published by The Macmillan Company. Reprinted by permission of the estate of Edgar Lee Masters.

"Carl Hamblin" from *Spoon River Anthology.* Copyright, 1914, 1942, 1944, by Edgar

Lee Masters. Published by The Macmillan Company. Reprinted by permission of the estate of Edgar Lee Masters.

"Silas Dement" from *Spoon River Anthology*. Copyright, 1914, 1942, 1944, by Edgar Lee Masters. Published by The Macmillan Company. Reprinted by permission of the estate of Edgar Lee Masters.

"Stephen Spalding" from *The New Spoon River* by Edgar Lee Masters. Copyright, 1924, by Liveright Publishing Corporation. Reprinted by permission of the Liveright Publishing Corporation and the estate of Edgar Lee Masters.

"Schroeder the Fisherman" from *Spoon River Anthology*. Copyright, 1914, 1942, 1944, by Edgar Lee Masters. Published by The Macmillan Company. Reprinted by permission of the estate of Edgar Lee Masters.

"Catherine Ogg" from *The New Spoon River* by Edgar Lee Masters. Copyright, 1924, by Liveright Publishing Corporation. Reprinted by permission of the Liveright Publishing Corporation and the estate of Edgar Lee Masters.

"Fiddler Jones" from *Spoon River Anthology*. Copyright, 1914, 1942, 1944, by Edgar Lee Masters. Published by The Macmillan Company. Reprinted by permission of the estate of Edgar Lee Masters.

"Harry Wilmans" from *Spoon River Anthology*. Copyright, 1914, 1942, 1944, by Edgar Lee Masters. Published by The Macmillan Company. Reprinted by permission of the estate of Edgar Lee Masters.

"To a Contemporary Bunkshooter" from *Chicago Poems* by Carl Sandburg. Copyright, 1916, by Henry Holt and Company, Inc. Copyright, 1944, by Carl Sandburg. Reprinted by permission of the publishers.

"Chicago" from *Chicago Poems* by Carl Sandburg. Copyright, 1916, by Henry Holt and Company, Inc. Copyright, 1944, by Carl Sandburg. Reprinted by permission of the publishers.

"Buttons" from *Chicago Poems* by Carl Sandburg. Copyright, 1916, by Henry Holt and Company, Inc. Copyright, 1944, by Carl Sandburg. Reprinted by permission of the publishers.

"Mamie" from *Chicago Poems* by Carl Sandburg. Copyright, 1916, by Henry Holt and Company, Inc. Copyright, 1944, by Carl Sandburg. Reprinted by permission of the publishers.

"General William Booth Enters into Heaven" from *Collected Poems* by Vachel Lindsay. Copyright, 1923, by The Macmillan Company.

"Simon Legree" from *Collected Poems* by Vachel Lindsay. Copyright, 1923, by The Macmillan Company.

Lines from "Sew the Flags Together" from *Collected Poems* by Vachel Lindsay. Copyright, 1923, by The Macmillan Company.

"A Net to Snare the Moonlight" from *Collected Poems* by Vachel Lindsay. Copyright, 1923, by The Macmillan Company.

Part I of "The Congo" from *Collected Poems* by Vachel Lindsay. Copyright, 1923, by The Macmillan Company.

■ CHAPTER 15

Quotation from *Tiger at the Gates* by Jean Giraudoux, translated by Christopher Fry. Copyright, 1955, by Christopher Fry and reprinted by permission of Oxford University Press, Inc.

PREFACE

The growing enthusiasm for interpretative reading is one of the heartening aspects of the generally increased interest in the arts of oral communication. This enthusiasm emphasizes the importance of oral interpretation, the oldest form of the speech arts and the original means by which literary experience was communicated. Man has once again learned that the values of most good literature are best appreciated when that literature is communicated orally.

In our century two major shifts of emphasis in the teaching of oral interpretation have occurred. The first was away from the elocutionist's emphasis upon vocal and bodily display to an emphasis upon content alone—with a consequent belief in the invalidity of most techniques of expression. The second shift has been to a modern belief that techniques derived from meaning do achieve desired audience responses to literature. This concept is basic to our text.

We have employed the commonly accepted procedure for the study of interpretative reading: namely that the reader must first find the meaning of literature and then develop the techniques for communicating that meaning. Preliminary to the study of finding the meaning of a selection are the chapters dealing with the principles of the art form and the discovery of suitable literary materials. Therefore, we think that Parts I, II, and III of the text should be used in the order provided. However, opportunities exist for flexibility in the employment of the chapters within the individual parts, in the employment of exercises and readings, and in supplementing instruction with material from Parts IV and V. We have intended this text for a beginning college course in interpretative reading, but the detailed treatment in Parts I through IV and the specialized materials in Part V are suitable for more advanced study also.

Numerous illustrative quotations and exercises will guide the student to creative experiences with literature. We think that students do their best work when skillfully guided in choosing their own selections for reading. Therefore, we have provided a varied and extensive body of literature closely associated with specific exercises and selected to motivate interest, but we have had no intention of compiling a comprehensive anthology. Teachers differ in their choices of selections for instructional purposes. Consequently, we have provided many old favorites as well as a generous amount of new quoted material.

The reader's enjoyment of oral interpretation results from his thorough understanding and appreciation of a literary selection; from the mastery of his own thoughts, feelings, body, and voice in effective communication; and from the achievement of the desired audience response. We have tried to write a book which will assist the teacher in meeting the student at his own level and in guiding him to intelligent and pleasurable oral reading experiences.

Modern interpretative theory and practice have evolved from the contributions of many writers and teachers of oral interpretation, speech in general, dramatics, literary criticism, psychology, and aesthetics. We are deeply indebted to all of them, but we shall not try to list their names. References to some of them appear in suggested readings throughout the text.

We are also appreciative of the cooperation of the copyright owners who have generously given their permission for the inclusion of quoted materials.

■ PREFACE TO THE SECOND EDITION

We are grateful to our professional colleagues throughout the country who have used the first edition of this book in sufficient numbers to justify the second edition. We have, therefore, retained the original philosophy and approach for the teaching of the beginning course in interpretative reading. The changes which we have made are those of implementation.

In an effort to teach more effectively, we have modified the organization, revised sections of chapters, written new discussions of matters not covered in the first edition, and brought numerous materials up-to-date. In addition, we have provided many new literary selections, hoping thus to keep up with the dynamic advance of modern literature and to furnish the student with more interesting and illustrative examples for oral interpretation. These modifications have been made in order that training in communicative reading will be more successful.

With the improvement in content, has appropriately come a new and more attractive format, for which we thank our publisher.

Otis J. Aggertt
Elbert R. Bowen

CONTENTS

PART I. EXPLORING INTERPRETATIVE READING

PART II. FINDING THE MEANING

PART III. EXPRESSING THE MEANING

PART IV. INTENSIFYING THE MEANING

PART V. INTERPRETING THE BASIC FORMS OF LITERATURE

Part I

EXPLORING INTERPRETATIVE READING

1

■ WHAT IS INTERPRETATIVE READING?

We are all aware of the importance of the spoken word in the traffic of practical life, but we should not overlook its significance as a vital aspect of our cultural-aesthetic life, as well. In addition to the speaker and actor, as communicators of vicarious experience, we can find a third speech artist: the interpretative reader. He has been a welcome guest for centuries. Originally, he was the poet, singing his own verses, or the wandering storyteller, communicating literary experiences long before books were printed, or even written. After man learned to read and, finally, to print, he still liked to listen to an effective interpreter weave a spell with his expressive voice and vibrant personality, making a story or poem *live*. In recent years we have seen a rebirth in this form of literary communication. In spite of the almost overwhelming emphasis on physical activity in our culture, authors, actors, and others are reading to us on the platform, through records, and even on television! Their audiences, though comparatively small by mass media standards, listen enthusiastically.

At a relatively simple level, interpretative reading is practiced when the parent or baby-sitter reads a bedtime story. At a much more complex level, it occurs when the accomplished reader communicates the intricate mental and emotional significances of such a passage as:

> Good friends, sweet friends, let me not stir you up
> To such a sudden flood of mutiny.
> They that have done this deed are honourable:
> What private griefs they have, alas, I know not,
> That made them do it: they are wise and honourable,
> And will, no doubt, with reasons answer you.
> I come not, friends, to steal away your hearts:
> I am no orator, as Brutus is;
> But, as you know me all, a plain blunt man,
> That love my friend; and that they know full well
> That gave me public leave to speak of him:
> For I have neither wit, nor words, nor worth,
> Action, nor utterance, nor the power of speech,
> To stir men's blood: I only speak right on;
> I tell you that which you yourselves do know;
> Show you sweet Caesar's wounds, poor poor dumb mouths,
> And bid them speak for me: but were I Brutus,
> And Brutus Antony, there were an Antony
> Would ruffle up your spirits and put a tongue
> In every wound of Caesar that should move
> The stones of Rome to rise and mutiny.
>
> —SHAKESPEARE, *Julius Caesar*

The principles in this textbook should help you learn to read aloud well, regardless of the nature of the reading material. Most of the principles discussed here apply to all forms of oral reading. Some of them go beyond the problems in reading simple expository materials and deal with the complex art of interpreting the best of prose as well as poetic and dramatic literature to a public audience. The authors hope that you will not only achieve some skill in the simple forms of oral reading but will also learn to enjoy the *art* of interpretative reading, both as a reader and as a listener.

The art of interpretative reading concerns itself with more than the mere translation of written words into sounds. It concerns itself with the communication of human *experience*. Consider, for example, the functions of the novelist, poet, painter, sculptor, musician, actor—in fact, any artist—and you will find that all artists endeavor to communicate human experience to others. Experience is translatable in terms of ideas and feelings, and it is these that artistic expression communicates from the artist to the viewer or hearer.

The simplest definition of interpretative reading would be the broad statement that it is "reading aloud." This would account for any instance in which the reader changes written symbols into oral symbols. We usually think of him doing this for the benefit of an audience, but we should not ignore the value of the reader reading aloud for his own understanding and appreciation. Most of us know that an aid to the study of difficult material is to read it aloud, suddenly discovering meanings not apparent in the silent, passive contemplation of the symbols on the page. Furthermore, since a part of the value of good literature, especially poetry and drama, lies in the *speech* implicit in the symbols, reading aloud helps us to participate physically, hence more completely, in the author's language. Thus, without really being at all farfetched, we can assert that a reader at times can and should read aloud to himself. Therefore, although we speak of interpretative reading as being a form of communication, always keep in mind that we communicate with ourselves as well as with others when we read aloud.

We can be more precise in constructing a definition of interpretative reading. Let us say, for the time being, that it is "the oral communication of ideas and feelings from the printed page to an audience, so that the listeners will understand the ideas and will experience the feelings."

The definition of interpretative reading is not yet complete, but it will be with the addition of three concepts. The first concept is that the interpreter communicates both audibly and visibly: he appeals to both the ears and the eyes of his listeners. Not only does he utter meaningful sounds, but he also uses his entire visible personality in meaningful ways.

The second concept pertains to the ideas and feelings that we have said are obtained from the printed page. Of course, ideas and feelings are not actually on the page: they exist only inside *human beings*. What is found on the printed page are words and punctuation marks so arranged as to attempt to arouse within the reader ideas and feelings the same as or similar to those existing within the writer. Words are not actualities, but only symbols. Since the writer cannot transport what he thinks from his brain to another, and since symbols are relatively poor transmitters of such intangibles, the reader really perceives only what he *thinks* the writer is saying. The oral interpreter therefore tries to communicate the author's ideas as he himself understands them.

The third and last concept needed to complete our definition of interpretative reading concerns appreciation. One of the goals of reading to others is the contagious transference of appreciation from reader to listener. For example, you may enjoy reading a certain story; therefore you wish to share it with someone else. This desire to share appreciation is quite natural to us. We see a movie and like it; therefore we do our best to get our friends to see it, too. We'll even see it a second time in order to get them to go! We like a certain phonograph record; therefore we insist that our friends listen to it. If they do not appreciate it, we are disappointed. Likewise, if we enjoy a story by O. Henry or Damon Runyon, or a poem by Dorothy Parker or Robert Frost, or a play by Eugene O'Neill or Shakespeare, we wish to share it with others; we have a desire to communicate. And we know that we not only must communicate the ideas and feelings suggested to us by the author's symbols, but we also have the responsibility of making our listeners appreciate the way in which the author has expressed himself.

If we will now put the above concepts together properly, we shall have a fairly complete definition of interpretative reading. It is "the communication of the reader's impression of the author's ideas and feelings to the eyes and ears of an audience, so that the audience understands the ideas, experiences the feelings, and appreciates the author's literary skill."

INTERPRETATIVE READERS IN ACTION

Perhaps a few word pictures of student readers in action will serve to describe further the nature of interpretative reading.

Bob became interested in literature about life in the military services, particularly the army, because he expected to be drafted in the near future. He read James Jones's best-selling novel *From Here to Eternity* and was impressed by the author's realistic treatment of the American soldier. This reading stimulated Bob to do some research in his major field of interest: dramatic literature. He decided to find the first ultra-realistic war play. After some searching and study, he discovered the play to be *What Price Glory?* by Maxwell Anderson and Laurence Stallings. Bob planned to read a scene from that play to his class. His purposes were to entertain his audience and to communicate the playwrights' realistic yet admiring picture of the professional American soldier during World War I. He selected a suitable scene from the play, studied it thoroughly, and practiced reading it, perhaps when alone and perhaps also to his roommates. When the time came for him to read in class, Bob walked to the front of the room carrying the playbook. He paused to describe his interest in war literature and how he happened to read *What Price Glory?* He explained that the authors had used some strong language in the play, not to shock or attract attention, but to reproduce the true speech of the soldier. Then he read the scene from the book, using enough suggestion of facial and bodily expression and vocal change to enable the audience to keep each character separate in its mind. When he finished, he had accomplished his purpose, for the audience appreciated the honesty and sincerity of the authors' writing, enjoyed the humor of the scene, and acknowledged having received a more profound understanding of the soldier.

Mary Ellen found herself excited by the writing of Stephen Vincent Benét. Upon reading some accounts of Benét's life and philosophy, she found that his and her ideas on democracy coincided. She was also impressed by his patriotism. One day in a class in interpretative reading, she read Benét's poem "Nightmare at Noon," and she succeeded in communicating the poet's love for America coupled with his fear of attack by the enemies of democracy. Reading from the book, yet knowing her material well enough to look at her audience, Mary Ellen made Benét's ideas and emotions very vivid to her listeners.

Duane had read a short firsthand account of a tiger hunt. He thought the class would enjoy the story, for it was one of intense adventure and suspense. When he read it aloud, his classmates and instructor visualized the scenes of the hunting expedition and especially the climactic episode in which the ferocious tiger was killed.

From these examples we can see that all three student readers put something of themselves into their reading; in other words, they participated in the experiences suggested by the author's symbols. All three were strongly motivated to read what they did: they had a desire to communicate. All were apparently successful in enlisting the cooperative attention of their audiences and in getting their audiences to think and feel as they believed their authors intended. All three readers and all three audiences enjoyed the experience.

WHAT INTERPRETATIVE READING IS NOT

Interpretative reading is a form of communication, not an exhibition of skill. Not so many years ago the "art" of elocution led public reading into disrepute simply because the techniques of presentation, such as beautiful gestures and pure vocal tones, became more important to the performer than the content of the literature he was reading. Audiences were impressed with the accomplishments of the reader rather than with the significance or beauty of his selection. The following bit of light verse aptly tells the story:

AN OVERWORKED ELOCUTIONIST

CAROLYN WELLS

Once there was a little boy whose name was Robert Reese;
And every Friday afternoon he had to speak a piece.
So many poems thus he learned, that soon he had a store
Of recitations in his head and still kept learning more.

And now this is what happened: He was called upon one week
And totally forgot the piece he was about to speak.
His brain he cudgeled. Not a word remained within his head!
And so he spoke at random, and this is what he said:

"My beautiful, my beautiful, who standest proudly by,
It was the schooner Hesperus—the breaking waves dashed high!
Why is this Forum crowded? What means this stir in Rome?
Under a spreading chestnut tree, there is no place like home!

When freedom from her mountain height cried, 'Twinkle, little star,'
Shoot if you must this old gray head, King Henry of Navarre!
Roll on, thou deep and dark blue castled crag of Drachenfels,
My name is Norval, on the Grampian Hills, ring out, wild bells!

If you're waking, call me early, to be or not to be,
The curfew must not ring tonight! Oh, woodman, spare that tree!
Charge, Chester, charge! On, Stanley, on! and let who will be clever!
The boy stood on the burning deck, but I go on forever!"

His elocution was superb, his voice and gestures fine;
His schoolmates all applauded as he finished the last line.
"I see it doesn't matter," Robert thought, "what words I say,
So long as I declaim with oratorical display."

Elocutionary recitation has almost disappeared because we now value sincerity and naturalness in public performance. Just as we laugh at the artificial gestures of actors in old movies, we refuse to take seriously the reader who overdoes his manner and forgets his message. Our tastes today favor some restraint.

Interpretative reading is also not acting. Although these two forms of speech art are close cousins, since they both interpret literature, they do possess distinguishable differences. Both the reader and the actor use impersonation—the assumption of the traits of another personality. The actor uses complete impersonation, for he gives the impression of actually being the character he portrays. The reader, on the other hand, uses impersonation only when trying to suggest a character and then uses only selected elements of characterization. The actor attempts to make the audience see the character in himself; the reader attempts to make his listeners see the character in their own imaginations.

The question arises: "How much impersonation does the interpretative reader use?" The answer to this question is far more important to the reader than the application of the age-old labels of "acting" and "reading." To answer it, however, we must ask and try to answer two other questions: "How much impersonation *can* a given reader use?" and "How much impersonation *should* he use in a given situation?"

How much he *can* use depends on the reader's own personality. Some persons do not impersonate with ease; they just never "perform" in public. Others glory in impersonation—they have animated personalities; they can tell stories or jokes with vividness; and they are relatively uninhibited in social situations. (In extreme forms, they are exhibitionists, the life-of-the-party type.) It is obvious, is it not, that the latter type of person will tend to use more impersonation when reading orally to an audience? Remember, though, that you are not unalterably limited by your present personality; you can learn to be more dynamic in your speaking; you can learn to read more vividly than you have read before; you can develop the ability to be animated and colorful in oral reading. Read with a strong desire to communicate literary experience. Provide whatever audible and visible cues your audience needs for a lively visualization.

How much impersonation the reader *should* use is determined by three factors: the type of literature, the composition of the audience, and the aesthetic distance inherent in the reading situation.

Some literary selections will permit, even demand, considerable impersonation; other forms will permit none. For example, humorous materials invariably permit more impersonation than serious ones; the reader can slice the ham a bit thicker when he has his audience laughing. It should be very clear that dramatic materials from plays or fiction, where characters speak, will profit from impersonative assistance to suggestion. On the other hand, expository materials, lyric poetry, and simple narration practically devoid of personality usually offer little or no raw material for impersonation.

Some audiences will delight in lively, animated impersonative techniques by the reader whereas others will enjoy only the most restrained forms of presentation. The more sophisticated, or culturally aware, an audience is, the more subtle and restrained it prefers its art and entertainment. Younger listeners and audiences not highly educated seem to appreciate impersonative help from the reader.

Some reading situations will provide better opportunities for impersonation than will others. Generally speaking, the reader will increase his degree of impersonation when reading in a large room or to a large audience, or when using a stage, platform, reading stand, or lighting effects because these factors all increase what we call *aesthetic distance*. This term refers to the psychic separation needed between a work of art and the observer in order for appreciation of the work to take place. A few simple examples should explain aesthetic distance. If you wish to appreciate the beauty of a great bridge or huge building, you cannot do it by standing under the bridge or on the sidewalk directly in front of the building. You must move away some considerable distance in order to experience the object as an artistic whole. Likewise, in an art gallery you must stand back to appreciate a fine painting. (You may move closer to study the brush strokes, but that is a study of technique, not artistic participation.) In the theatre most persons like to sit back at least a few rows from the stage. Being too close can often ruin the effect of the scene or, in the case of highly dramatic action, actually be uncomfortable.

The theatre almost always provides greater aesthetic distance than does the interpretative reading platform, and in this difference lie some of the explanations of the dissimilarity between the arts of the actor and the interpretative reader. The greater psychic separation between actor and audience in the theatre is provided by such elements as: the greater physical distance between stage and audience, the raised level of the stage, the presence of the proscenium arch and, sometimes, footlights, the contrast between the lighted stage and the darkened auditorium, the use of properties, scenery, and the actor's make-up and costumes: in short, by the simulation of a make-believe world distinctly separate from the real world of the auditorium in which the audience sits. The actor is sufficiently removed from his audience to lose his own identity and to be accepted as the character he portrays. Therefore, he can use whatever visible and audible manners are appropriate to the character.

The interpretative reader, on the other hand, usually finds himself in an intimate situation reading to a small audience in a small room. (At times he will even be reading directly to the eyes of specific individuals.) He is essentially a member of his own audience who, for practical purposes, holds the book and reads aloud; his attitude is one of: "Since we can't all read this together, let me read it to you." Lacking all the actor's exterior means of creating a make-believe world, he can never pretend to be another person; the audience accepts him only as himself. He can now use impersonation only as an aid to imaginative suggestion, not as a means for portrayal. Therefore, the reader can use only those visible and audible techniques which seem appropriate to himself. Whereas the theatre audience will accept the actor's scene of high emotionalism as a genuine aspect of a fictional event, the reader's audience, being psychologically closer to him and therefore more aware of his techniques, prefers to imagine the scene for itself, if he will only provide the necessary stimuli.

Although students of acting and interpretative reading should be aware of the theoretical distinctions between the arts, they should not permit the theory to ruin the practice. Do not be a dull reader in order to avoid "acting." The way to be an effective reader is not to try to avoid a label but to make an intelligent analysis of the factors governing effective reading. Develop the ability to use impersonation, then analyze your literature, your audience, and the aesthetic distance inherent in a reading situation, in order to use an effective degree of impersonation.

WHY SHOULD I STUDY INTERPRETATIVE READING?

"But I don't want to be a professional oral reader!" you say. Let us be realistic. Although most students will never read literary programs publicly, you as an individual will probably read aloud many times during your lifetime. As a parent you will read stories to your children at home. If you are to be a teacher, the ability to read aloud well is indispensable. If you are to be a minister, you will wish to avoid the pitiful reading of the Scriptures so common in today's churches. If you are to be a lawyer, a doctor, an engineer, a home economist, a social worker, a politician, for example, you will find yourself before other people with a report, an article, a written appeal, or even a speech to read aloud. Observe the people around you in everyday life. Notice how many occasions demand effective communication in the reading situation. Also notice how often this form of communication is bungled by persons who are most uncomfortable while reading to others.

Aside from the value of mastering a different form of oral communication, there are other justifications for your study and practice. You should certainly improve your speaking skills, both public and private, for the basic techniques of expression, visible and audible, of all forms of oral communication, are the same. Practice in interpretative reading should sharpen your diction, improve your voice, facilitate your use of facial expression and gesture, and improve your poise and confidence. Most of all, such study will help you develop the ability to think on your feet under stress. The person who can learn to concentrate on ideas while speaking is in possession of an immeasurable asset. Thus, oral reading is good exercise for the improvement of speaking in general.

Practice in interpretative reading is excellent training for radio, television, and the theatre. In addition to developing the ability to read lines with facility and meaning, the student actor sharpens his sensitivity to character, to emotion, and to fine literature. He learns how to study literature, how to derive ideas and feelings from it, and how to communicate those ideas and feelings by means of his voice and his visible personality. If all students of dramatics, radio, and television classes could study interpretative reading early in their training, much of the present work of the teachers of those fields would be done, and they would have much more time to train their students in such specialized techniques as the art of pantomime, and microphone and camera procedures.

Interpretative reading is also a form of communication which should be mastered by every public speaker. Public officials and politicians often find that they must read their speeches in order to speak precisely without fear of misinterpretation. They find that to meet the requirements of time, particularly for radio and television appearances, they must read their speeches from manuscript. Their reading must, of course, be convincing. Furthermore, it must have the quality of spontaneity. Even the extemporaneous speaker must be able to read authoritative and statistical evidence with clarity and communicative persuasiveness. Thus, the public speaker can profit from a study of interpretative reading.

Even more important to the student, however, are certain personal values. One of the most important is training in the means of enriching our own lives. The person who has no appreciation of the arts, who cannot listen attentively to a piece of good music, who cannot sit comfortably with a good book, who can see nothing meaningful in a great painting, nor anything significant in a well-designed building, is an unfortunate individual, indeed. You, who are studying interpretative reading, are in an admirable position to develop or increase your own responsiveness to—hence appreciation of—good prose, poetry, and drama. The goal of this study is somewhat different from that of a survey course in literature. The emphasis is upon savoring good writing rather than upon consuming volumes of literature. Study here is intensive rather than extensive. The oral reader tries to increase his appreciation and then to communicate that appreciation to others. Experience in interpretative reading should be regarded as an ideal liberal arts study because it offers a fusion of literature and communication. Literature has held the position of prime emphasis in liberal education throughout its history; effective communication has been an attribute of the effective individual since man began; and the oral communication of literary content even antedates written literature itself.

Perhaps the most important reason for studying interpretative reading is the training the student receives in finding the meaning on the printed page. Because today we derive our information from so many sources other than the printed page, such as radio, television, films, and travel, we are frequently ill-equipped to cope with fine distinctions of meaning intended by a writer. Training in interpretative reading will help us learn how to determine what an author says in print, for we must understand what we read before we can read it intelligently to an audience.

While considering the values of studying interpretative reading, we should consider briefly why we do read. Reading is a worthwhile activity for several reasons.

We read to understand ourselves. Life can be not only difficult but perplexing as well. If we read good literature, written by persons who can interpret life, we often find solutions to our own problems through understanding other persons, fictional or real. In a good novel, you perhaps have found a hero somewhat like yourself. You understood him, felt for him, suffered with him, rejoiced at the solution of his difficulties, and somehow felt better after you laid the book aside. You may have been disturbed rather than pleased with the novel, but that disturbance may have brought you satisfying insights into life.

We read to get away from ourselves—for escape. We find that it is occasionally good—even necessary!—to get away from our own troubled existence merely for the purpose of escaping; hence the popularity of motion pictures, stage plays, radio and television programs, and exciting books. Perhaps you have read accounts of adventure. Although you may be a person who has "never been anywhere or done anything," the authors took you all over the world: climbing mountains, exploring jungles, and sailing the high seas. Such escape, taken in reasonable doses, is healthful. We thus read to enlarge our existence through experiencing secondhand the adventures others have but which are far removed from our own lives. We read, therefore, to participate in experiences we might otherwise never have. The range of human experience is far too great for any one life to encompass. Most of us lead rather narrow, sheltered lives, but we need to know how other types of persons think and feel. We may never climb a mountain, but it is good for us to climb one vicariously, not only for the secondhand experience but also to understand the person whose life mission seems to be the reaching of places where most of us will never go.

We read for the pleasure of experiencing beauty. Literature at its best is an art, and one of the functions of art is to communicate beauty. What is beauty? We are privileged to choose from the hundreds of definitions debated by the philosophers. To some, beauty is found in what gives pleasure to the senses: attractive sights, sounds, smells. To appreciate a writer's skill in using words in a way which delights us constitutes one value of reading.

Beauty is often given a deeper significance than mere pleasurable sensation, however. John Keats made the poetic observation that "Beauty is truth, truth beauty. . . ." Some persons believe that beauty in nature is a representation of spiritual truth, that beauty in a work of art is also a representation of truth in nature, or truth in man, or truth in spirit. If we accept the idea that the artist can communicate spiritual truth, we find an additional value in reading beyond sensation. We find that we are intellectually and emotionally awakened by the great writer.

To learn to appreciate good writing is to learn to appreciate the effective expressions of sensitive and articulate men who can experience and communicate ideas and feelings which most of us cannot express. To learn to read this literature aloud effectively is to bring these same experiences to others. To learn to read to others is to have the pleasure of eating a good meal with friends at the table rather than to eat alone.

Summary

Interpretative reading is the communication of the reader's impression of the author's ideas and feelings to the eyes and ears of an audience, so that the audience understands the ideas, experiences the feelings, and appreciates the author's literary skill. We must constantly keep in mind that interpretative reading is a form of communication, not an exhibition of speaking skills. It is suggestive in nature rather than portraitive. In other words, the reader always maintains his own identity and never attempts to "become" a fictitious character. Interpretative reading is thus different from acting. There are many reasons for studying interpretative reading: to learn to read aloud; to improve speaking skills; to learn techniques useful in public speaking, or on the stage, radio, or television; to learn how to find the meaning in literature; to develop or increase an appreciation for good literature; and to learn how to share literary experience with others.

Exercises

1. Write a short essay describing the times you have read aloud during the past two or three years. If you have taken part in interpretative or dramatic reading contests, you will have much to say about your experiences. If you have not participated in reading contests, you may feel that your experience is too limited for this exercise, but you have probably read more often than you realize. Describe the instances when you have read from a textbook in the classroom, from a storybook to a child, from a newspaper or magazine to friends or relatives, etc. Were you comfortable in this form of communication? Were you successful in communicating meaning, feeling, or appreciation?

2. Think over your past teachers and instructors. Which ones read aloud well? In what ways were some good readers? Some poor?

3. Consider the political speakers you have heard on the radio or seen and heard on television or in person. Which ones were persuasive? Which were not? Can you determine why? Were not most of them reading their speeches? Were not some of them actually reading "ghost-written" speeches? Which ones read effectively? Which were thinking as they read? Which ones communicated to *you?*

4. Find a paragraph in a magazine, newspaper, or book which contains primarily ideas alone, with relatively little emotional coloring. Study it and get a firm grasp of the ideas involved. Try communicating these ideas to a listener.

5. Find a paragraph in a story or novel which contains feelings which stir you. Study it and practice reading it aloud. Then read it to the class with the goal of making your listeners feel as you feel.

6. Find a paragraph or short piece of writing which you enjoy thoroughly. Read it so well that your listeners like it, too. Study and practice before you attempt any reading to others!

7. Prepare for a class discussion on the relative merits of radio, tele-

vision, theatre, movies, stage, and platform as media for speech and dramatic presentation. What are the advantages of each? What are the disadvantages?

8. Write about your experience in reading silently a thrilling adventure story which helped you escape your own life for a few precious hours.

9. Write about your experience in reading a story which seemed to help you better understand yourself.

10. Write about your experience in reading a fictional character portrayal which helped you understand or appreciate a type of person quite different from yourself.

11. Prepare to read in class a literary selection, of any type, which demonstrates the great need for a liberal education in today's civilization.

12. Bring to class a piece of writing which expertly expresses ideas or feelings which seem "true" to you. For example, find a paragraph which seems to you to express a fundamental "truth," which makes you say to yourself: "I've always felt that, but I've never put it into words!" The author of the following quotation seems to have made a sound observation of a truth about some of today's students:

ON THE DEATH OF A STUDENT HOPELESSLY FAILING MY COURSE

GEORGE CUOMO

He died the day before the last exam,
Leaving parents a lifetime of saying
"He could have made it, poor boy!" Poor boy, he
Could not. How little he could do in life!
He lacked whole galaxies of talents, lacked
Quickness of hand or foot or eye or mind,
Lacked will and ambition, lacked height and strength,
Lacked even hope, lacked means of being hurt.
He could swim well, he told me, and tried out,
And did not make the team, and did not mind.
Failure themed his small life, comforting him.
He died racing a fire-red sports car,
Soaring from the mountain roadway to spread
A giant arc across the still night sky.

13. Find in this textbook a literary selection which you enjoy reading. Begin studying it now with the intention of reading it to your class in the near future.

14. Using one of the following poems, each of which is quoted in this book, demonstrate two distinctly different modes of presenting it: suggestion

of character and portrayal of character. Discuss with your instructor and the class the relative effectiveness of the presentations.

"The Creation" by James Weldon Johnson
"Jim Bludso" by John Hay
"My Last Duchess" by Robert Browning

15. Make a list of ten selections quoted in this book which might permit a considerable degree of impersonation when read by some readers to some audiences.

16. Make a list of ten selections quoted in this book which will not permit any impersonative treatment by the reader.

17. Compare the effectiveness of the reader described in the following poem with the one described in "The Poetry Reading" on pages 53–54. Obviously, the two performers are quite different personalities, using quite different techniques, and being quite different in effectiveness. Write an analysis of each performance.

GIELGUD READING LEAR

PETER KANE DUFAULT

He comes on with a keening moan
as if all stops upon his pipe
but the last falsetto vent
were choked by grief,
and with poor grasping-empty
lingering-loosening hands delineates
dead Cordelia . . . What is she
to him that he should weep for her?—A corpse of air.
And no more there (stage left)
than say at rear right of the mezzanine
or lobby, equally empty, or
the street outside, or anywhere-
under-the-moon vacant. Yet he weeps for her,
with seeming-helpless hands conducts
a whole mighty orchestra of eyes
to weep for her . . . Something lies there—
Cordelia, Hecuba, the abstract
and distillate of loss—an element
invisible, but as real to character
as waves to fish or fire to salamanders?
He cannot face it but the blast
contorts his features to a mask

of Heracles gone mad or Oedipus . . .
Gielgud, you take the wind
out of our question: Not
"Why does he weep?" but, "Why—
since we're all fathers, sons,
daughters, to lose or to be lost—why
are we tonight only come to tears?"

Suggested Readings

Bowen, Elbert R. "The General Education Approach to Interpretative Reading," *Central States Speech Journal* (Autumn 1958), 33–6.

Dolman, John, Jr. *The Art of Play Production.* (Revised edition) New York: Harper, 1946, Chapter III, "The Principle of Aesthetic Distance."

Grimes, Wilma H., and Alethea Smith Mattingly. *Interpretation: Writer, Reader, Audience.* Belmont, Cal.: Wadsworth Publishing Co., 1961, Chapter II, "The Literary Object."

Harrington, Elbert W. "The Role of Speech in Liberal Education," *Quarterly Journal of Speech* (October 1955), 219–22.

Marshman, John T. "Art Approach to Reading Aloud," *Quarterly Journal of Speech* (February 1951), 35–40.

Ness, Ordean G. "The Value of Oral Interpretation to the Student in General Speech," *The Speech Teacher* (September 1956), 209–13.

Pooley, Robert C. "The English Teacher's Preparation in Speech," *The Speech Teacher* (September 1956), 186–93.

Rarig, Frank M. "Some Elementary Contributions of Aesthetics to Interpretative Speech," *Quarterly Journal of Speech* (December 1940), 528–39.

Tassin, Algernon. *The Oral Study of Literature.* New York: Crofts, 1947, Introduction.

Tripp, Walter Bradley. "Impersonation versus Interpretation." In *Studies in the Art of Interpretation* (Gertrude E. Johnson, ed.) New York: Appleton-Century-Crofts, 1940, pp. 131–37.

Wallace, Karl R., *et al.* (eds.) *A History of Speech Education in America.* New York: Appleton-Century-Crofts, 1954. Chapters V, VII, VIII, IX, X, XIV, and XIX are of particular interest to the student of interpretative reading.

2

■ WHAT SHALL I READ?

In his delightful novel *The Human Comedy* William Saroyan tells of two little boys who wander into the public library just to look at the books. The older boy, Lionel, tells the librarian that he and little Ulysses are friends because neither one of them can read. Lionel's forthright admission that they are there to look at the books, simply because they like to, astonishes the librarian, but since she can think of no law against it, she sends them into the stacks to fulfill their mission. Saroyan's description of the ensuing scene deftly recreates in us the awe that most of us feel as we look at the thousands of many-colored volumes on library shelves. Read it, and put your past-present self into the picture:

> The two friends moved off into still greater realms of mystery and adventure. Lionel pointed out more books to Ulysses. "These," he

> said. "And those over there. And these. All books, Ulysses." He stopped a moment to think. "I wonder what they say in all these books." He pointed out a whole vast area of them, five shelves full of them. "All these," he said—"I wonder what they say."

A pretty book with a green cover "like fresh grass" caught Lionel's eye. He had no way of knowing what was inside the book, judging by title or the name of the author. Only the color of the cover had meaning for one so young.

> A little frightened at what he was doing, Lionel lifted the book out of the shelf, held it in his hands a moment and then opened it. "There, Ulysses!" he said. "A book! There it is! See? They're saying something in here." Now he pointed to something in the print of the book. "There's an 'A,' " he said. "That's an 'A' right there. There's another letter of some sort. I don't know what that one is. Every letter's different, Ulysses, and every word's different." He sighed and looked around at all the books. "I don't think I'll ever learn to read," he said, "but I sure would like to know what they're saying in there. Now here's a picture," he said. "Here's a picture of a girl. See her? Pretty, isn't she?" He turned many pages of the book and said, "See it? More letters and words, straight through to the end of the book. This is the pubalic liberry, Ulysses," he said. "Books all over the place." He looked at the print of the book with a kind of reverence, whispering to himself as if he were trying to read. Then he shook his head. "You can't know what a book says, Ulysses, unless you can read, and I can't read," he said.

No one who has observed a first-grader learning to read can fail to sense his thrill of mastering a new mode of communication. Long has this youngster known that words mean something, but now, suddenly, he can *read* them and get meaning for himself. Like a toddler on his first steps, he falters often and needs assistance, but it is not long until he races through those words which are within his grasp, and he is deliriously independent in a new world where people he likes can do things he cannot do. No one who reads Saroyan's story can fail to realize that if Lionel is given the chance, he will someday soon be spending his time reading books. Most children love to learn to read. Unfortunately, somehow and at sometime during their formative years, many of them lose their love for books. Reading should be an ever-unfolding process of achievement, pleasure, and experience.

As a beginning student of interpretative reading you may already be an avid silent reader. You may need no encouragement to read, and you may have no difficulty in finding prose, poetry, or dramatic literature which you will wish to read to your classmates. If you are a habitual reader, you are to be congratulated. You have already passed the first two hurdles: motivating yourself and finding materials. You may, however, find the contents of this chapter, particularly the booklists and exercises, helpful.

On the other hand, you may be one of the many students who are stricken with the somewhat panicky notion that they have no idea where to start in reading. You need not be ashamed if you are, for you are not alone. Like the student of English composition, who asks: "What shall I write about?" and the beginning student of public speaking, who asks: "What shall I talk about?" the student of oral interpretation often asks: "What shall I read?"

CONSULT YOUR INTERESTS

When faced with these questions, the teacher frequently counters with: "What are you interested in?" Consult yourself on this point. Your own interests and activities should offer you clues as to what kinds of reading materials are most likely to please you. (And you must please yourself in reading before you can hope to please a listener!)

The library nearest you has books and periodicals to fit almost every human interest and a librarian to assist you in finding what you might like to read. Nearly every drugstore has a rack of magazines and inexpensive paperback editions of books of every description, some of which are quite worthwhile. Before you lies the entire field of human knowledge and literary experience. Explore it.

For your first experience in reading to others, read a selection already familiar to you. Nearly everyone reads newspapers and magazines. Choose an article or a story you have enjoyed reading to yourself. Try it on your classmates. Then, as you progress in this course, explore other forms of writing: essays, short stories, novels, poems, and plays. If you have not liked poetry heretofore, you will do yourself a personal favor if, during this course, you discover at least one good poem and enjoy sharing it with other people.

Although there are always instances in which you must read what is good for you, the first test of your selection will be your own appreciation. Within the limits of the techniques you know, the greater your appreciation, the greater your communicative effectiveness. The more sincerely the salesman believes in his product, the better he will sell it. The more a teacher believes in his subject, the better he is likely to teach it. The more a speaker feels personally interested in his topic, the more persuasive his speaking will be. Enthusiastic appreciation of a story will boost the reader's effectiveness by giving him a sharpened and concentrating mind, a bodily alertness, and a personal magnetism—all of which are necessary for persuading his listeners to enjoy it, too. Read what you really enjoy and wish to share with others, and you will conquer the most common difficulty faced by the beginner: the burdensome task of reading aloud only because the course requires it.

CONSULT YOUR CAPACITIES

The second requirement for the choice of good reading material is this: never attempt to read a selection to others unless you are confident that you understand it yourself. To do so is to be like the optimistic fellow who attempts to bluff his way through a classroom discussion without first having studied the subject. If the material is beyond you, do not expect your reading of it to make sense to your listeners. Ignorance cannot be concealed in reading any more than it can in conversation. This warning does not mean that one must always read simple stuff; it does mean that study may be necessary before understanding is developed. Few of us would have difficulty in reading the following aloud with some confidence: "John went to the store to buy some cake flour for his wife." We get the idea easily. Although we may not know the full story, we know where John went and what for, and probably also why he went. But most of us would have to study and think a good deal before we could make sense, even to ourselves, out of this single sentence from Nietzsche:

> It may be necessary for the education of the real philosopher that he himself should have once stood upon all those steps upon which his servants, the scientific workers of philosophy, remain standing, and *must* remain standing: he himself must perhaps have been critic, and dogmatist, and historian, and besides, poet, and collector, and traveller, and riddle-reader, and moralist, and seer, and "free spirit," and almost everything, in order to traverse the whole range of human values and estimations, and that he may *be able* with a variety of eyes and consciences to look from a height to any distance, from a depth up to any height, from a nook into any expanse.

CONSULT YOUR AUDIENCE

The first two requirements for choosing materials for oral interpretation, therefore, lie within the interpreter's capacity to understand and to appreciate. The third and fourth requirements concern the same capacities in the listeners, for the understanding and appreciation of the audience are the fundamental goals of oral interpretation. The reader should analyze his audience as carefully as the public speaker does, and, in this analysis, he should consider such characteristics of the audience as its predominant age, social and economic strata, sex, religion, nationality, race, and geographical location. One would not usually read the same materials to a church sewing circle that he would to a group of Boy Scouts, nor to a men's smoker the same selection he would read to the sixth-grade children in an elementary school. On the other hand, it is rather surprising to the interpreter to discover that he can read many types of selections to many different kinds of groups, if only he has a great degree of personal enthusiasm for his material. If he is skilled, he can often "sell" a piece of literature to his audience. Until you learn the skill, however, you should pick "sure-fire" selections—that is, material which you are confident will appeal to your audience.

In consulting your audience you will do well to consider the time it spends listening to you. An audience of twenty will spend an hour and forty minutes in listening to your five-minute reading. Do not waste your listeners' time—or your energy—on unworthy or unappealing literature. Whether your material is comic or tragic, make it good comedy or good tragedy. Good literature is so voluminous that the choice of poor-quality material is unfortunate and wholly unnecessary.

CONSULT THE REQUIREMENTS OF ORAL COMMUNICATION

The interpretative reader must consult the requirements of oral communication. He must choose literature which is, for the most part, easy to read aloud and easy to listen to. The oral and aural mechanisms make demands not made by the eye. The speech mechanism, for example, falls easy victim to undue complications of sound. To read aloud Swinburne's extended use of alliteration in the following lines is to invite the twisted tongue:

> From the depth of the dreamy decline of the dawn through a notable
> nimbus of nebulous noonshine,
> Pallid and pink as the palm of the flagflower that flickers with fear of
> the flies as they float,
> Are they looks of our lovers that lustrously lean from a marvel of
> mystic miraculous moonshine,
> These that we feel in the blood of our blushes that thicken and threaten
> with throbs through the throat?
>
> —ALGERNON CHARLES SWINBURNE, *Nephelidia*

The ear, furthermore, cannot relisten as the eye can reread. When the mind of a silent reader does not comprehend ideas, the eye can backtrack, reconsider relationships, and even consult a dictionary or encyclopedia in the pursuit of understanding. The ear, however, must perceive meaning the first time it hears—perhaps not the whole meaning, but enough meaning to make the effort satisfying.

We must consider the preferences of the ear, which are few but assertive. The ear prefers simplicity to complication, either in vocabulary or syntax. It prefers images to abstractions, and drama to thought. Apply these requirements to the following excerpts from two O. Henry stories, and they become evident. Read the passages aloud. Do they flow with equal ease from your lips? Read them aloud to a friend. Are they equally meaningful to the ear?

from THE GREEN DOOR

O. HENRY

Suppose you should be walking down Broadway after dinner, with ten minutes allotted to the consummation of your cigar while you are choosing between a diverting tragedy and something serious in the way of vaudeville. Suddenly a hand is laid upon your arm. You turn to look into the thrilling eyes of a beautiful woman, wonderful in diamonds and Russian sables. She thrusts hurriedly into your hand an extremely hot buttered roll, flashes out a tiny pair of scissors, snips off the second button of your overcoat, meaningly ejaculates the one word "parallelogram!" and swiftly flies down a cross street, looking back fearfully over her shoulder.

from THE COP AND THE ANTHEM

O. HENRY

The hibernatorial ambitions of Soapy were not of the highest. In them were no considerations of Mediterranean cruises, of soporific Southern skies or drifting in the Vesuvian Bay. Three months on the Island was what his soul craved. Three months of assured board and bed and congenial company, safe from Boreas and blue-coats, seemed to Soapy the essence of things desirable.

For years the hospitable Blackwell's had been his winter quarters. Just as his more fortunate fellow New Yorkers had bought their tickets to Palm Beach and the Riviera each winter, so Soapy had made his humble arrangements for his annual hegira to the Island. And now the time was come. On the previous night three Sabbath newspapers, distributed beneath his coat, about his ankles and over his lap, had failed to repulse the cold as he slept on his bench near the spurting fountain in the ancient square. So the Island loomed big and timely in Soapy's mind. He scorned the provisions made in the name of charity for the city's dependents. In Soapy's opinion the Law was more benign than Philanthropy. There was an endless round of institutions, municipal and eleemosynary, on which he might set out and receive lodging and food accordant with the simple life. But to one of Soapy's proud spirit the gifts of charity are encumbered. If not in coin you must pay in humiliation of spirit for every benefit received at the hands of philanthropy. As Caesar had his Brutus, every bed of charity must have its toll of a bath, every loaf of bread its compensation of a private and personal inquisition. Wherefore it is better to be a guest of the law, which, though conducted by rules, does not meddle unduly with a gentleman's private affairs.

CONSULT THE REQUIREMENTS OF LITERARY QUALITY

When selecting literature to read to an audience, the reader must consider the quality of the material. Most college students feel inept in attempting to evaluate literary worth. Part of the explanation for this difficulty probably lies in the fact that courses in literature seldom deal with a consideration of *relative* quality; everything quoted in the textbook anthology is supposed to be good writing. Students are not required to weigh one selection against another or to compare a good piece of writing with a poor one. Since critical judgment is rarely developed, or even exercised, the student feels at a loss in selecting material for oral reading where the job of evaluation is his. Yet, it is unfortunate when a reader wastes his audience's time and his own with material that is unworthy.

What constitutes literary quality? The answer would, of course, be too extensive to include in this textbook, for it would fill a book of its own; however, a few basic principles can be stated here, perhaps to your advantage. First, a good piece of writing is original. A good writer has something new and unique to say, or he has a new way of dealing with an old concept. Compare T. S. Eliot's poem "Journey of the Magi," quoted and discussed in Chapter 5, with the following verse:

CHRISTMAS EVERYWHERE

PHILLIPS BROOKS

Everywhere, everywhere, Christmas tonight!
Christmas in lands of the fir-tree and pine,

Christmas in lands of the palm-tree and vine,
Christmas where snow peaks stand solemn and white,
Christmas where cornfields stand sunny and bright.
Christmas where children are hopeful and gay,
Christmas where old men are patient and gray,
Christmas where peace, like a dove in his flight,
Broods o'er brave men in the thick of the fight;
Everywhere, everywhere, Christmas tonight!

For the Christ-child who comes is the Master of all;
No palace too great, no cottage too small.

Eliot added new and significant thought to the old Christmas story; Brooks had only one, comparatively superficial, idea: "Christmas is everywhere." Although some readers and audiences might find some charm in Brooks's delight in the overwhelming presence of Christmas, all who know literature will agree that Eliot probed deeper and with more originality into the meaning of Christmas.

In addition, the original writer is not content to imitate another writer, for he values his own creative spirit too highly to copy. He prefers to create his own style, his own characters, situations, images, figures of speech, rhythms, symbolism, etc. In *The Caine Mutiny* Herman Wouk wrote one of the most dramatic courtroom scenes found in modern fiction. It was so powerful that it later became a successful Broadway play. A recent novel proved to be rather interesting to one of your authors until the climax of the book arrived, which was in a scene almost identical to Wouk's trial scene, even to the mental breakdown of a major character exactly like the breakdown of Captain Queeg on the stand. The second writer apparently did not have the originality to create something new for his climax. His lack of originality at the crucial point of his book is doubly sad since he showed considerable literary skill in the rest of his novel. Of course, writers cannot always be completely original; even Shakespeare borrowed his plots liberally, but he was so inventive in characterization, imagery, and language that few persons object to his use of old stories for his great plays. Good writers are original where originality is most important.

Second, good writing has something significant to say. This does not mean that it must be world-shaking in importance, or even serious, for light, humorous, or satirical writing may be significant. "Jenny Kissed Me," quoted elsewhere in this textbook, is not profound—in fact, it is quite light—but it is significant, for in a few deft lines Leigh Hunt expertly communicates the universal delight of an aging person in a child's kiss. The concrete picture of Jenny's action and the poet's consequent thoughts about his age furnish fine contrast to Brooks's generalized shouts about Christmas. James

Thurber's humor usually shows an incisive view of man's frailties. Phyllis McGinley's light verses are also the result of astute observation of life. Fathers of girls can vouch for the validity of her "Girl's-Eye View of Relatives: First Lesson," quoted on page 362.

Third, good writing is a result of accuracy and honesty in the writer's perception of life. Some assembly-line writers, because they wear colored glasses of one tint or another, either deliberately or ignorantly, do not make very accurate observations. For example, a newspaper versifier once philosophized about a neighbor who had a beautifully landscaped home. The "poet" came to the conclusion that a man who took such care of the outside of his home *must* unconditionally be a good man. One reader took issue with this specious bit of homey reasoning, reporting that in his boyhood he had once had a neighbor whose green thumb had been responsible for a magnificent lawn and garden. The man was generous with his garden produce and was even kind to the neighborhood children. But, he was not in all ways a good man: regularly, he beat his wife, and he was a bootlegger, as well. Such a jingling paean to man's goodness as had appeared in that newspaper column is guaranteed to appear in popular publications because it pleasantly reassures unsophisticated readers by telling them what they *want* to hear about their fellow men. Just as dishonest are those writers who pander to the tastes of readers who want only a constant diet of criticism of mankind. Thus, these authors show man only in his lurid moments of utter bestiality not because they genuinely see man that way but because they know that their stories will sell.

We interpretative readers cannot choose our reading materials uncritically. We must attempt the often difficult task of sorting the valid from the phony. When, because of our own limitations, we cannot determine literary quality, we should consult the opinions of those who should know, such as scholars in all fields, including literary critics.

Fourth, when good writing solicits emotional reaction by the reader, it offers sufficient reason for that emotion: a situation which justifies the emotion. Compare the following pieces of writing:

THE SPIRES OF OXFORD

(As seen from the train)

WINIFRED M. LETTS

I saw the spires of Oxford
  As I was passing by,
The grey spires of Oxford
  Against a pearl-grey sky;
My heart was with the Oxford men
  Who went abroad to die.

The years go fast in Oxford,
  The golden years and gay;
The hoary colleges look down
  On careless boys at play,
But when the bugles sounded—War!
  They put their games away.

They left the peaceful river,
  The cricket field, the quad,
The shaven lawns of Oxford,
  To seek a bloody sod.
They gave their merry youth away
  For country and for God.

God rest you, happy gentlemen,
  Who laid your good lives down,
Who took the khaki and the gun
  Instead of cap and gown.
God bring you to a fairer place
  Than even Oxford town.

THE DEATH OF THE BALL TURRET GUNNER

RANDALL JARRELL

From my mother's sleep I fell into the State,
And I hunched in its belly till my wet fur froze.
Six miles from earth, loosed from its dream of life,
I woke to black flak and the nightmare fighters.
When I died they washed me out of the turret with a hose.

In "The Spires of Oxford" the writer gives no *personal* reason for being so disturbed about the deaths of the Oxford students. Was one of them her son, or her lover? Of course, it is true that we all may think, momentarily, of the great waste of human lives in war, but we do not *feel* the loss unless we are given a tragic figure. We cannot feel much for a generalized group of Oxford students; we might have felt sorry for the loss of *one* of them if the author had really brought one to life for us. In Jarrell's fine little poem, we can feel the tragic loss of a young man who tells us so tersely that he did not wake up to life until the moment he was killed. We can feel the tragic irony of this boy's death. Letts merely talks about war deaths; Jarrell gets inside the individual and expresses the stark tragedy with unique symbolism.

Fifth, good writing comes to us in a form that is appropriate to its message. Consider the last two selections again. The rhythm of the former is inappropriate for a message of tragedy: an unrelieved ta-tah, ta-tah, ta-tah that jangles rather jauntily along. The regular rime scheme also contributes to a merry kind of atmosphere. The verses are filled with trite expressions that sound very familiar to us: "As I was passing by," "pearl-grey sky," "My heart was with," "The years go fast," "The golden years and gay," "the bugles sounded," "For country and for God," "God rest you, happy gentlemen," "laid your good lives down," and others. Surely, some of these must seem overfamiliar to you. Jarrell, on the other hand, has used no monotonous meter, only one rime—for a concluding unity—and no clichés. In a title and five lines, he has said all that needs to be said.

This is as far as we shall pursue this subject now; however, you should keep literary quality in mind. Make interpretative reading a profitable experience for both the audience and yourself by reading good materials. You will find that many other parts of this book will furnish insights into literary quality. Chapter 5 will be particularly helpful.

CONSULT THE AUTHORITIES

"But how do I find suitable reading materials?" you may ask. The answer is simple: "Look for them." One systematic way to start would be for you to consult a selected booklist of recommended books. One of the best was prepared by the Committee on College Reading and is now published in revised edition by Mentor Books under the title *Good Reading*. You can buy this paper-bound volume at most bookstores and at many newsstands for less than a dollar. In addition to the extensive list of readings known to be popular with college students are included interesting, helpful essays on good reading.

Another type of book which you will find of great help in your search for reading matter is the "guidance" book in the art of reading. Guidance books not only suggest titles to read but also tell you how to go about reading them. If you purchase *Good Reading,* mentioned above, look for its companion volume *The Wonderful World of Books,* also a Mentor Book. Most libraries have books which will guide you in good reading; a few of the helpful ones on shelves today are listed.

Enjoying Poetry (Mark Van Doren). New York: Sloane, 1951.

Enjoyment of Poetry, with *Anthology for Enjoyment of Poetry* (Max Eastman), 2 vols. in 1. New York: Scribner, 1951.

Exploring Poetry (M. L. Rosenthal and A. J. M. Smith). New York: Macmillan, 1955.

In Pursuit of Poetry (Robert Hillyer). New York: McGraw-Hill, 1960.

On Reading Shakespeare (Logan Pearsall Smith). New York: Harcourt, Brace, 1933.

Pleasure Dome; On Reading Modern Poetry (Lloyd Frankenberg). Boston: Houghton Mifflin, 1949.

Reading Drama; A Method of Analysis with Selections for Study (Fred B. Millett). New York: Harper, 1950.

Reading Fiction; A Method of Analysis with Selections for Study (Fred B. Millett). New York: Harper, 1950.

Reading for Life; Developing the College Student's Lifetime Reading Interest (Jacob M. Price, ed.). Ann Arbor: University of Michigan Press, 1959.

Reading Poetry; A Method of Analysis with Selections for Study (Fred B. Millett). New York: Harper, 1950.

Studies in Poetry (Neal Frank Doubleday, ed.). New York: Harper, 1949.

The Art of Book Reading (Stella Center). New York: Scribner, 1952.

The Reading of Books (Holbrook Jackson). New York: Scribner, 1947.

Understanding Drama (Cleanth Brooks and Robert B. Heilman). New York: Holt, 1948.

Understanding Fiction (Cleanth Brooks and Robert Penn Warren). New York: Appleton-Century-Crofts, 1959.

Understanding Poetry (Cleanth Brooks and Robert Penn Warren). New York: Holt, Rinehart and Winston, 1960.

These books are only guides to help you find reading materials. Do not overlook the fact that you must be your own authority for determining what *you* should read. It is to be hoped that it will not be long before you will have the courage to strike beyond the tried, old, and recommended materials, and read refreshingly new ones to your audiences.

CONSULT POPULAR BOOKS

You will probably find interesting reading materials if you investigate books of proved popularity. Lists of best-sellers appear regularly in many newspapers. Most libraries have such lists posted, and most librarians will cheerfully refer you to the most popular books in your field of interest. The following list of one hundred and ten books of twenty-two types is a composite list of the most popular books circulating from eight of the major public libraries in the nation in late 1961: Boston, Dallas, Denver, Detroit, New Orleans, New York, San Francisco, and Seattle.[1] Study the list carefully. Several of the books may provide good reading for you.

[1] Librarians who submitted materials from which this list was prepared were: John M. Carroll, Chief Librarian, Division of Home Reading and Community Services, Boston Public Library; James D. Meeks, Library Director, and Mrs. Lillian Moore Bradshaw,

ADVENTURE

Cousteau, Jacques. *The Silent World*. New York: Harper.
Freuchen, Peter. *Adventures in the Arctic*. New York: Messner.
Heyerdahl, Thor. *Kon-Tiki*. Chicago: Rand McNally.
Lord, Walter. *A Night to Remember*. New York: Holt.
Moorhead, Alan. *The White Nile*. New York: Harper.

THE ARTS

Blake, Peter. *The Master Builders*. New York: Knopf.
Brion, Marcel. *Art Since 1945*. London: Thames and Hudson.
Gardner, Helen. *Art through the Ages*. New York: Harcourt, Brace.
Malraux, André. *The Metamorphosis of the Gods*. New York: Doubleday.
Wright, Frank Lloyd. *A Testament*. New York: Horizon Press.

BIOGRAPHY

Gann, Ernest K. *Fate is the Hunter*. New York: Simon and Schuster.
Jenkins, Elizabeth. *Elizabeth the Great*. New York: Coward-McCann.
Kennedy, John F. *Profiles in Courage*. New York: Harper.
Marshall, Catherine. *A Man Called Peter*. New York: McGraw-Hill.
Pope-Hennessy, James. *Queen Mary, 1867–1953*. New York: Knopf.

BIZARRE AND UNUSUAL FICTION

Bradbury, Ray. *The Martian Chronicles*. New York: Doubleday.
Jackson, Shirley. *The Haunting of Hill House*. New York: Viking.
Orwell, George. *Nineteen Eighty-Four*. New York: Harcourt, Brace.
Shute, Nevil. *On the Beach*. New York: Morrow.
Wells, H. G. *Seven Science Fiction Novels*. New York: Dover.

COLLECTIONS OF ESSAYS

Camus, Albert. *Resistance, Rebellion, and Death*. New York: Knopf.
Emerson, Ralph Waldo. *Essays*. [Various publishers.]
Golden, Harry L. *Only in America*. New York: World.
Highet, Gilbert. *The Powers of Poetry*. New York: Oxford.
Huxley, Aldous L. *Collected Essays*. New York: Harper.

Acting Director, Dallas Public Library; John T. Eastlick, Librarian, and Walter N. Babbitt, Supervisor, Central Adult Services, Denver Public Library; Ralph A. Ulveling, Director, Harriet Goode, Chief of Book Selection Department, Detroit Public Library; Jerome Cushman, Librarian, New Orleans Public Library; John Mackenzie Cory, Chief, Circulation Department, and Mary Hatch, Readers' Adviser, New York Public Library; Dorothy Weed, Senior Circulation Librarian, Geraldine Whitney, and James Cleghorn, San Francisco Public Library; Willard O. Youngs, Librarian, Seattle Public Library.

COLLECTIONS OF SHORT STORIES

Foley, Martha (ed.) *The Best American Short Stories.* Boston: Houghton Mifflin.

Gold, Herbert (ed.) *Fiction of the Fifties.* New York: Doubleday.

Poe, Edgar Allan. *Tales.* New York: Dodd, Mead.

Saturday Evening Post Stories, 1961. New York: Doubleday.

Stories from the New Yorker, 1950–1960. New York: Simon and Schuster.

ENTERTAINMENT WORLD

Clausen, Connie. *I Love You Honey, but the Season's Over.* New York: Holt, Rinehart and Winston.

Hardwicke, Sir Cedric. *Victorian in Orbit.* New York: Doubleday.

Hart, Moss. *Act One.* New York: Random House.

Hemingway, Ernest. *Death in the Afternoon.* New York: Scribner.

Tynan, Kenneth. *Curtains.* New York: Atheneum.

HISTORY

Catton, Bruce. *Grant Moves South.* New York: Little, Brown.

Churchill, Winston L. S. *Memoirs of The Second World War.* Boston: Houghton Mifflin.

Mattingly, Garrett. *The Armada.* Boston: Houghton Mifflin.

Shirer, William L. *The Rise and Fall of the Third Reich.* New York: Simon and Schuster.

White, Theodore H. *The Making of the President.* New York: Atheneum.

HUMOR

Armour, Richard W. *The Classics Reclassified.* New York: McGraw-Hill.

Kerr, Jean. *Please Don't Eat the Daisies.* New York: Doubleday.

———. *The Snake Has All the Lines.* New York: Doubleday.

Parkinson, Cyril N. *Parkinson's Law, and Other Studies in Administration.* Boston: Houghton Mifflin.

Thurber, James. *Lanterns and Lances.* New York: Harper.

INTERNATIONAL AFFAIRS

Kennan, George F. *Russia and the West under Lenin and Stalin.* Boston: Little, Brown.

Lederer, William J. *A Nation of Sheep.* New York: Norton.

Morganthau, Hans J. *Politics Among Nations.* New York: Knopf.

Strausz-Hupé, Robert. *Protracted Conflict.* New York: Harper.

Ward, Barbara. *Five Ideas That Change the World.* New York: Norton.

JOURNALISM

Amory, Cleveland, and Frederic Bradlee (eds.) *Vanity Fair*. New York: Viking.

Hohenberg, John. *The Pulitzer Prize Story*. New York: Columbia.

Lindstrom, Carl E. *The Fading American Newspaper*. New York: Doubleday.

Matthews, Thomas S. *The Sugar Pill; An Essay on Newspapers*. New York: Simon and Schuster.

Thurber, James. *The Years with Ross*. Boston: Little, Brown.

MUSIC

Bernstein, Leonard. *The Joy of Music*. New York: Simon and Schuster.

Copland, Aaron. *What to Listen for in Music* and *Copland on Music*. New York: McGraw-Hill and Doubleday.

Grout, Donald J. *A History of Western Music*. New York: Norton.

Hentoff, Nat. *The Jazz Life*. New York: Dial.

Stearns, Marshall. *The Story of Jazz*. New York: Oxford.

MYSTERY AND MURDER

Ambler, Eric. *Passage of Arms*. New York: Knopf.

Christie, Agatha. [Works.]

Doyle, Arthur Conan. *The Complete Sherlock Holmes* (2 vols.) New York: Doubleday.

Greene, Graham. *Our Man in Havana*. New York: Viking.

Tey, Josephine. *Daughter of Time*. New York: Berkley Books.

NATURE

Adamson, Joy. *Born Free, A Lioness of Two Worlds*. New York: Pantheon.

Carson, Rachel. *The Sea Around Us*. New York: Oxford.

Maxwell, Gavin. *Ring of Bright Water*. New York: Dutton.

Moorehead, Alan. *No Room in the Ark*. New York: Harper.

Teale, Edwin Way. *Journey into Summer*. New York: Dodd, Mead.

NOVELS

Lederer, William J., and Eugene Burdick. *The Ugly American*. New York: Norton.

Lee, Harper. *To Kill a Mockingbird*. Philadelphia: Lippincott.

Michener, James A. *Hawaii*. New York: Random House.

Stone, Irving. *The Agony and the Ecstasy*. New York: Doubleday.

Uris, Leon. *Exodus*. New York: Doubleday.

PHILOSOPHY

Barrett, William. *Irrational Man; A Study in Existential Philosophy.* New York: Doubleday.

Barzun, Jacques. *The House of Intellect.* New York: Harper.

Durant, Will. *The Story of Philosophy.* New York: Simon and Schuster.

Le Comte du Noüy, Pierre. *Human Destiny.* New York: Longmans, Green.

Russell, Bertrand A. *Wisdom of the West.* New York: Doubleday.

POETRY

Eliot, T. S. *Collected Poems.* New York: Harcourt, Brace.

Frost, Robert. *Complete Poems.* New York: Holt.

Graves, Robert. *Collected Poems.* London: Cassell.

McGinley, Phyllis. *Times Three.* New York: Viking.

Sandburg, Carl. *Complete Poems.* New York: Harcourt, Brace.

PSYCHOLOGY

Fromm, Erich. *The Art of Loving.* New York: Harper.

Jones, Ernest. *The Life and Work of Sigmund Freud* (3 vols.) New York: Basic Books.

Menninger, Karl. *The Human Mind.* New York: Knopf.

Osborn, Alexander F. *Applied Imagination.* New York: Scribner.

Woolson, Arthur. *Good-by, My Son.* New York: Harper.

RELIGION

Brown, Robert M., and Gustave Weigel. *An American Dialogue: A Protestant Looks at Catholicism and a Catholic Looks at Protestantism.* New York: Doubleday.

Burrows, Millar. *The Dead Sea Scrolls.* New York: Viking.

Dooley, Tom. *The Night They Burned the Mountain.* New York: Farrar, Straus & Cudahy.

The New English Bible. New York: Oxford.

Wouk, Herman. *This is My God.* New York: Doubleday.

SCIENCE

Asimov, Isaac. *The Intelligent Man's Guide to Science* (2 vols.) New York: Basic Books.

Eiseley, Loren. *The Firmament of Time.* New York: Atheneum.

Moore, Ruth E. *The Earth We Live On* and *Man, Time, and Fossils.* New York: Knopf.

Snow, Charles. *The Two Cultures and the Scientific Revolution*. London: Cambridge.

Sullivan, Walter. *Assault on the Unknown; The International Geophysical Year*. New York: McGraw-Hill.

SOCIOLOGY

Galbraith, John K. *The Affluent Society*. Boston: Houghton Mifflin.

Hoover, J. Edgar. *Masters of Deceit; The Story of Communism in America*. New York: Holt.

Mumford, Lewis. *The City in History*. New York: Harcourt, Brace.

Packard, Vance. *The Status Seekers* and *The Waste Makers*. New York: David McKay.

Whyte, William H. *The Organization Man*. New York: Simon and Schuster.

TRANSPORTATION

Abdill, George B. *Rails West*. Seattle: Superior Publishing Co.

Beebe, Lucius, and Charles Clegg. *Narrow Gauge in the Rockies*. Berkeley, Cal.: Howell-North Books.

Hornung, Clarence. *Wheels Across America*. New York: A. S. Barnes.

Keats, John. *The Insolent Chariots*. Philadelphia: Lippincott.

Ley, Willy. *Rockets, Missiles, and Space Travel*. New York: Viking.

CONSULT THE LIBRARY

Another systematic technique is to look up subjects and authors in the card catalogue of the library. These drawers look imposing, but, since every item is arranged alphabetically by author's name and also subject, your search through them can be both easy and interesting.

The most satisfactory method of looking for something to read, however, is to browse in the books themselves, for by so doing you not only catch Lionel's enthusiasm for the presence of books, but you also have freedom of movement, a chance to look the book over before drawing it out of the library, and a delightful degree of solitude away from the bustling circulation desk. If your library permits your entrance to the stacks, locate the shelves holding the type of book you think you want. Then enjoy yourself! Look the books over. Pick out one; leaf through it; read a line here, a paragraph there. If it appeals to you, check it out for home use, and give it a real chance to interest you. If it does not, keep looking.

In fiction, you will find many shelves of novels, old and new, good and bad, dull and exciting. You will also find many collections of short stories, classified by authors, by types, and by subject matter. If you do not know any authors well, take out an anthology which appeals to you. In it you will probably find some stories which you will enjoy. Then go back to the library and search for more stories by the same author. At this point, that alphabetical card catalogue comes in very handy. You can follow exactly the same procedure in respect to poetry and drama.

The library contains volumes of the works of individual poets and dramatists, but the beginning student will usually prefer to make his first selection from an attractive anthology, which often assists him with helpful information about the writer and his writings. The following list of anthologies—selected at random in a college library—is provided merely to suggest to the student how many different and specialized types of collections are in the library. Study this list carefully, for some book in it—or some book like one of these—may be your "open sesame" to many hours of enjoyment.

A Harvest of World Folk Tales (Milton Rugoff, ed.). New York: Viking, 1949.

A Renaissance Treasury (Hiram Haydn and John Charles Nelson, eds.). New York: Doubleday, 1953.

A Southern Harvest: Short Stories by Southern Writers (Robert Penn Warren, ed.). Boston: Houghton Mifflin, 1937.

A Subtreasury of American Humor (E. B. White and Katharine S. White, eds.). New York: Coward-McCann, 1941.

A Treasury of British Humor (Morris Bishop, ed.). New York: Coward-McCann, 1942.

A Treasury of Friendship: Sentiment, Philosophy, Humor, Inspiration, Observation, Counsel, Analysis, Idealism, and Friendship in Action (Ralph L. Woods, comp. and ed.). New York: David McKay, 1957.

A Treasury of Great Reporting; Literature Under Pressure from the Sixteenth Century to Our Own Time (Louis L. Snyder and Richard B. Morris, eds.). New York: Simon and Schuster, 1949.

A Treasury of Great Russian Short Stories (Avrahm Yarmolinsky, ed.). New York: Macmillan, 1946.

A Treasury of Jewish Folklore (Nathan Ausubel, ed.). New York: Crown, 1948.

A Treasury of New England Folklore (B. A. Botkin, ed.). New York: Crown, 1947.

A Treasury of Railroad Folklore: The Stories, Tall Tales, Traditions, Ballads and Songs of the American Railroad Man (B. A. Botkin and Alvin F. Harlow, eds.). New York: Crown, 1956.

A Treasury of Satire (Edgar Johnson, ed.). New York: Simon and Schuster, 1945.

A Treasury of the Familiar (Ralph L. Woods, ed.). New York: Macmillan, 1942.

A Treasury of the World's Great Letters (M. Lincoln Schuster, comp.). New York: Simon and Schuster, 1940.

A Treasury of the World's Great Speeches (Houston Peterson, ed.). New York: Simon and Schuster, 1954.

American Legend: A Treasury of Our Country's Yesterdays (Robert Van Gelder and Dorothy Van Gelder, eds.). New York: Appleton-Century, 1946.

As I Pass, O Manhattan; An Anthology of Life in New York (Esther Morgan McCullough, ed.). Coley Taylor, 1956.

Canadian Poetry in English (Chosen by Bliss Carman, Lorne Pierce, & V. B. Rhodenizer). Toronto, Canada: Ryerson, 1954.

Continent's End; A Collection of California Writing (Joseph Henry Jackson, comp.). New York: Whittlesey, 1944.

Country Matters (Barbara Webster, ed.). Philadelphia: Lippincott, 1959.

Famous Chinese Short Stories; Retold by Lin Yutang. New York: John Day, 1952.

40 Best Stories from Mademoiselle, 1935–1960 (Cyrilly Abels and Margarita G. Smith, eds.). New York: Harper, 1960.

Gentlemen, Scholars and Scoundrels: A Treasury of the Best of Harper's Magazine, from 1850 to the Present (Horace Knowles, ed.). New York: Harper, 1959.

Ghosts, Grim and Gentle: A Collection of Moving Ghost Stories (Joseph Lewis French, comp.). New York: Dodd, Mead, 1926.

Great Adventures and Explorations: From the Earliest Times to the Present, as Told by the Explorers Themselves (Vilhjalmur Stefansson, ed.). New York: Dial Press, 1952.

Hoosier Caravan: A Treasury of Indiana Life and Lore (R. E. Banta, ed.). Bloomington: Indiana University Press, 1951.

Jubilee: One Hundred Years of the Atlantic (Edward Weeks and Emily Flint, eds.). Boston: Little, Brown, 1957.

Literature for Interpretation (Wallace A. Bacon and Robert S. Breen, eds.). New York: Holt, Rinehart and Winston, 1961.

Living Literature for Oral Interpretation (Moiree Compere, ed.). New York: Appleton-Century-Crofts, 1949.

Love Songs of Asia (Powers Mathers, trans.). New York: Knopf, 1946.

Masterpieces of Religious Verse (James Dalton Morrison, ed.). New York: Harper, 1948.

Medieval Narrative: A Book of Translation (Margaret Schlauch). Englewood Cliffs, N.J.: Prentice-Hall, 1934.

Men at War; The Best War Stories of All Time (Ernest Hemingway, ed.). New York: Crown, 1942.

Midland Humor; A Harvest of Fun and Folklore (Jack Conroy, ed.). New York: Wyn, 1947.

Modern American Poetry; Modern British Poetry: A Critical Anthology (Louis Untermeyer, ed.). New York: Harcourt, Brace and World, 1962.

New Directions [*Year*]. New Directions, [Year].

North, East, South, West; A Regional Anthology of American Writing (Charles Lee *et al.*, eds.). New York: Howell, Soskin, 1945.

O. Henry Memorial Award Prize Stories of [*Year*]. New York: Doubleday, [Year].

1000 Years of Irish Poetry (Kathleen Hoagland, ed.). New York: Devin-Adair, 1947.

Parodies, An Anthology from Chaucer to Beerbohm—and After (Dwight MacDonald, ed.). New York: Random House, 1960.

Reading I've Liked (Clifton Fadiman, ed.). New York: Simon and Schuster, 1941.

Reveille: War Poems by Members of Our Armed Forces (Daniel Henderson, John Kieran, and Grantland Rice, eds.). New York: A. S. Barnes, 1943.

Roundup Time; A Collection of Southwestern Writing (George Sessions Perry, ed.). New York: Whittlesey, 1943.

Short Novels of the Masters (Charles Neider, ed.). New York: Rinehart, 1948.

Short Stories from the New Yorker. New York: Simon and Schuster, 1940.

Sky Clears; Poetry of the American Indians (Arthur Grove Day). New York: Macmillan, 1951.

Spearhead: 10 Years' Experimental Writing in America. New York: New Directions, 1947.

The Astounding Science Fiction Anthology (John W. Campbell, Jr., ed.). New York: Simon and Schuster, 1952.

The Best Short Stories of [*Year*] (Martha Foley, ed.). Boston: Houghton Mifflin Company, [Year].

The Book of Negro Folklore (Langston Hughes and Arna Bontemps, eds.). New York: Dodd, Mead, 1958.

The Fireside Book of Fishing; A Selection from the Great Literature of Angling (Raymond R. Camp, ed.). New York: Simon and Schuster, 1959.

The Great Detective Stories: A Chronological Anthology (Willard Huntington Wright, ed.). New York: Scribner, 1928.

The Great Prisoners; The First Anthology of Literature Written in Prison (Isidore Abramowitz, ed.). New York: Dutton, 1946.

The Greatest Stories of All Time: Tellers of Tales (W. Somerset Maugham, ed.). Garden City, N.Y.: Garden City, 1939.

The Negro Caravan (Sterling A. Brown, Arthur P. Davis, and Ulysses Lee, eds.). New York: Dryden Press, 1941.

The New Poetry; An Anthology of Twentieth-Century Verse in English

(Harriet Monroe and Alice Corbin Henderson, eds.). New York: Macmillan, 1947.

The Oxford Book of American Verse (F. O. Matthiessen, ed.). New York: Oxford, 1950.

The Oxford Book of Light Verse (Chosen by W. H. Auden). New York: Oxford, 1952.

The Poetry of the Negro (Langston Hughes and Arna Bontemps, eds.). New York: Doubleday, 1949.

The Practical Cogitator; or the Thinker's Anthology (Charles P. Curtis, Jr. and Ferris Greenslet, eds.). Boston: Houghton Mifflin, 1950.

The Saturday Review Treasury: A Volume of Good Reading Selected from the Complete Files (John Haverstick and editors of *The Saturday Review*, eds.). New York: Simon and Schuster, 1957.

The Seas of God (Whit Burnett, ed.). Philadelphia: Lippincott, 1944.

The Spell of the Pacific: An Anthology of Its Literature (Carl Stroven and A. Grove Day, eds.). New York: Macmillan, 1949.

The World's Great Catholic Literature (George N. Shuster, ed.). New York: Halcyon House, 1947.

The World's Great Religious Poetry (Caroline Miles Hill, ed.). New York: Macmillan, 1938.

The World's Great Speeches (Lewis Copeland and Lawrence Lamm, eds.). New York: Dover, 1958.

Thus Be It Ever: A Heritage of Freedom (Clara A. Molendyk and Major Benjamin C. Edwards, eds.). New York: Harper, 1942.

Triumph over Odds: An Anthology of Man's Unconquerable Spirit (J. Donald Adams, ed.). New York: Duell, Sloan and Pearce, 1957.

Twentieth Century Parody: American and British (Burling Lowrey, comp.). New York: Harcourt, Brace, 1960.

Virginia Reader; A Treasury of Writings, From the First Voyages to the Present (Francis Coleman Rosenberger, ed.). New York: Dutton, 1948.

CONSULT YOUR POCKETBOOK

In addition to recommending the foregoing procedures for finding books to read, we should like to suggest that you will enjoy reading more if you have some books of your own handy at all times. A good book on a table in your room is often as welcome as a candy bar tucked away in the desk drawer. During a late-night study period, we find it inconvenient to run to a store for something to eat, yet breakfast seems a *long* time away. When we wish to read something entertaining, we find it equally disconcerting to think of a trip to the library at that particular moment. The solutions to these two problems, then, are simple: keep some snacks on hand for nutritional needs and a book handy for intellectual needs.

Fortunately, most of us can find a few cents to spend on luxuries, such as magazines, shows, and refreshments. And, these days, a little money will go a long way toward building an inexpensive library. During recent years, modest editions of good literature have been published in paperback form and are available on most newsstands for thirty-five cents to a dollar. Buy a couple of volumes which interest you, put them on your study table, and read them when you have spare moments.

You will be surprised at how much more reading you will do, and at how much more you will enjoy doing it, when you have your own books as permanent fixtures in your room. You will also be surprised to discover what an excellent and extensive library you can build with the occasional expenditure of a quarter, half-dollar, or dollar.

Summary

You are fortunate if you read a great deal, but you are typical of your generation if you have lost your childhood enthusiasm for reading. When seeking materials for oral reading: read selections you and your audience will understand and appreciate; read good literature; consult literary authorities for suggestions as to what to read; search the library personally and systematically to find suitable reading materials. Begin with anthologies, for they may suggest authors and types of literature you will enjoy. Stimulate yourself to additional enjoyable reading by building your own library; you may do it modestly and inexpensively. As you follow these procedures, you will probably find reading materials you will wish to share with your classmates.

Suggested Readings

Compere, Moiree. *Living Literature for Oral Interpretation.* New York: Appleton-Century-Crofts, 1949, Introduction.

Geiger, Don. "Oral Interpretation in the Liberal Arts Context," *Quarterly Journal of Speech* (April 1954), 137–44.

Grimes, Wilma H. "Choosing Literature for Oral Reading; A Psychological Basis," *Quarterly Journal of Speech* (April 1956), 133–38.

Lee, Charlotte I. *Oral Interpretation.* (2nd edition) Boston: Houghton Mifflin, 1959, Chapter II, "Selection and Evaluation of Material."

3

■ COMMUNICATING WITH THE AUDIENCE

Before studying the necessarily detailed procedures for analyzing literature for effective interpretative reading, to be discussed in Chapters 4 and 5, you will probably be reading relatively simple materials in class and can make use of some suggestions on basic platform techniques.

BEGINNING AND STOPPING

The wise public speaker plans his introduction and conclusion carefully, so that when he speaks he can skillfully enlist the attention of his audience and effectively utilize it at the end of his speech. On the other hand, the poor speaker merely jumps into his argument and out of it again. The good interpreter avoids the latter's errors and provides an introduction to his reading which readies his listeners for the type of reading to follow. Likewise, he somehow lets his audience know that he is concluding. If you get ahead of your audience, you will lose it. If you quit abruptly, you will destroy any illusion you have created. Always prepare your audience for whatever you are going to do.

The introduction must be consistent with the type of material you are to read. If the selection is dignified, your manner of introducing it must also be dignified. If the material is light and informal, the introductory remarks should be so, too. What, then, should an introduction contain? Obviously, the title and author, if they have not been announced by a chairman or included on a printed program. But just as valuable are a few remarks concerning the reason you have chosen to read this particular selection to this particular audience. Is it appropriate to the times? Does it lead to an understanding or appreciation of a current happening? Do you enjoy it because of an experience it brings to mind? What needs to be said about the author, the literary form, any linguistic or stylistic peculiarities, or other significant matters to help your audience understand it?

Such remarks should be made in a natural, spontaneous manner, even though you may have chosen your words carefully, ahead of time. The introduction is important in establishing *your relationship* with your audience; do not let it sound as if you have memorized a statement someone else has written for you to say. The introduction is your best opportunity to meet your audience personally in a conversational way. While it may be wise to extemporize your remarks, prepare sufficiently so that you do not flounder. One student in an interpretation class gave the following appropriate introduction:

> About ten or twelve years ago, I used to go with my parents to visit my grandfather and grandmother on their farm. I remember one spring vacation when I went with my grandfather as he repaired the rail fences on the farm. I got a big thrill out of riding on the wagon, holding the horse's reins in my small hands. Strangely enough, that was about all I did remember of the experience until about a year ago, when I happened to read Robert Frost's poem "Mending Wall." While reading the poem, I began to recall the scenes in which the fence was repaired, and I cherish my childhood experiences on Grandfather's farm all the more. Frost's poem concerns a situation similar to the one I saw, firsthand. A farmer and his neighbor are walking along on opposite sides of the stone wall which lies between their properties. They are repairing the wall, which has broken apart during the winter. The poet is philosophizing upon the uselessness of this wall, and he also has some observations to make about the narrow views of his

neighbor, who repeats over and over again an old cliché: "Good fences make good neighbors."

A good introduction may be extremely simple, if it says all that needs to be said:

> Ogden Nash's light verse is not only funny, but it sometimes contains some rather sharp satire upon people in today's world. The other day I read his "The Seven Spiritual Ages of Mrs. Marmaduke Moore" and laughed so hard that my roommates insisted that I read it to them. They seemed to enjoy it, and I hope you will, too.

If you have a job of persuasion to do, you may introduce it like this:

> I suppose everyone has a pet peeve, a prejudice, a mindset, or a fear. Well, I, too, have an obsession. I believe in the American principle of freedom of speech, but I have a strong fear that we are losing it. To me, no other freedom is so precious as our privilege and right to speak our minds, as long as we do not abuse that privilege by speaking irresponsibly. Well, with this strong desire for the preservation of freedom of speech, and with a parallel fear that we are about to lose that freedom, I'd like to read to you what I consider to be one of the most pertinent observations I've read on our losing battle. It is an editorial published in a recent edition of *The New Yorker* magazine. It deals with controversy.

Sometimes a poem may be so short that your reading of it will be completed before the audience can "get the drift" of it. An introduction which gives the listeners a head start will be conducive to successful communication. Here is a simple example:

> As college students we find ourselves falling in love and sometimes out of love. Some of us take defeat in a cavalier manner, but others of us take it hard. In listening to this poem, imagine the scene to be a men's dormitory room. A happy-go-lucky fellow is giving advice to a disconsolate lover. The poem is Sir John Suckling's verse entitled "Encouragements to a Lover."

The introduction, as these examples illustrate, should reveal your relationship with the material you read, but it may also deal with the author and his creation of the selection. The backgrounds for his writing, such as the biographical, historical, philosophical, sociological, linguistic, and literary, may be essential to the listeners' understanding and appreciation of the literature you read aloud. Elizabeth Barrett Browning's tender sonnets are best appreciated when one is familiar with her love for Robert Browning. Walt Whitman's poems "O Captain! My Captain!" and "When Lilacs Last in the Dooryard Bloom'd" are fully comprehended only when one knows that they were inspired by the death of Abraham Lincoln. Matthew Arnold's "Dover Beach" is most significant when one is familiar with Arnold's philosophical reaction to the modern world. Clifford Odets' plays are powerful when one considers the economic and sociological conditions of the 1930's. Shakespeare's rhetorical greatness is best realized when one is aware that he was the greatest of many great writers of the Renaissance, when men explored the world of words as well as the world of Nature. Walter de la Mare's poetry and stories are most meaningful when we know that his greatest skill is with imagery.

Remember: the eye can backtrack and retrace the printed line, but your listeners' ears are limited to one hearing. In your introduction give them all that they need in order to understand and appreciate what you read while you read it.

Stopping effectively presents a more delicate problem, for you will seldom speak after you finish reading. Two suggestions may be pertinent. The first is: try to show by the manner of reading that you are approaching the final idea. You can use a change in time, pitch, loudness, or quality. Perhaps a slight pause before reading the final idea will tip off the listener to the fact that the last thought is approaching.

I know not if thy heart my heart will greet:
I ask not if thy love my love can meet:
Whate'er thy worshipful soft tongue shall say,
I'll kiss thine answer, be it yea or nay:
I do but know I love thee, and I pray
To be thy knight // until my dying day.

—SIDNEY LANIER, *The Symphony*

A slow rate of reading the last thought phrase, with well-placed pauses, is often effective.

Over the cobbles he clatters and clangs in the dark inn-yard;
And taps with his whip on the shutters, but all is locked and barred;
He whistles a tune to the window, and who should be waiting there
But the landlord's black-eyed daughter,
Bess, the landlord's daughter,
Plaiting a dark red love-knot // into her long / black / hair.

—ALFRED NOYES, *The Highwayman*

But equally important is your manner immediately following the conclusion. Rushing to your seat shocks your listeners, whose minds should still be upon the content of the material. The important principle to remember is: do not *distract* their attention. Stop. Pause. Close the book silently. Lower it. Turn slowly and walk away.

MEMORIZATION—FAMILIARIZATION

Students of interpretative reading often ask: "Shall I memorize?" The answer will probably depend on the teaching methods of the instructor since there are two valid approaches to the subject. Some instructors require complete memorization, because they believe that this permits the reader to be free to concentrate on communicating. Complete memorization has another advantage: it enables the reader to remember worthwhile literature, perhaps for a lifetime. It is often pleasant for a person to be able to quote passages of great literature from memory. We all know older persons, trained in schools where memorization was a constant requirement, who seem to derive great pleasure from reciting Shakespeare, the Bible, or other classics from memory. Not many college students of today can do this, and, from some points of view, this is regrettable.

Familiarization, which is really a partial memorization gained through study and practice, is used much more commonly by interpretative readers today. There seem to be three reasons for this preference. First, because today's students have had so little experience in memorizing, they do it rather badly, tending to commit the words mechanically so that the reading is automatic and lacks the spontaneity so essential to effective communication. Familiarization through concentration on meaning seems to be a more natural method of gaining command of important phraseology. Second, the time spent in memorizing is usually thought to be better spent in analysis of material and attention to the communication of precise meanings. Third, since most teachers of the subject feel that the reader should have the manuscript before him as he reads (as is indicated in the next section of this chapter), they feel that the reader ought actually to use it.

It is possible for an interpreter to read from a manuscript and yet be sufficiently free from it to communicate to an audience if he has studied and practiced *enough;* thus most readers now depend on familiarization rather than complete memorization.

We should admire the person who can do either well. We should criticize the reader who does either poorly. If one can memorize easily and still convey literary content as he speaks, while giving the impression of reading from the manuscript, he should not be criticized for memorizing. If one can become so familiar with the manuscript that he can communicate to his audience—while, of course, participating in his material—he should not be criticized for not memorizing. The important thing is not the technique but the communication.

A suggestion to the memorizer: Remember always to concentrate on meaning, not on words.

A suggestion to the familiarizer: Do not look back to the manuscript in the middle of a thought-unit. Avoid the bad habit of killing thoughts and images by breaking contact with your listeners.

THE MANUSCRIPT

The presence of the book is to be desired, even though the reader may have memorized everything. Charles Laughton certainly memorized his program, yet he had the books in front of him for atmosphere. Their presence was a constant reminder to the listener that what Laughton was saying came from the books, not from him. People like books; why should we hide them?

Whatever the manuscript may be—newspaper article, magazine article or story, play, novel, poem, essay—it should be one which you can handle. To juggle a big, floppy magazine while reading to others is distracting. Double-spaced typing of the article onto reasonable-sized sheets of paper will make your task easier. Another method is to type the story onto the sheets of a small—not tiny!—looseleaf notebook, which you can hold easily in your hands. This procedure can be used very well, too, for copying material from large books, too heavy to hold while reading. Another method is to type it onto sheets of paper which can be fastened inside a smaller book, one which you can handle with ease.

THE READING STAND

Teachers of interpretative reading differ on the use of reading stands. Some prefer to have their students hold their reading materials in their hands so that they do not become so accustomed to having a stand that they feel naked when forced to read without one. Others permit their students to use stands at all times. And still others insist upon their use. Of course, there are reasons for using them under certain circumstances: when the manuscript is too large or too heavy to handle with ease, when the reader's hands should be free for gesturing, or when the stand would add a desirable degree of aesthetic distance by further separating the reader from his audience. If you do employ one, let us hope that it is a thin one, so that your body can communicate emotional significance. Good readers often have to struggle valiantly behind large lecterns in order to communicate to listeners who can see only their faces. How much better they could communicate if their bodies were also visible! Whatever stand you use, do not permit it to become a leaning post or an anchor for your hands. Although the hands can be most expressive, most readers who use stands permit their hands to freeze upon the stand. Mr. Laughton had an interesting technique: he used two tables, a small one on top of a large one. This device enabled his audiences to see his body through the table legs, and Mr. Laughton's body, though rotund, was *very* expressive. He, of course, never permitted a table to immobilize his hands.

AUDIENCE CONTACT

Since interpretative reading is a form of communication, it is obvious that the reader must have effective contact with his audience. All of the suggestions in this text are designed to facilitate the reader's contact with his listeners; therefore it is always important to remember our admonition: never bury your nose in a book.

You must learn to hold the book low enough for your audience to see your face, yet high enough for you to see the audience *and* the book by shifting only your eyes. Avoid bobbing your head when referring to the book. You must learn to read ahead in order to look up from the manuscript as much as possible. If you are reading to a small group, establish eye contact with as many individuals as possible. If you are reading to a large audience, establish eye contact with individuals in representative sections of the audience. No listener likes to feel slighted. Try to make each listener feel that you are communicating with him.

The most direct form of audience contact is with the eyes of the audience member. Most literature demands this very personal form of contact. Certainly no obstacle should prevent eye contact when you read expository or narrative materials. On the other hand, some forms of literature will require less directness of communicative approach. Many authorities feel that some forms of writing, such as lyric poetry and dialogue, are effectively communicated if the reader uses a lesser personal form of audience contact than person-to-person eye contact, which can become an intrusion at times, an obstacle to communication. Let us assume, for example, that you are to read Elizabeth Barrett Browning's sonnet "How do I love thee?"

> How do I love thee? Let me count the ways.
> I love thee to the depth and breadth and height
> My soul can reach, when feeling out of sight
> For the ends of Being and ideal Grace.
> I love thee to the level of every day's
> Most quiet need, by sun and candlelight.
> I love thee freely, as men strive for Right;

I love thee purely, as they turn from Praise.
I love thee with the passion put to use
In my old griefs, and with my childhood's faith.
I love thee with a love I seemed to lose
With my lost saints,—I love thee with the breath,
Smiles, tears, of all my life!—and, if God choose,
I shall but love thee better after death.

Whom is the poet addressing? Obviously, someone very dear rather than just anyone; obviously, a single individual rather than a group of persons. The members of the audience will be aware of this relationship as they listen to you read. They will never assume either that you are the poet or that the poet is speaking to them. This poem contains the intimate thoughts and feelings of Elizabeth Barrett Browning, thoughts and feelings that all of us wish we could express as well as she has, but nevertheless they are hers and only hers. Because she was an artist, she was able to objectify her experience and write it down in a form for us to see, read, feel, and appreciate.

How will you read it? By addressing the reading to Bill Jones and Sally Smith? You might. But if you do, you may find that when your eyes meet theirs, you and they come too directly into the picture. You may find that you intrude upon the poet: upon *her* personal thoughts and feelings. Embarrassment on your part, or on the part of your listeners, may result, and the tenderness of the sonnet may be lost. The most beautiful literature can become ludicrous in such circumstances. How else might you read it? By reading in such a way as to suggest that you and your listeners are—in your imagination—listening to one of the greatest expressions of love ever to be recorded. The revelations of intimacy found in lyric poetry deserve the finest of oral treatment. They must be handled with delicacy, so avoid direct eye-to-eye relationships with specific listeners when reading them. Through effective visible communication and vocal projection, you can still achieve audience contact, even without eye contact.

SPONTANEITY AND ENJOYMENT

In Chapter 2, it was stressed that your interests and appreciation were prime requisites for the choice of materials to read aloud, for only if you are interested and enjoying what you read will you do a good job of appealing to the interests and enjoyment of your audience. You are reminded of that admonition at this point, for if you are like many conscientious students, you may become so involved in developing effective techniques that you will overplan and underenjoy. A student of music could work so hard to execute a run on the keyboard efficiently that he would play it with little personal inspiration or enthusiasm. Check on yourself now, to see if you are making the same mistakes. Try to retain initial experience and pleasure in your public reading. Keep your work alive, fresh, and do not be afraid to let others see that you enjoy reading.

One negative example may be enough to impress you with the importance of spontaneity. Not long ago, a young man prepared to read in a statewide collegiate reading festival. He was so ambitious in his preparation that he carefully planned how to make each move from the time he left his seat until he returned to it. His preparation, unfortunately, "showed." All spontaneity was lost. His listeners could see only his technique and consequently their pleasure was somewhat spoiled. Even the young man's appreciation seemed artificial, although it had once been quite genuine. Do not let that happen to you. Always keep in mind that your technique is only the means to the ends of appreciation and enjoyment.

On the other hand, this advice should not be leaned upon as an excuse for inadequate practice. There is no such thing as too much preparation; only too much improper preparation. If you will strive to rethink the thoughts, revisualize the images, and refeel the emotions expressed by the author *each* time you read a selection aloud, you will not go stale. Your *enjoyment* will be greatest when you have prepared well.

Summary

The oral interpreter can facilitate his expression of meaning by means of good platform technique. He establishes favorable audience attention by means of a well-planned, but spontaneous, introduction, and closes his reading in such a way as not to distract his audience from the content of his material. In addition, he uses a manuscript which he can handle with ease and which will actually add to the effectiveness of his reading. If he memorizes, he will learn the sequence of thought in the words of the author: he will not be satisfied with mechanical memorization. If he does not hold the book in his hands, he uses a reading stand which will not interfere with his communication. He maintains contact with his audience directly with his eyes whenever the reading materials demand conversational communication; he never buries his nose in a manuscript. He does all he can to avoid letting his reading seem mechanically prepared, for he knows that spontaneity and freshness are necessary for the audience's enjoyment of his reading. He never lets technique become an end in itself. He enjoys reading to others, for he has prepared well.

Exercises

1. Start a personal notebook of literary selections and articles of interest which you can use in interpretative reading.

2. Turn in a written report explaining how following three different procedures for finding literary selections of oral interpretation recommended in Chapter 2 have led you to three good selections.

3. Watch your fellow classmates to see whether their manuscripts or reading stands aid or interfere with the effectiveness of their communication. Plan your own platform work to make yourself comfortable and your own communication effective.

4. Find a selection quoted in this textbook, possibly one from the pages which follow, and prepare to read it to your class. Make a special effort to plan a good introduction, but do not read it. Speak it extemporaneously and spontaneously.

5. What manner of audience contact would you establish and maintain in reading each of the following selections? Would you use eye contact or a less direct form of audience contact? When would you change forms of contact during the reading of a single selection?

from THE AUTOBIOGRAPHY OF WILL ROGERS

December 7 [1924]:

Well, we were all last week trying to sink our greatest Battleship, the Washington.

Here is a Boat we had spent 35 millions on, and we go out and sink it. And the funny part is that it cost us more to sink it than it did to build it. We shot all the ammunition we had left over from the war into it and those big Guns on the Texas they were using, they only are good for so many shots during their lifetime. So we spoiled the Guns of our next best boat trying to sink the best one.

A great many people don't understand just how this sinking come about. You see we had a conference over here a few years ago. It was called by America. We were building a lot of Battleships and we had plenty of money to do it on, and it looked like in a couple of years we might have the largest Navy in the World. Well, the League of Nations gathering in Paris had attracted a lot of attention and got quite a lot of publicity, none of which had been shared in this country by the Democrats. So, when the Republicans got in, they conceived the idea of a publicity stunt for the Republicans. Why not then have a conference? But what would they confer about? The League of Nations had conferred about six months, and in that time had taken up about every question on the Calendar.

So Secretary Hughes happened to think of an idea: "Let us confer on sinking Battleships." Well, the idea was so original that they immediately made him the Toastmaster. You see, up to then, Battleships had always been sunk by the enemy, and when he proposed to sink them yourself it was the most original thought that had ever percolated the mind of a Statesman. So, when we communicated the idea to England and Japan that we had an idea whereby we would sink some of our own Battleships, why they come over so fast, even the Butler wasn't dressed to receive them when they arrived.

England was willing to tear her blueprints on planned building into half, Japan was willing to give up her dreams of having more ships on the seas than any nation and stop building up to 3/5 of the size of England and America, and Secretary Hughes met that with, "Now, Gentlemen, I will show you what America is prepared to do. FOR EVERY BATTLESHIP YOU FELLOWS DON'T BUILD AMERICA WILL SINK ONE."

Now they are talking of having another Naval Disarmament Conference. We can only stand one more. If they ever have a second one we will have to borrow a Boat to go to it.

You see, we don't like to ever have the start on any Nation in case of war. We figure it looks better to start late and come from behind. If we had a big Navy some Nation would just be picking on us all the time. Sinking your own Boats is a military strategy that will always remain in the sole possession of America.

CHRISTMAS AFTERNOON

(Done in the Manner, if Not the Spirit, of Dickens)

ROBERT C. BENCHLEY

What an afternoon! Mr. Gummidge said that, in his estimation, there had never *been* such an afternoon since the world began, a sentiment which was heartily endorsed by Mrs. Gummidge and all the little Gummidges, not to mention the relatives who had come over from Jersey for the day.

In the first place, there was the *ennui*. And such *ennui* as it was! A heavy, overpowering *ennui,* such as results from a participation in eight courses of steaming, gravied food, topping off with salted nuts which the little old spinster Gummidge from Oak Hill said she never knew when to stop eating—and true enough she didn't—a dragging, devitalizing *ennui,* which left its victims strewn about the living-room in various attitudes of prostration suggestive of those of the petrified occupants in a newly unearthed Pompeiian dwelling; an *ennui* which carried with it a retinue of yawns, snarls and thinly veiled insults, and which ended in ruptures in the clan spirit serious enough to last throughout the glad new year.

Then there were the toys! Three and a quarter dozen toys to be divided among seven children. Surely enough, you or I might say, to satisfy the little tots. But that would be because we didn't know the tots. In came Baby Lester Gummidge, Lillian's boy, dragging an electric grain-elevator which happened to be the only toy in the entire collection which appealed to little Norman, five-year-old son of Luther, who lived in Rahway. In came curly-headed Effie in frantic and throaty disputation with Arthur, Jr., over the possession of an articulated zebra. In came Everett, bearing a mechanical negro which would no longer dance, owing to a previous forcible feeding by the baby of a marshmallow into its only available aperture. In came Fonlansbee, teeth buried in the hand of little Ormond, which bore a popular but battered remnant of what had once been the proud false-bosom of a hussar's uniform. In they all came, one after another, some crying, some snapping, some pulling, some pushing—all appealing to their respective parents for aid in their intramural warfare.

And the cigar smoke! Mrs. Gummidge said that she didn't mind the smoke from a good cigarette, but would they mind if she opened the windows for just a minute in order to clear the room of the heavy aroma of used cigars? Mr. Gummidge stoutly maintained that they were good cigars. His brother, George Gummidge, said that he, likewise, would say that they were. At which colloquial sally both the Gummidge brothers laughed testily, thereby breaking the laughter record for the afternoon.

Aunt Libbie, who lived with George, remarked from the dark corner of the room that it seemed just like Sunday to her. An amendment was offered to this statement by the cousin, who was in the insurance business, stating that it was worse than Sunday. Murmurings indicative of as hearty agreement with this sentiment as their lethargy would allow came from the other members of the family circle, causing Mr. Gummidge to suggest a walk in the air to settle their dinner.

And then arose such a chorus of protestations as has seldom been heard. It was too cloudy to walk. It was too raw. It looked like snow. It looked like rain. Luther Gummidge said that he must be starting along home soon, anyway, bringing forth the acid query from Mrs. Gummidge as to whether or not he was bored. Lillian said that she felt a cold coming on, and added that something they had had for dinner must have been undercooked. And so it went, back and forth,

forth and back, up and down, and in and out, until Mr. Gummidge's suggestion of a walk in the air was reduced to a tattered impossibility and the entire company glowed with ill-feeling.

In the meantime, we must not forget the children. No one else could. Aunt Libbie said that she didn't think there was anything like children to make a Christmas; to which Uncle Ray, the one with the Masonic fob, said, "No, thank God!" Although Christmas is supposed to be the season of good cheer, you (or I, for that matter) couldn't have told, from listening to the little ones, but what it was the children's Armageddon season, when Nature had decreed that only the fittest should survive, in order that the race might be carried on by the strongest, the most predatory and those possessing the best protective coloring. Although there were constant admonitions to Fonlansbee to "Let Ormond have that now; it's his," and to Arthur, Jr., not to be selfish, but to "give the kiddie-car to Effie; she's smaller than you are," the net result was always that Fonlansbee kept the whistle and Arthur, Jr., rode in permanent, albeit disputed, possession of the kiddie-car. Oh, that we mortals should set ourselves up against the inscrutable workings of Nature!

Hallo! A great deal of commotion! That was Uncle George stumbling over the electric train, which had early in the afternoon ceased to function and which had been left directly across the threshold. A great deal of crying! That was Arthur, Jr., bewailing the destruction of his already useless train, about which he had forgotten until the present moment. A great deal of recrimination! That was Arthur, Sr., and George fixing it up. And finally a great crashing! That was Baby Lester pulling over the tree on himself, necessitating the bringing to bear of all of Uncle Ray's knowledge of forestry to extricate him from the wreckage.

And finally Mrs. Gummidge passed the Christmas candy around. Mr. Gummidge afterward admitted that this was a tactical error on the part of his spouse. I no more believe that Mrs. Gummidge thought they wanted that Christmas candy than I believe that she thought they wanted the cold turkey which she later suggested. My opinion is that she wanted to drive them home. At any rate, that is what she succeeded in doing. Such cries as there were of "Ugh! Don't let me see another thing to eat!" and "Take it away!" Then came hurried scramblings in the coat-closet for overshoes. There were the rasping sounds made by cross parents when putting wraps on children. There were insincere exhortations to "come and see us soon" and to "get together for lunch some time." And, finally, there were slammings of doors and the silence of utter exhaustion, while Mrs. Gummidge went about picking up stray sheets of wrapping paper.

And, as Tiny Tim might say in speaking of Christmas afternoon as an institution, "God help us, every one."

THE POETRY READING

KARL SHAPIRO

He takes the lectern in his hands
And, like a pilot at his instruments,
Checks the position of his books, the time,
The glass of water, and the slant of light;
Then, leaning forward on guy-wire nerves,
He elevates the angle of his nose
And powers his soul into the evening.

Now, if ever, he must begin to climb
To that established height
Where one hypnotically remains aloft,
But at the thought, as if an engine coughed,
He drops, barely clearing the first three rows,
Then quakes, recovers, and upward swerves,
And hangs there on his perilous turning fans.

O for more altitude, to spin a cloud
Of crystals, as the cloud writes poetry
In nature's wintry sport!
Or for that hundred-engined voice of wings
That, rising with a turtle in its claws,
Speeds to a rock and drops it heavily,
Where it bursts open with a loud report.

O for that parchment voice of wrinkled vowels,
The voice of all the ages, polyglot,
Sailing death's boat
Past fallen towers of foreign tours—
The shrouded voice troubled with stony texts,
Voice of all souls and of sacred owls,
Darkly intoning from the tailored coat!

Or for the voice of order, witty and good,
Civilizing the ears of the young and rude,
Weaving the music of ideas and forms,
Writing encyclopedias of hope.

Or for that ever higher voice that swarms
Like a bright monkey up religion's rope
To all those vacant thrones.

But he who reads thinks as he drones his song:
What do they think, those furrows of faces,
Of a poet of the middle classes?
Is he a poet at all? His face is fat.
Can the anthologies have his birthday wrong?
He looks more like an aging bureaucrat
Or a haberdasher than a poet of eminence.

He looks more like a Poet-in-Residence. . . .

O to be *déclassé,* or low, or high,
Criminal, bastard, or aristocrat—
Anything but the norm, the in-between!
Oh, martyr him for his particular vice,
Make him conspicuous at any price,
Save him, O God, from being nice.

Whom the gods love die young. Too late for that,
Too late also to find a different job,
He is condemned to fly from room to room
And, like a parakeet, be beautiful,
Or, like a grasshopper in a grammar school,
Leap for the window that he'll never find,
And take off with a throb and come down blind.

A TONVERSATION WITH BABY

MORRIS BISHOP

"Was it a little baby
With wide, unwinking eyes,
Propped in his baby carriage,
Looking so wise?

"Oh, what a pwitty baby!
Oh, what a sweety love!
What is oo thinkin', baby,
And dweamin' of?

"Is oo wond'rin' 'bout de doggie
  A-fwiskin' here 'n dere?
Is oo watchin' de baby birdies
  Everywhere?

" 'N all de funny peoples
  'N a funny sings oo sees?
What is oo sinkin' of, baby?
  Tell me, please.

" 'Z oo sinkin' of tisses, tunnin',
  'N wannin' 'n wannin' for some?
O tweety goo swimmy doodle,
  O yummy yum!"

Then spoke that solemn baby,
  Wise as a little gnome:
"You get in the baby carriage;
  I'll push you home."

END OF SUMMER

STANLEY KUNITZ

An agitation of the air,
A perturbation of the light
Admonished me the unloved year
Would turn on its hinge that night.

I stood in the disenchanted field
Amid the stubble and the stones,
Amazed, while a small worm lisped to me
The song of my marrow-bones.

Blue poured into summer blue,
A hawk broke from his cloudless tower,
The roof of the silo blazed, and I knew
That part of my life was over.

Already the iron door of the north
Clangs open: birds, leaves, snows
Order their populations forth,
And a cruel wind blows.

MY LAST DUCHESS

ROBERT BROWNING

Ferrara

That's my last Duchess painted on the wall,
Looking as if she were alive; I call
That piece a wonder, now: Frà Pandolf's hands
Worked busily a day, and there she stands.
Will't please you sit and look at her? I said
'Frà Pandolf' by design, for never read
Strangers like you that pictured countenance,
The depth and passion of its earnest glance,
But to myself they turned (since none puts by
The curtain I have drawn for you, but I)
And seemed as they would ask me, if they durst,
How such a glance came there; so, not the first
Are you to turn and ask thus. Sir, 'twas not
Her husband's presence only, called that spot
Of joy into the Duchess' cheek: perhaps
Frà Pandolf chanced to say 'Her mantle laps
Over my Lady's wrist too much,' or 'Paint
Must never hope to reproduce the faint
Half-flush that dies along her throat;' such stuff
Was courtesy, she thought, and cause enough
For calling up that spot of joy. She had
A heart . . . how shall I say? . . . too soon made glad,
Too easily impressed; she liked whate'er
She looked on, and her looks went everywhere.
Sir, 'twas all one! My favour at her breast,
The dropping of the daylight in the West,
The bough of cherries some officious fool
Broke in the orchard for her, the white mule
She rode with round the terrace—all and each
Would draw from her alike the approving speech,
Or blush, at least. She thanked men,—good; but thanked
Somehow . . . I know not how . . . as if she ranked
My gift of a nine-hundred-years-old name
With anybody's gift. Who'd stoop to blame
This sort of trifling? Even had you skill
In speech—(which I have not)—to make your will

Quite clear to such an one, and say 'Just this
Or that in you disgusts me; here you miss,
Or there exceed the mark'—and if she let
Herself be lessoned so, nor plainly set
Her wits to yours, forsooth, and made excuse,
—E'en then would be some stooping, and I choose
Never to stoop. Oh, Sir, she smiled, no doubt,
Whene'er I passed her; but who passed without
Much the same smile? This grew; I gave commands;
Then all smiles stopped together. There she stands
As if alive. Will't please you rise? We'll meet
The company below, then. I repeat,
The Count your Master's known munificence
Is ample warrant that no just pretence
Of mine for dowry will be disallowed;
Though his fair daughter's self, as I avowed
At starting, is my object. Nay, we'll go
Together down, Sir! Notice Neptune, though,
Taming a sea-horse, thought a rarity,
Which Claus of Innsbruck cast in bronze for me.

from ROMEO AND JULIET

WILLIAM SHAKESPEARE

JULIET. Gallop apace, you fiery-footed steeds,
Towards Phoebus' lodging: such a waggoner
As Phaethon would whip you to the west,
And bring in cloudy night immediately.
Spread thy close curtain, love-performing night,
That runaways' eyes may wink, and Romeo
Leap to these arms, untalk'd of and unseen!
Lovers can see to do their amorous rites
By their own beauties; or, if love be blind,
It best agrees with night. Come, civil night,
Thou sober-suited matron, all in black,
And learn me how to lose a winning match,
Play'd for a pair of stainless maidenhoods:
Hood my unmann'd blood, bating in my cheeks,
With thy black mantle; till strange love, grown bold,
Think true love acted simple modesty.
Come, night; come, Romeo; come, thou day in night;
For thou wilt lie upon the wings of night

Whiter than new snow on a raven's back.
Come, gentle night, come, loving, black-brow'd night,
Give me my Romeo; and, when he shall die,
Take him and cut him out in little stars,
And he will make the face of heaven so fine
That all the world will be in love with night
And pay no worship to the garish sun.
O! I have bought the mansion of a love,
But not possess'd it, and, though I am sold,
Not yet enjoy'd: so tedious is this day
As is the night before some festival
To an impatient child that hath new robes
And may not wear them.

ELEGY ON THE DEATH OF A MAD DOG

OLIVER GOLDSMITH

Good people all, of every sort,
Give ear unto my song;
And if you find it wond'rous short,
It cannot hold you long.

In Islington there was a man,
Of whom the world might say,
That still a godly race he ran,
Whene'er he went to pray.

A kind and gentle heart he had,
To comfort friends and foes;
The naked every day he clad,
When he put on his clothes.

And in that town a dog was found,
As many dogs there be,
Both mongrel, puppy, whelp, and hound,
And curs of low degree.

This dog and man at first were friends;
But when a pique began,
The dog, to gain some private ends,
Went mad and bit the man.

Around from all the neighboring streets
  The wond'ring neighbors ran,
And swore the dog had lost its wits,
  To bite so good a man.

The wound it seem'd both sore and sad
  To every Christian eye;
And while they swore the dog was mad,
  They swore the man would die.

But soon a wonder came to light,
  That showed the rogues they lied:
The man recover'd of the bite,
  The dog it was that died.

THE CAMPUS ON THE HILL

W. D. SNODGRASS

Up the reputable walks of old established trees
They stalk, children of the *nouveaux riches;* chimes
Of the tall Clock Tower drench their heads in blessing:
"I don't wanna play at your house;
I don't like you any more."
My house stands opposite, on the other hill,
Among meadows, with the orchard fences down and falling;
Deer come almost to the door.
You cannot see it, even in this clearest morning.
White birds hang in the air between
Over the garbage landfill and those homes thereto adjacent,
Hovering slowly, turning settling down
Like the flakes sifting imperceptibly onto the little town
In a waterball of glass.
And yet, this morning, beyond this quiet scene,
The floating birds, the backyards of the poor,
Beyond the shopping plaza, the dead canal, the hillside lying tilted in the air,
Tomorrow has broken out today:
Riot in Algeria, in Cyprus, in Alabama;
Aged in wrong, the empires are declining,
And China gathers, soundlessly, like evidence.
What shall I say to the young on such a morning?—
Mind is the one salvation?—also grammar?—

No; my little ones lean not toward revolt. They
Are the Whites, the vaguely furiously driven, who resist
Their souls with such passivity
As would make Quakers swear. All day, dear Lord, all day
They wear their godhead lightly.
They look out from their hill and say,
To themselves, "We have nowhere to go but down;
The great destination is to stay."
Surely the nations will be reasonable;
They look at the world—don't they?—the world's way?
The clock just now has nothing more to say.

LOVELIEST OF TREES

from *A Shropshire Lad*

A. E. HOUSMAN

Loveliest of trees, the cherry now
Is hung with bloom along the bough,
And stands about the woodland ride
Wearing white for Eastertide.

Now, of my threescore years and ten,
Twenty will not come again,
And take from seventy springs a score,
It only leaves me fifty more.

And since to look at things in bloom
Fifty springs are little room,
About the woodlands I will go
To see the cherry hung with snow.

TO HIS COY MISTRESS

ANDREW MARVELL

Had we but World enough, and time,
This coyness, Lady, were no crime.
We would sit down, and think which way
To walk, and pass our long Love's Day.
Thou by the *Indian Ganges* side
Should'st Rubies find: I by the Tide

Of *Humber* would complain. I would
Love you ten years before the Flood:
And you should if you please refuse
Till the Conversion of the *Jews*.
My vegetable Love should grow
Vaster than Empires, and more slow.
An hundred years should go to praise
Thine Eyes, and on thy Forehead Gaze.
Two hundred to adore each Breast:
But thirty thousand to the rest.
An Age at least to every part,
And the last Age should show your Heart.
For Lady, you deserve this State,
Nor would I love at lower rate.
    But at my back I always hear
Time's wingèd Chariot hurrying near:
And yonder all before us lie
Desarts of vast Eternity.
Thy Beauty shall no more be found,
Nor, in thy marble Vault, shall sound
My echoing Song. Then Worms shall try
That long preserv'd Virginity,
And your quaint Honour turn to dust,
And into ashes all my Lust.
The Grave's a fine and private place,
But none, I think, do there embrace.
    Now therefore, while the youthful hue
Sits on thy skin like morning dew,
And while thy willing Soul transpires
At every pore with instant Fires,
Now let us sport us while we may;
And now, like am'rous birds of prey,
Rather at once our Time devour,
Than languish in his slow-chapt pow'r.
Let us roll all our Strength, and all
Our sweetness, up into one Ball,
And tear our Pleasures with rough strife
Thorough the Iron gates of Life.
Thus, though we cannot make our Sun
Stand still, yet we will make him run.

DEATH, BE NOT PROUD

JOHN DONNE

Death, be not proud, though some have callèd thee
Mighty and dreadful, for thou art not so;
For those whom thou think'st thou dost overthrow
Die not, poor Death; nor yet canst thou kill me.
From rest and sleep, which but thy pictures be,
Much pleasure; then from thee much more must flow;
And soonest our best men with thee do go—
Rest of their bones, and souls' delivery!
Thou'rt slave to fate, chance, kings, and desperate men,
And dost with poison, war, and sickness dwell;
And poppy or charms can make us sleep as well
And better than thy stroke. Why swell'st thou then?
    One short sleep past, we wake eternally,
    And Death shall be no more: Death, thou shalt die.

Selected Readings

Compere, Moiree. *Living Literature for Oral Interpretation.* New York: Appleton-Century-Crofts, 1949, Part VI, "Introduction to the Lecture-Recital," Part VII, "Poetry and Laughter: A Lecture-Recital."

Grimes, Wilma H., and Alethea Smith Mattingly. *Interpretation: Writer, Reader, Audience.* Belmont, Cal.: Wadsworth Publishing Co., 1961, Chapter XII, "Programing."

Lowrey, Sara, and Gertrude E. Johnson. *Interpretative Reading.* (Revised edition) New York: Appleton-Century-Crofts, 1953, Chapter VI, "Illlusion in Interpretative Reading," Chapter IX, "Backgrounds, Introductions, and Programs."

Smith, Joseph F., and James R. Linn. *Skill in Reading Aloud.* New York: Harper, 1960, Chapter VIII, "Visibility."

Part II

FINDING THE MEANING

4

DISCOVERING THE NATURE OF MEANING

IMPORTANCE OF UNDERSTANDING THE MEANING

Your most important task as an interpreter is to understand what you read. While it may be an exaggeration to say that if you understand an idea you can explain it to someone else, it is certainly no exaggeration to say that if you do *not* understand it you *cannot* explain it. No one doubts this necessity on the level of everyday experiences. You would not try to give a tourist instructions on how to reach the spots of interest in your town unless you first knew where those places were. You would not try to explain the ablative case to your roommate who is struggling with Latin unless you had been exposed to that grammatical construction yourself. Perhaps you have tried to answer a little child's question about "How does the grass grow?"

or "Who made God?" and found that you simply could not do so because you did not understand the matter yourself. Beginning teachers sometimes discover with a shock that they must restudy their subject matter for full comprehension before they can begin to teach their students.

As students of speech many of you already know how hopeless it is to try to make a point clear to an audience if you do not grasp it yourself. Probably you have been told that the very best material for speech making is personal experience, for with it you are most likely to understand what you are trying to tell others. All the techniques for effective public speaking are doomed to failure unless the speaker knows his subject.

Just as certainly, the techniques of oral interpretation will fail unless you first thoroughly understand the meaning of the literature you are reading. For this reason we must be concerned with what are called "techniques of impression" before studying the use of voice and body in the actual process of communication. Quite often the poor reader knows only the relatively simple mechanical process of translating black marks on a page to sound waves. This inadequate process suggests the definition of the lecture method so often used in college classes: the process of transferring the words in the notes of the professor to the notes of the student without passing through the mind of either. Good reading is never the process of transferring mere symbols to the listeners' ears without involving the minds of both reader and listeners. Your expression of a piece of literature can never exceed your impression.

THE NATURE OF MEANING

The psychologist will tell you that the essence of meaning is response. In a laboratory experiment a fish may be subjected to a tiny electric shock. In response he feels pain and withdraws from the stimulus. His pain and withdrawal constitute the innate and unlearned meaning of the shock. If food is placed on the surface of the water and the stimulus of that food reaches his senses, his response may be to approach the food; perhaps he may even begin to secrete the appropriate digestive juices. These responses then are the meanings which he attaches to these elements injected into his environment. Further experimentation can result in conditioning his reactions. Conceivably he may so often be shocked and then immediately given food that his responses may be associated: eventually he may respond to the shock as if it were food. The shock treatment may become a call to lunch. In the same way a dog can be conditioned to respond to his master's voice or to the sight of his feeding pan.

So it is on any level of life that meaning is the response—sometimes innate and sometimes learned—which an organism makes to a stimulus:

to a baby the meaning of a hot stove may be pain and the meaning of a spoon unpleasant medicine. The child who is only beginning to use language again illustrates this principle on an elementary level. Already he has learned that the presence of his mother is accompanied by the satisfaction of his needs: she gives him food or soothes his troubled spirit. Always she says, "Mamma feed baby," or "Mamma help." Soon the words alone are enough to soothe him. Then, perhaps rather suddenly, he begins to say "Mamma" himself, for the word means hunger pangs alleviated or cares dissolved. He can as easily learn to respond with fear to the word "Mamma" or any other. Meaning at the word level too is response, whether it be physical, mental, or emotional.

When the child is older, the same principle is repeated endlessly as he responds to the stream of things and activities which make up his environment. The meaning of a dish of cereal may be pleasurable eating; on the contrary, if the oatmeal is hot when he first feels it within his mouth, the meaning may be a very unpleasant one, which to the frustration of his parents may persist for a long time. Thus he may have as unfavorable—even unhealthful—a response to the word "cereal" as he has to the food itself. In that event he may have to learn all over again the meaning of a dish of cereal. Through a process of *conditioning,* his meanings gradually change so that the sight of the oatmeal box may come to produce much the same response as the food itself. In this way words are learned. Eventually the word "eat" may provoke the same response he earlier experienced only in connection with the food itself.

In the course of our learning a language this process is repeated over and over again until we have mastered a long and involved set of word symbols with which we have come to associate certain responses. The baby hears "No" and desists from what he is doing. "Hot" or "Hurt" may produce the same general response. "Come" is followed by outstretched arms, "Pretty" by a smile, "Bye-Bye" by waving, and "Kiss" by an obediently offered cheek. Soon the responses have become fixed so that they are combined into intelligent reactions to phrases, sentences, and even extended patterns of speech. The eighteen-months-old baby may react quite accurately to "Love Daddy," "Go to Mamma," "Build a house," "Get your shoes," "Put it in the waste basket," and even more complicated sentences. Eventually he learns that he can employ the same symbols himself to express the responses within him. After building his house he may say, "See." When he wants the door opened, he says, "In." If a toy is damaged, he runs to tell Mother, "Broke." Soon he is saying "Read book," and "Rock baby." Thus oral language is mastered by the association of responses with the word symbols.

Then we are exposed to written language, and we learn a new step in the stimulus-response pattern. To use the illustration already employed, we now learn to respond to the printed word "cereal" by making the sounds of the word, which in turn evoke the response already learned for cereal. For a long time we are able to complete only the first step in reading, which is to say the word when we see it written. (Pity the reader who never gets beyond this stage!) Slowly then the pattern is completed, and we learn to respond to the printed symbol with a whole set of reactions dictated and limited by the experiences that have happened to us.

The point of this discussion is that for the reader, and the listener too, meaning is simply response. It may include purely logical designations (if such there be!) and the most involved emotional reactions. It is almost never solely one or the other but is nearly always both. Meaning is as complicated as the experiences of the reader and often may include a multitude of them. It must remain forever the great uncertain, immeasurable quantity in communication. There is so much of reality for which language tries to stand that, while literary men and dictionary makers alike may try to refine meanings, responses to words will remain always personalized and varied. They will include all of the experiences of all the minds involved in communication. For this reason "finding the meaning" is the single most significant and difficult part of oral interpretation.

WHAT DOES IT MEAN TO YOU?

Let us suppose that you wish to read narrative prose to your oral interpretation class. Luckily you find the following selection.

from A SENSE OF SHELTER

JOHN UPDIKE

in *Pigeon Feathers and Other Stories*

The two hours of the school afternoon held Latin and a study hall. In study hall, while the five people at the table with him played tic-tac-toe and sucked cough drops and yawned, he did all his homework for the next day. He prepared thirty lines of Vergil, Aeneas in the Underworld. The study hall was a huge low room in the basement of the building; its coziness crept into Tartarus. On the other side of the fudge-colored wall the circular saw in the woodworking shop whined and gasped and then whined again; it bit off pieces of wood with a rising, somehow terrorized inflection—*bzzzzzp!* He solved ten problems in trigonometry. His mind cut nearly through their knots and separated them, neat stiff squares of answer, one by one from the long but finite plank of problems that connected Plane Geometry with Solid. Lastly, as the snow on a ragged slant drifted down into the cement pits outside the steel-mullioned windows, he read a short story by Edgar Allan Poe. He closed the book softly on the pleasing sonority of its final note of horror, gazed at the red, wet, menthol-scented inner membrane of Judy Whipple's yawn, rimmed with flaking pink lipstick, and yielded his conscience to the snug sense of his work done, of the snow falling, of the warm minutes that walked through their shelter so slowly. The perforated acoustic tiling above his head seemed the lining of a long tube that would go all the way: high school merging into college, college into graduate school, graduate school into teaching at a college—section man, assistant, associate, *full* professor, possessor of a dozen languages and a thousand books, a man brilliant in his forties, wise in his fifties, renowned in his sixties, revered in his seventies, and then retired, sitting in the study lined with acoustical books until the time came for the last transition from silence to silence, and he would die, like Tennyson, with a copy of *Cymbeline* beside him on the moon-drenched bed.

After school he had to go to Room 101 and cut a sports cartoon into a stencil for the school paper. He liked the building best when it was nearly empty, when the casual residents—the real commuters, the do-nothings, the trash—had cleared out. Then the janitors went down the halls sowing seeds of red wax and making an immaculate harvest with broad brooms, gathering all the fluff and hairpins and wrappers and powder that the animals had dropped that day. The basketball team thumped in the hollow gymnasium; the cheerleaders rehearsed behind drawn curtains on the stage. In Room 101 two empty-headed typists with stripes bleached into their hair banged away between giggles and mistakes. At her desk Mrs. Gregory, the faculty sponsor, wearily passed her pencil through misspelled news copy on tablet paper. William took the shadow box from the top of the filing cabinet and the styluses and little square plastic shading screens from their drawer and the stencil from the closet where the typed stencils hung, like fragile scarves, on hooks. B-BALLERS BOW, 57-42, was the headline. He drew a tall b-baller bowing to a stumpy pagan idol, labelled "W" for victorious Weiserton High, and traced it in the soft blue wax with the fine loop stylus. His careful breath grazed his knuckles. His eyebrows frowned while his heart bobbed happily on the giddy prattle of the typists. The shadow box was simply a black frame holding a pane of glass and lifted at one end by two legs so the light blub, fitted in a tiny tray, could slide under; it was like a primitive lean-to sheltering a fire. As he worked, his eyes smarting, he mixed himself up with the light bulb, felt himself burning under a slanting roof upon which a huge hand scratched. The glass grew hot; the danger in the job was pulling the softened wax with your damp hand, distorting or tearing the typed letters. Sometimes the center of an *o* stuck to your skin like a bit of blue confetti. But he was expert and cautious. He returned the things to their places feeling airily tall, heightened by Mrs. Gregory's appreciation, which she expressed by keeping her back turned, in effect stating that other staff members were undependable but William did not need to be watched.

In the hall outside Room 101 only the shouts of a basketball scrimmage reverberated; the chant of the cheerleaders had been silenced. Though he had done everything, he felt reluctant to leave.

WHAT IS YOUR ROLE?

Just what is your personal role in this reading situation? What do you do? This is the problem we face: not necessarily the reader's role in reading "A Sense of Shelter" but his role in reading any selection aloud. You may at first think the problem is so simple that it can be answered in a word or two, but that is not the case. In fact, many reading experiences are ruined because the reader cannot adequately answer the question, "What is my role?"

IS THERE ABSOLUTE MEANING?

In trying to determine the reader's role we must first discover whether any particular piece of literature has clear, specific, unquestionable meanings. In the whole or in any part of "A Sense of Shelter" is there absolute meaning? This profound question we can simplify by applying it to a short sentence rather than to an entire selection. The following sentence will serve our purpose.

I am going to Chicago.

Does it not have a clear, definite, unquestionable meaning? Is it not an example of the expression of an absolute meaning? Apparently so, for the words are in normal order and among the simplest and most easily recognized in English. A readily understood definition of each may be easily found. Surely it therefore follows that we know positively the meaning of that sentence. Suppose, however, that you read it aloud just to make sure: "I am going to Chicago."

On which word did you focus attention by raising the volume or changing the pitch? Did you read it this way? "I am going to *Chicago*." If you did, you probably meant that you are headed for Chicago rather than going to any other city. Perhaps you stressed one of the other words. At any rate, try reading the sentence in these different ways:

> *I* am going to Chicago. (You in particular are going while others may not.)
> I *am* going to Chicago. (Despite obstacles, you are determined to go.)
> I am *going* to Chicago. (You are on your way.)
> I am going *to* Chicago. (You are going to Chicago rather than coming away from there.)

The meaning we at first thought might be absolute has become five possibilities. As a matter of fact, there are many more possible meanings. You can, for example, stress two or more words in one reading and convey a distinctive meaning: "I *am* going to *Chicago*." Make some other combinations which convey different meanings.

Thus far we have experimented with only two of the speech variables, pitch and loudness. If you will employ the other variables, rate and quality, the idea of absolute meaning will become even less tenable. Say the sentence slowly and then rapidly to convey other meanings. Now say it in a tired, nasal voice. Try it with a breathy quality. Say it enthusiastically. Whisper it with secrecy. Notice that the meanings you achieve differ both logically and emotionally.

In all of our experimenting with voice we may have forgotten that speech is a matter of face and body too. See how you can repeat our sentence and give it distinctive meanings with varying facial expressions. Use a smile, a frown, a sneer, raised eyebrows, and any other expressions which may alter meaning. What variety of body movements could you employ with the sentence? Say it as you raise and clench your fist. Experiment with other body movements.

Theoretically, we could go on indefinitely demonstrating different meanings possible in our much-used sentence. Furthermore, we could do the same with any word, sentence, paragraph, story, or poem. See if you can convey several different meanings with the word "yes." Make it mean "no." (Men often think that women have a special talent for saying "yes" or "no" and meaning the opposite.) Say it in such a way as to mean "I certainly do," "Sometimes I do," "Of course, but it doesn't matter," and "I challenge you to deny it." Reread aloud "A Sense of Shelter," using some of the devices we have tried in order to convey different meanings. Invariably you will find not one absolute meaning for any statement but a multitude of meanings from which you must choose.

Is there, then, no definite, clear, absolute meaning? Cannot words on a page say this and only this, no more and no less? To put it a little more academically, can words or phrases ever be completely *denotative* or literal rather than *connotative* in their meanings? What does the word "rose" mean to you? The dictionary defines the noun form alone in six different ways, from a sixty-four word definition of the flower to a much shorter one of the nautical compass card called a rose. It defines a rose as "a perforated nozzle for delivering water in fine jets." A rose is also "a form in which diamonds and other gems are cut." Even the words of these definitions are only symbols. Words which define words are symbols and must in turn be defined with word symbols. The process goes on interminably. Thus there is really so much chance for misinterpretation that it is a wonder that we ever understand anything that anyone ever says! Any definition can only approximate that concept of a rose which you have in your mind and which you have acquired and retained in terms of your *senses* as they have been involved in experiences. To you the word symbol "rose" may mean the red roses on Grandmother's casket or the yellow ones that Dad loves. To someone else "rose" may call to mind the rose thorns he got in his hands as a youngster. Others may be reminded of the pink roses in a special corsage. The service man may think of the compass card he used in the Navy. To more than a few people "rose" means rose fever sniffles and sneezes. You cannot say that "a rose is a rose," for to each person it means something different. In a military or industrial order for material or in a legal document every effort is made to employ languages symbols which cannot be misinterpreted. Qualifying phrases and detailed definitions mount into long paragraphs in the interest of accuracy of meaning, as the following paragraph demonstrates.

> If any premium or installment of premium be not paid as herein provided, and if there be at the expiration of the time herein provided for such payment accumulated cash dividends credited on account of this Policy at least equal to the payment required, then said payment shall be made by the application of an equal amount of such credit, or if such credit be less than the required payment then out of such credit, if sufficient, shall be paid a semiannual or quarterly installment of the annual premium. If such credit shall not be sufficient to pay a quarterly installment of the annual premium, this paragraph shall not apply.

The fact that misinterpretations still occur with disturbing frequency, even when such paragraphs are written, is evidence enough that most words abound in meanings. We call these many meanings *connotations:* they are the personal meanings that we bring to our reading. Because they are so abundant, we must conclude that seldom, if ever, may an absolute meaning be ascribed to any word.

RELATIONSHIP OF EXPERIENCE TO MEANING

Our problem now is to determine the role of experience in the choice of meaning. Here is a portion of a letter.

> Dad is better every day. He has been helping Helen elevate corn and is so happy that he can do it. Helen brings the corn in from the field. Her foot still bothers, especially at night, but nothing serious.
>
> I went to a tea yesterday afternoon at Anna Hessler's church in Galesburg. Six of us neighbors went, and we rode with Marie Swanson. It was a Swedish affair—"a little bit of Sweden." I'd rather have stayed home but couldn't let Anna down.
>
> Frost again last night and 25 this morning. Have you had snow yet?

In all probability it means very little to you. If, however, you had known "Dad"—his character, his appearance, his age, the sound of his voice—and the pathetic story of his many illnesses, you could read the letter more intelligently. If you had painted and used that corn elevator or a similar one, or even if you had only seen one used, you would know what the story is about. Apparently, Helen's foot has been injured. How? What is the story? Knowing it would make you a more appreciative reader. If you had ever been a part of that rural community, you could better appreciate its neighborly relations. If you knew Mother, who wrote the letter, you would understand why she says, "I'd rather have stayed home." Is she bored with her neighbors or does she simply love her home and want to participate in its every activity? Finally, suppose that you knew the thermometer on the front porch and remembered the biting chill of twenty-five degrees on a fall day in northern Illinois. Surely if you had had all these experiences you could draw at will upon your memories as you read the letter, making its words literally come alive, and you could approach an understanding of what the word symbols meant as Mother wrote them.

We suggest that you press this point further. Read the beautiful lyric poem "Barter" by Sara Teasdale on page 106. It will be most meaningful to you if you can draw upon a well-stocked memory of lovely impressions: leaping, sizzling flames of a campfire in the night, blue waves churned white against a cliff, the gentle wonder of a little child's face, and the firm grip of loving arms. "Old Women" by Babette Deutsch may be most truly poignant if you have seen your own sick mother's hands fumble helplessly at the sheets where once she knew romance with her husband and expectant joy at the birth of her child. The poem is real as you remember guiding those nearly lifeless hands to find what they sought. Read Norman Mailer's novel *The Naked and the Dead* and find breath-taking, provocative reality in this novel of war in the Pacific primarily in terms of sensations, thoughts, and emotions you have previously known either in war or elsewhere.

"But," you say, "'Barter,' 'Old Women,' *The Naked and the Dead,* and a simple letter from home are charged with emotions. Surely the more prosaic forms of composition make no such requirements of the reader. Might not I pick up a piece of writing that you would not call 'literature' at all and read it with understanding without all of this reference to previous experience?" Suppose we find out. The following is an exact quotation from a booklet on the operation of a household refrigerator. Notice the words we have underlined and ask yourself whether this paragraph would be meaningful to you without the experiences they inevitably call to mind.

> Wash the exterior with a clean cloth and water. Soap will discolor and scouring powders eventually cut the gloss. Polish with a good wax base polish. Wash the interior, ice trays, shelves, and freezing unit with a lukewarm baking soda solution. Never use hot water on any part of the refrigerator. Ice trays have a treated surface (to aid in removing cubes) which will be destroyed by hot water, soap, or scouring powders.

If each of these underlined words calls to mind a clear memory of an experience, even these instructions become far more understandable. Does not the reference to removing ice cubes call up the sensations of an experience? Actually the simplest word is definable only in terms of some kind of experience. The words themselves are only symbols for experience. Without experiences, full appreciation—yes, even simple understanding—is impossible. Understanding of all meaning centers in the experiences which have created the personality of the reader. The psychologist would say that such understanding is *egocentric*.

A KEY TO UNDERSTANDING

The *one great key* to the understanding and appreciation of literature is this: *we think in terms of our personal and our secondhand experiences.* Rarely, if ever, do we think outside of these experiences. Our comprehension of the thought and the emotion of a piece of literature exists in terms of our direct experience: what we have actually done, felt, and thought; or our indirect experience: what we have participated in vicariously through the medium of listening to and watching others, reading what others have written, listening to the radio, watching television, movies, and plays. Understanding that all meaning is egocentric is the key to the appreciation of literature, and all the other arts as well.

Our fullest thinking is that which employs most intensely the most experience. If you and several other students have recently endured the rigors of registration in a college or university, you will certainly be able to sit down together and decide on improvements you would like to see made in this traditional headache of higher education. Your registrar and the registration officers could also think about their job and perhaps more fully than you because they have had even more experiences with it. The most adequate thinking about the problems of living in a fraternity house is likely to occur in those who have had and can vividly recall fraternity experiences. Your understanding and appreciation of the novel by Harper Lee, *To Kill a Mockingbird,* will depend on the vivid recollection of your own experiences. If you have had military experience, you may be better able to enter into *The Caine Mutiny,* quoted in Chapter 12.

Some of us, however, can employ vicarious experiences more vividly than others can employ personal ones. Often we who have had many vicarious experiences, and have learned to marshal them at will, can find more pleasure in a piece of literature than another person who has had direct personal experience with the people, places, events, and ideas involved. Your appreciation of the book *Anna and the King of Siam,* by Margaret Landon, may be greater than that of the Asiatic traveler—if your indirect experiences are adequate and at your command when needed.

READER'S FREEDOM

Are you as the reader entitled to pick any of those meanings which your experiences enable you to conceive and then try to convey those meanings to your audience? Theoretically, yes, but the context, the author's motivation for writing, his philosophy, his experiences, and perhaps many other factors must guide you in choosing the meaning. In any event, you can choose and express meanings only in terms of your own abilities and experiences, personal and vicarious. There is no absolute meaning, for all understanding is egocentric within the limitations just explained. It is up to you to choose the meaning you are to convey.

READER'S RESPONSIBILITIES

Having observed that there is no absolute meaning inherent in language, that response to language symbols is egocentric, and that the reader is free to choose and express meanings in terms of his abilities and experiences, we must immediately examine the responsibilities of the reader.

Anyone who practices the speech skills is responsible for their honest use. Any public speaker ought to be responsible for the validity of the responses he elicits from his hearers. Any good training in public speaking emphasizes the necessity for reliability in the speaker. In like manner, you, the interpreter, must also be a responsible moral agent. You must choose meaning intelligently. You must try to be faithful to the author's intent. While like the artist you must create truth as you see it, you have no right to betray either the author or your audience. You have the right and the responsibility to say, *"I think this is what the author meant."* The next chapter provides the steps in an intelligent and responsible search for meaning.

IMPLICATIONS

The egocentric nature of meaning also provides an effective clue to the quality of literature. That literature is best which most effectively suggests the significant details to the reader. It challenges him to interpret egocentrically. The role of good literature is the achievement of vital experiences for the reader. Literature even provides so-called new experiences: you are enabled to climb Mt. Everest with Hillary or visit the South Pole with Admiral Byrd. These literary excursions into different worlds are made possible, however, only as you draw on experiences you have already had. Just as a child learns that a mountain (which he has never seen) is a high hill (which he *has* seen), so adults have new experiences in terms of the old. The challenge of good literature is the challenge to egocentric interpretation. More of this is discussed near the end of the next chapter.

Summary

The most important requisite of good oral reading is maximum experience of meaning. Because meaning is response, it is ever individualized and personal. There is no absolute meaning. All appreciation of meaning is egocentric. Understanding is always greatest when you draw generously and with facility upon your relevant experiences. In your role as an oral reader you are free to interpret meaning as you are able and see fit, *but* you must assume the obligation and make a genuine effort to be faithful to the author. Try to find the meaning within yourself. Test that meaning with research. Add to it and modify it accordingly.

Exercises

1. Practice reading aloud the following sentences to see how many different meanings you can convey with each.

Do you hate me?
I love you.
Look at the beautiful girl.
I shall speak when I am ready.
The price is always higher than you think.
Professor Thompson's examinations are easier to understand than his lectures.
No, I don't think so.

2. Read the following excerpt from "University Days" by James Thurber and be ready to tell the class how your appreciation of it is egocentric.

> Another course that I didn't like, but somehow managed to pass, was economics. I went to that class straight from the botany class, which didn't help me any in understanding either subject. I used to get them mixed up. But not as mixed up as another student in my economics class who came there direct from a physics laboratory. He was a tackle on the football team, named Bolenciecwcz. At that time Ohio State University had one of the best football teams in the country, and Bolenciecwcz was one of its outstanding stars. In order to be eligible to play it was necessary for him to keep up in his studies, a very difficult matter, for while he was not dumber than an ox he was not any smarter. Most of his professors were lenient and helped him along. None gave him more hints, in answering questions, or asked him simpler ones than the economics professor, a thin, timid man named Bassum. One day when we were on the subject of transportation and distribution, it came Bolenciecwcz's turn to answer a question. "Name one means of transportation," the professor said to him. No light came into the big tackle's eyes. "Just any means of transportation," said the professor. Bolenciecwcz sat staring at him. "That is," pursued the professor, "any medium, agency, or method of going from one place to another." Bolenciecwcz had the look of a man who is being led into a trap. "You may choose among steam, horse-drawn, or electrically propelled vehicles," said the instructor. "I might suggest the one which we commonly take in making long journeys across land." There was a profound silence in which everybody stirred uneasily, including Bolenciecwcz and

Mr. Bassum. Mr. Bassum abruptly broke his silence in an amazing manner. "Choo-choo-choo," he said, in a low voice, and turned instantly scarlet. He glanced appealingly around the room. All of us, of course, shared Mr. Bassum's desire that Bolenciecwcz should stay abreast of the class in economics, for the Illinois game, one of the hardest and most important of the season, was only a week off. "Toot, toot, too-tooooooot!" some student with a deep voice moaned, and we all looked encouragingly at Bolenciecwcz. Somebody else gave a fine imitation of a locomotive letting off steam. Mr. Bassum himself rounded off the little show. "Ding, dong, ding, dong," he said, hopefully. Bolenciecwcz was staring at the floor now, trying to think, his great brow furrowed, his huge hands rubbing together, his face red.

"How did you come to college this year, Mr. Bolenciecwcz?" asked the professor. "*Chuf*fa chuffa, *chuf*fa chuffa."

"M'father sent me," said the football player.

"What on?" asked Bassum.

"I git an 'lowance," said the tackle, in a low, husky voice, obviously embarrassed.

"No, no," said Bassum. "Name a means of transportation. What did you *ride* here on?"

"Train," said Bolenciecwcz.

"Quite right," said the Professor. "Now, Mr. Nugent, will you tell us . . ."

3. Read the following essay by William Allen White, the late editor of *The Emporia Gazette,* and be ready to tell the class how your appreciation of it is egocentric.

HOW TO EAT WATERMELON

A young person of the female persuasion, who signs herself Guinevere but whose real name is Molly, writes to the *Gazette* to know what is the proper way to eat a watermelon.

The Gazette is no Hill's Manual of Etiquette; neither is it a Gaskell's Compendium of Special Forms. Still it does know how to eat a watermelon. First you slough off thirty years; then get a ten-acre field adjoining a cornfield which borders a creek; prepare carefully, and be sure to insert in the ten-acre field one acre of watermelons; then take three or four large dark green pot-bellied watermelons, insert them gently but firmly in the arms of a similar number of young gentlemen just at that age; slip the young gentlemen deftly through the large commodious cornfield to the banks of the deep, wet creek. Remove the outer covering of the young gentlemen down to that buff cutaneous substance beneath the husks; let them put the melons in the spring under the sycamore tree, and then soak the young gentlemen in the creek from two until half-past four, taking care not to sunburn their backs, nor to remove any of the cutaneous substance on the slippery side. At four-thirty take the young gentlemen out and drain them as they duck through the high horse weeds two hundred yards up stream, still wearing that buff cutaneous substance, and stand them in a row by the railroad bridge waiting for the five o'clock passenger train. As it arrives let the young gentlemen stand waving their arms and yelling to attract the attention of the passengers, and as the sleeper passes let them duck head first, patting their backs as they disappear in the water. After floating downstream at five-thirty take the melons from the spring, break them on a big limestone ledge, give each young gentleman half a melon to hold in his lap, let him gouge out the heart and souse his face in the hole and swill it down. Next, let the first boy who gets down to the rind begin breaking it up and throwing it at the others until all are as sticky and dirty as pigs; take them to the high mud bank over the turtle hole, and shove them off one at a time, then take out and dry clean and serve raw for supper.

That, Guinevere, is the best way to eat watermelon. Try it someday, it is fine.

4. Bring to class all or part of a personal letter with which you can demonstrate how your own experiences enhance appreciation of meaning.

5. Do the same with a poem.

6. Using a musical composition or a painting, demonstrate that here too appreciation of meaning is egocentric. This is a rewarding experience.

7. Ask a friend to tell you his initial response to each of the following words. Ask him what it calls to mind.

rocket	candidate	drink
tobacco	oratory	vault
prayer	flower	graft
war	bomb	work

Now find dictionary definitions of the words and prepare to illustrate for the class the differences between denotation and connotation. You will need to make a note of each response and each definition.

8. Make a serious attempt to find or write a paragraph in which the meaning or meanings will be absolute. You can achieve only very limited success in the attempt, but do your best. Be prepared to measure your success by asking the members of the class to interpret the paragraph for you.

9. What experiences would you have had to have in order to appreciate the following selection as much as you did "A Sense of Shelter" or "How to Eat Watermelon"?

from THE BABY PARTY

F. SCOTT FITZGERALD

He was in a good humor today—all the things in his life were going better than they had ever gone before. When he got off the train at his station he shook his head at an importunate taxi man, and began to walk up the long hill toward his house through the crisp December twilight. It was only six o'clock but the moon was out, shining with proud brilliance on the thin sugary snow that lay over the lawns.

As he walked along drawing his lungs full of cold air his happiness increased, and the idea of a baby party appealed to him more and more. He began to wonder how Ede compared to other children of her own age, and if the pink dress she was to wear was something radical and mature. Increasing his gait he came in sight of his own house, where the lights of a defunct Christmas tree still blossomed in the window, but he continued on past the walk. The party was at the Markeys' next door.

As he mounted the brick step and rang the bell he became aware of voices inside, and he was glad he was not too late. Then he raised his head and listened—the voices were not children's voices, but they were loud and pitched high with anger; there were at least three of them and one, which rose as he listened to a hysterical sob, he recognized immediately as his wife's.

"There's been some trouble," he thought quickly.

Trying the door, he found it unlocked and pushed it open.

The baby party began at half past four, but Edith Andros, calculating shrewdly that the new dress would stand out more sensationally against vestments already rumpled, planned the arrival of herself and little Ede for five. When they appeared it was already a flourishing affair. Four baby girls and nine baby boys, each one curled and washed and dressed with all the care of a proud and jealous heart, were dancing to the music of a phonograph. Never more than two or three were dancing at once, but as all were continually in motion running to and from their mothers for encouragement, the general effect was the same.

As Edith and her daughter entered, the music was temporarily drowned out by a sustained chorus, consisting largely of the word *cute* and directed toward little Ede, who stood looking timidly about and fingering the edges of her pink dress. She was not kissed—this is the sanitary age—but she was passed along a row of mamas each one of whom said "cu-u-ute" to her and held her pink little hand before passing her on to the next. After some encouragement and a few mild pushes she was absorbed into the dance, and became an active member of the party.

Edith stood near the door talking to Mrs. Markey, and keeping one eye on the tiny figure in the pink dress. She did not care for Mrs. Markey; she considered her both snippy and common, but John and Joe Markey were congenial and went in together on the commuting train every morning, so the two women kept up an elaborate pretense of warm amity. They were always reproaching each other for "not coming to see me," and they were always planning the kind of parties that began with "You'll have to come to dinner with us soon, and we'll go in to the theatre," but never matured further.

"Little Ede looks perfectly darling," said Mrs. Markey, smiling and moistening her lips in a way that Edith found particularly repulsive. "So *grown-up*—I can't *believe* it!"

Edith wondered if "little Ede" referred to the fact that Billy Markey, though several months younger, weighed almost five pounds more. Accepting a cup of tea she took a seat with two other ladies on a divan and launched into the real business of the afternoon, which of course lay in relating the recent accomplishments and insouciances of her child.

Suggested Readings

Compere, Moiree. *Living Literature for Oral Interpretation.* New York: Appleton-Century-Crofts, 1949, Introduction.

Geiger, Don. "The Oral Interpreter as a Creator," *The Speech Teacher* (November 1954), 269–277.

Lee, Charlotte I. *Oral Interpretation.* Boston: Houghton Mifflin, 1952, Chapter II, "Selection and Evaluation of Material."

Smith, Joseph F., and James R. Linn. *Skill in Reading Aloud.* New York: Harper, 1960, Chapter II, "What's in a Word?"

Woolbert, Charles H., and Severina E. Nelson. *The Art of Interpretative Speech.* (4th edition) New York: Appleton-Century-Crofts, 1956, Chapter II, "Control in Interpretation."

5

■ FINDING THE MEANING

Although it is hard to separate one aspect of meaning from another, an effort to do so is necessary for the sake of clarity and simplicity. Actually any one part of meaning is involved in every other part, but the procedure for finding the meaning may be organized in thirteen steps: five for the primary essentials of meaning, five for the refinements of meaning, and three for the literary quality.

PRIMARY ESSENTIALS OF MEANING

Step one. The *first step* in finding the meaning of a piece of literature is to read it completely through in order to begin to enjoy it and to grasp the over-all meaning. If your selection is a part of a longer whole, you will usually find it essential to read the entire piece.

Let us suppose that you have chosen to read the following poem. Read it now to get the over-all meaning.

THE GREAT LOVER

RUPERT BROOKE

I have been so great a lover: filled my days
So proudly with the splendor of Love's praise,
The pain, the calm, the astonishment,
Desire illimitable, and still content,
And all dear names men use, to cheat despair,
For the perplexed and viewless stream that bears
Our hearts at random down the dark of life.
Now, ere the unthinking silence on that strife
Steals down, I would cheat drowsy Death so far,
My night shall be remembered for a star
That outshone all the suns of all men's days.
Shall I not crown them with immortal praise
Whom I have loved, who have given me, dared with me
High secrets, and in darkness knelt to see
The inenarrable godhead of delight?
Love is a flame—we have beaconed the world's night;
A city—and we have built it, these and I;
An emperor—we have taught the world to die.
So, for their sakes I loved, ere I go hence,
And the high cause of Love's magnificence,
And to keep loyalties young, I'll write those names
Golden forever, eagles, crying flames,
And set them as a banner, that men may know,
To dare the generations, burn, and blow
Out on the wind of Time, shining and streaming.
These I have loved:
White plates and cups, clean-gleaming,
Ringed with blue lines; and feathery, faery dust;
Wet roofs, beneath the lamplight; the strong crust
Of friendly bread; and many-tasting food;
Rainbows; and the blue bitter smoke of wood;
And radiant raindrops couching in cool flowers;
And flowers themselves, that sway through sunny hours,
Dreaming of moths that drink them under the moon;
Then, the cool kindliness of sheets, that soon
Smooth away trouble; and the rough male kiss

Of blankets; grainy wood; live hair that is
Shining and free; blue-massing clouds; the keen
Unpassioned beauty of a great machine;
The benison of hot water; furs to touch;
The good smell of old clothes; and other such—
The comfortable smell of friendly fingers,
Hair's fragrance, and the musty reek that lingers
About dead leaves and last year's ferns—
Dear names,
And thousand others throng to me! Royal flames;
Sweet water's dimpling laugh from tap or spring;
Holes in the ground; and voices that do sing—
Voices in laughter, too; and body's pain,
Soon turned to peace; and the deep-panting train;
Firm sands; the little dulling edge of foam
That browns and dwindles as the wave goes home;
And washen stones, gay for an hour; the cold
Graveness of iron; moist black earthen mold;
Sleep; and high places; footprints in the dew;
And oaks; and brown horse chestnuts, glossy-new;
And new-peeled sticks; and shining pools on grass—
All these have been my loves. And these shall pass.
Whatever passes not, in the great hour,
Nor all my passion, all my prayers, have power
To hold them with me through the gate of Death.
They'll play deserter, turn with the traitor breath,
Break the high bond we made, and sell Love's trust
And sacramental covenant to the dust.
—Oh, never a doubt but, somewhere, I shall wake,
And give what's left of love again, and make
New friends, now strangers—
But the best I've known,
Stays here, and changes, breaks, grows old, is blown
About the winds of the world, and fades from brains
Of living men, and dies.
Nothing remains.

O dear my loves, O faithless, once again
This one last gift I give: that after men
Shall know, and later lovers, far-removed,
Praise you, "All these were lovely"; say, "He loved."

As a part of your reading for over-all meaning you ought to discover and write down whatever theme you find. In this poem the author is expressing his exultation in the thousand little details of life, familiar and dear through memory—a zest for living. He wants us to remember him as one who loved the experiences of his senses. If the lines to be read were a part of a larger whole, you would want to determine the theme of the whole and the relationship of the part to the whole.

Now let us read another poem.

from CREATE GREAT PEACE

JAMES OPPENHEIM

Would you end war?
Create great Peace . . .
The Peace that demands all of a man,
His love, his life, his veriest self;
Plunge him in the smelting fires of a work that becomes his child. . . .

Give him a hard Peace: a Peace of discipline and justice. . . .
Kindle him with vision, invite him to joy and adventure:
Set him at work, not to create *things*
But to create *men:*
Yea, himself.

Go search your heart, America. . . .
Turn from the machine to man,
Build, while there is yet time, a creative Peace . . .
While there is yet time! . . .
For if you reject great Peace,
As surely as vile living brings disease,
So surely shall your selfishness bring war.

What is the theme? These lines are a part of a longer poem and the theme of the part is the same as that of the whole selection. If you did not know the theme, however, you would have to find the entire poem and determine it. Poems, like other writings, have different meanings for different people, but this one seems to say: "If we want to end war, we must make peace as challenging as war and our goal the building of better people, not better things." What do you think the poem means? Study it again. Be able to explain your understanding of it. When you have made your own statement of the theme, you are ready to discover how every portion of the poem contributes to that theme. The remaining steps will enhance both your understanding and your enjoyment of the selection.

Step two. The *second step* in finding the meaning is to make sure that you understand the meaning of every word as it is used in the selection. Doing this is not usually so simple as it sounds. We find only one really unusual word in "The Great Lover": *inenarrable* in the fifteenth line means "indescribable." Words need not be long or unfamiliar, however, to be inadequately understood. The very title could be easily misunderstood, for it does not refer as might first be imagined to a famous romantic lover but to one who has an intense affection for the experience of the senses.

Go on through the whole selection to get the most out of every word employed. Be sure to understand *desire illimitable* (unrestricted wants and curiosity), *perplexed and viewless, random, immortal, godhead* (the dictionary will tell you this means "essence"), *beaconed* (notice how this means more than just "illuminated" and suggests the searching ray of a lighthouse), *many-tasting food* (the meaning here is as broad as your eating experience!), *unpassioned, benison* (here we have not only a synonym for "blessing" but also a suggestion of dignity), *reek, dimpling laugh, deep-panting train* (do you see the comparison with a great dog gasping for its breath?), *browns, dwindles, washen* (do not let a passive present participle floor you!), *deserter, and sacramental covenant*. Every word, like the brick in the wall, is a part of the whole.

Did you notice the capitalized words? In this case *Death, Love,* and *Time* were all personifications of those realities: each was referred to as a personality. Sometimes the capitalized words are references and allusions, as in the following quotations:

> What was Lincoln's mysterious power, and whence? . . . Inspired, he was truly, as Shakespeare was inspired; as Mozart was inspired; as Burns was inspired; each, like him, sprang directly from the people.
>
> —HENRY WATTERSON, *The Secret of Lincoln's Power*

> And yet, in the El Dorado of which I have told you, but fifteen per cent of lands are cultivated.
>
> —HENRY GRADY, *The Race Problem in the South*

THE WORLD IS TOO MUCH WITH US

WILLIAM WORDSWORTH

The world is too much with us; late and soon,
Getting and spending, we lay waste our powers:
Little we see in Nature that is ours;
We have given our hearts away, a sordid boon!
This Sea that bares her bosom to the moon,
The winds that will be howling at all hours
And are up-gather'd now like sleeping flowers,
For this, for everything, we are out of tune;
It moves us not.—Great God! I'd rather be
A Pagan suckled in a creed outworn,
So might I, standing on this pleasant lea,
Have glimpses that would make me less forlorn;
Have sight of Proteus rising from the sea;
Or hear old Triton blow his wreathéd horn.

Lincoln, Shakespeare, Mozart, Burns, El Dorado, Pagan, Proteus, and *Triton* are not words to skip: find the background of each, for it is essential. If you have tried to read John Milton's poems such as "L'Allegro," "Il Penseroso," or "Paradise Lost," you know that you are helpless to understand them until you have refreshed yourself in classic mythology. References and allusions are probably more important in reading Milton than in reading any other English writer, but they must be understood in all reading whether they are emphasized with capital letters or not.

Surely you have noticed by now that in many instances words are not clear if you use only a literal, dictionary definition. These matter-of-fact definitions, which are so often inadequate, we call "denotative meanings." As we learned in Chapter 4 on "Discovering the Nature of Meaning," the clearest and most important meanings are those that refer to experience: these we call "connotative meanings." This kind of meaning is demonstrated in Brooke's line from "The Great Lover"—*radiant raindrops couching in cool flowers*—if you have ever seen a great crimson rose with the jewels of a recent rain nestling among its petals. Other brilliant connotations might be found for *grainy wood, live hair, blue-massing clouds,* and *body's pain,* to mention only a few. Eventually all meaning partakes of this connotative quality and is most poignant only when it does. The best words in literature are usually those that tell whole stories in themselves—and personal stories at that.

Now try applying the second step to "Create Great Peace." Check on every word about which you have the slightest doubt. Don't miss *smelting fires, discipline, machine, creative,* and *vile.*

Step three. Our *third step* in finding the meaning is to understand word grouping. This process involves an understanding of English usage and idiom: which words go together and what they mean together. Let us use "Create Great Peace" to illustrate our point. Turn back to it and follow as we discuss its constructions. In the third line the word *Peace* is a parallel equivalent of the word *Peace* in the second line. (The grammarian would call it an appositive.) Lines two, three, and four are all one main clause, but this includes a minor clause, *that demands all of a man, his love, his life, his veriest self.* Notice that the minor clause works as an adjective to describe *Peace.* You will see that the fifth line is a complete thought with a "you" understood for the subject. In fact the later groups which begin with *Give, Kindle, invite, Set, Go, Turn,* and *Build* all suppose the use of "you." Notice that when you read *Give him a hard Peace* the following group of *a Peace of discipline and justice* is but an explanatory equivalent of the first.

Go on through the whole poem and analyze the word groups. See which words belong together and what relation they have to other words or word groups. If we were grammarians, we would speak here about simple, complex, and compound sentences, modifiers, prepositional phrases and clauses, subordination, coordination, and many more such technicalities. Our concern with grammar, however, is not with mechanics, but with structure: which words go together to make the sense?

When you have made a careful analysis of the world grouping in the poem, you will have recognized that some groups of words and single words are more important than others. For example, *Create Great Peace* is the most meaningful part of the first stanza. The next three lines of subordinate clauses are amplification of the main idea. Within the main idea, *great* carries the major burden of meaning: you might call it the thought-center. In stanza two the author uses a similar construction in *Give him a hard peace.* This clause expresses the key idea of the whole stanza, and *hard* is the thought-center. Do you think we might call line four another key idea and *men* the thought-center? How about *himself?* Notice the contrasting ideas of *to create things* and *to create men.* The last stanza has a number of important word groups. Would you consider the third line the most important? The last line is the climax and certainly a key idea, with *selfishness* and *war* thought-centers. Many kinds of subordinate words and groups of words are found in the poem: *While there is yet time* and *For if you reject great Peace* are conditional; and *as surely as vile living brings disease* is comparative.

In the following selections we have separated word groups with virgules, and we have underscored the thought-centers. Obviously it is impossible for a marking system fully to indicate which words go together in what relationships, but the lines used here will help you to understand how you can devise your own system. Do you find any occasions to disagree with our choice of groups and centers?

THE UNKNOWN CITIZEN

(To JS/07/M/378 This Marble Monument Is Erected by the State)

W. H. AUDEN

He was found by the Bureau of Statistics to be
One against whom there was no official complaint,/
And all the reports on his conduct agree
That,/ in the modern sense of an old-fashioned word,/ he was a saint,/
For in everything he did/ he served the Greater Community./
Except for the War/till the day he retired/
He worked in a factory and never got fired,/
But satisfied his employers,/ Fudge Motors Inc./
Yet he wasn't a scab/ or odd in his views,/
For his Union reports that he paid his dues,/
(Our report on his Union shows it was sound)/
And our Social Psychology workers found
That he was popular with his mates/ and liked a drink./
The Press are convinced that he bought a paper every day/
And that his reactions to advertisements were normal in every way./
Policies taken out in his name prove that he was fully insured,/
And his Health-card shows he was once in hospital/but left it cured./
Both Producers Research and High-Grade Living declare
He was fully sensible to the advantages of the Installment Plan/
And had everything necessary to the Modern Man,/
A phonograph,/a radio,/ a car/ and a frigidaire./
Our researchers into Public Opinion are content
That he held the proper opinions for the time of year;/
When there was peace,/ he was for peace;/ when there was war,/ he went./
He was married/ and added five children to the population,/
Which our Eugenist says was the right number for a parent of his generation,/
And our teachers report that he never interfered with their education./
Was he free?/ Was he happy?/ The question is absurd:/
Had anything been wrong,/ we should certainly have heard.

from THE SCHOLAR IN A REPUBLIC

WENDELL PHILLIPS

We all agree in the duty of scholars to help those less favored in life,/ and that this duty of scholars to educate the masses/ is still more

> imperative in a republic,/ since a republic trusts the State wholly to the intelligence and moral sense of the people./ The experience of the last forty years/ shows every man that law has no atom of strength,/ either in Boston or New Orleans,/ unless, and only so far as, public opinion indorses it,/ and that your life, goods, and good name/ rest on the moral sense, self-respect, and law-abiding mood/ of the men that walk the streets,/ and hardly a whit on the provisions of the statute-book./ Come,/ any one of you/ outside of the ranks of popular men,/ and you will not fail to find it so./ Easy men dream that we live under a government of law./ Absurd mistake!/ We live under a government of men and newspapers./ Your first attempt to stem dominant and keenly-cherished opinions/ will reveal this to you.

The matter of word grouping and discovering thought-centers is extremely important in finding the meaning of any writing, especially the more involved selections. If you master the process now, you will be ready for succeeding chapters in which you will learn how to employ the elements of voice to communicate the grouping and the centering to your listeners.

Step four. The *fourth step* in finding the meaning is to uncover the author's organization. You need to repeat the process of composition approximately as the author must have experienced it. Any work of literary art is planned. If the literature is good, it must have had a blueprint. That organization will show you how the writer has established his theme. Just as a public speaker must first set up his purpose and central idea, like the runway of a great bridge, and then make sure that every major point in his organization directly supports that idea, like the pilings under a bridge, so has your author planned his poem or story. The job now is to find his bridging! In "Create Great Peace" you will find the following plan: an initial question and answer stating the theme, the necessity for devotion, the need for a hard peace, the fact it must be man's task to develop his personality. Then comes a challenge, and finally a look at the prospects if man refuses to devote himself to peace.

In any language composition the function of an outline is to assist the author in establishing his theme. Compare the ramblings of Walt Whitman in "There Was a Child Went Forth" on page 293 with the tight structure of a sonnet such as Shakespeare's "When in Disgrace with Fortune" on page 115. If you discover the outline in either of these, you will not only know how the author accomplishes his purpose, but you will enable yourself to share his experience as you recreate the piece for an audience.

Never leave out step four. Eventually you may be able to do it in your mind without writing, but do it even then!

Step five. The *fifth step* is to write a paraphrase of the selection. The purpose of this paraphrase is to express in your own words precisely what the selection means to you. Putting ideas into your own words is the surest way to prove your understanding of them. The process of making a paraphrase usually consists of simplification and modernization. You attempt to translate the material into your own thought processes. Consequently the good paraphrase avoids the original author's own words although it is written as if he were saying it. Do not use such expressions as "the author says" but try to employ a clear-cut phrasing of what he says. Keep as close as possible to the form and tone of the original as you understand it. Proceed sentence by sentence.

You will find that different kinds of literature require different types of paraphrase: you may want to use either the *condensative* paraphrase, often called the précis, or the *expansive* paraphrase. In most prose materials, such as exposition or narration, you can boil down the author's words to roughly one-third the length of the original. On the other hand, some pieces of literature, such as most good verse or especially terse prose writings, are already quite concise. In such writing, the author has already distilled experience into fewer and more effective words than could the rest of us. For example, it is unlikely that you could rewrite "The World Is Too Much with Us" in fewer words than Wordsworth used. In this instance a paraphrase will undoubtedly be an expansive one.

> The activities of every day are excessively important in our lives; constantly acquiring and expending, we exhaust our resources: our appreciation of nature is minimal; we have devoted ourselves to that which is not worthwhile. Our lives are ugly and wasted! The great sweep of the ocean in the moonlight, the mighty winds that can break into a roar but are calm and peaceful now like endless fields of quiet and drowsing flowers, for these and for all the magnificence of nature we are not receptive; they are not meaningful to us.
>
> Almighty God! I'd rather I were a believer in falsehoods, nurtured from the cradle in archaic conceptions, if by being so, I could from this lovely spot see things that would give me joy and direction—if I could have here a vision of mythical Proteus, the ancient sea-god who could assume different forms, coming up out of the sea; or if I could hear Triton, a classical sea-god too, with the head and trunk of a man and the tail of a fish, blowing his conch-shell trumpet to raise or calm the waves.

Of course, we must recognize the paraphrase for what it is: a self-disciplinary effort to probe for and to conceive meanings. When we must write them in our own words, we test our own comprehension. Sometimes, of course, we find a selection so simple, the vocabulary and language constructions so near our own, and the meaning so clear that to write a paraphrase would be a waste of time. As our experiences with literature increase, these instances become more common. However, if we find we cannot write a paraphrase, we probably do not understand the author's words.

We must also acknowledge that the paraphrase, no matter how expertly written, is not the entire meaning, for, when one eliminates the original words, phrases, style, and form, one inevitably loses some of the aspects of the author's meanings. The best literature really has an amazing identity of form and meaning: the writer seems to have chosen the inevitable word. We shall speak of this fact again near the end of the chapter.

REFINEMENTS OF MEANING

Next we are concerned with the emotional meaning of language. When we were in grade school, we all learned the multiplication tables. Perhaps you mastered them quickly, or maybe you struggled over some of the combinations a long time. Remembering six times nine was about the hardest of all. Seven times nine was not much easier. Maybe, these two combinations were so difficult that you took them home and repeated them for Mother endlessly. To this day, those two sets of figures may mean not only fifty-four and sixty-three but also the image of Mother and child quietly conquering frustration together. These numbers connote a struggle. Because five times five and nine times nine were easy, they may suggest pleasure even now.

We are not suggesting that there is any emotional color innate in mathematics. Your slide rule obviously has no feelings. The mechanical brains of modern industry and research, which can perform in an instant functions that would require a lifetime of human calculation, have no feelings either. However, we have seen that figures in the experience of a person can involve feelings. In fact, any number has significance to a person that it could never have to a slide rule or calculating machine. The difference lies in the fact that a person has an intricate nervous system which does not isolate impressions and experiences but combines them and, as we have seen in our discussion of the nature of meaning, often alters responses with conditioning and association. Furthermore, the body is equipped with a thalamus, a part of the brain which is involved in the autonomic nervous system and makes every experience in some degree an emotional one. Sometimes this emotional aspect of meaning is so tiny as to be insignificant, but always it is there. This fact is evidence that man is basically an emotional creature.

"But," you say, "I try to be logical, unemotional, and objective about many of my experiences and problems." And so you do; so do we all. It is often necessary that we attempt to be unemotional, but it is always a struggle and never a completely successful one. If you are interested in learning more about the role of language in man's efforts to communicate accurately, ask your librarian for *Language Habits in Human Affairs* by Irving Lee. This stimulating book will show you how difficult it is to engage in objective and logical communication. Our purpose in bringing up the matter here is merely to underline the fact that while we may quite properly try sometimes to employ language symbols without emotional meaning, the attempt is contrary to our natures. More often than not, we are emotional and may expect others to be. This characteristic is a natural and desirable part of being human.

If any piece of writing is to be understood fully, we must look not only to its logical designations but to the emotional refinements of meaning as well. Being the kind of creatures we are, we necessarily respond to both kinds of meaning. For this reason the second section of this chapter is just as important as the first.

Step six. The *sixth step* in finding the meaning is to get acquainted with the personality of the author. Any good encyclopedia or perhaps the introductory commentary in the anthology where the poem is found should be of help. You will find that Rupert Brooke was one of the more promising young English poets in the early part of this century. In college he was known as a brilliant and attractive young man enthralled with the experience of living and dedicated to a career of writing. His teachers expected great things of him, and in 1913 with the publication of his first slight volume of verse they proudly saw their hopes being realized: Rupert Brooke would go far. But when Britain declared war, he enlisted at once. He died in 1915 aboard a hospital ship in the Mediterranean Sea. A man who delighted in life, as few men have, gave it up at twenty-eight. His love of this world was never withered by age: in his poetry he remains an exuberant youth. Now look at the poem again in the light of what you know about the man.

Learn to go through a process like this when you prepare to interpret a piece of literature. Let's do it now for "Create Great Peace." James Oppenheim, modern American poet, novelist, and short story writer, was proud of his Hebrew heritage and said that the *Bible,* together with the writings of Walt Whitman, had been the chief influence upon his writing. Indeed the style of his free verse often takes on the bold freedom of the *Old Testament.* There is a prophetic tone to much of his poetry. Being interested in the psychological aspects of life, he probed deep into human behavior. "The Slave," for example, proclaims the importance of the inner life of a man, how the slavery of man is "not in the chains, but in himself." As you get acquainted with an author, why not read other writings by him? Turn to "Create Great Peace" again, and you will recognize the *Old Testament* style and the prophetic character of the lines. You can see too how Oppenheim employs his knowledge of psychology as he tells us that peace must be challenging. Are you not better able to appreciate the poem than you were before learning about the author?

Step seven. The *seventh step* in finding the meaning is to answer the question, "Why did the author write this?" Like other people, writers often work for money, but because language is a tool of communication you always find that the writer who is worth reading is trying to convey some message. Among the general reasons for writing are to inform, to describe, to convince, to persuade, to interest, to amuse, to entertain, to stimulate, and to impress. But always the purpose is more specific. What do you think it is in "The Great Lover"? Perhaps it was to describe some of the aspects of living that the author loved and to persuade us to remember him for his love of life. What do you think was his reason for writing the poem? Out of your experiences you may see other purposes. How about "Create Great Peace"? What does Oppenheim want us to think and feel when we have read his lines?

Step eight. The *eighth step* in finding the meaning is to decide upon the mood or moods of whatever you are to read. This decision will be easy in "The Great Lover." Obviously it is written in a serious, rather than a tragic, mood, for the simple joy of the senses pervades the whole of it. Even in the last lines when the writer contemplates his death, he indulges in no sorrow but just wants to be remembered as one who loved. Turn once more to "Create Great Peace." Do you find that it has a mood of frightened urgency? Determine the predominant mood before attempting to read a selection to someone else. Even the matter of fact has a mood!

Actually the predominant mood may prove elusive. There may be an underlying mood which upon early reading does not *seem* dominant. You may, for example, miss the underlying mood of "When in Disgrace with Fortune and Men's Eyes" on page 115 because only the last lines are given to the exultant happiness that is basic to the poem. Upon first reading "Dover Beach" on page 232 you may have the same experience. The setting is so beautiful and romantic that your own experiences suggest that the mood is one of basic faith and security. Again the last lines give the lie to this conclusion. The effective oral interpreter will always seek to sense the overriding mood of the total selection he is reading, elusive though that mood may be.

You have probably noticed that portions of "Create Great Peace" are colored by minor moods which vary from one section of the poem to another. You might consider much of the second stanza exalted or inspiring in mood. The first two lines of the last stanza seem solemn and pleading. The last three lines of that stanza are almost brutal and seem to communicate a shudder with *vile living, disease, selfishness,* and *war.* Look not only for the predominant mood but for the minor moods as well. Awareness of them often distinguishes vivid and intense interpretation from that which is colorless and dull.

Step nine. The contemporary poet-critic John Ciardi has written: "It is almost safe to say that a poem is never about what it seems to be about." [1] To find out the less obvious meanings requires that the student study the symbolism in a piece of literature, since many of the deeper meanings lie in symbols rather than in the literal meanings of the words. To make this discovery is the *ninth step* in finding the meaning.

Surely the story of Jonah and the whale has more significance than the mere events of the story seem to express: there must be a "moral." Its exact meaning is, of course, subject to the interpretation placed upon it by the individual reader, but one writer has analyzed it this way:

> The story is told as if these events had actually happened. However, it is written in symbolic language and all the realistic events described are symbols for the inner experiences of the hero. We find a sequence of symbols which follow one another: going into the ship, going into the ship's belly, falling asleep, being in the ocean, and being in the fish's belly. All these symbols stand for the same inner experience: for a condition of being protected and isolated, of safe withdrawal from communication with other human beings. They represent what could be represented in another symbol, the fetus in the mother's womb. Different as the ship's belly, deep sleep, the ocean, and fish's belly are realistically, they are expressive of the same inner experience, of the blending between protection and isolation.
>
> In the manifest story events happen in space and time: *first,* going into the ship's belly; *then,* falling asleep; *then,* being thrown into the ocean; *then,* being swallowed by the fish. One thing happens after the other, and although some events are obviously unrealistic, the story has its own logical consistency in terms of time and space. But if we understand that the writer did not intend to tell us the story of external events, but of the inner experience of a man torn between his conscience and his wish to escape from his inner voice, it becomes clear that his various actions following one after the other express the same mood in him; and that *sequence in time* is expressive of *growing intensity* of the same feeling. In his attempt to escape from his obligation to his fellow men Jonah isolates himself more and more until in the belly of the fish, the protective element has so given way to the imprisoning element that he can stand it no longer and is forced to pray to God to be released from where he had put himself.[2]

[1] John Ciardi, "Robert Frost: The Way to the Poem," *The Saturday Review of Literature,* April 12, 1958, p. 13.

[2] Erich Fromm, *The Forgotten Language: An Introduction to the Understanding of Dreams, Fairy Tales and Myths* (New York: Rinehart, 1951), pp. 22–23.

Employment of symbolic meanings may range from the extremely simple use of a simile to language structures so abstruse that only the most erudite critics bother to argue their exact meanings. Let us look at three rather simple uses of the rose as a symbol of woman's beauty. The first is a simile, a comparison that no one can miss:

MY LOVE IS LIKE A RED RED ROSE

ROBERT BURNS

My love is like a red red rose
  That's newly sprung in June:
My love is like the melodie
  That's sweetly played in tune.

So fair art thou, my bonnie lass,
  So deep in love am I:
And I will love thee still, my dear,
  Till a' the seas gang dry.

Till a' the seas gang dry, my dear,
  And the rocks melt wi' the sun:
And I will love thee still, my dear,
  While the sands o' life shall run.

And fare thee weel, my only love,
  And fare thee weel awhile!
And I will come again my love,
  Tho' it were ten thousand mile.

A more subtle use of the same symbol is provided in the following poem:

GO, LOVELY ROSE!

EDMUND WALLER

  Go, lovely Rose!
Tell her, that wastes her time and me,
  That now she knows,
When I resemble her to thee,
How sweet and fair she seems to be.

  Tell her that's young
And shuns to have her graces spied,

That hadst thou sprung
In deserts, where no men abide,
Thou must have uncommended died.

Small is the worth
Of beauty from the light retired:
Bid her come forth,
Suffer herself to be desired,
And not blush so to be admired.

Then die! that she
The common fate of all things rare
May read in thee:
How small a part of time they share
That are so wondrous sweet and fair!

Another poet has more briefly made a similar use of the rose:

PIAZZA PIECE

JOHN CROWE RANSOM

—I am a gentleman in a dustcoat trying
To make you hear. Your ears are soft and small
And listen to an old man not at all;
They want the young men's whispering and sighing.
But see the roses on your trellis dying
And hear the spectral singing of the moon;
For I must have my lovely lady soon.
I am a gentleman in a dustcoat trying.

—I am a lady young in beauty waiting
Until my true love comes, and then we kiss.
But what grey man among the vines is this
Whose words are dry and faint as in a dream?
Back from my trellis, Sir, before I scream!
I am a lady young in beauty waiting.

Here, the rose is not something the lady is "like" but a mirror in which the lady is supposed to see her own beauty. Its dying is a symbol of the lady's imminent death. Death (amid other clues of her identity: *dustcoat, old, spectral, grey, dry, faint, dream*) awaits her, rather impatiently.

Incidentally, you might like to wonder if the old man in the poem is a symbol of death. Perhaps on the other hand he could be just what he seems to be—an evil old man trying to seduce the young lady. To interpret the poem you would have to decide which is the case.

Even more subtle is William Blake's use of the worm-eaten rose to symbolize the corruption of physical love:

O Rose, thou art sick!
The invisible worm
That flies in the night,
In the howling storm,

Has found out thy bed
Of crimson joy,
And his dark secret love
Does thy life destroy.

Great writers often become much involved with expressing their meanings symbolically, however, and students of literature will often have to dig deep to perceive their meanings. In the following poem, the writer has given new significance to an old story, which is only partially evident from a first or second reading:

JOURNEY OF THE MAGI

T. S. ELIOT

"A cold coming we had of it,
Just the worst time of the year
For a journey, and such a long journey:
The ways deep and weather sharp,
The very dead of winter."
And the camels galled, sore-footed, refractory,
Lying down in the melting snow.
There were times we regretted
The summer palaces on slopes, the terraces,
And the silken girls bringing sherbet.
Then the camel men cursing and grumbling
And running away, and wanting their liquor and women,
And the night-fires going out, and the lack of shelters,
And the cities hostile and the towns unfriendly
And the villages dirty and charging high prices:
A hard time we had of it.
At the end we preferred to travel all night,
Sleeping in snatches,

With the voices singing in our ears, saying
That this was all folly.

Then at dawn we came down to a temperate valley,
Wet, below the snow line, smelling vegetation;
With a running stream and a water-mill beating the darkness,
And three trees on the low sky,
And an old white horse galloped away in the meadow.
Then we came to a tavern with vine-leaves over the lintel,
Six hands at an open door dicing for pieces of silver,
And feet kicking the empty wine-skins.
But there was no information, and so we continued
And arrived at evening, not a moment too soon
Finding the place; it was (you may say) satisfactory.

All this was a long time ago, I remember,
And I would do it again, but set down
This set down
This: were we led all that way for
Birth or Death? There was a Birth, certainly,
We had evidence and no doubt. I had seen birth and death,
But had thought they were different; this Birth was
Hard and bitter agony for us, like Death, our death.
We returned to our places, these Kingdoms,
But no longer at ease here, in the old dispensation,
With an alien people clutching their gods.
I should be glad of another death.

Even on a first reading, the perceptive reader will recognize the *three trees on the low sky* as the three crosses on Golgotha and the *pieces of silver* as the currency for which Christ was sold, and this should convince him that many other items in the poem must also be symbolic. A student of interpretative reading analyzed the second part of this poem as follows: [3]

Then at dawn we came down to a temperate valley,
Wet, below the snow line, smelling vegetation;

Valleys, caves, and other depressions are ancient symbols for woman. This valley has vegetation in it, in other words, life resulting from the woman.

With a running stream—

[3] The authors extend their appreciation to Mr. Lynn Hagman for permission to use his analysis here.

Water is also an old symbol for woman and also for spiritual rebirth; hence, life. *A running stream* would symbolize the eternal life. This stream would represent Christ, issued from Mary.

and a water-mill beating the darkness,

This mill is powered by Christ's promise of everlasting life and is beating at ignorance and evil indicated by *darkness*.

And three trees on the low sky,

This is a grim prophecy of Christ's death. The crosses, themselves, were ancient symbols for trees, which are, in turn, religious symbols, looking upward toward God. The *three trees* might also stand for the Tree of Life, the Tree of Knowledge, and the Tree of Heaven.

An old white horse galloped away in the meadow.

A white horse has long been a symbol associated with a Saviour God. Among many others, Christ has been pictured as riding a white horse. The white horse in this poem is old and is running *away*, probably another prophecy of Christ's death amidst the symbols of his birth. The end of the poem makes much of the relationship of this Birth and Death, of Death *being* Birth, etc.

Then we came to a tavern with vine-leaves over the lintel,

Ivy also symbolizes eternal life.

Six hands at an open door dicing for pieces of silver,

Six hands means that there were three beings. They could be either the Fates or the Christian Trinity. Three is an ancient sacred number. These beings are at an open door, an opening to knowledge, another symbol for Christ. They are gambling for pieces of silver, the currency for which Christ was sold. Perhaps the outcome of this game will decide the fate of Christ.

And feet kicking the empty wine skins.

From Mark 2:22: "And no man putteth new wine into old skins: else the new wine doth burst the skins, and the wine is spilled, and the skins will be marred; but new wine must be put into new skins." Perhaps the empty wine-skins stand for the archaic, rigid customs and laws of ancient Judaism, which were cracked and made useless when the new wine of Christianity was poured into them. After Christ's death, Christianity had apparently died out but it had ruined the old system and left it marred beyond repair. The feet are kicking the old skins, thus demonstrating further contempt for the old dispensation.

Whether the poet would agree with the student's interpretation of his poem, we do not know, but we can see that the student's research in ancient symbols does reveal many interesting significances to this part of the poem, and they are seemingly consistent with the Christian theme and apparently with the rest of the poem.

Various sources exist for one who wishes to pursue the study of symbolism in literature. It can be an interesting pursuit, necessary if Mr. Ciardi's statement is true.

While it is possible that the search for symbols can become such a fascinating obsession that the student attempts to ascribe meaning to "symbols" which do not really exist, it is even greater folly to ignore the symbolic meanings in great literature.

Step ten. The *tenth step* is experiencing the images, which are, perhaps, the most interesting aspect of literature. It is primarily the images in language that vivify and personalize. If it were not for images, we would react to language symbols like a calculating machine in response to figures, or a photo-electric cell in response to a beam of light. Instead we are forever different from the mechanical device, which retains nothing from experience, for we respond out of the experience of our senses. This is what we were talking about in Chapter 4 on the nature of meaning.

For some illustrations of imagery we need look no farther than the classic examples to be found in "The Great Lover." In the middle section of the poem there are about fifty distinct images. The words in parentheses identify them for you. Some of these pictures depend upon eye recollections, and so we shall call them sight images. Others are images of hearing, smell, taste, and touch. A little later we shall have a more exhaustive listing of the kinds of images possible.

These I have loved:

White plates and cups, clean-gleaming,
(sight)
Ringed with blue line; and feathery, faery dust;
(sight) (sight and touch)
Wet roofs, beneath the lamp-light; the strong crust
(sight and touch) (sight) (touch)
Of friendly bread; and many tasting food;
(taste)
Rainbows: and the blue bitter smoke of wood;
(sight) (sight) (smell)

And radiant raindrops couching in cool flowers;
(sight) (movement) (temperature and sight)
And flowers themselves, that sway through sunny hours,
(sight) (movement) (sight and temperature)
Dreaming of moths that drink them under the moon;
(sight) (movement) (sight)
Then, the cool kindliness of sheets, that soon
(temperature) (touch)
Smooth away trouble; and the rough male kiss
(movement) (touch)
Of blankets; grainy wood; live hair that is
(touch and sight) (touch)
Shining and free; blue massing clouds; the keen
(sight) (sight)
Unpassioned beauty of a great machine;
(sight)
The benison of hot water; furs to touch;
(touch and temperature) (touch)
The good smell of old clothes; and other such—
(smell)
The comfortable smell of friendly fingers,
(smell)
Hair's fragrance, and the musty reek that lingers
(smell) (smell)
About dead leaves and last year's ferns—
Dear names,
And thousand others throng to me! Royal flames;
(movement) (sight)
Sweet water's dimpling laugh from tap or spring;
(taste) (sight) (hearing) (sight) (sight)
Holes in the ground; and voices that do sing—
(sight) (hearing)
Voices in laughter, too; and body's pain,
(hearing) (pain)
Soon turned to peace; and the deep-panting train;
(hearing)
Firm sands; the little dulling edge of foam
(touch) (touch)
That browns and dwindles as the wave goes home.
(sight) (sight) (movement)

What is an image? The best answer we know is to be found in this well-known poem.

DAFFODILS

WILLIAM WORDSWORTH

I wander'd lonely as a cloud
That floats on high o'er vales and hills,
When all at once I saw a crowd,
A host, of golden daffodils,
Beside the lake, beneath the trees,
Fluttering and dancing in the breeze.

Continuous as the stars that shine
And twinkle on the Milky Way,
They stretch'd in never-ending line
Along the margin of a bay:
Ten thousand saw I at a glance
Tossing their heads in sprightly dance.

The waves beside them danced, but they
Outdid the sparkling waves in glee:
A poet could not but be gay,
In such a jocund company!
I gazed—and gazed—but little thought
What wealth the show to me had brought:

For oft, when on my couch I lie
In vacant or in pensive mood,
They flash upon that inward eye
Which is the bliss of solitude;
And then my heart with pleasure fills,
And dances with the daffodils.

Like Wordsworth, you surely have had the experience of recollecting an impressive sight. The pictures that flashed upon his *inward eye* were images. He re-experienced the sight of the daffodils within his mind. But as we have seen in "The Great Lover," imagery may have to do with senses other than sight. Can you recall the taste of an onion? That recollection is imagery too. Can you re-experience the touch of a dog's silky ear, the odor of rotten eggs, the feeling of oppressive heat on a humid day, or the movement involved in a dance step you know? All of these are images.

The following list may serve to review for you some of the possibilities of imagery. See if you can call to mind an example of each type of image.

sight	pain
hearing	temperature
smell	balance
taste	movement
touch	hunger
thirst	

This list includes some not mentioned before. Can you think of any more types? We know a successful college student who is blind. He tells us that he can sense the presence of another person or of an obstruction before him. He is also able to recreate an image of that sensation, to produce it in his mind when the reality is not present. This is imagery too. May there not also be images of frustration, anger, fear, joy, and many more? Your experiences with imagery need not be confined to any list.

Imagery is part of meaning, for it is part of your response to language symbols. The great difficulty in ascertaining the meaning of language comes from the diversity of images aroused in us according to our various experiences. The image exists only as the reader or listener is able to recall some experience or combination of experiences, either personal or secondhand. Therefore, the images which come to your mind will be different from those of someone else. In fact, the image in your mind may or may not be the same as that intended by the author. As we have already observed in talking about your personal role in reading, you should try to reproduce as nearly as possible the author's intention, to recapture his images, but those pictures will eternally remain *your personal* possessions. They will be appealing and vital in proportion to your experience and ability to recall.

LITERARY QUALITY

As we have seen in the first chapter of this book, the ability to appreciate good literature is one of the potential outcomes of a course in oral interpretation. If you want to improve your own appreciation of the skill that has gone into the composition of literature that you choose to read aloud, you will want to know what to look for.

Step eleven. To begin with, certain factors of literary art, which C. C. Cunningham calls the extrinsic ones of literary skill, take the reader beyond the bounds of the particular selection and relate him to the whole range of human experience.[4] They are universality, individuality, and suggestion. Al-

[4] If you are interested in what Cunningham has to say about the factors of literary skill, see his book entitled *Making Words Come Alive,* which is listed in the Suggested Readings on page 140. It is sufficient for our purpose here to name them and to point them out in sample selections.

though your ability to appreciate these factors will be determined by your knowledge of people, the extent of your experiences, and the degree of your acquaintance with literature, the recognition of them is the *eleventh step* in finding the meaning.

The most easily recognized of these qualities is universality. Good literature refers to human motives and experiences common to all men. The public speaker learns that he is most effective when he appeals to such basic motives as the desire to possess things, the need for security, and the desire to show up well in others' eyes. He finds too that he is likely to be most effective when he employs illustrations that touch on feelings and experiences all men have had or will have, such as love, hate, hope, fear, loneliness, childhood, and death. These motives, feelings, and experiences tend to assure him a universality of response, and they are the same features you must look for to discover the potential appeal inherent in a selection you are to read aloud. Certainly "The Great Lover" has a high degree of universality in its many references to our common experiences.

Suppose we look for universality in "Create Great Peace." The first line, *Would you end war?* touches a desire or motive that is vital to all of us in these days of international suspicion and fear. Surely every one of us would like to end war. Are there any other references to motives or experiences common to all of us? How about *justice, joy and adventure, vile living brings disease,* and the idea that selfishness brings war? If you have seen the movie called *La Dolce Vita,* you certainly understand the reference to vile living.

The second of the extrinsic factors of literary skill is known as individuality. It is revealed in the unique way the author treats the material he has chosen to write about. What is there about his writing that makes it stand out from the commonplace? What does it have that makes it more appealing than other writings on the same or a similar theme? Your ability to see freshness and originality of expression depends on the breadth of your acquaintance with literature. Read this paraphrase of some lines from "The Great Lover" and see how inferior it is to the original: "Clean, blue and white plates and cups; dust; wet roofs shining in the light; hard bread crust; foods with many flavors; rainbows; smoke; drops of water lying in flowers; bending flowers in the sunshine, pleasantly cool sheets; the feel of blankets; rough wood; hair that is shiny and messed; banks of blue clouds; a machine; the blessing of hot water; the feel of furs; smelly clothes, etc." These lines lack individuality, but the original ones have it. This factor of individuality is largely responsible for some books appealing to generation after generation and others exhausting their usefulness in a fortnight. Individuality distinguishes the work of the artist from the work of the hack. Look for it in anything you expect to read aloud.

The third of the extrinsic factors of literary skill, and perhaps the most rewarding one, is suggestion. The mark of a good book or poem is often not so much what it says as what it leaves unsaid and prompts you to think for yourself. Imagery is a part of suggestion, but often images are only means to the suggestion of larger concepts not literally expressed. Look for the between-the-lines ideas the author suggests to you. In them an author wins your participation in his book or poem. What images does he prompt you to recall? What thoughts does he provoke without wrapping them up and tying them down with his words, commas, and periods? Look for these thoughts and then try to get your listener to do his own thinking too. Suggestion is the mark of art.

Universality, individuality, and suggestion will be easily seen in the following samples of modern American literature. In the first one you will see that Sara Teasdale has dealt with ideas and motives appealing to all of us. Furthermore, she has treated them with a charm and delicacy all her own. Finally, her poem has far more between the lines than in the lines themselves: to read it is to make it yours with all the thoughts and experiences she prompts you to recall.

BARTER

SARA TEASDALE

Life has loveliness to sell—
    All beautiful and splendid things,
Blue waves whitened on a cliff,
    Climbing fire that sways and sings,
And children's faces looking up
Holding wonder like a cup.

Life has loveliness to sell—
    Music like a curve of gold,
Scent of pine trees in the rain,
    Eyes that love you, arms that hold,
And for your spirit's still delight,
Holy thoughts that star the night.

Spend all you have for loveliness,
    Buy it and never count the cost,
For one white singing hour of peace
    Count many a year of strife well lost,
And for a breath of ecstasy
Give all you have been or could be.

The pen of John Dos Passos is rich in universality, individuality, and suggestion.

from MANHATTAN TRANSFER

JOHN DOS PASSOS

Three gulls wheel above the broken boxes, orangerinds, spoiled cabbage heads that heave between the splintered plank walls, the green waves spume under the round bow as the ferry, skidding on the tide, crashes, gulps the broken water, slides, settles slowly into the slip. Hand-winches whirl with jingle of chains. Gates fold upwards, feet step out across the crack, men and women press through the manuresmelling wooden tunnel of the ferry-house, crushed and jostling like apples fed down a chute into a press. . . .

Glowworm trains shuttle in the gloaming through the foggy looms of spiderweb bridges, elevators soar and drop in their shafts, harbor lights wink.

Like sap at the first frost at five o'clock men and women begin to drain gradually out of the tall buildings downtown, grayfaced throngs flood subways and tubes, vanish underground.

All night the great buildings stand quiet and empty, their million windows dark. Drooling light the ferries chew tracks across the lacquered harbor. At midnight the fourfunneled express steamers slide into the dark out of their glary berths. Bankers blearyeyed from secret conferences hear the hooting of the tugs as they are let out of side doors by lightningbug watchmen; they settle grunting into the back seats of limousines, and whisked uptown into the Forties, clinking streets of ginwhite whiskey-yellow ciderfizzling lights. . . .

Dusk gently smooths crispangled streets. Dark presses tight the steaming asphalt city, crushes the fretwork of windows and lettered signs and chimneys and watertanks and ventilators and fire escapes and moldings and patterns and corrugations and eyes and hands and neckties into blue chunks, into black enormous blocks. Under the rolling heavier heavier pressure windows blurt light. Night crushes bright milk out of arclights, squeezes the sullen blocks until they drip red, yellow, green into streets resounding with feet. All the asphalt oozes light. Light spurts from lettering on roofs, mills dizzily among wheels, stains rolling tons of sky. . . .

Seeping in red twilight out of the Gulf Stream fog, throbbing brassthroat that howls through the stiff-fingered streets, prying open glazed eyes of skyscrapers, splashing red lead on the girdered thighs of the five bridges, teasing caterwauling tugboats into heat under the toppling smoketrees of the harbor.

Spring puckering our mouths, spring giving us gooseflesh grows gigantic out of the droning of sirens, crashes with enormous scaring din through the halted traffic, between attentive frozen tiptoe blocks. . . .

They pair off hurriedly. STANDING UP IN CARS STRICTLY FORBIDDEN. The climbing chain grates, grips the cogs; jerkily the car climbs the incline out of the whirring lights, out of the smell of crowds and steamed corn and peanuts, up jerkily grating up through the tall night of September meteors.

Sea, marshsmell, the lights of an Iron Steamboat leaving the dock. Across wide violet indigo a lighthouse blinks. Then the swoop. The sea does a flipflop, the lights soar. Her hair in his mouth, his hand in her ribs, thighs grind together.

The wind of their falling has snatched their yells, they jerk rattling upwards through the tangled girder-structure. Swoop. Soar. Bubbling lights in a sandwich of darkness and sea. Swoop. KEEP YOUR SEATS FOR THE NEXT RIDE.

Did you notice in the second and fifth paragraphs the pictures of city lights at night? Here is a universal experience in modern living. Can you find any more elements of universality? How about individuality? In paragraph six we are impressed by the unique and brilliant description of how twilight comes to New York City. Are there other especially well-said phrases or lines? Notice how Dos Passos often condenses the noun and the adjective into a single word: it is one of his most famous characteristics. Some good examples of his noun-adjectives are *ginwhite, whiskey-yellow,* and *ciderfizzling*. Of course the suggestion lies in the way the lines call to your mind whatever city scenes you may have experienced, whether in Manhattan or elsewhere, and prompt you to think between the lines of the wonder, beauty, and even the futility of it all.

Carl Sandburg, too, is one of the larger figures in modern literature, and much of his stature lies in his employment of the three qualities we have been talking about. There is often a large element of universal truth in his poetry, especially in the poems about the working class. Examine "Chicago" in Chapter 14 for elements of universality, individuality, and suggestion.

One of the stalwarts of American literature is John Greenleaf Whittier. His writing has an enduring appeal in part at least because of its universality, individuality, and suggestion. Look for these qualities in the following poem. Perhaps, when you have read it, you will want to reread "Snow-

Bound," his best-known poem and part of our rich heritage from the nineteenth century.

from THE ETERNAL GOODNESS

JOHN GREENLEAF WHITTIER

O friends! with whom my feet have trod
The quiet aisles of prayer,
Glad witness to your zeal for God
And love of man I bear.

I trace your lines of argument;
Your logic linked and strong
I weigh as one who dreads dissent,
And fears a doubt as wrong.

But still my human hands are weak
To hold your iron creeds:
Against the words ye bid me speak
My heart within me pleads.

Who fathoms the Eternal Thought?
Who talks of scheme and plan?
The Lord is God! He needeth not
The poor device of man.

I walk with bare, hushed feet the ground
Ye tread with boldness shod;
I dare not fix with mete and bound
The love and power of God.

Ye praise His justice; even such
His pitying love I deem:
Ye seek a king; I fain would touch
The robe that hath no seam.

Ye see the curse which overbroods
A world of pain and loss;
I hear our Lord's beatitudes
And prayer upon the cross.

. . . .

I see the wrong that round me lies,
    I feel the guilt within;
I hear, with groan and travail-cries,
    The world confess its sin.

Yet, in the maddening maze of things,
    And tossed by storm and flood,
To one fixed trust my spirit clings;
    I know that God is good!

. . . .

O brothers! if my faith is vain,
    If hopes like these betray,
Pray for me that my feet may gain
    The sure and safer way.

And Thou, O Lord! by whom are seen
    Thy creatures as they be,
Forgive me if too close I lean
    My human heart on Thee!

Step twelve. Other marks of literary quality you will want to be aware of we shall call the intrinsic factors, those that are part and parcel of the author's skill with words. They include easily read and flowing language, combinations of words that create a melody expressive of the same meaning as that intended by the sense, and appealing rhythms. Take another look at "Barter" for these qualities.

Lincoln's "Gettysburg Address" is rich in these intrinsic factors. You remember it easily and can say it fluently because of these qualities. Someone has printed this speech in poetic lines and so revealed its flowing style, melody, and rhythm, but you have only to say the lines to sense these evidences of the speaker's skill with words. Find a copy of it, or write down the words from memory, and study it. Could you change any words without impeding its easy flow, destroying its melody, or changing its rhythm? The answer is "No," for Lincoln had the happy faculty of choosing the inevitable word for its place, and the result is a masterpiece of intrinsic literary art. Do not expect many selections you may want to read to compare with this speech, but notice always the intrinsic factors of literary quality. This looking for the author's skill with words is the *twelfth step* we suggest you employ in finding the meaning of any selection you may want to read to others.

Step thirteen. The *thirteenth and last step* is to make yourself aware of the literary unity your selection may have. Edgar Allan Poe, who was a foremost literary critic of his day as well as one of our first-ranking American writers, said that in a good short story every feature contributes to the one purpose of the story. By following this principle he was able to produce the best horror stories in the language. Every detail of plot, characters, setting, vocabulary, and sentence structure in "The Masque of the Red Death" contributes to the one purpose of producing a horrified reader. Now look again at the selections from Brooke, Oppenheim, Wordsworth, Teasdale, Dos Passos, Whittier, and Sandburg to see how each of these authors attempts to achieve that same quality of unity. Observe the way one produces delightful reminiscence, another challenge, others beauty, and the last poise and good will. Of course, you do not always find the perfect unity that exists in Poe, but be aware of such unity as there is. Always try to sense it as you find the meaning of a piece of literature. It has been achieved by the conscious effort of the writer: do not miss it.

Summary

The process of finding the meaning of any selection you expect to read to others may be reduced to these simple steps:

1. Read the whole selection quickly and silently to grasp the over-all meaning.
2. Make sure you understand the meaning of each word used.
3. Determine the word grouping or phrasing.
4. Discover the author's organization.
5. Write a paraphrase.
6. Get acquainted with the personality of the author.
7. Determine the reason the selection was written.
8. Decide on the predominant and minor moods of the writing.
9. Understand the symbolism.
10. Try to experience the images.
11. Study the universality, individuality, and suggestion employed in the selection.
12. Mark well the flow of language, its melody, and its rhythm.
13. Discover how the author has achieved literary unity in his writing.

These steps may look like an enormous task, but remember that you cannot effectively read a selection to someone else unless you first understand it yourself. Before you consider your study of this chapter completed, carry out the thirteen steps on several more pieces of writing you might like to read to others. Sometimes all steps may not apply, but usually most of them will. You will find suggested materials in the exercises which follow.

Exercises

1. Find the thought-centers in the following sentences. Be sure you know which word groups belong together and what relation they have to other words or groups of words. Look for contrasts, climaxes, and subordinations.

a. Ability involves responsibility; power, to its last particle, is duty. —A. MACLAREN

b. What I admire in Columbus is not his having discovered a world, but his having gone to search for it on the faith of an opinion. —A. R. J. TURGOT

c. Falsehoods not only disagree with truths, but usually quarrel among themselves.—DANIEL WEBSTER

d. As love increases, prudence diminishes.—FRANÇOIS, DUC DE LA ROCHEFOUCAULD

e. A father's heart is tender, though the man's is made of stone. —EDWARD YOUNG

f. Love is the hardest lesson in Christianity; but, for that reason, it should be most our care to learn it.—WILLIAM PENN

g. The history of Jesus is the history of every man written large. —RALPH WALDO EMERSON

h. For what are they all, in their high conceit,
When man in the bush with God may meet?—RALPH WALDO EMERSON

i. All I have seen teaches me to trust the creator for all I have not seen.—RALPH WALDO EMERSON

j. What is excellent,
As God lives, is permanent;
Hearts are dust, hearts' loves remain:
Heart's love will meet thee again.—RALPH WALDO EMERSON

k. If eyes were made for seeing,
Then Beauty is its own excuse for being.—RALPH WALDO EMERSON

l. Fear not, then, thou child infirm,
There's no god dare wrong a worm.—RALPH WALDO EMERSON

m. O Wild West Wind, thou breath of Autumn's being,
Thou, from whose unseen presence the leaves dead
Are driven, like ghosts from an enchanter fleeing,

Yellow, and black, and pale, and hectic red,
Pestilence-stricken multitudes: O thou,
Who chariotest to their dark wintry bed

The wingéd seeds, where they lie cold and low,
Each like a corpse within its grave, until
Thine azure sister of the spring shall blow

Her clarion o'er the dreaming earth, and fill
(Driving sweet buds like flocks to feed in air)
With living hues and odours plain and hill:
Wild Spirit, which art moving everywhere;
Destroyer and preserver; hear, Oh, hear!—PERCY BYSSHE SHELLEY, *Ode to the West Wind*

n. A good name is to be chosen rather than great riches, and favor is better than silver or gold.—PROVERBS

o. The wicked flee when no one pursues, but the righteous are bold as a lion.—PROVERBS

p. A wise son makes a glad father, but a foolish son is a sorrow to his mother.—PROVERBS

q. The way of a fool is right in his own eyes, but a wise man listens to advice.—PROVERBS

r. He who guards his mouth preserves his life; he who opens wide his lips comes to ruin.—PROVERBS

s. If a man has a talent and cannot use it, he has failed. If he has a talent and uses only half of it, he has partly failed. If he has a talent and learns somehow to use the whole of it, he has gloriously succeeded, and won a satisfaction and a triumph few men ever know.—THOMAS WOLFE

t. A powerful agent is the right word. Whenever we come upon one of those intensely right words in a book or a newspaper the resulting effect is physical as well as spiritual, and electrically prompt.—MARK TWAIN

u. My method is to take the utmost trouble to find the right thing to say, and then to say it with utmost levity.—GEORGE BERNARD SHAW

v. Good name in man and woman, dear my lord,
Is the immediate jewel of their souls:
Who steals my purse steals trash; 'tis something, nothing,
'Twas mine, 'tis his, and has been slave to thousands;
But he that filches from me my good name

Robs me of that which not enriches him,
And makes me poor indeed.—SHAKESPEARE, *Othello*

w. When you sell a man a book you don't sell him just twelve ounces of paper and ink and glue—you sell him a whole new life.—CHRISTOPHER MORLEY

x. Wartime is a bad time for writers, artists and thinking people. No clear or beautiful thought is possible in any country in Europe because of the curse of war, a more fatal disease than cholera, typhoid fever and the rest put together.—JOHN MASEFIELD

y. A teacher who can arouse a feeling for one single good action, for one single good poem, accomplishes more than he who fills our memory with rows on rows of natural objects, classified with name and form.—GOETHE

z. Since I do not foresee that atomic energy is to be a great boon for a long time, I have to say that for the present it is a menace. Perhaps it is well that it should be. It may intimidate the human race into bringing order into its international affairs, which, without the pressure of fear, it would not do.—ALBERT EINSTEIN

2. In the Selections for Practice in Finding the Meaning on the pages which follow, study numbers 4, 7, 8, and 16, and determine the meaning of every word with which you are not thoroughly familiar. Be sure the meaning fits the context.

3. Among the same selections study numbers 1, 2, 3, 13, 14, 18, and 21, and determine word grouping.

4. Briefly outline the author's organization in number 1. Do the same for number 18.

5. Write a paraphrase for each of the following: 3, 5, 6, and 12.

6. In the instances of selections 3, 9, 10, 15, 17, 19, and 21, the personalities of the authors are even more important than in most literature. Read each of these selections, find out about the author, and explain how knowledge of his personality is significant in understanding the selection.

7. Read all of the Selections for Practice in Finding the Meaning and state the predominant mood of each. Note variations in that mood.

8. Why do you think number 9 was written? Ask yourself the same question about numbers 11, 16, 18, 19, and 20.

9. Notice the imagery in the following selections: 2, 9, 10, 14, 15, 16, 17, 18, 19, 22, and 23.

10. Copy at least two of the selections on alternate lines, underline each example of imagery, and label it as in "The Great Lover."

11. Which two or three of all the Selections for Practice in Finding the Meaning seem to be most distinguished for flow, melody, and rhythm of

language? Account for your choice in each instance with specific references to lines.

12. In which two or three selections has unity been most successfully achieved?

SELECTIONS FOR PRACTICE IN FINDING THE MEANING

1

WHEN IN DISGRACE WITH FORTUNE

WILLIAM SHAKESPEARE

When, in disgrace with fortune and men's eyes,
I all alone beweep my outcast state,
And trouble deaf heaven with my bootless cries,
And look upon myself, and curse my fate;
Wishing me like to one more rich in hope,
Featured like him, like him with friends possess'd,
Desiring this man's art, and that man's scope,
With what I most enjoy contented least;
Yet in these thoughts myself almost despising,
Haply I think on thee—and then my state,
Like to the lark at break of day arising
From sullen earth, sings hymns at heaven's gate;
For thy sweet love remember'd such wealth brings
That then I scorn to change my state with kings.

2

from THE EVE OF ST. AGNES

JOHN KEATS

St. Agnes' Eve—Ah, bitter chill it was!
The owl, for all his feathers, was a-cold;
The hare limped trembling through the frozen grass,
And silent was the flock in woolly fold:
Numb were the Beadsman's fingers, while he told
His rosary, and while his frosted breath,
Like pious incense from a censer old,
Seemed taking flight for heaven, without a death,
Past the sweet Virgin's picture, while his prayer he saith.

3

THE HEIGHT OF THE RIDICULOUS

OLIVER WENDELL HOLMES

I wrote some lines once on a time
In wondrous merry mood,
And thought, as usual, men would say
They were exceeding good.

They were so queer, so very queer,
I laughed as I would die;
Albeit, in the general way,
A sober man am I.

I called my servant, and he came;
How kind it was of him
To mind a slender man like me,
He of the mighty limb!

"These to the printer," I exclaimed,
And, in my humorous way,
I added (as a trifling jest),
"There'll be the devil to pay."

He took the paper, and I watched,
And saw him peep within;
At the first line he read, his face
Was all upon the grin.

He read the next; the grin grew broad,
And shot from ear to ear;
He read the third; a chuckling noise
I now began to hear.

The fourth; he broke into a roar;
The fifth; his waistband split;
The sixth; he burst five buttons off,
And tumbled in a fit.

Ten days and nights, with sleepless eye,
I watched that wretched man,

And since, I never dare to write
As funny as I can.

4

MRS. MERRITT

EDGAR LEE MASTERS

Silent before the jury,
Returning no word to the judge when he asked me
If I had aught to say against the sentence,
Only shaking my head.
What could I *say* to people who thought
That a woman of thirty-five was at fault
When her lover of nineteen killed her husband?
Even though she had said to him over and over,
"Go away, Elmer, go far away,
I have maddened your brain with the gift of my body:
You will do some terrible thing."
And just as I feared, he killed my husband;
With which I had nothing to do, before God!
Silent for thirty years in prison!
And the iron gates of Joliet
Swung as the gray and silent trusties
Carried me out in a coffin.

5

A GLASS OF BEER

JAMES STEPHENS

The lanky hank of a she in the inn over there
Nearly killed me for asking the loan of a glass of beer:
May the devil grip the whey-faced slut by the hair,
And beat bad manners out of her skin for a year.

That parboiled imp, with the hardest jaw you will see
On virtue's path, and a voice that would rasp the dead,
Came roaring and raging the minute she looked at me,
And threw me out of the house on the back of my head!

If I asked her master he'd give me a cask a day;
But she with the beer at hand, not a gill would arrange!
May she marry a ghost and bear him a kitten and may
The High King of Glory permit her to get the mange.

6

SONG

CHRISTINA ROSSETTI

When I am dead, my dearest,
    Sing no sad songs for me;
Plant thou no roses at my head,
    Nor shady cypress tree;
Be the green grass above me
    With showers and dewdrops wet;
And if thou wilt, remember,
    And if thou wilt, forget.

I shall not see the shadows,
    I shall not feel the rain;
I shall not hear the nightingale
    Sing on, as if in pain;
And dreaming through the twilight
    That doth not rise nor set,
Haply I may remember,
    And haply may forget.

7

from PARADISE LOST

JOHN MILTON

Of Man's first disobedience, and the fruit
Of that forbidden tree, whose mortal taste
Brought death into the world, and all our woe,
With loss of Eden, till one greater Man
Restore us, and regain the blissful seat,
Sing, heavenly muse, that on the secret top
Of Oreb, or of Sinai, didst inspire

That shepherd who first taught the chosen seed,
In the beginning how the heavens and earth
Rose out of Chaos; or, if Sion hill
Delight thee more, and Siloa's brook that flowed
Fast by the oracle of God; I thence
Invoke thy aid to my adventurous song,
That with no middle flight intends to soar
Above th' Aonian mount, while it pursues
Things unattempted yet in prose or rhyme.
And chiefly thou, O Spirit, that dost prefer
Before all temples th' upright heart and pure,
Instruct me, for thou knowest; thou from the first
Wast present, and, with mighty wings outspread,
Dove-like sat'st brooding on the vast abyss,
And madest it pregnant: what in me is dark,
Illumine; what is low, raise and support;
That, to the height of this great argument,
I may assert eternal Providence,
And justify the ways of God to men.

8

THE NEOLITHIC MAN

from *Similar Cases*

CHARLOTTE PERKINS GILMAN

There was once a Neolithic Man,
    An enterprising wight,
Who made his chopping implements
    Unusually bright.
Unusually clever he,
    Unusually brave,
And he drew delightful Mammoths
    On the borders of his cave.
To his Neolithic neighbors,
    Who were startled and surprised,
Said he, "My friends, in course of time,
    We shall be civilized!
We are going to live in cities!
    We are going to fight in wars!
We are going to eat three times a day
    Without the natural cause!

We are going to turn life upside down
About a thing called gold!
We are going to want the earth, and take
As much as we can hold!
We are going to wear great piles of stuff
Outside our proper skins!
We are going to have diseases!
And Accomplishments!! And Sins!!!"
Then they all rose up in fury
Against their boastful friend,
For prehistoric patience
Cometh quickly to an end.
Said one, "This is chimerical!
Utopian! Absurd!"
Said another, "What a stupid life!
Too dull, upon my word!"
Cried all, "Before such things can come,
You idiotic child,
You must alter Human Nature!"
And they all sat back and smiled.
Thought they, "An answer to that last
It will be hard to find!"
It was a clinching argument
To the Neolithic Mind!

9

from THE PREMATURE BURIAL

EDGAR ALLAN POE

For some minutes after this fancy possessed me, I remained without motion. And why? I could not summon courage to move. I dared not make the effort which was to satisfy me of my fate—and yet there was something at my heart which whispered me *it was sure*. Despair—such as no other species of wretchedness ever calls into being—despair alone urged me, after long irresolution, to uplift the heavy lids of my eyes. I uplifted them. It was dark—all dark. I knew that the fit was over. I knew that the crisis of my disorder had long passed. I knew that I had now fully recovered the use of my visual faculties—and yet it was dark—all dark—the intense and utter raylessness of the Night that endureth for evermore.

I endeavoured to shriek; and my lips and my parched tongue

moved convulsively together in the attempt—but no voice issued from the cavernous lungs, which oppressed as if by the weight of some incumbent mountain, gasped and palpitated, with the heart, at every elaborate and struggling inspiration.

The movement of the jaws, in this effort to cry aloud, showed me that they were bound up, as is usual with the dead. I felt, too, that I lay upon some hard substance; and by something similar my sides were, also, closely compressed. So far, I had not ventured to stir any of my limbs—but now I violently threw up my arms, which had been lying at length, with the wrists crossed. They struck a solid wooden substance, which extended above my person at an elevation of not more than six inches from my face. I could no longer doubt that I reposed within a coffin at last.

And now, amid all my infinite miseries, came sweetly the cherub Hope—for I thought of my precautions. I writhed, and made spasmodic exertions to force open the lid; it would not move. I felt my wrists for the bell-rope: it was not to be found. And now the Comforter fled for ever, and still sterner Despair reigned triumphant; for I could not help perceiving the absence of the paddings which I had so carefully prepared—and then, too, there came suddenly to my nostrils the strong peculiar odour of moist earth. The conclusion was irresistible. I was *not* within the vault. I had fallen into a trance, while absent from home—while among strangers—when, or how—I could not remember—and it was they who had buried me as a dog—nailed up in some common coffin—and thrust, deep, deep, and for ever, into some ordinary and nameless grave.

10

from SPARK OF LIFE

ERICH MARIA REMARQUE

The cell was small and unbearably hot. It had a central heating apparatus turned on full blast. A man was chained by the hands and feet to the pipes. He hung unconscious just above the floor. Breuer contemplated him for a while; then he fetched a watering can from the corridor and sprayed the man as though he were a parched plant. The water sizzled on the hot pipes and evaporated. Luebbe didn't stir. Breuer unlocked the chains. The burned hands fell down. He sprayed the remains of the water in the can over the figure on the floor. A puddle formed. Breuer walked out with the can to fill it again. Outside, he stood still. Two cells further on someone moaned. He put down the can, unlocked the second cell and strolled leisurely in. He could be heard muttering; then came the muffled sounds of kicking; then a thumping, shoving, knocking, clanking, and suddenly howls and screams that slowly merged into the gasps of choking. There were a few more hollow thuds and Breuer appeared again. His right boot was wet. He filled the watering can and strolled back to Cell Seven.

"Well, well!" he said. "You're awake!"

Luebbe lay flat on the ground, face down. He was trying with both hands to scrape together the water on the floor to lick it up. He moved clumsily like a half-dead toad. Suddenly he saw the full watering can. With a low squawk he arched himself, lunged round and made a grab for it. Breuer trod on his hand. Luebbe failed to pull it out from under the boot. He craned his neck as far as he could toward the can; his lips quivered, his head trembled, and he squawked with great effort.

Breuer contemplated him with the expert's eye. He realized that Luebbe was almost finished. "Go on, then—guzzle," he growled. "Guzzle your last breakfast!"

He grinned at his joke and stepped off the hand. Luebbe threw himself at the can with such haste that it rocked. He couldn't believe his luck. "Guzzle slowly," said Breuer. "We have time."

Luebbe drank and drank. He had just gone through chapter six of Breuer's educational program—several days of feeding on nothing but salted herring and salt water; and in addition to this, chained to the hot pipes with the heat full on.

"Enough!" declared Breuer at last and pulled away the can. "Get up. Follow me."

Luebbe stumbled up. He swayed and leaned back and vomited water. "You see," said Breuer, "I told you to drink slow. Move!"

He pushed Luebbe in front of him down the corridor into his room. Luebbe fell into it. "Get up!" said Breuer. "Sit down on that chair!"

Luebbe crawled onto the chair. He swayed and leaned back and waited for the next torture. He no longer knew anything else.

11

from A SOLDIER LOOKS AT THE CHURCH

RUSSELL C. STROUP

It is the function of the Church to convict the world of sin and call men to repentance, but what are the sins which are damning the world to hell in our time? Today fear clutches the heart of humanity as it dimly conceives of the awful horror threatening to destroy every vestige of Christian civilization and send us reeling back into barbarism. But while the world is on fire, the Church fiddles. With irritating monotony we play over the same silly tune unheard above the roaring of the flames. We continue to condemn those evils of the flesh which are only secondary symptoms of a deep-seated disease which threatens the very life of humanity.

Is it any wonder that soldiers facing death in the grim reality of the greatest bloodletting in human history should be unconcerned at the prattle of the chaplains—and there are many—who lecture them on the evils of stud poker, profanity, and jungle juice? Most of the soldiers would not defend as good their language, appetites, or diversions, but all of them must feel that the evil which has brought them to this hour, threatening their lives and the life of the world, is not contained in these paltry sins. They know the awful necessity of war has made them wreckers and killers. They have been taught to shoot, stab, and throttle their enemies. They have been exiled from peaceful homes and the creative work they knew to live like rats in muddy holes. They feel instinctively that the physical and spiritual suffering of war in which they have shared must result from the sins of the world. They would like to know what these sins are. They would like to hear them condemned in themselves as well as others. They long to understand the reason for the cross on which they hang and that other Cross where goodness, justice, mercy, beauty, honor, and love are crucified. They desperately hope that the world may be saved; but how? And the Padre says, "Naughty, naughty for getting drunk."

Before God, what sort of preaching is that? Worse, I have heard a chaplain, God forgive him, preaching to men in the valley of the shadow of death the absolute necessity of baptism by total immersion! Is it any wonder that the soldier is only irritated by the pathetic pipings of such pitiful prophets? While Christ suffers on the Cross for the sins of the world we hurl our polemics at the soldiers shooting craps for His robe. And the tragedy is that the men expect more from His disciples.

12

THE PARABLE OF THE GOOD SAMARITAN

LUKE 10:30–36

REVISED STANDARD VERSION

A man was going down from Jerusalem to Jericho, and he fell among robbers, who stripped him and beat him, and departed, leaving him half-dead. Now by chance a priest was going down that road; and when he saw him he passed by on the other side. So likewise a Levite, when he came to the place and saw him, passed by on the other side. But a Samaritan, as he journeyed, came to where he was; and when he saw him, he had compassion, and went to him and bound up his wounds, pouring on oil and wine; then he set him on his own beast and brought him to an inn, and took care of him. And the next day he took out two denarii and gave them to the innkeeper, saying, "Take care of him; and whatever more you spend, I will repay you when I come back." Which of these three, do you think, proved neighbor to the man who fell among the robbers?

13

PSALM 148

REVISED STANDARD VERSION

Praise the Lord!
Praise the Lord from the heavens,
praise him in the heights!
Praise him, all his angels,
praise him, all his host!

Praise him, sun and moon,
praise him, all you shining stars.
Praise him, you highest heavens,
and you waters above the heavens.

Let them praise the name of the Lord!
For he commanded and they were created.
And he established them for ever and ever;
he fixed their bounds which cannot be passed.

Praise the Lord from the earth,
you sea monsters and all deeps,
Fire and hail, snow and frost,
stormy wind fulfilling his command!

Mountains and all hills,
fruit trees and all cedars!

Beasts and all cattle,
    creeping things and flying birds!

Kings of the earth and all peoples,
    princes and all rulers of the earth!
Young men and maidens together,
    old men and children!

Let them praise the name of the Lord,
    for his name alone is exalted;
    his glory is above earth and heaven.

14

THE TREE

RICHARD M. ROTHMAN

A tree took root in barren soil,
and flourished.

The earth shook and trembled, but the tree stood,
green leaves undaunted.

A wind moaned low from out of the East
then howled at the tree in roaring glee
and struck it in tidal fury.

But the wind passed, and the tree stood,
a green goddess of beauty.

A jagged white bayonet pounced from the blue,
in a terrible streak it shot to the base
and twisted and seared and tore at the tree.

But the bolt passed, and the tree stood,
its ancient green unaltered.

Yet look you at this tree.
Its leaves are withered, its branches shrivelled,
The tree has fallen, dead.

Man came.

15

from THE RIME OF THE ANCIENT MARINER

SAMUEL TAYLOR COLERIDGE

"The fair breeze blew, the white foam flew,
The furrow followed free;
We were the first that ever burst
Into that silent sea.

"Down dropped the breeze, the sails dropped down,
'Twas sad as sad could be;
And we did speak only to break
The silence of the sea!

"All in a hot and copper sky,
The bloody Sun, at noon,
Right up above the mast did stand,
No bigger than the Moon.

"Day after day, day after day,
We stuck, nor breath nor motion;
As idle as a painted ship
Upon a painted ocean.

"Water, water, everywhere,
And all the boards did shrink;
Water, water, everywhere,
Nor any drop to drink.

"The very deep did rot; O Christ!
That ever this should be!
Yea, slimy things did crawl with legs
Upon the slimy sea.

"About, about, in real and rout
The death fires danced at night;
The water, like a witch's oils,
Burnt green, and blue and white."

16

DELIGHT IN DISORDER

ROBERT HERRICK

A sweet disorder in the dress
Kindles in clothes a wantonness:
A lawn about the shoulders thrown
Into a fine distraction:
An erring lace, which here and there
Enthralls the crimson stomacher:
A cuff neglectful, and thereby

Ribands to flow confusedly:
A winning wave (deserving note)
In the tempestuous petticoat:
A careless shoestring in whose tie
I see wild civility:
Do more bewitch me, than when art
Is too precise in every part.

17

TAKE-OFF

ANNE MORROW LINDBERGH

The spray sluiced over the windshield as we started to take off—faster now—we were up on the step—we were trying to get off the water. I held my breath after each pounding spank as the pontoons skipped along from wave to wave. Weighed down with its heavy test load of fuel, the plane felt clumsy, like a duck with clipped wings. It met the coming wave quivering after each effort to rise. Now the spanks were closer together—quick, sharp jolts. I put my hand on the receiving set. It was shaking violently. Suddenly all vibration smoothed out. Effortlessly we rose; we were off; a long curve upward. The squat ferryboats below plowed across our wake, and great flat barges carrying rectangular mounds of different colored earth like spools of gold and tawny silk. I found the little black mass of people on the pier where we had been. Small and insignificant it looked, now I could see the whole life of the river: many piers and crowded ferryboats, ships and roofs and fields and barges, dredges and smokestacks and the towers of New York. We looked insignificant, also, and small to them, I knew, now that our bulk on the end of the pier no longer blocked the horizon. I had become simply a boat in the river of many boats; then a plane in the sky with other planes; now, only a speck against the blue, mistaken easily for a gull.

18

OWNERS AND TENANTS

from *The Grapes of Wrath*

JOHN STEINBECK

The owners of the land came onto the land, or more often a spokesman for the owners came. They came in closed cars, and they felt the dry earth with their fingers, and sometimes they drove big earth augers into the ground for soil tests. The tenants, from their sun-beaten dooryards, watched uneasily when the closed cars drove along the fields. And at last the owner men drove into the dooryards and sat in their cars to talk out of the windows. The tenant men stood beside the cars for a while, and then squatted on their hams and found sticks with which to mark the dust.

In the open doors the women stood looking out, and behind them the children—corn-headed children, with wide eyes, one bare foot on top of the other bare foot, and the toes working. The women and the children watched their men talking to the owner men. They were silent.

Some of the owner men were kind because they hated what they had to do, and some of them were angry because they hated to be cruel, and some of them were cold because they had long ago found that one could not be an owner unless one were cold. And all of them were caught in something larger than themselves. Some of them hated the mathematics that drove them, and some were afraid, and some worshiped the mathematics because it provided a refuge from thought and from feeling. If a bank or a finance company owned the land, the owner man said, The Bank—or the Company—needs—wants—insists—must have—as though the Bank or the Company were a monster, with thought and feeling, which had ensnared them. These last would take no responsibility for the banks or the companies because they were men and slaves, while the banks were machines and masters all at the same time. Some of the owner men were a little proud to be slaves to such cold and powerful masters. The owner men sat in the cars and explained. You know the land is poor. You've scrabbled at it long enough. God knows.

The squatting tenant men nodded and wondered and drew figures in the dust, and yes, they knew, God knows. If the dust only wouldn't fly. If the top would only stay on the soil, it might not be so bad.

The owner men went on leading to their point: You know the land's getting poorer. You know what cotton does to the land; robs it, sucks all the blood out of it.

The squatters nodded—they knew. God knew. If they could only rotate the crops they might pump blood back into the land.

Well, it's too late. And the owner men explained the workings and thinkings of the monster that was stronger than they were. A man can hold land if he can just eat and pay taxes; he can do that.

Yes, he can do that until his crops fail one day and he has to borrow money from the bank.

But—you see, a bank or a company can't do that, because those creatures don't breathe air, don't eat side-meat. They breathe profits; they eat the interest on money. If they don't get it, they die the way you die without air, without side-meat. It is a sad thing, but it is so. It is just so.

The squatting men raised their eyes to understand. Can't we just hang on? Maybe the next year will be a good year. God knows how much cotton next year. And with all the wars—God knows what price cotton will bring. Don't they make explosives out of cotton? And uniforms? Get enough wars and cotton'll hit the ceiling. Next year, maybe. They looked up questioningly.

We can't depend on it. The bank—the monster has to have profits all the time. It can't wait. It'll die. No, taxes go on. When the monster stops growing, it dies. It can't stay one size.

Soft fingers began to tap the sill of the car window, and hard fingers tightened on the restless drawing sticks. In the doorways of the sun-beaten tenant houses, women sighed and shifted feet so that the one that had been down was now on top, and the toes working. Dogs came sniffing near the owner cars and wetted on all four tires one after another. And the chickens lay in the sunny dust and fluffed their feathers to get the cleansing dust down to the skin. In the little sties the pigs grunted inquiringly over the muddy remnants of the slops.

The squatting men looked down again. What do you want us to do? We can't take less share of the crop—we're half starved now. The kids are hungry all the time. We got no clothes, torn an' ragged. If all the neighbors weren't the same, we'd be ashamed to go to meeting.

And at last the owner men came to the point. The tenant system won't work any more. One man on a tractor can take the place of twelve or fourteen families. Pay him a wage and take all the crop. We have to do it. We don't like to do it. But the monster's sick. Something's happened to the monster.

But you'll kill the land with cotton.

We know. We've got to take cotton quick before the land dies. Then we'll sell the land. Lots of families in the East would like to own a piece of land.

The tenant men looked up alarmed. But what'll happen to us? How'll we eat?

You'll have to get off the land. The plows'll go through the dooryard.

And now the squatting men stood up angrily. Grampa took up the land, and he had to kill the Indians and drive them away. And Pa was born here, and he killed weeds and snakes. Then a bad year came and he had to borrow a little money. An' we was born here. There in the door—our children born here. And Pa had to borrow money. The bank owned the land then, but we stayed and we got a little bit of what we raised.

We know that—all that. It's not us, it's the bank. A bank isn't like a man. Or an owner with fifty thousand acres, he isn't like a man either. That's the monster.

Sure, cried the tenant men, but it's our land. We measured it and broke it up. We were born on it and we got killed on it, died on it. Even if it's no good, it's still ours. That's what makes it ours—being born on it, working it, dying on it. That makes ownership, not a paper with numbers on it.

We're sorry. It's not us. It's the monster. The bank isn't like a man.

Yes, but the bank is only made of men.

No, you're wrong there—quite wrong there. The bank is something else than men. It happens that every man in a bank hates what the bank does, and yet the bank does it. The bank is something more than men, I tell you. It's the monster. Men made it, but they can't control it.

The tenants cried: Grampa killed Indians, Pa killed snakes for the land. Maybe we can kill banks—they're worse than Indians and snakes. Maybe we got to fight to keep our land, like Pa and Grampa did.

And now the owner men grew angry. You'll have to go.

But it's ours, the tenant men cried. We—

No. The bank, the monster owns it. You'll have to go.

We'll get our guns, like Grampa when the Indians came. What then?

Well—first the sheriff, and then the troops. You'll be stealing if you try to stay, you'll be murderers if you kill to stay. The monster isn't men, but it can make men do what it wants.

But if we go, where'll we go? How'll we go? We got no money.

We're sorry, said the owner men. The bank, the fifty-thousand-acre owner can't be responsible. You're on land that isn't yours. Once over the line maybe you can pick cotton in the fall. Maybe you can go on relief. Why don't you go on west to California? There's work there, and it never gets cold. Why, you can reach out anywhere and pick an orange. Why, there's always some kind of crop to work in. Why don't you go there? And the owner men started their cars and rolled away.

The tenant men squatted down on their hams again to mark the dust with a stick, to figure, to wonder. Their sun-burned faces were dark, and their sun-whipped eyes were light. The women moved cautiously out of the doorways toward their men, and the children crept behind the women, cautiously, ready to run. The bigger boys squatted beside their fathers, because that made them men. After a time the women asked, What did he want?

And the men looked up for a second, and the smolder of pain was in their eyes. We got to get off. A tractor and a superintendent. Like factories.

Where'll we go? the women asked.

We don't know. We don't know.

And the women went quickly, quietly back into the houses and herded the children ahead of them. They knew that a man so hurt and so perplexed may turn in anger, even on people he loves. They left the men alone to figure and to wonder in the dust.

After a time perhaps the tenant man looked about—at the pump put in ten years ago, with a goose-neck handle and iron flowers on the spout, at the chopping block where a thousand chickens had been killed, at the hand plow lying in the shed, and the patent crib hanging in the rafters over it.

The children crowded around the women in the houses. What we going to do, Ma? Where we going to go?

The women said: We don't know, yet. Go out and play. But don't go near your father. He might whale you if you go near him. And the women went on with the work, but all the time they watched the men squatting in the dust—perplexed and figuring.

The tractors came over the roads and into the fields, great crawlers moving like insects, having the incredible strength of insects. They crawled over the ground, laying the track and rolling on it and picking it up. Diesel tractors, puttering while they stood idle; they thundered when they moved, and then settled down to a droning roar. Snub-nosed monsters, raising the dust and sticking their snouts into it, straight down the country, through fences, through dooryards, in and out of gullies in straight lines. They did not run on the ground, but on their own roadbeds. They ignored hills and gulches, water courses, fences, houses.

The man sitting in the iron seat did not look like a man; gloved, goggled, rubber dust mask over the nose and mouth, he was a part of the monster, a robot in the seat. The thunder of the cylinders sounded through the country, became one with the air and the earth, so that earth and air muttered in sympathetic vibration. The driver could not control it—straight across country it went, cutting through a dozen farms and straight back. A twitch at the controls could swerve the cat, but the driver's hands could not twitch because the monster that built the tractor, the monster that sent the tractor out, had somehow got into the driver's hands, into his brain and muscle, had goggled him and muzzled him—goggled his mind, muzzled his speech, goggled his perception, muzzled his protest. He could not see the land as it was, he could not smell the land as it smelled; his feet did not stamp the clods or feel the warmth and power of the earth. He sat in an iron seat and stepped on iron pedals. He could not cheer or beat or curse or encourage the extension of his power, and because of this he could not cheer or whip or curse or encourage himself. He did not know or own or trust or beseech the land. If a seed dropped did not germinate, it was nothing. If the young thrusting plant withered in drought or drowned in a flood of rain, it was no more to the driver than to the tractor.

He loved the land no more than the bank loved the land. He could admire the tractor—its machined surfaces, its urge of power, the roar of its detonating cylinders; but it was not his tractor. Behind the tractor rolled the shining disks, cutting the earth with blades—not plowing but surgery, pushing the cut earth to the right where the second row of disks cut it and pushed it to the left; slicing blades shining, polished by the cut earth. And pulled behind the disks, the harrows combing with iron teeth so that the little clods broke up and the earth lay smooth. Behind the harrows, the long seeders—twelve curved iron penes erected in the foundry, orgasms set by gears, raping methodically, raping without passion. The driver sat in his iron seat and he was proud of the straight lines he did not will, proud of the tractor he did not own or love, proud of the power he could not control. And when that crop grew, and was harvested, no man had crumbled a hot clod in his fingers and let the earth sift past his fingertips. No man had touched the seed, or lusted for the growth. Men ate what they had not raised, had no connection with the bread. The land bore under iron, and under iron gradually died; for it was not loved or hated, it had no prayers or curses.

At noon the tractor driver stopped sometimes near a tenant house and opened his lunch: sandwiches wrapped in waxed paper, white bread, pickle, cheese, Spam, a piece of pie branded like an engine part. He ate without relish. And tenants not yet moved away came out to see him, looked curiously while the goggles were taken off, and the rubber dust mask, leaving white circles around the eyes and a large white circle around nose and mouth. The exhaust of the tractor puttered on, for fuel is so cheap it is more efficient to leave the engine running than to heat the Diesel nose for a new start. Curious children crowded close, ragged children who ate their fried dough as they watched. They watched hungrily the unwrapping of the sandwiches, and their hunger-sharpened noses smelled the pickle, cheese, and Spam. They didn't speak to the driver. They watched his hand as it carried food to his mouth. They did not watch him chewing; their eyes followed the hand that held the sandwich. After a while the tenant who could not leave the place came out and squatted in the shade beside the tractor.

"Why, you're Joe Davis's boy!"

"Sure," the driver said.

"Well, what you doing this kind of work for—against your own people?"

"Three dollars a day. I got damn sick of creeping for my dinner—and not getting it. I got a wife and kids. We got to eat. Three dollars a day, and it comes every day."

"That's right," the tenant said. "But for your three dollars a day fifteen or twenty families can't eat at all. Nearly a hundred people have to go out and wander on the roads for your three dollars a day. Is that right?"

And the driver said, "Can't think of that. Got to think of my own kids. Three dollars a day, and it comes every day. Times are changing, mister, don't you know? Can't make a living on the land unless you've got two, five, ten thousand acres and a tractor. Crop land isn't for little guys like us any more. You don't kick up a howl because you can't make Fords, or because you're not the telephone company. Well, crops are like that now. Nothing to do about it. You try to get three dollars a day some place. That's the only way."

The tenant pondered. "Funny thing how it is. If a man owns a little property, that property is him, it's part of him, and it's like him. If he owns property only so he can walk on it and handle it and be sad when it isn't doing well, and feel fine when the rain falls on it, that property is him, and some way he's bigger because he owns it. Even if he isn't successful he's big with his property. That is so."

And the tenant pondered more. "But let a man get property he doesn't see, or can't take time to get his fingers in, or can't be there to walk on it—why, then the property is the man. He can't do what he wants, he can't think what he wants. The property is the man, stronger than he is. And he is small, not big. Only his possessions are big—and he's the servant of his property. That is so, too."

The driver munched the branded pie and threw the crust away. "Times are changed, don't you know? Thinking about stuff like that don't feed the kids. Get your three dollars a day, feed your kids. You got no call to worry about anybody's kids but your own. You get a reputation for talking like that, and you'll never get three dollars a day. Big shots won't give you three dollars a day if you worry about anything but your three dollars a day."

"Nearly a hundred people on the road for your three dollars. Where will we go?"

"And that reminds me," the driver said, "you better get out soon. I'm going through the dooryard after dinner."

"You filled in the well this morning."

"I know. Had to keep the line straight. But I'm going through the dooryard after dinner. Got to keep the lines straight. And—well, you know Joe Davis, my old man, so I'll tell you this. I got orders wherever there's a family not moved out—if I have an accident—you know, get too close and cave the house in a little—well, I might get a couple of dollars. And my youngest kid never had no shoes yet."

"I built it with my hands. Straightened old nails to put the sheathing on. Rafters are wired to the stringers with baling wire. It's mine. I built it. You bump it down—I'll be in the window with a rifle. You even come too close and I'll pot you like a rabbit."

"It's not me. There's nothing I can do. I'll lose my job if I don't do it. And look—suppose you kill me? They'll just hang you, but long before you're hung there'll be another guy on the tractor, and he'll bump the house down. You're not killing the right guy."

"That's so," the tenant said. "Who gave you orders? I'll go after him. He's the one to kill."

"You're wrong. He got his orders from the bank. The bank told him, 'Clear those people out or it's your job!' "

"Well, there's a president of the bank. There's a board of directors. I'll fill up the magazine of the rifle and go into the bank."

The driver said, "Fellow was telling me the bank gets orders from the East. The orders were, 'Make the land show profit or we'll close you up.' "

"But where does it stop? Who can we shoot? I don't aim to starve to death before I kill the man that's starving me."

"I don't know. Maybe there's nobody to shoot. Maybe the thing isn't men at all. Maybe, like you said, the property's doing it. Anyway I told you my orders."

"I got to figure," the tenant said. "We all got to figure. There's some way to stop this. It's not like lightning or earthquakes. We've got a bad thing made by men, and by God that's something we can change." The tenant sat in his doorway, and the driver thundered his engine and started off, tracks falling and curving, harrows combing, and the phalli of the seeder slipping into the ground. Across the dooryard the tractor cut, and the hard, foot-beaten ground was seeded field, and the tractor cut through again; the uncut space was ten feet wide. And back he came. The iron guard bit into the housecorner, crumbled the wall, and wrenched the little house from its foundation so that it fell sideways, crushed like a bug. And the driver was goggled and a rubber mask covered his nose and mouth. The tractor cut a straight line on, and the air and the ground vibrated with its thunder. The tenant man stared after it, his rifle in his hand. His wife was beside him, and the quiet children behind. And all of them stared after the tractor.

19

SEA-FEVER

JOHN MASEFIELD

I must go down to the seas again, to the lonely sea and the sky,
And all I ask is a tall ship and a star to steer her by,
And the wheel's kick and the wind's song and the white sail's shaking,
And a grey mist on the sea's face and a grey dawn breaking.

I must go down to the seas again, for the call of the running tide
Is a wild call and a clear call that may not be denied;
And all I ask is a windy day with the white clouds flying,
And the flung spray and the blown spume, and the sea-gulls crying.

I must go down to the seas again to the vagrant gypsy life,
To the gull's way and the whale's way where the wind's like a whetted knife;
And all I ask is a merry yarn from a laughing fellow-rover,
And quiet sleep and a sweet dream when the long trick's over.

20

SEA-CHILL

ARTHUR GUITERMAN

I must go down to the seas again, where the billows romp and reel,
So all I ask is a large ship that rides on an even keel,
And a mild breeze and a broad deck with a slight list to the leeward,
And a clean chair in a snug nook and a nice, kind steward.

I must go down to the seas again, the sport of wind and tide,
As the gray wave and the green wave play leapfrog over the side.
And all I want is a glassy calm with a bone-dry scupper,
A good book and a warm rug, and a light, plain supper.

I must go down to the seas again, though there I'm a total loss,
And can't say which is worst, the pitch, the plunge, the roll, the toss.
But all I ask is a safe retreat in a bar well tended,
And a soft berth and a smooth course till the long trip's ended.

21

THIS MOMENT

WALT WHITMAN

This moment yearning and thoughtful sitting alone,
It seems to me there are other men in other lands yearning and thoughtful,
It seems to me I can look over and behold them in Germany, Italy, France, Spain,
Or far, far away in China, or in Russia or Japan, talking other dialects,
And it seems to me if I could know those men I should become attached to them
As I do to men in my own lands.
Oh I know we should be brethren and lovers,
I know I should be happy with them.

22

THE FAIR

from *The Wapshot Chronicle*

JOHN CHEEVER

Coverly was excited to see so many lights burning after dark and by the apparatus for the tightrope artist—a high pole secured by guy wires with a summit of fringed platforms and pedestals, all of it standing in the glare of two up-angled searchlights in whose powdery beams moth millers could be seen to swim like scraps of gum paper. There a girl with powdery skin and straw hair and a navel (Leander thought) deep enough to put your thumb into, and with rhinestones burning blue and red at her ears and breasts, walked and rode a bicycle over the tightwire, pushing her hair back now and then and hurrying a little it seemed, for the thunder was quickening and the gusty wind smelled clearly of rain and now and then people who were anxious or old or wearing their best clothes were leaving the bleachers and looking for shelter although not a drop of rain had fallen. When the high-wire act was over Leander took Coverly down to the head of the midway, where the argument for the cootch show had begun.

Burlymaque, burlymaque, see them strip the way you like, see them do the dance of the ages. If you're old you'll go home to your wife feeling younger and stronger and if you're young you'll feel happy and full of high spirits as youth should feel, said a man whose sharp face and sharp voice seemed wholeheartedly dedicated to chicanery and lewdness and who spoke to the crowd from a little red pulpit although they stayed at a safe distance from him as if he were the devil himself or at least the devil's advocate, a serpent. Lashed to poles at his back and billowing in the rain wind like idle sails were four large paintings of women in harem dress, so darkened by time and weather that the lights played on them to no purpose and they might have been advertising cough syrup and cure-alls. In the center was a gate in which some lights spelled GAY PAREE—the gate scuffed and battered from its long summer travels up and down New England. Burlymaque, burlymaque, hootchie cootch, hootchie cootch, said the devil, striking the top of his little red pulpit with a roll of unsold tickets. I'm going to ask the little ladies out here just once more, just one more time, to give you some idea, a little idea of what you'll see when you get inside.

Reluctantly, talking among themselves, shyly, shyly, as children called on to recite "Hiawatha" or the "Village Blacksmith," a pair of girls, dressed in skirts of some coarse, transparent cloth like the cloth hung at cottage windows, side by side for company, one adventuresome and one not so, their breasts hung lightly in cloth so that you could see the beginning of the curve, climbed up onto a ramshackle platform, the boards of which gave under their weight, and looked boldly and cheerfully into the crowd, one of them touching the back of her hair to keep it from blowing in the rain wind and holding with her other hand the opening in her skirt. . . . Coverly followed his father up to the stand and then into a little tent where perhaps thirty men were standing apathetically around a little stage not so unlike the stage where he had seen his beloved Judy hit Punch over the head when he was younger. The roof of the tent was so shot with holes that the lights of the carnival shown through it like the stars of a galaxy—an illusion that charmed Coverly until he remembered what they were there for. Whatever it was, the crowd seemed sullen. Leander greeted a friend and left Coverly. . . . "Burlymaque, hootchie cootch—I'm going to ask these little ladies out here just one more time before the show begins. . . ."

They waited and waited while the girls climbed up onto the platform and down again—up and down and the evening and the fair passed outside. A little rain began to fall and the walls of the tent to luff but the water did not cool the tent and sent up only in Coverly's mind memories of some mushroom-smelling forest where he wished he was. Then the girls retired, one of them to crank a phonograph and the other to dance. She was young—a child to Leander—not pretty but so fully in possession of the bloom of youth that it couldn't have mattered. Her hair was brown and as straight as a cow hand's except at the side where she had made two curls. She swore when she pricked her finger with a pin that held her skirt together and went on dancing with a drop of blood on her thumb. When she dropped her skirt she was naked.

. . . .

The fair was persevering in spite of the rain, which had left a pleasant, bitter smell in the air. The merry-go-round and the Ferris wheel were still turning. At his back Coverly could hear the scratchy music of the cootch show where his father was. To get out of the rain he wandered into the agricultural exhibit. There was no one there but an old man and nothing that he wanted to see. Squashes, tomatoes, corn, and lima beans were arranged on paper plates with prizes and labels. The irony of admiring squashes, under the circumstances, was not wasted on him. "Second prize. Olga Pluzinski," he read, staring miserably at a jar of tomato pickles. "Golden Bantam Corn. Raised by Peter Covell. Second prize, Jerusalem Artichokes . . ." He could still pick out, past the noise of the merry-go-round and the rain, the music where the girl was dancing. When the music stopped he went back and waited for his father.

23

from RAINTREE COUNTY

ROSS LOCKRIDGE, JR.

FIGHTING FOR FREEDOM
FROM SHILOH TO SAVANNAH

is the name of the goddam thing, the General said. I happen to have a few hundred pages of it stuffed into my coatpocket here, Shawnessy, and if you have a little time, I'd like to have you glance it over and tell me frankly what you think of it. There you are.

—Thanks, General. Be glad to look at it.

—By the way, you were in the War, weren't you? the General said.

—Yes, Mr. Shawnessy said.

He and some fifty other members of the Raintree County Post of the Grand Army of the Republic were standing in a shapeless mass at the middle of the intersection, waiting to form ranks and march down to the Schoolhouse for the outdoor banquet. General Jacob J. Jackson, Raintree County's outstanding military figure, a hero of two wars, had arrived in Waycross only a few minutes before to lead the march.

The General, a hearty man in his middle sixties, was a little shorter than Mr. Shawnessy. Broadshouldered, deepchested, he was built like an athlete except for the hard bulge of his belly. Freeflowing gray hair fell thickly from his thinning dome to lie upon his shoulders and blend over his ears into the great ball of a beard. Out of this beard his voice blew like a horn of cracked brass, having no variations in pitch or volume between a hard bray and a hoarse whisper. The General was now standing in one of his characteristic postures, arms folded over chest, head thrust back, left foot forward. One could see the bulge of his right calfmuscle in the army trousers. His small blue eyes glared. The muscles around his cheekbones twitched as if under his beard the General were gritting his jaw teeth. A dress sword and two Colt revolvers hung from his belt. He held a broad Western hat adorned with military cord.

The General made everyone else look like a supernumerary. Most of the other veterans were in uniform too, but only the General seemed clothed in heroic dignity.

—I'm a practical man, the General was saying, a man of action, and I hate like hell to write.

—For a man who hates to write, General, you've ground out a lot of copy in your time, Mr. Shawnessy said. Let's see, how many books is it now?

The General's chest swelled, and there burst from his throat a series of distinct hahs, of exactly the same timbre as his speaking voice.

—Well, let's see, he said. I began with *Fighting for the Flag,* and followed it up with *Memoirs of a Fighting General.* Then there was *Four Years at the Front or Fighting for the Cause* and of course *A Fighting Man's History of the War in the West.* I've also done that series called *Fights I have Fought from Chapultepec to Chickamauga or Tales of Two Wars.* Then, there's that goddam thing my publishers have had me doing called *Fifteen Historic Fights from Marathon to Manassas.*

—I hadn't seen that one, General, Mr. Shawnessy said. I didn't know you went in for European battles.

—Once you understand war, the General said, one goddam battle is like another. By the way, it's time to march, isn't it?

—Just about, Mr. Shawnessy said. I think the band's about ready.

—Fall in, boys! the General barked.

Suggested Readings

Beebe, Maurice (ed.) *Literary Symbolism; An Introduction to the Interpretation of Literature.* Belmont, Cal.: Wadsworth Publishing Co., 1960.

Burkland, Carl E. "The Presentation of Figurative Language," *Quarterly Journal of Speech* (December 1955), 383–90.

Clark, Solomon Henry, and Maud May Babcock. *Interpretation of the Printed Page.* Englewood Cliffs, N.J.: Prentice-Hall, 1946, Chapter I, "The Speech Unit—Grouping," Chapter II, "The Speech Paragraph—Group Sequence," Chapter III, "Group Value," Chapter IV, "The Important Idea."

Cobin, Martin. *Theory and Technique of Interpretation.* Englewood Cliffs, N.J.: Prentice-Hall, 1959, Chapter IV, "Thought Impact," and Chapter V, "Emotion Impact."

Cunningham, Cornelius Carman. *Making Words Come Alive.* Dubuque, Iowa: William C. Brown, 1951, Chapter II, "Grasping the Significance of the Whole," Chapters III, IV, V, VI, "Using the Means of Association," and Chapter VII, "Making the Thoughts Your Own."

Geiger, Don. "A 'Dramatic' Approach to Interpretative Analysis," *Quarterly Journal of Speech* (April 1952), 189–94.

Grimes, Wilma H., and Alethea Smith Mattingly. *Interpretation: Writer, Reader, Audience.* Belmont, Cal.: Wadsworth Publishing Company, 1961, Chapter III, "Understanding the Literary Object."

Parrish, Wayland Maxfield. *Reading Aloud.* (3rd edition) New York: Ronald Press, 1953, Chapter II, "Meaning," Chapter XI, "Emotion."

Rosenthal, M. L., and A. J. M. Smith. *Exploring Poetry.* New York: Macmillan, 1955, Chapter VI, "Poetic Symbolism."

Smith, Joseph F., and James R. Linn. *Skill in Reading Aloud.* New York: Harper, 1960, Chapter II, "What's in a Word?" and Chapter III, "What's in the Text?"

Winans, J. A. *Public Speaking.* New York: Century, 1917, Chapter XIV, "The Study and Delivery of Selections."

Woolbert, Charles H., and Severina E. Nelson. *The Art of Interpretative Speech.* (4th edition) New York: Appleton-Century-Crofts, 1956, Chapter III, "The Author," Chapter IV, "The Author's Meaning."

Part III

EXPRESSING THE MEANING

6

VISIBLE COMMUNICATION

ITS PRIMACY

Anthropologists tell us that primitive man once had no audible speech. He communicated with his own and other forms of life largely by visible means. Teeth bared in a snarl or an upraised hand bearing a stone conveyed by sight the spirit of defiance. By sight he recognized pleasure and anger, fear and defiance. Perhaps somewhere in the grass roots of his past, man came to accept the gesture of the extended open palm as a sign of weaponless friendliness. It would seem probable that in the beginning man's communication was, like that of his primitive relatives in the animal kingdom, almost entirely visible.

However, we need not look to vague conjecture for evidence that audible speech is a fairly recent acquisition. The various parts of the so-called speech mechanism—the tongue, teeth, lips, mandible, maxilla, soft palate, hard palate, lungs, and even the larynx itself—have far more fundamental functions than the formation of speech sounds. The tongue is used in tasting, in manipulating food while it is in the mouth, and in sucking. The teeth, mandible, and maxilla seem designed primarily for the mastication of food. The hard palate is employed in sucking and as a wall between the mouth and the nasal cavity. The soft palate is contractible and permits normal breathing through the nose or enforced respiration through the mouth when more oxygen is required. The lungs are organs of respiration. Finally the fundamental function of the larynx is a valvular one. It is employed to close the tracheal passageway from the lungs in order that pressure may be created for such basic acts as lifting, defecation, and childbirth. This function may be readily understood if you will grasp the edges of the chair seat on which you sit and try to lift yourself, chair and all. In making the exertion you involuntarily close the vocal folds and shut off the exit of air from the lungs. When the muscular tension is eased, the breath is expelled in a grunt.

These basic processes of tasting, sucking, chewing, breathing, exertion, and childbearing are ones of survival and appear to be the functions for which the organs we have discussed were originally evolved. Some authorities tell us that the speech production in which these parts of the body are now employed is an overlaid function, that we have found an additional role for the organs beyond the more basic ones. They point out that no animal has a true organ of voice except certain birds.

Why discuss all of these factors now? The reason is merely to demonstrate clearly and forcefully that historically man's speech was first of all visible and that to this day visible speech is most "natural."

If other evidence of the basic nature of visible speech were necessary, an analysis of typical human behavior would show that visible speech was not only prior in man's evolution but remains prior to this day. A careful timing of effective gestures in speaking will reveal that they precede momentarily the utterance of the idea with which they are associated. It seems right to point with the hand a fraction of a second before shouting, "Look there!" but observe how foolish you appear if first you shout and then point. As any student of theatre will tell you, the action must precede the word. To reverse the process is to create the style of acting we associate with old-time melodrama. What better evidence could there be of the basic nature of visible speech? It is right and proper; it belongs, even more surely than the speech sounds you produce. Proceeding from this conclusion, let us begin our study of the visible action of speech, remembering that this mode of expression is fundamental in oral communication.

EMPATHY

Many people saw and heard Charles Laughton in his celebrated reading tours. If you saw him, perhaps you did not notice his platform behavior. After all, he was an accomplished artist and did not call attention to himself as much as to what he was reading, but it was especially interesting to notice how he achieved his amazing audience response. Informality seemed to be his motto, for he came to the platform laden with a huge and awkward assortment of books tucked high under his chin. Smiling broadly he flung them onto the waiting table, leaned on the improvised speaker's stand, and said, "Hello." He seemed to engage us in conversation for a few moments before beginning his "speech." We hardly knew when his program began and his visiting ended. Smiling with us, he read Thurber. When he had finished a humorous piece, he laughed with us, shifted his position as if to relax, scratched himself comfortably, and searched with us for another. His face mirrored his thoughts and feelings, and our faces mirrored his face. We saw during Mr. Laughton's entire program an excellent example of the role of empathy in public speaking and reading. By means of empathy he promoted our relaxation, prompted our anticipation, enhanced our pleasure, made us laugh, and helped us to love books.

Now although we have spoken rather glibly of empathy, it is most difficult to define. It occurs only spontaneously; in fact, the empathic response takes place on an unconscious level. It is fundamentally what the muscles of one person do to the muscles of another who is watching him. It is not subject to the will of the second person but is rather a natural impulse, a kind of involuntary imitative reaction. We tended to do what we saw Mr. Laughton doing. Perhaps the simplest illustration of empathic response occurs when you smile at someone who smiles at you. It is the way a baby learns to smile and the reason that most adults smile at babies. It accounts for epidemics of yawns when people are together. Sometimes coughing, clearing the throat, and sniffing come in epidemics too. If you watch such a phenomenon sometime and can be at all objective about the matter, you will see that it takes place in response to the initial behavior of some one or a few people present: one coughs and others follow suit.

Several years ago in a high school speech class there was a good looking, intelligent young man who prepared his speech with great care and then spoke clearly and emphatically. There was just one difficulty, however. This young man's audience could never relax to listen. Always they squirmed in their seats and gave the speaker a most unsatisfactory response. The difficulty was that this speaker scratched: every time he faced the class he systematically but unobtrusively scratched. No wonder his listeners could not sit still and listen: they scratched too. Empathy is sometimes a negative matter for the speaker.

One more illustration may serve to underline the startling power of empathy. One time a college class in interpretation decided to employ the principle of empathy in a number of stunts about the campus. One good actor pulled an old trick. He stood on the campus during the rush to the noon meal and gazed intently at the tower on one of the buildings. More than fifty people collected about him to examine the same tower and the sky beyond. Of course, imaginations went to work, tongues began to wag, and many were late to lunch—all because people stopped to do what they saw others doing. That handful of interpretation students was responsible for other peculiar happenings on the campus that day. Unexplained fits of coughing swept classes. Several groups of students were seen actually running to classes. Some ordinarily serious philosophy sessions gave way to fits of giggling.

Empathy is a part of our daily lives in many small ways. Have you sat in a movie as the heroine smiled into the face of her beloved, and smiled too? Have you watched a football game and strained every muscle as Number Nineteen dodged, twisted, dashed, stumbled, and careened down the field to a touchdown? Have you seen a boxing match in person or on television and felt your own fists drawn tight and your breaths quick and short? Have you watched a television comic and observed yourself with his silly expression on your face? In each of these instances your enjoyment of these experiences is probably directly in proportion to your empathic participation in them.

Often we like another person to the degree to which his behavior causes us to do as we like to do, to be correct, proper, and stimulating. It may be that much of the personal appeal of Franklin D. Roosevelt was of that very kind. He somehow made those with whom he came in contact feel strong, ambitious, clean, proud of their manhood. Often this ability is the secret of a teacher's success. Perhaps it is the appeal of Col. John Glenn. Surely you have heard the expression, "He makes his associates ladies and gentlemen."

We have seen from many examples that empathy is that phenomenon common to human nature wherein the muscles of an observer tend to repeat the activity he observes in others. The "activity" may vary from the most strenuous exertion to a very limited degree of muscular tension or relaxation. In one respect this definition is not complete, for it fails to take into account the statement of psychologists that we learn and think with our whole bodies. You are surely familiar with this idea in the public schools where *progressive* educators are recognizing that they must educate the "whole child." If we do think with the whole of ourselves, those muscular reactions that we have referred to as empathic responses must be a part of our thought processes. When empathy prompts us to smile, we must to a degree be thinking a smile. When our faces reflect the approval we see in the face of a good public speaker, our minds tend to think approval. If this line of reasoning is true, as modern psychology would indicate, empathy goes much deeper than mere muscular response and becomes a matter of attitudes and thought patterns. Thus its significance is manifold. Seen in this light, empathy may be the most important mental and emotional factor in communication whether it is conversation, public speaking, or reading.

Empathy functions in at least three ways. First, it operates to guide the reader's response to his material. The degree to which he participates in the attitudes and behavior of his story will show in his face, his hands, his posture, in fact, in his general body response. To this degree he is not simply revealing his appreciation of his selection, but he is fully engaged in the activity of the story at the moment he reads. Every thought and action is *vital* to him *now,* while he reads. He experiences the bodily tensions implied by the literature. If the reader gives a full empathic response to his material, his chances for effective reading are good. This is not to say that if a speaker knows an idea he can express it, or that if a reader understands a text he can read it. On the other hand, he cannot be an effective speaker or reader without a full empathic response to or participation in the selection he reads.

Second, empathy functions in communicative reading in the audience response to the reader. As we have already seen in our general discussion of the nature of empathy, an audience tends to duplicate the tensions, responses, attitudes, and feelings of the speaker. If, therefore, the speaker wants his listeners to be relaxed, he must appear relaxed. If he wants them to experience tensions, he must show those tensions himself. If he wants them to smile, he must smile. If he wants them to be vitally concerned for a solution of his problem, he must show concern.

Third, if genuine communication is taking place, the speaker will experience an empathic response to his audience. It is essentially impossible for either to avoid reflecting the muscular and emotional experiences of the other. The very nature of the speech situation is implicit in the word "communication" which means an *inter*course or exchange of ideas and feelings. We must recognize the modern emphasis on *speech to communicate:* perhaps the outstanding identifying characteristic of today's study of speech is the recognition that the speaking situation always involves at least two personalities and that fundamentally speech has no purpose other than the exchange of ideas and feelings. The fact that the speaker is reading does not eliminate this exchange feature. Although the speaker is responding to words from a page, he still responds and adjusts to his audience.

We should recognize that perhaps the speaker experiences a response to himself. Who has not heard the axiom, "To look like is to feel like"? To smile is to feel like smiling more. To laugh is to laugh more. To express anger is to feel angry. To show concern is to be concerned. Certainly the principle is subject to its limitations: we cannot work mood miracles just by pretending, but the speaker's response to himself offers basic help to better speech. He may add to his calmness by acting calm. He may enhance his own feelings by expressing with his body those feelings. Again the explanation lies in the "whole person" concept of thought and emotion. It would be interesting to pursue this idea in a good psychology text and see that it truly may profit a speaker to use this means of making his speech more vivid to himself and others. For example, you may be startled to discover that you not only shake because you are afraid but *are afraid* because you *shake.* There is something in the old advice to whistle as you pass a cemetery; for if you run, you will become more and more afraid the faster you run. Indeed, the individual seems to experience a response to himself.

ONE CRITERION OF EFFECTIVENESS

It has taken a long time to see how empathy works when one person reads to another. Now let us reduce the whole matter of visible action in speech, indeed all aspects of speech, to one criterion of effectiveness. If the purpose of speech is "to tell somebody something," we can determine the effectiveness of speech only in terms of the response of the person to whom something is told. That is, the only reliable criterion for the effectiveness of any speaking is the response of the audience. If your listeners feel when you finish the way you want them to feel, you have succeeded. If they are inspired when you want them to be inspired, you have succeeded. If they rush out and picket the city hall, and that is what you wanted them to do, you have succeeded. By these terms Antony's funeral oration is a perfect example of the successful speech. Although complete success is indeed rare, applied relatively the criterion of *audience response* is the *one measure of effectiveness in speaking.* It is therefore the moral responsibility of the speaker to set up worthy goals in order that the audience response may be socially desirable. Without a sense of such responsibility the effective speaker is a dangerous person.

If we accept the response criterion of effectiveness as true, we can measure any aspect of a speech presentation in terms of whether or not it has promoted the desired audience response. If a feature of voice helps to achieve the audience reaction you desire, it is good to have that feature. If it does not help or if it detracts, it is bad to have it. So it is with the visible aspect of speech too. Any appearance or behavior which helps the audience to respond as you wish is desirable. Any facial expression, gesture, body position, step, or even item of dress which works to the contrary is undesirable and may be referred to as "negative visible action." This term includes mannerisms of face, hands, and body which draw attention away from the thought and feeling expressed. Any violation of the indefinite but nevertheless important criterion of good taste may seriously interfere with communication. Effective speakers and readers are careful not to offend their audiences with behavior which seems unsuitable or calls special attention to itself. Even the best speakers, however, often have habitual negative visible actions such as slouching, keeping their hands always in their pockets, removing their glasses, and contorting their faces. Such speakers may succeed in their speaking but

Gloria – 8 pt.

Nice, well-done opening. Paced well with good emphasis.

Good feeling of tension.

Watch posture when sitting on stool. Don't slump – let your body reflect the tension of the mood,

do so *in spite of* these liabilities of visible action. They should strive to eliminate from their speech any habitual behavior which detracts and distracts.

The moment the audience becomes conscious of your attempts to employ empathy to your ends, then the facial expression or the behavior involved in that attempt becomes a distraction from your purpose and constitutes negative visible action. Techniques of speech must never call attention to themselves. When they do, the techniques have become liabilities, not assets. So it is with visible action.

PERSONAL APPEARANCE

For the purpose of discussion we shall divide the specific aspects of visible action employed in speaking and reading into the following categories: personal appearance, posture, gesture, and total bodily response. By the term personal appearance we mean the reader's attitude, manner, grooming, and dress. From the very moment the audience becomes aware of his physical presence these features communicate meaning. The psychologist would say that by these means he establishes a "set" or a readiness for the message he is to convey. Of course he is not specifically communicating his own personality, but, if he can achieve to any degree at all audience acceptance of himself before he speaks, his subsequent success is all the more likely. When the salesman first faces the housewife who has just opened the door, he is wise to try for an affirmative response, even before he mentions his product. In the terms of the trade, he should "sell himself first." It is no less incumbent upon the speaker to achieve acceptance of himself. When you come before an audience to read, you can help your audience to accept you by being well groomed and pleasant but sufficiently dignified to elicit respect. You can help yourself by dressing in such a way as to satisfy whatever standards are maintained in the group. It is generally true that an audience likes a speaker who shows by his dress that he considers the occasion an important one. This is not to say that finery is a prerequisite to success—indeed it may be a deterrent, but it is merely to recognize that even the smallest detail of appearance can make a contribution to your success.

Your attitude, too, is a part of personal appearance. By the expression on your face and the set of your body you can make observers consider you unpleasantly cocky or disconcertingly unsure. Certainly you will want your audience to feel that you have something worth saying and that you want to say it, that you are fully prepared, and that you regard this audience as fully capable of appreciating what you are about to say. If your behavior reflects uncertainty on any of these points, the audience will sense that uncertainty. Let your manner bespeak appropriate confidence but not arrogance.

In those moments before you speak you can incline an audience in your favor or you can create obstacles later to be surmounted.

POSTURE

The second aspect of visible action is posture. Simply expressed, posture is the arrangement of the bones and muscles of the body. How are you standing? How are you sitting? Your posture is good if it promotes the most effective use of your body. Can you breathe freely and deeply? Can you speak calmly and forcefully? Can you use your hands, arms, shoulders, trunk, and head readily and with ease? Can you step quickly and gracefully? If the answer to each of these questions is "yes," your posture is probably satisfactory for reading and speaking. Good posture is that arrangement of the parts of your body which enables you to employ them with maximum effectiveness. Good posture is good physical readiness.

If, however, you have formed poor posture habits, the best posture may not seem natural to you. One of the worst kinds of posture is the stoop. If you stand with your shoulders hunched and your head forward, you restrict your breathing by confining the chest cavity and pushing the rib cage down against the abdomen. The result may be inadequate loudness of voice and inability to sustain voice as long as you may need to. You may even cause a tension in the region of your larynx which will result in a tight, inflexible voice, unpleasant both to you and to your listeners. The sway-back posture is probably just as poor for health as for speech. If you allow your spine to sway forward at the middle of the back, your pelvis will be tipped out of its normal alignment, your abdomen will protrude unduly, your neck will thrust forward, and speech will be as difficult as in the stooped position. Another kind of poor posture often results from the teaching of well-meaning parents and teachers. We call this the ramrod or military posture. Perhaps you have been told to stand up straight, throw your shoulders back, and pull your abdomen in. Of course this position is uncomfortable to maintain, for throwing the shoulders back upsets the normal balance of the body, and pulling the abdomen in may confine the muscles of the diaphragm. In any event the position produces such tensions as to make speech difficult. If you have any of these bad habits of posture, it is desirable to correct them.

Imagine you are a puppet which your master has grasped by the hair of the head and lifted from its feet. Now let your shoulders fall into a natural position. Allow your whole body to relax. Lift your chin until the eyes look out on a horizontal plane. The result should be good posture characterized by relaxation and muscular readiness. Every demand which speech will make upon you can be easily met. You can breathe, gesture, bend, or step without hesitation. Some speakers find it helpful to place one foot slightly ahead of the other and to rest the weight on the balls of the feet. In this position the heels only balance the body. The speaker is ready to move forward or backward easily. Others prefer to place the feet together with the heels about two inches apart and the feet forming an angle of about forty-five degrees. The choice of stance is a personal one governed only by the need for relaxation and muscular readiness.

GESTURE

The third aspect of visible action in oral reading or speaking is gesture. Many years ago the elocutionist taught a long and involved catalogue of gestures in much the same manner as primary teachers taught the alphabet. A certain movement meant repulsion. Another meant challenge. There were gestures for fear, pleading, dismay, and a multitude of other moods and assertions. The student practiced long hours to learn specific movements. In order to execute the hand movements gracefully, he was enjoined to lead with the wrist, form an ellipsis, curve the fingers, and in general to pose. There were similar standards for the use of the trunk, the shoulders, the face, the legs, and the feet. The result of such instruction was often gesture, not of the whole body, but of isolated members of the body. All too frequently gesture was obviously a "thing apart." Of course such practices became stylized and were expected by audiences. Consequently speech behavior that would seem absurd to us could often pass unnoticed or be highly admired for its own sake.

Popular taste, however, was eventually pushed to the breaking point by the excesses of the elocutionist, and a revulsion set in. Today it is recognized that gesture should be a matter of the whole body, that it should be a part of and spring from the thought. The whole organism of man is involved in thinking. The mind is not an isolated part of the body. It is an activity, a function. Aristotle said that the mind is to the body what cutting is to the ax. When the ax is not in use, there is obviously no cutting. So it is with the mind. Thought does not involve the brain alone, or even the nervous system alone. The brain, nerves, glands, and muscles work together as a whole. Full experience of the thought involves, theoretically at least, full employment of the body. Since experience of the thought is the goal of the oral interpreter, he must involve his whole body in that thought.

Total bodily activity is necessary for thinking. Total activity is also necessary for communicating thought from one person to another. It is inherent in the act of speech. Watch a small child as he quivers with excitement, jumps up and down, smiles broadly, and uses his hands, arms, torso, and legs to voice a simple idea. His parents and teachers will expend much effort in the frustrating task of calming down the expert communicator, but as an adult engaged in conversation he will still make extensive use of his whole body in the process of communicating. Notice how people go about ordinary conversation. If you have never really paid attention to conversational behavior, you, most likely, will be surprised. People conversing shake their heads, lift their eyebrows, and changes of feeling play across their faces. They shrug their shoulders. Their hands are almost never still. They are not trying to make speeches but are merely trying to make others understand what they have in mind. Unconscious of using action, they are talking the way people have always talked.

In brief, thought is an "all-of-the-body" process, and so too is speaking. Within limits imposed by the presence of a manuscript, oral reading also involves total bodily activity.

Since classical times students of oral communication have recognized three kinds of gesture: descriptive, suggestive, and emphatic. Descriptive gestures point out physical placement, proportion, or detail. We use our body to indicate where something is: perhaps we use our eyes, head, shoulder, or all three. We use our hands and arms to indicate relative sizes. We gesture to show shape. We gesture to show movement. Such visible action may have been the earliest form of speech and is certainly one of the most common forms today. The second kind of gesture is suggestive. It is much like descriptive gesture but is used for less concrete subject matter. We may shrug our shoulders to indicate indifference or throw up our arm to show that someone has departed. We may cast our eyes upward as we speak of God. The third kind, emphatic, is employed to underline what our words say and may be typified by a clenched fist, nodding head, or even stamping our foot. These three kinds of gesture are as appropriate in oral interpretation as in any other kind of speech. Look objectively at your own visible action in reading aloud. Do you employ the three kinds of gesture in those places where they will promote the effectiveness of your interpretation? Strive for a fuller employment of your body within the limits imposed by a manuscript.

The presence of that manuscript and the understanding that gesture must be a part of thought and spring from thought, together with the fact that movement must never call attention to itself, prompt many oral interpreters to prefer *covert* gesture rather than *overt*. That is, they think that the most communicative movement is change in the general body tonicity, in the diffused and the over-all degree of tension and relaxation. Anger is expressed, not with a clenched fist alone, but with a general heightening of body tension. Such covert action may actually be far more effective than wide, sweeping movements. The body speaks as a whole. To gain freedom in the use of the body, the reader may want to use large and full movements in his practice. On the actual occasion of reading to an audience, he will probably exercise some restraint. Restraint is meaningful, however, only when there is something to be restrained. For most of us there is little or no danger of employing too much visible action in oral reading. Indeed we need to enlarge or "project" our normal visible action. Practicing in the way suggested may help us to use more bodily action before the audience despite stage fright, which may tend to subdue us.

It should be recognized that two factors usually determine what constitutes effective gesture. The first and most important is the speaker's personality. If you are an active, aggressive individual, you probably employ far more gesture than the average person. On the other hand, if you are more quiet in your behavior, it is right and proper for you to use less gesture. No one can tell you that you must gesture just as someone else does, for we are all different. Nothing is so characteristic of individual personality as the use of one's body. The second factor to determine what constitutes effective gesture is the material being read. For example, broad humor ordinarily requires far larger action than most other forms of reading material. By contrast, covert body action is often more suitable for abstract and serious content. Your sense of propriety must be your guide.

STAGE FRIGHT

Perhaps you call it tension, but if you are like most of us you do have an experience that many people refer to as stage fright. You might be surprised at the tensions suffered by experienced teachers when facing new classes. Most of our great speakers and actors have told us they have known the same feeling. Do not think that your own fear before an audience is unique or even that it is greater than many others feel. Actually, you would be a peculiar, vegetable-like creature indeed if you were a stranger to stage fright.

Fear of an audience usually shows up first in the speaker's visible action. He tends to freeze, to become immobile, or else his muscles respond unreliably, and he engages in ridiculous, repetitious gesticulations. The audience *sees* that he has stage fright.

What can you do about stage fright? First, you must realize that elimination of all tension is not desirable. You need only to *utilize* your nervous energy to increase instead of hinder your effectiveness. Second, do not forget that the way you feel is nothing new or different but is common to all speakers. Third, prepare—prepare—prepare. Give yourself reason for confidence. Without much preparation you may, it is true, be able to "fool part of the people part of the time," but if you want to be confident you must be satisfied with no less than a thoroughgoing study of the content and then much conscientious practice in actually reading your selection aloud. It is only the rank novice who feels that he can interpret confidently and effectively without several hours of preparation for every quarter hour of reading. Fourth, act as if you are confident. Remember that, as observed earlier, you respond to yourself. Instill courage in yourself by employing positive movements. Do not hesitate nor shrink from your audience. Fifth, consciously focus your attention on the meaning of the words you are reading at the moment you are reading. If your mind is filled with the feelings and ideas in your selection, there will be no room for thoughts about yourself. Sixth, try to replace fear with another emotion. Your psychology professor will tell you that if the thalamus, which is the seat of your emotions, is filled with hate, for example, there is no room for fear. Witness the angry fighter! Apply this principle to yourself as you speak: replace stage fright with strong emotional feelings associated with the ideas you are expressing. When you can do it, *it works perfectly*. Seventh, and last, remember at all times that oral reading is communication and that you must focus all of your energy on conveying the meaning. There can be little time or strength to waste in self-consciousness and fear.

PRINCIPLES

Study the following nine principles of effective visible communication.

1. Prestige. The good speaker or reader will behave in such a way and maintain such an appearance as to inspire confidence in the minds of his observers.

2. Self-confidence. He will have confidence in himself and that confidence will show through his actions. He will not be overbearing.

3. Communication. His goal will always be to communicate, never to show off. For most selections he will look into the eyes of his audience.

4. Animation. He will be alive and alert. His posture, facial expression, and movement will show that he is capable of full physical control. He will be ready.

5. Appropriateness. He will look and act in keeping with his own personality, the material he is reading, and the occasion.

6. Coordination. His visible action will involve all of him. There will be no isolated gestures, steps, or facial expressions.

7. Seeming naturalness. No matter how much afraid he is, he will not show it. He will try to avoid self-consciousness by giving his full attention to the communication of his reading to his audience.

8. Projection. He will strive for sufficient distinctness of visible action for others to receive the ideas and feelings he is experiencing.

9. Practice. He will realize that practice is the secret of success in visible speech as in audible speech.

Summary

Visible communication is a basic ingredient of man's speech. It is his most "natural" mode of communication. Through the employment of empathy it may be his most effective. This effectiveness is measurable only in terms of the response secured. Personal appearance, posture, and gesture are the aspects of visible communication. A person talking or reading aloud, like a person thinking, engages in total bodily activity. General bodily tonicity in keeping with the thought is his aim. Restraint is appropriate although the degree of movement is determined by several factors. Stage fright is normal and can be controlled. The principles of effective visible action in oral communication are: prestige, self-confidence, communicativeness, animation, appropriateness, coordination, seeming naturalness, projection, and practice.

Exercises

1. Observe several speakers or readers in person or on television and analyze their visible action by the one criterion of effectiveness. Look for examples of negative visible action.

2. Attend a movie or observe a speaker and watch the empathic responses of the audience. Notice the responses which the speaker or actor must have wanted. Does he receive any empathic responses he would consider undesirable?

3. For a striking demonstration of empathy, go to some athletic event and watch the faces and bodies of the observers. What relation does empathy seem to have to their enjoyment?

4. Try some of these empathy experiments and report the results to the class.

a. Cough quietly and frequently in an uninteresting lecture. See if you can make others do it too as an empathic response.
b. If you are very brave, try the same stunt with a giggle or a bored yawn.
c. Post yourself at some busy campus spot and pretend to become engrossed in the ground, the sky, or some object. You need not say a word to get others curious too. See how many stop. Empathy will be in part responsible.
d. Tell a short moderately funny joke to a friend while you have present a second friend who has been coached to "enjoy it thoroughly." Then tell it to someone else with the second friend warned to show no reaction at all. Do this several times to see how laughter is contagious.
e. Devise a stunt of your own to demonstrate empathy.

5. Select two people in the presence of each of whom you usually behave quite differently. Explain the difference and account for it. To what degree is empathy responsible?

6. Observe a speaker before he goes into action and analyze the response you make before he says a word. Look for personal appearance and attitude.

7. Stand before a mirror as you think you would before an audience and evaluate your own posture.

8. Observe one or more speakers in person or on television and note examples of the three different kinds of gesture. Which is most common? Which least?

9. Describe with gestures the size and shape of an apple, the height of your father, the size of this book, the way to throw a ball, how to hold a golf club, how to swing a ball bat, how to use a table fork, the way to sight a gun, how to light a cigarette, how to shave, how to powder your face, and the way to dial a telephone.

10. For freedom of communicative bodily activity, plan and tell a complete story without words. Perhaps you will want to explain the setting before you begin.

11. Together with some classmates compose, rehearse, and present an original play without words—a pantomime.

12. Prepare a charade with each syllable in a word or each word in a title represented by some dramatic action. Be ready to play charades in class. Perhaps you'd like to play the popular game, "Pantomime Quiz."

13. To increase your feel for the employment of visible action with the spoken word, take the members of your class on a four-minute imaginary visit to your own living room. Stand up as you speak and make a conscious effort to employ all of yourself in the process of describing the room.

14. Speak the following sentences with visible action. Remember that your purpose is simply to communicate effectively. Within the limits of good taste, use your whole body.

a. On one side sat all the men, and on the other the women.

b. Mankind must make its choice: either peace with freedom or war with the gradual destruction of all rights.

c. Why you rat! I could knock your teeth out!

d. This is where we grew the zinnias, and over there the marigolds.

e. "When he came up out of the water, immediately he saw the heavens opened and the Spirit descending upon him like a dove; and a voice came from heaven, 'Thou art my beloved Son; with thee I am well pleased.' "

f. "Rise, take up your pallet and walk!"

g. "Who is this that speaks blasphemies? Who can forgive sins but God only?"

h. "Why are you troubled, and why do questionings rise in your hearts? See my hands and my feet, that it is I myself; handle me, and see; for a spirit has not flesh and bones as you see that I have."

i. "Give me thy hand, Kate: I will unto Venice, To buy apparel 'gainst the wedding day."

j. "I swear I'll cuff you, if you strike again."

k. "Go get some water,
And wash this filthy witness [blood] from your hand."

l. He swept down the field, shouldering his way through the opposition.

m. Be he wise or foolish, the law's the law.

n. Me? Why, I wouldn't hurt a baby!

o. Stop, thief!

p. You're a liar!

15. Now try reading some of the above lines again, this time experimenting with the timing of gestures. In general, does it seem best to make the movement a fraction of a second before the word, just during the word, or right after it? Decide for yourself.

16. Turn back to the "Selections for Practice in Finding the Meaning" at the end of Chapter 5 and practice reading numbers 2, 14, and 18 with appropriate visible action.

17. Practice reading the following selections with appropriate visible actions that communicate and do not detract.

THE CREATION

(A Negro Sermon)

JAMES WELDON JOHNSON

And God stepped out on space,
And he looked around and said:
I'm lonely—
I'll make me a world.
And as far as the eye of God could see
Darkness covered everything,
Blacker than a hundred midnights
Down in a cypress swamp.

Then God smiled,
And the light broke,
And the darkness rolled up on one side,
And the light stood shining on the other,
And God said: That's good!

Then God reached out and took the light in his hands,
And God rolled the light around in his hands
Until he made the sun;
And he set that sun a-blazing in the heavens.
And the light that was left from making the sun
God gathered it up in a shining ball
And flung it against the darkness,
Spangling the night with the moon and stars.
Then down between
The darkness and the light
He hurled the world;
And God said: That's good!

Then God himself stepped down—
And the sun was on his right hand,
And the moon was on his left;
The stars were clustered about his head,
And the earth was under his feet.
And God walked, and where he trod
His footsteps hollowed the valleys out
And bulged the mountains up.

Then he stopped and looked and saw
That the earth was hot and barren.
So God stepped over to the edge of the world
And he spat out the seven seas;
He batted his eyes, and the lightnings flashed—
He clapped his hands, and the thunders rolled—
And the waters above the earth came down,
The cooling waters came down.
Then the green grass sprouted,
And the little red flowers blossomed,
The pine tree pointed his finger to the sky,
And the oak spread out his arms,
The lakes cuddled down in the hollows of the ground,
And the rivers ran down to the sea;
And God smiled again,

And the rainbow appeared,
And curled itself around his shoulder.

Then God raised his arm and he waved his hand
Over the sea and over the land,
And he said: Bring forth! Bring forth!
And quicker than God could drop his hand,
Fishes and fowls
And beasts and birds
Swam the rivers and the seas,
Roamed the forests and the woods,
And split the air with their wings.
And God said: That's good!

Then God walked around,
And God looked around
On all that he had made.
He looked at his sun,
And he looked at his moon,
And he looked at his little stars;
He looked on his world
With all its living things,
And God said: I'm lonely still.

Then God sat down—
On the side of a hill where he could think;
By a deep, wide river he sat down;
With his head in his hands,
God thought and thought,
Till he thought: I'll make me a man!

Up from the bed of the river
God scooped the clay;
And by the bank of the river
He kneeled him down;
And there the great God Almighty
Who lit the sun and fixed it in the sky,
Who flung the stars to the most far corner of the night,
Who rounded the earth in the middle of his hand;
This Great God,
Like a mammy bending over her baby,
Kneeled down in the dust

Toiling over a lump of clay
Till he shaped it in his own image;

Then into it he blew the breath of life,
And man became a living soul.
Amen. Amen.

TO THE TERRESTRIAL GLOBE

(by a Miserable Wretch)

SIR W. S. GILBERT

Roll on, thou ball, roll on!
Through pathless realms of Space
        Roll on!
What though I'm in a sorry case?
What though I cannot meet my bills?
What though I suffer toothache's ills?
What though I swallow countless pills?
    Never *you* mind!
        Roll on!
Roll on, thou ball, roll on!
Through seas of inky air
        Roll on!
It's true I have no shirts to wear;
It's true my butcher's bill is due;
It's true my prospects all look blue—
But don't let that unsettle you:
    Never *you* mind!
        Roll on!

It rolls on!

CONCERT IN THE PARK

E. B. WHITE

Another hot night I stop off at the Goldman Band concert in the Mall in Central Park. The people seated on the benches fanned out in front of the band shell are attentive, appreciative. In the trees the night wind stirs, bringing the leaves to life, endowing them with speech; the electric lights illuminate the green branches from the under side, translating them into a new language. Overhead a plane passes dreamily, its running lights winking. On the bench directly in front of me, a boy sits with his arm around his girl; they are proud of each other and are swathed in music. The cornetist steps forward for a solo, begins, "Drink to me only with thine eyes . . ." In the wide, warm night the horn is startlingly pure and magical. Then from the North River another horn solo begins—The *QUEEN MARY* announcing her intentions. She is not on key; she is a half tone off. The trumpeter in the bandstand never flinches. The horns quarrel savagely, but no one minds having the intimation of travel injected into the pledge of love. "I leave," sobs Mary. "And I will pledge with mine," sighs the trumpeter. Along the asphalt paths strollers pass to and fro; they behave considerately, respecting the musical atmosphere. Popsicles are moving well. In the warm grass beyond the fence, forms wriggle in the shadows, and the skirts of the girls approaching on the Mall are ballooned by the breeze, and their bare shoulders catch the lamplight. "Drink to me only with thine eyes." It is a magical occasion, and it's all free.

THE MOUNTAIN WHIPPOORWILL

(*Or, How Hillbilly Jim Won the Great Fiddler's Prize*)

A GEORGIA ROMANCE

STEPHEN VINCENT BENÉT

Up in the mountains, it's lonesome all the time,
(Sof' win' slewin' thu' the sweet-potato vine).

Up in the mountains, it's lonesome for a child,
(Whippoorwills a-callin' when the sap runs wild).

Up in the mountains, mountains in the fog,
Everythin's as lazy as an old houn' dog.

Born in the mountains, never raised a pet,
Don't want nuthin' an' never got it yet.

Born in the mountains, lonesome-born,
Raised runnin' ragged thu' the cockleburrs and corn.

Never knew my pappy, mebbe never should.
Think he was a fiddle made of mountain-laurel wood.

Never had a mammy to teach me pretty-please,
Think she was a whippoorwill, a-skitin' thu' the trees.

Never had a brother ner a whole pair of pants,
But when I start to fiddle, why, yuh got to start to dance!

Listen to my fiddle—Kingdom Come—Kingdom Come!
Hear the frogs a-chunkin' "Jug o' rum, Jug o' rum!"
Hear that mountain whippoorwill be lonesome in the air,
An' I'll tell yuh how I traveled to the Essex County Fair.

Essex County has a mighty pretty fair,
All the smarty fiddlers from the South come there.

Elbows flyin' as they rosin up the bow
For the First Prize Contest in the Georgia Fiddlers' Show.

Old Dan Wheeling, with his whiskers in his ears,
Kingpin fiddler for nearly twenty years.

Big Tom Sargent, with his blue walleye,
An' Little Jimmy Weezer that can make a fiddle cry.

All sittin' roun', spittin' high an' struttin' proud,
(Listen, little whippoorwill, yuh better bug yore eyes!)
Tun-a-tun-a-tunin' while the jedges told the crowd
Them that got the mostest claps 'd win the bestest prize.

Everybody waitin' for the first tweedle-dee,
When in comes a-stumblin'—hillbilly me!

Bowed right pretty to the jedges an' the rest,
Took a silver dollar from a hole inside my vest,

Plunked it on the table an' said, "There's my callin' card!
An' anyone that licks me—well, he's got to fiddle hard!"

Old Dan Wheeling, he was laughin' fit to holler,
Little Jimmy Weezer said, "There's one dead dollar!"

Big Tom Sargent had a yaller-toothy grin,
But I tucked my little whippoorwill spang underneath my chin
An' petted it an' tuned it till the jedges said, "Begin!"

Big Tom Sargent was the first in line;
He could fiddle all the bugs off a sweet-potato vine.
He could fiddle down a possum from a mile-high tree,
He could fiddle up a whale from the bottom of the sea.

Yuh could hear hands spankin' till they spanked each other raw,
When he finished variations on "Turkey in the Straw."

Little Jimmy Weezer was the next to play;
He could fiddle all night, he could fiddle all day.

He could fiddle chills, he could fiddle fever,
He could make a fiddle rustle like a lowland river.

He could make a fiddle croon like a lovin' woman.
An' they clapped like thunder when he'd finished strummin'.

Then came the ruck of the bobtailed fiddlers,
The let's-go-easies, the fair-to-middlers.

They got their claps an' they lost their bicker,
An' they all settled back for some more corn licker.

An' the crowd was tired of their no-count squealing,
When out in the center steps Old Dan Wheeling.

He fiddled high and he fiddled low,
(*Listen, little whippoorwill; yuh got to spread yore wings!*)
He fiddled and fiddled with a cherry-wood bow.
(*Old Dan Wheeling's got bee honey in his strings.*)

He fiddled the wind by the lonesome moon,
He fiddled a most almighty tune.

He started fiddling like a ghost,
He ended fiddling like a host.

He fiddled north and he fiddled south,
He fiddled the heart right out of yore mouth.

He fiddled here an' he fiddled there.
He fiddled salvation everywhere.

When he was finished the crowd cut loose.
(Whippoorwill, they's rain on yore breast.)
An' I sat there wonderin' "What's the use?"
(Whippoorwill, fly home to yore nest.)

But I stood up pert an' I took my bow,
An' my fiddle went to my shoulder, so.

An'—they wasn't no crowd to get me fazed—
But I was alone where I was raised.

Up in the mountains, so still it makes yuh skeered.
Where God lies sleepin' in his big white beard.

An' I heard the sound of the squirrel in the pine,
An' I heard the earth a-breathin' thu' the long nighttime.

They've fiddled the rose, and they've fiddled the thorn,
But they haven't fiddled the mountain corn.

They've fiddled sinful an' fiddled moral,
But they haven't fiddled the breshwoodlaurel.

They've fiddled loud, and they've fiddled still,
But they haven't fiddled the whippoorwill.

I started off with a *dump-diddle-dump,*
(Oh, hell's broke loose in Georgia!)
Skunk cabbage growin' by the bee-gum stump,
(Whippoorwill, yo're singin' now!)

Oh, Georgia booze is mighty fine booze,
The best yuh ever pourd yuh,
But it eats the soles right offen yore shoes,
For Hell's broke loose in Georgia.

My mother was a whippoorwill pert,
My father, he was lazy,
But I'm Hell broke loose in a new store shirt
To fiddle all Georgia crazy.

Swing yore partners—up an' down the middle!
Sashay now—oh, listen to that fiddle!
Flapjacks flippin' on a red-hot griddle,

An' hell broke loose,
Hell broke loose,
Fire on the mountains—snakes in the grass.
Satan's here a-bilin'—oh, Lordy, let him pass!
Go down, Moses, set my people free;
Pop goes the weasel thu' the old Red Sea!
Jonah sittin' on a hickory bough
Up jumps a whale—an' where's yore prophet now?
Rabbit in the pea patch, possum in the pot,
Try an' stop my fiddle, now my fiddle's gettin' hot!
Whippoorwill, singin' thu' the mountain hush,
Whippoorwill, shoutin' from the burnin' bush,
Whippoorwill, cryin' in the stable door,
Sing tonight as yuh never sang before!
Hell's broke loose like a stompin' mountain shoat,
Sing till yuh bust the gold in yore throat!
Hell's broke loose for forty miles aroun'
Bound to stop yore music if yuh don't sing it down.
Sing on the mountains, little whippoorwill,
Sing to the valleys, an' slap 'em with a hill,
For I'm struttin' high as an eagle's quill,
An' Hell's broke loose,
Hell's broke loose,
Hell's broke loose in Georgia!

They wasn't a sound when I stopped bowin',
(*Whippoorwill, yuh can sing no more*).
But, somewhere or other, the dawn was growin',
(*Oh, mountain whippoorwill!*)

An' I thought, "I've fiddled all night an' lost,
Yo're a good hillbilly, but yuh've been bossed."

So I went to congratulate old man Dan,
—But he puts his fiddle into my han'—
An' then the noise of the crowd began!

SUNRISE

MARK TWAIN

I had myself called with the four-o'clock watch, mornings, for one cannot see too many summer sunrises on the Mississippi. They are enchanting. First, there is the eloquence of silence; for a deep hush broods everywhere. Next, there is the haunting sense of loneliness, isolation, remoteness from the worry and bustle of the world. The dawn creeps in stealthily; the solid walls of black forest soften to gray, and vast stretches of the river open up and reveal themselves; the water is glass-smooth, gives off spectral little wreaths of white mist, there is not the faintest breath of wind, nor stir of leaf; the tranquility is profound and infinitely satisfying. Then a bird pipes up, another follows, and soon the pipings develop into a jubilant riot of music. You see none of the birds; you simply move through an atmosphere of song which seems to sing itself. When the light has become a little stronger, you have one of the fairest and softest pictures imaginable. You have the intense green of the shade in front of you; upon the next projecting cape, a mile off or more, the tint has lightened to the tender young green of spring; the cape beyond that one has almost lost color, and the farthest one, miles away under the horizon, sleeps upon the water a mere dim vapor, and hardly separable from the sky above it and about it. And all this stretch of river is a mirror, and you have the shadowy reflections of the leafage and the curving shores and the receding capes pictured in it. Well, that is all beautiful; soft and rich and beautiful; and when the sun gets well up, and distributes a pink flush here and a powder of gold yonder and a purple haze where it will yield the best effect, you grant that you have seen something that is worth remembering.

from THE CIRCUS OF DR. LAO

CHARLES G. FINNEY

Sonorously the great bronze gong banged and rang; and from all over the circus ground the people, red and black and white, left the little sideshow tents and shuffled through the dust. The midway was thick with them for a minute or two as they crowded toward the big tent. Then the midway was desolate, save for its wreath of dust, as the people all disappeared beneath the canvas. And the ringing of the bronze gong diminuendoed and died.

The big tent was a dull creamy lacquer within. Black swastikas were painted on it and winged serpents and fish eyes. There were no circus rings. In the center of the floor was a big triangle instead, a pedestal adorning each angle. Doctor Lao, in full showman's dress of tails and high hat and cracking whip, attained the top of one of the pedestals and blew on a whistle. At a far entrance a seething and a rustling was heard. Chinese music, monotonous as bagpiping, teetled through the tent. Figures could be seen massing at the far entrance. The grand march was starting. The main performance had begun.

Snorting and damping, the unicorn came leading the grand march. Its hoofs had been gilded and its mane combed.

"Notice it!" screamed Doctor Lao. "Notice the unicorn. The giraffe is the only antlered animal that does not shed its antlers. The pronghorn antelope is the only horned animal that sheds its horns. Unique they are among the deciduous beasts. But what of the unicorn? Is it not unique? A horn is hair; and antler is bone; but that thing on the unicorn's head is metal. Think that over, will you?"

Then came the sphinx, ponderous and stately, shaking its curls.

"Say something to them!" hissed Majordomo Lao.

"What walks on four legs, two legs, three legs?" simpered the androgyne.

Mumbo Jumbo and his retinue came. The satyr syrinxed. The nymphs danced. The sea serpent coiled and glided. Fluttering its wings, the chimera filled the tent with smoke. Two shepherdesses drove their sheep. A thing that looked like a bear carried the kiss-blowing mermaid in its arms. The hound of the hedges barked and played. Apollonius cast rose petals. Her eyes blindfolded, her snakes awrithe, the medusa was led by the faun. Cheeping, the roc chick gamboled. On the golden ass an old woman rode. A two-headed turtle, unable to make up either of its minds, wandered vaguely. It was the damnedest collection Abalone, Arizona, had ever seen.

Mr. Etaoin, sitting behind Larry Kamper, said to Miss Agnes Birdson: "Well, that's the whole outfit, I guess, except for the werewolf. I wonder where it is?"

Larry turned around. "See that old woman on the donkey's back? There's yer goddam werewolf."

Round and round the great triangle the animals walked, danced, pranced, fluttered, and crawled, Master of Ceremonies Lao directing them from his pedestal. They roared and screamed and coughed; rising from strings and reeds the Chinese music teetled monotonously and waveringly whined. Too close upon the fastidious unicorn, the sphinx accidently nuzzled its rump; and the unicorn exploded with a tremendous kick, crashing its heels into the sphinx's side. The hermaphrodite shrieked. With its great paws it struck and roweled the unicorn's neck and back. The unicorn leaped like a mad stallion, whirled and centered its horn in the sphinx's lungs. Nervous, the chimera dodged about, its flapping wings fanning up dust clouds. The sea serpent reared into a giant S, launched a fifty-foot strike, caught the chimera by a forefoot, and flung seven loops about its wings and shoulders. The hound of the hedges curled in a tight ball, looking like a stray grass hummock. The Russian passionately kissed the mermaid. Lowering his horns, taking a short run for it, the satyr spiked Mumbo Jumbo in the rump when the black god's back was turned. The old woman changed back into a wolf and ravened at the roc chick. The little faun threw stones at Dr. Lao. The nymphs and shepherdesses and lambs hid and whimpered. From the face of the medusa the blindfold fell; eleven people turned to stone.

"Oh, misery!" screamed the doctor. "Why do they have to fight so when there is nothing to fight about? They are as stupid as humans. Stop them, Apollonius, quickly, before someone gets hurt!"

The thaumaturge hurled spell after spell among the hysterical beasts. Spells of peace, mediation, rationality, arbitration, and calmness flashed through the feverish air and fell like soft webs about the battlers. The din lessened. Withdrawing his horn from the sphinx's lungs, the unicorn trotted away and cropped at sparse grass. The sphinx licked at its lacerated side. The sea serpent loosed the chimera, yawned his jaws back into place. Shaking itself, the hound of the hedges arose and whined. The mermaid patted the bear. Mumbo Jumbo forgave the satyr. The werewolf remetamorphosed. The faun stopped throwing rocks. Back came the nymphs and shepherdesses and lambs. Once again the medusa assumed her blindfold.

After the storm, tranquillity. Peace after battle. Forgiveness after hate.

POEM

WILLIAM CARLOS WILLIAMS

As the cat
climbed over
the top of

the jamcloset
first the right
forefoot

carefully
then the hind
stepped down

into the pit of
the empty
flowerpot

18. Elsewhere in this book are many selections suitable for reading with appropriate visible actions. Prepare to read some of the following and then

practice aloud with visible action which communicates and does not distract: "My Last Duchess" by Robert Browning in Chapter 3, "Nightmare at Noon" by Stephen Vincent Benét in Chapter 12, and part of *Tiger at the Gates* by Jean Giraudoux in Chapter 15.

Suggested Readings

Bacon, Wallace A., and Robert S. Breen. *Literature as Experience.* New York: McGraw-Hill, 1959, Chapter II, "The Physical Nature of the Individual."

Grimes, Wilma H., and Alethea Smith Mattingly. *Interpretation: Writer, Reader, Audience.* Belmont, Cal.: Wadsworth Publishing Co., Chapter VIII, "The Interpreter's Use of His Body."

Lee, Charlotte I. *Oral Interpretation.* Boston: Houghton Mifflin, 1952, Chapter IV, "Use of the Body in Oral Interpretation."

Lynch, Gladys E., and Harold C. Crain. *Projects in Oral Interpretation.* New York: Holt, 1959, Chapter IV, "Projects in Physical Expressiveness."

Monroe, Alan H. *Principles and Types of Speech.* (3rd edition) Chicago: Scott Foresman, 1955, Chapter III, "Bodily Action in Interpretative Reading."

Smith, Joseph F., and James R. Linn. *Skill in Reading Aloud.* New York: Harper, 1960, Chapter VIII, "Visibility."

Woolbert, Charles H., and Severina E. Nelson. *The Art of Interpretative Speech.* (3rd edition) New York: Appleton-Century-Crofts, 1945, Chapter V, "Meaning through Bodily Action."

7

AUDIBLE COMMUNICATION: GENERAL PRINCIPLES

Although visible communication is primary in every public performance, the interpretative reader communicates most of the color and substance in a literary selection by means of his voice. He makes impressions, strengthens his meaning, and produces proper empathic responses visibly, but he communicates ideas and feelings fundamentally with sound. Just as his visible communication will be only as effective as his use of his entire visible personality, so his oral communication will be only as effective as his use of his vocal mechanism in producing sounds.

Effective sounds may be likened to effective lines and masses drawn by the painter. The interpreter's silence is similar to a painting's neutral background. The reader must make significant sounds prominent, just as the painter must make important details stand out from the background of the painting. Both artists must likewise make unimportant details fade into the background. Learning this technique is the first step in learning to communicate through sound.

When a child learns to read aloud, he reads each word separately, and he treats each word in exactly the same way: "SEE—THE—CAT. SEE—THE—CAT—RUN." No one will contend that this reading is either communicative or interesting. No one admires the performance of a pianist who hits every note with the same force or the product of a painter who executes all lines with the same width or in the same direction. When each word is read separately or when each word is emphasized without relation to meaning, nothing stands out; nothing seems to be more important than anything else; hence, nothing is communicated and nothing is beautiful. It takes time for a child reader to learn to group words into thoughts and to master emphasis. It takes time for him to learn to focus his mind upon meaning and feeling. Some persons never learn how.

This chapter enlarges upon the principles of the thought-group and thought-center, which were discussed in Chapter 5 as aspects of finding the meaning, but treats them now as aspects of expressing the meaning. The chapters which follow this one will attempt to show how the reader can accomplish phrasing and centering through the elements of audible communication: time, loudness, pitch, and quality.

THE THOUGHT-GROUP

A thought-unit is a word or a series of words expressing an idea which may be held in the human consciousness indefinitely. The interpretative reader has the responsibility of tying words together into groups that will register and remain in the minds of himself and his listeners.

Written and spoken words may or may not mean anything to a reader or listener, depending on the way in which they are used. We have already seen that words are mere symbols which may be utilized to stir up definite meanings or feelings in the reader and listener. The word "fire" calls to mind in most of us merely an abstract concept of a physical phenomenon. But, printed in a different way—"FIRE!"—it is likely to mean more to most of us, either because we have heard it used as a frantic warning or we have been conditioned to such a possible use of the word by vicarious experiences or fire prevention programs. All of us know what "FIRE!" means.

Uttered one way, the word actually means little to us; uttered another, it calls to mind vivid imaginings. In the one case, the sound is a symbol for generalized concepts; in the other, it is a complete thought, which we may retain in our consciousness indefinitely. In using sound and silence, the interpretative reader is not concerned directly with sound and the absence of sound alone, but with the *thoughts* which the use of sound and silence can convey.

The flat utterance of the sound "dog" means nothing to a foreigner who knows no English, but if said in a cursing manner to him—Dog!—he would sense the insult even if he did not know the meaning of the word. The use of the sound, coupled with sight certainly, would mean more to him than the animal the word symbolizes. The flat utterance of this word would also carry a very hazy meaning to most of us. To make the meaning more concrete, other sounds and silences must be incorporated with it. For example, consider how much more each successive expression means to you:

dog

little dog

little Cocker Spaniel

little brown Cocker Spaniel

the little brown Cocker Spaniel from across the street

the little brown Cocker Spaniel from across the street ran

The little brown Cocker Spaniel from across the street ran up to me.

The little brown Cocker Spaniel from across the street ran up to me, wiggled all over, licked his chops, and whined for affection.

Each successive expression means more to you than the preceding ones because in each case the idea becomes *more complete, concrete,* and *specific.* In each successive one you are able to picture the situation more fully. Each of us has had such an experience with a "dog." "Dog" cannot be held in mind very long. "Little dog" will remain there a bit longer. "The little brown Cocker Spaniel from across the street" is quite complete as an idea; therefore it is a concrete and specific thought-group which stirs up a vivid and specific picture in your mind. "Ran" is indefinite in meaning, but "ran up to me" is specific—a definite thought. So are "wiggled all over," "licked his chops," and "whined for affection."

A word by itself may or may not be a thought-unit. More often than not, words properly fitted together stimulate more complete and concrete thoughts. As a reader you are more concerned with thought-groups than with separate words. Words, as words, lie inert upon the page. Thought-groups whine for interpretation.

Apply our definition of a thought-group—a series of words expressing an idea which may be held in the human consciousness indefinitely—to the following sentence from W. H. Hudson's *Far Away and Long Ago:*

> One hot day in December I had been standing perfectly still for a few minutes among the dry weeds when a slight rustling sound came from near my feet, and glancing down I saw the head and neck of a large black serpent moving slowly past me.

The sentence has thirteen possible thought-groups, some more specific and image-provoking than others: (1) *One hot day* creates an image which we may think about for some time. (2) *In December* is a clear-cut concept. It is not hard to visualize (3) *I had been standing,* (4) *perfectly still,* (5) *for a few minutes,* and (6) *among the dry weeds,* as they follow in a logical progression, gradually building a more complete image. The phrase (7) *when a slight rustling sound* adds a new element to the total picture, but it is an element which may be held in the consciousness alone, nevertheless. The same is true of the next phrase, (8) *came from near my feet,* as it adds a new idea to the preceding one. (9) *And glancing down* describes a specific act which is easily visualized. The subject and verb (10) *I saw* of the second main clause describe another act which might conceivably stand alone in the consciousness. The longest thought-group in the sentence is (11) *the head and neck of a large black serpent.* (Why can this thought-group not be divided into shorter ones?) When thinking of the serpent, one can easily see in his mind's eye the last two thought-groups: (12) *moving slowly* and (13) *past me.*

Do not assume that any intelligent person would read the sentence as it is divided here; we have merely exhausted all possibilities in this example. Short thought-groups are often linked together into longer, more meaningful groups. This sentence will again be used as illustrative material in the following chapter, in a discussion of the pause and phrasing. When you study that material, you should review this analysis.

EMPHASIS AND SUBORDINATION

In addition to learning to recognize thought-groups you must learn to distinguish between the important and the unimportant. Within thought-groups are words of varying significance. Some are vitally essential to the meaning; some only tie the essential words together. The reader must be able to focus attention by means of emphasis and subordination. A few years ago, a popular song expressed the philosophy that we should accentuate the positive and eliminate the negative. The rules for effective emphasis and subordination are admirably stated here, and they are just that simple. They are, in fact, so simple that they are constantly adhered to by almost everyone in his daily conversation. Few persons must think consciously of which words to emphasize or de-emphasize. We should realize that emphasis is a physical expression of mental activity. When the mind centers upon the idea expressed by a significant word, the physical result—audibly and visibly—is emphasis. In the words of Tin Pan Alley, again, we all "do what comes naturally" when we speak our minds. But in the world of the arts, to do what comes naturally is often the most difficult. Actors soon learn that it is hard to seem natural upon the stage. It is often far easier to act a part far removed from our own personality than it is to "be ourselves" satisfactorily before an audience. To seem natural is the object of as much practice in interpretative reading as it is in acting. Some readers quite naturally group words effectively and also emphasize and subordinate effectively. Others must restudy the fundamentals. What follows is a simple but thorough analysis of emphasis and subordination.

For purposes of illustration, let us consider a simple declarative sentence:

> I am sending Christmas cards and gifts.

(We can recognize immediately that the sentence is one single thought-group. At no place would the speaker try to divide it into more than one thought.)

Which words are important? Which are unimportant? That depends on what the speaker has in mind and is trying to communicate, but assuming that the meaning is quite simple, probably these words are of greatest importance:

> *I* am *sending Christmas cards* and *gifts.*

Although "I" is the subject of the sentence and states who is sending the items mentioned, it hardly needs much stress. We often speak in the first person, of ourselves, and we do not naturally stress the pronoun unless we are abnormally egotistical or are being emphatic and saying that *we* have done something in contrast to someone else who has not. "Sending" is the important verb, which states the action of the subject. Additional emphasis would be placed on this word if the speaker were indicating that he was *sending* them rather than *receiving* them. "Christmas" is, of course, a very important adjective, stating the kind of cards and gifts. (The further away from Christmas one is, the more emphasis he would place upon this word. Do you see why?) "Cards" and "gifts" carry the whole point of the sentence, stating the things being sent.

The good reader would make all these words stand out, but he would throw additional weight upon the particular word or words which convey the specific meaning he has in mind for the sentence; he would give greatest emphasis to the thought-centers.

Next let us consider the same sentence in regard to subordinating the remaining unimportant words. "Am" is an auxiliary verb, probably of little importance, unless the speaker were strongly asserting that he *is* sending out the articles, in which case we would emphasize "am": "I *am* sending. . . ." When the basic verb carries the meaning, as "sending" does here, we quite naturally in conversation contract the auxiliary with the subject: "I'm sending. . . ." (This principle of contraction is one of the most prominent characteristics of informal, easy, conversation-like speaking. The effective radio and television speaker contracts—*can't, won't, wouldn't, couldn't,* etc. —whereas the amateur reads *cannot, will not, would not, could not,* etc., as they appear in print but seldom in speech.) Skip lightly over "and," a word which is seldom stressed. In this sentence, "and" becomes only a nasal sound [n] between the two nouns. When emphasized or stressed, words retain their distinctive identities; when unstressed, their forms are changed—often radically—in pronunciation. You will find a thorough discussion of the principles of stressing and unstressing in the opening pages of *Webster's New International Dictionary,* Second Edition. Unnatural, pedantic speech results from the stressing of each syllable of each word. In conversation the above sentence would sound somewhat as represented here: "I'm *send*ing *Christ*mas *cardz'*n *gifts.*" We could very well draw a line under the particular word to be emphasized in order to convey the particular meaning we wish to communicate, in other words, under the thought-center.

Effective grouping and emphasizing depend on the meaning. (This principle is so important that it deserves frequent repetition.) Only if the reader obtains the meaning, will he be able to read effectively. Some authorities go so far as to contend that if a reader does not read intelligently, he simply does not understand the meaning. For those who habitually read all words with undiscerning stress or for those who unstress the important and emphasize the unimportant, a study of the fundamentals is necessary.

The effective audible communication of meaning is completely dependent on adequate comprehension of the material read at the moment of utterance. Therefore, the principles outlined in this chapter are akin to and dependent on the principles outlined in Chapter 5, "Finding the Meaning." The principles of the two chapters overlap; in fact, we may say that the accurate determination of meaning and the accurate expression of meaning are parts of the same process. For purposes of illustration and clarity of instruction, however, we have arbitrarily separated the two processes into "Finding" and "Expressing." Hence, Chapter 5 dealt with the mental processes of discovering meaning, particularly during study, and the present chapter with the audible expression of those symbols which convey the author's meaning. Food for thought: does not the reader discover meaning while reading aloud?

Types of words. Any word may be important; any word may be unimportant. The meaning determines relative importance. *Generally speaking,* however, we may make these observations regarding word emphasis:

Nouns are usually important words, since they are the names of things discussed. Eliminate the nouns and you have little left.

EXAMPLES: Nouns are underlined in these examples. Study them; read them aloud. Would *you* emphasize them all? Try reading only the words which are *not* underlined to see what happens when nouns are omitted.

> The poetry in the doctrines of Jesus Christ, and the mythology and institutions of the Celtic conquerors of the Roman empire, outlived the darkness and the convulsions connected with their growth and victory, and blended themselves in a new fabric of manners and opinion.
>
> —PERCY BYSSHE SHELLEY, *A Defence of Poetry*

To him who in the love of Nature holds
Communion with her visible forms, she speaks
A various language; for his gayer hours
She has a voice of gladness, and a smile
And eloquence of beauty, and she glides
Into his darker musings, with a mild
And healing sympathy, that steals away
Their sharpness, ere he is aware.

—WILLIAM CULLEN BRYANT, *Thanatopsis*

The day is done, and the darkness
Falls from the wings of Night,
As a feather is wafted downward
From an eagle in his flight.

—HENRY WADSWORTH LONGFELLOW, *The Day Is Done*

Verbs are usually important words, for they communicate all action, occurrence, and mode of being. Beware, however, of placing stress upon auxiliary or copulative verbs unless the sense demands that they be emphasized.

EXAMPLES: Verbs are underlined in these examples. Read them aloud to determine the importance of stressing verbs. "Did" in the first example, "have" in the second, "can" and "could" in the third, are auxiliary verbs. Try stressing them and notice the unnatural effect achieved.

A bird came down the walk:
He did not know I saw;
He bit an angle-worm in halves
And ate the fellow, raw.

And then he drank a dew
From a convenient grass,
And then hopped sidewise to the wall
To let a beetle pass.

—EMILY DICKINSON, *A bird came down the walk*

Have you heard of the wonderful one-hoss shay,
That was built in such a logical way
It ran a hundred years to a day,
And then, of a sudden, it—ah, but stay,
I'll tell you what happened without delay,
Scaring the parson into fits,
Frightening people out of their wits,—
Have you ever heard of that, I say?

—OLIVER WENDELL HOLMES, *The Deacon's Masterpiece*

He stripped the body of its armour and fastening cords to the feet tied them behind his chariot, leaving the body to trail along the ground. Then mounting the chariot he lashed the steeds and so dragged the body to and fro before the city. What words can tell the grief of King Priam and Queen Hecuba at this sight! His people could scarce restrain the old king from rushing forth. He threw himself in the dust and besought them each by name to give him way.

—*Bulfinch's Mythology*

Adjectives may be extremely important or of little importance. They describe nouns. Your judgment of the meaning will be your guide.

Adverbs should be treated the same as adjectives. They modify verbs or other modifiers and answer the questions: how? when? where? etc. Sometimes they are highly significant; sometimes insignificant. Use your own judgment.

EXAMPLES: Adjectives and adverbs are underlined in these examples. Although you would probably not emphasize them all, you may find that some may be the centers of your attention. Read the selections aloud and compare your treatment of these words with the reading of another student.

I am, in point of fact, a particularly haughty and exclusive person, of pre-Adamite ancestral descent. You will understand this when I tell you that I can trace my ancestry back to a protoplasmal primordial atomic globule. Consequently, my family pride is something inconceivable. I can't help it. I was born sneering. But I struggle hard to overcome this defect. I mortify my pride continually. When all the great officers of State resigned in a body, because they were too proud to serve under an ex-tailor, did I not unhesitatingly accept all their posts at once?

—GILBERT AND SULLIVAN, *The Mikado*

Let me have men about me that are fat;
Sleek-headed men and such as sleep o'nights:
Yon Cassius has a lean and hungry look;
He thinks too much: such men are dangerous.

—SHAKESPEARE, *Julius Caesar*

Articles are usually so unimportant that they are rarely emphasized. The habit of many beginning readers of giving the articles *a, an,* and *the* the same stress as nouns and verbs does more to obscure meaning and to make the reading seem childish and unnatural than any other mistake one could make. It is strange but true that most persons do not realize what is naturally done with articles in normal conversation. For example, we rarely pronounce the article *a* in its long form ā[e], except in the rare instance of pointing out a single item such as "There is *a* (meaning only one) table in the room." In all other cases, we would quite naturally pronounce *a* as an unaccented *uh* [ə]. (The article *a* precedes only words beginning with a consonant; before words beginning with a vowel, it is spelled *an.*) Our treatment of the article *the* is similar. We pronounce *the* as *thē* [ði] only in pointing out a single item, such as in "He is *the* authority on the subject." In all other instances, we use one of two other pronunciations of the word. When *the* precedes a word beginning with a vowel, we pronounce it as if its own vowel were a short *i* [ɪ] as in this sentence: "I saw a bird flying in the air." When *the* precedes a word beginning with a consonant, however, we normally pronounce it as an unaccented *thuh* [ðə] as in this sentence: "I saw a bird flying in the sky." These uses are normal, natural, and correct. You may find a discussion of this subject in your dictionary. Unfortunately, the distinctions are not commonly understood, and many persons when reading pronounce all *a*'s as *ā* [e] and all *the*'s as *thē* [ði]. Except when the meaning consists of pointing out a single item as important, slide over the articles, push them into the background, just as you normally do in conversational speech.

Prepositions should also be unstressed, except when the sense of the passage makes them important. Lincoln's "of the *people, by* the people, and *for* the people" is the most famous example of the sense being carried by important prepositions. When the sense depends upon prepositions, emphasize them, but otherwise, trip lightly over them.

Pronouns, which are words used in place of nouns, and which refer to a person, an idea, or an object already mentioned, are almost always unstressed. Only when some other principle—such as contrast, to be discussed shortly—throws the weight on a pronoun, should it be emphasized.

Connectives should usually be unstressed, especially when they are monosyllables such as *and, but, for, as, or*. Multisyllabic connectives such as *nevertheless, therefore,* and *consequently* will naturally have accented syllables, for it is impossible to speak them without accenting at least one of the syllables, but that is not thought-emphasis. Connectives may require emphasis in some instances, but they are often given too much importance by the unthinking neophyte.

EXAMPLES: The following examples contain articles, prepositions, pronouns, connectives, auxiliary verbs, and forms of the verb *to be* which are underscored. Try reading them aloud, emphasizing those words which are underlined. Notice the unnatural effect so obtained. Notice that false meaning or no meaning is communicated by such reading.

> Property is the fruit of labor; property is desirable, is a positive good in the world. That some should be rich shows that others may become rich, and hence is just encouragement to industry and enterprise. Let not him who is houseless pull down the house of another, but let him work diligently and build one for himself, thus by example assuring that his own shall be safe from violence when built.
>
> —ABRAHAM LINCOLN

QUESTION: Which of these words *do* deserve emphasis, according to your interpretation?

> The day is done, and the darkness
> Falls from the wings of Night,
> As a feather is wafted downward
> From an eagle in his flight.
>
> —HENRY WADSWORTH LONGFELLOW, *The Day Is Done*

Now read this stanza, emphasizing, in appropriate degree, the words indicated. Compare the difference!

> The day is done, and the darkness
> Falls from the wings of Night,
> As a feather is wafted downward
> From an eagle in his flight.

Although the principles just explained and illustrated are usually true, let us repeat our first statement of this section: "Any word may be important; any word may be unimportant. The meaning determines relative importance." A few samples from conversational speech will demonstrate that words which are usually insignificant may occasionally be vitally important:

BILL: You caught some fish?
JOE: (Sadly) I caught a fish.

FATHER: Now, Son, this is the way to putt.

MOTHER: Can't you, for once, throw waste into the basket instead of at it?

MARY: The new neighbor kids are named John, James, and Joan. She seems nice.

FATHER: Before I give you the key to the car, you will cut the grass, spade the garden, clean your room, and [pause for thought and impressiveness] anything else I think of!

HE: Let's stay home tonight.
SHE: I'd like to go to a movie.
HE: But I don't want to go to a movie.
SHE: We will go to a movie, if you know what's good for you!

SON (or DAUGHTER): I've tried every way I know, and this problem just won't work out.
FATHER (or MOTHER): Well, don't give up. There is a way to solve it, or it wouldn't have been assigned to you.

New ideas—old ideas. The distinction between new ideas and old ideas is very important! The interpretative reader must always emphasize new ideas in preference to old ones unless the old ideas are restatements for emphasis. In intelligent writing the train of thought is to be found in the flow from one new idea to another new idea. Mixed in with the succession of new ideas, however, are to be found repetitions or "echoes" of the old ideas. These should be unstressed, unless some other principle of emphasis throws the spotlight on them, in which case they cease to be echoes. Echoes are always unimportant.

EXAMPLE: Consider the use of the word *islands* in this paragraph:

All of us, without exception, live on islands. But some of these islands on our planet are so much larger than the others that we have decided to let them belong to a class of their own and have called them "continents." A continent therefore is an island which "contains" or "holds together" more territory than just an ordinary island like England or Madagascar or Manhattan.

—HENDRIK WILLEM VAN LOON, *Van Loon's Geography*

This is the first paragraph of a chapter. In the first line *islands* are mentioned for the first time. It is the word which focuses attention on the main point of the paragraph. It must be emphasized. In line 2, however, *islands* is used again, and here it is an echo of the preceding idea; *islands* is repeated only for coherence or clearness. The new idea in this sentence is to be found expressed in the word *some,* which should receive the emphasis. Throw the stress on *some,* but skim over *islands.* In line 2, *others* should be emphasized because it is the new idea in contrast to *some.* In line 4, *continents* becomes the new idea, but in the following sentence, both *continent* and *island* should be emphasized, for they are the important nouns in a highly significant definition, the author's main point. The author has repeated both to emphasize the relationship. In line 6, however, the word *island* is again an echo, to be unstressed, whereas the emphasis should be placed upon the new idea in the word *ordinary.* Now, read the above paragraph aloud to see how it sounds when you emphasize the words just discussed.

Consider another example in this piece of light verse entitled "Traffic."

He was right, dead right
As he hurried along.
But he's just as dead
As though he were wrong.

In death as in life
He fell for a cause;
At last has a country
Not of men but of laws.

—ANONYMOUS

The first new idea is *right,* followed by *dead,* the next new idea. The second *right* in line 1 is an echo of the first and should be subordinated. In line 2 the new idea is *hurried.* In line 3 *just* is the new idea, and *dead* the echo. In line 4 the new idea is *wrong.* In line 5 *death* and *life* are compared, and therefore both are emphasized. In line 6 the new idea is *cause.* In line 7 *last* and *country* are both new ideas. (Which is more important and should therefore receive the greater emphasis?) In the last line three new ideas occur: the negative and the contrast: *men* and *laws.*

Did you notice the pronouns in this verse? The first pronoun is unimportant because it is generalized or universal. It refers to anyone or everyone. After that, *he* is always an echo referring back. This is the principle of the unimportant pronoun: it is usually an echo. Notice also *her* and *she* referring to *moon* in "Silver" below.

Assertion—implication. This is similar to the principle of New Ideas—Old Ideas. The train of thought to be communicated is that which is asserted. On the other hand, those concepts which are obvious, therefore taken for granted, are implied. Implied material should not be centered on because it is not of greatest importance. For example, in Van Loon's paragraph on islands just discussed, *planet,* in line 2, is pure implication, for it is obvious to all that the author is speaking of our world. *Territory,* in line 5, is also implication because an island obviously contains, or holds together, territory. In de la Mare's little poem, which follows shortly, *night, sees, trees, beams, dog, water,* and *stream* are all implied. Why?

SILVER

WALTER DE LA MARE

Slowly, silently, now the moon
Walks the night in her silver shoon;
This way, and that, she peers, and sees
Silver fruit upon silver trees;
One by one the casements catch
Her beams beneath the silvery thatch;
Couched in his kennel, like a log,
With paws of silver sleeps the dog;
From their shadowy cote the white breasts peep
Of doves in a silver-feathered sleep;
A harvest mouse goes scampering by,
With silver claws and silver eye;
And moveless fish in the water gleam,
By silver reeds in a silver stream.

Repetitions for emphasis. Authors will often repeat a word or phrase in order to emphasize it or to create a desired psychological effect. (The wise public speaker also knows the persuasive value of well-planned and executed repetition.) De la Mare's frequent repetition—ten times in fourteen lines—of *silver* is certainly one of design. The word *silver* should receive careful consideration in each case. Not only is the idea "silver" predominant but also the sound value of the word is important. The same should be said for the *raven* and *nevermore* in Poe's "The Raven," quoted in Chapter 10, for *create, great,* and *peace* in "Create Great Peace," quoted in Chapter 4, and for the many uses of the word *silence* in the following poem:

SILENCE

EDGAR LEE MASTERS

I have known the silence of the stars and of the sea,
And the silence of the city when it pauses,
And the silence of a man and a maid,
And the silence for which music alone finds the word,
And the silence of the woods before the winds of spring begin,
And the silence of the sick
When their eyes roam about the room.
And I ask: For the depths
Of what use is language?
A beast of the field moans a few times
When death takes its young.
And we are voiceless in the presence of realities—
We cannot speak.

A curious boy asks an old soldier
Sitting in front of the grocery store,
"How did you lose your leg?"
And the old soldier is struck in silence,
Or his mind flies away
Because he cannot concentrate it on Gettysburg.
It comes back jocosely
And he says, "A bear bit it off."
And the boy wonders, while the old soldier
Dumbly, feebly lives over
The flashes of guns, the thunder of cannon,
The shrieks of the slain,
And himself lying on the ground,
And the hospital surgeons, the knives,
And the long days in bed.
But if he could describe it all
He would be an artist.
But if he were an artist there would be deeper wounds
Which he could not describe.

There is the silence of a great hatred,
And the silence of a great love,
And the silence of a deep peace of mind,
And the silence of an embittered friendship.
There is the silence of a spiritual crisis,
Through which your soul, exquisitely tortured,
Comes with visions not to be uttered
Into a realm of higher life,
And the silence of the gods who understand each other without speech.
There is the silence of defeat.
There is the silence of those unjustly punished;
And the silence of the dying whose hand
Suddenly grips yours.
There is the silence between father and son,
When the father cannot explain his life,
Even though he be misunderstood for it.

There is the silence that comes between husband and wife.
There is the silence of those who have failed;
And the vast silence that covers
Broken nations and vanquished leaders.
There is the silence of Lincoln,
Thinking of the poverty of his youth.
And the silence of Napoleon
After Waterloo.
And the silence of Jeanne d'Arc
Saying amid the flames, "Blessed Jesus"—
Revealing in two words all sorrow, all hope.
And there is the silence of age,
Too full of wisdom for the tongue to utter it
In words intelligible to those who have not lived
The great range of life.
And there is the silence of the dead.
If we who are in life cannot speak
Of profound experiences,
Why do you marvel that the dead
Do not tell you of death?
Their silence shall be interpreted
As we approach them.

You may have to make some difficult decisions as to whether words are meant to be treated as echoes to be suppressed or effective repetitions to be emphasized.

Contrasts, comparisons, and parallels. Whenever ideas are contrasted, compared, or paralleled, they should be emphasized. It is as important to recognize such elements as it is to emphasize new ideas and assertions. Ben Franklin's proverbs are full of such balancing of one idea with another. Study them and read them aloud, emphasizing the thought-centers.

> Fools need advice most, but Wise Men only are the better for it.
>
> You may delay, but Time will not.
>
> Virtue may not always make a Face handsome, but Vice will certainly make it ugly.
>
> The honest man takes pains, and then enjoys pleasures; the knave takes pleasures, and then suffers pains.
>
> Where there's marriage without love, there will be love without marriage.

In "The Red-Haired Man's Wife" on pages 199–200, notice in the last line of stanza 3 that *walk, obey,* and *smile* are important elements in parallel. So are *voice, command,* and *behest* at the end of stanza 5. So are the lines beginning with "I am. . . ." in stanzas 6, 7, and 8. There are even other paralleled elements in this poem which you can find for yourself. "The World," quoted on pages 355–56 also contains many parallel lines. Study them now in that sentimental-bitter poem.

Causal and conditional relationships. As a thinking being, man sees logical relationships in his society, his science, his philosophy, and his religion. Among these are the causal and the conditional. One action or state may cause another to occur: this relationship we call the causal, or cause and effect, relationship. One action or state may be necessary to the occurrence of another: this relationship we call the conditional. In the interpretative reading of literature, we must never fail to see such logical relationships and emphasize the key words, for they are invariably important.

EXAMPLES:
Causal:

> If you prick us, do we not bleed? if you tickle us, do we not laugh? if you poison us, do we not die? and if you wrong us, shall we not revenge?
>
> —SHAKESPEARE, *The Merchant of Venice*

> If a man can write a better book, preach a better sermon, or make a better mouse-trap than his neighbor, though he builds his house in the woods, the world will make a beaten path to his door.
>
> —RALPH WALDO EMERSON

I still remember the effect I produced on a small group of Galla tribesmen massed around a man in black clothes. I dropped an aerial torpedo right in the center, and the group opened up like a flowering rose. It was most entertaining.

—VITTORIO MUSSOLINI

Conditional:

To give a satisfactory answer to this mighty question, it is indispensable to have an accurate and thorough knowledge of the nature and the character of the cause by which the Union is endangered.

—JOHN C. CALHOUN

"Had he and I but met
By some old ancient inn,
We should have sat us down to wet
Right many a nipperkin!

"But ranged as infantry,
And staring face to face,
I shot at him as he at me,
And killed him in his place."

—THOMAS HARDY, *The Man He Killed*

The classic example of the conditional relationship carried to the extreme is, of course, Kipling's poem "If." The entire verse is only one sentence, with many conditional clauses.

Climax. Climactic structure always demands careful emphasis by the reader. A climax is a turning point, or a point of highest interest, or a point of greatest tension. Authors build words, phrases, clauses, sentences, paragraphs, or even chapters into suspenseful and emphatic climaxes. Climaxes are integral parts of essays, speeches, stories, novels, poems, and plays. The poor reader who fails to see the point of greatest importance or to feel the point of greatest tension or to realize the crucial moment, reads without regard for the over-all effect. A group of entrants in a sight-reading contest read—to a man—without climaxes, for they were prevented from knowing where the high points were to be found because they had no chance to study the material. The effective reader studies for the meaning not only of single words, phrases, sentences, and paragraphs but also for their relative degrees of importance. He then utilizes all the visible and audible techniques necessary to communicate climactic moments to the audience. Climaxes do not just happen in literature; they are constructed by good writers to create desired effects in readers and listeners. Never read with a uniformity of intensity. Locate all climaxes and study their relative degrees of importance. Build the appropriate degree of tension for each as if you were climbing mountains, through the foothills and small peaks, until you reach the highest peak: the main climax of the selection.

The pattern of most climactic interest is a rising interest which reaches the peak either at the end of a literary unit or very near the end:

or

If the peak of interest occurs too soon, what follows can only be anticlimactic, therefore, less interesting:

In reading tense scenes readers sometimes begin at too high a degree of vocal tension and have no place to go when the climax occurs; therefore, the climax lacks power through lack of contrast:

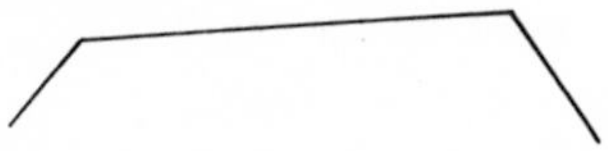

The tension, or interest value, of good writing is never this monotonous line:

Neither should your reading ever be a monotonous line of unvarying tension.

EXAMPLES: Study climaxes in the following examples:

> For, lo, the winter is past; the rain is over and gone; the flowers appear on the earth; the time of the singing of birds is come, and the voice of the turtle is heard in our land.
>
> —THE SONG OF SOLOMON

> There is no right to strike against the public safety by anybody, anywhere, anytime.
>
> —CALVIN COOLIDGE

> Dancing is the loftiest, the most moving, the most beautiful of the arts, because it is no mere translation or abstraction from life; it is life itself.
>
> —HAVELOCK ELLIS

> Hath not a Jew eyes? hath not a Jew hands, organs, dimensions, senses, affections, passions? fed with the same food, hurt with the same weapons, subject to the same diseases, healed by the same means, warmed and cooled by the same winter and summer, as a Christian is? If you prick us, do we not bleed? if you tickle us, do we not laugh? if you poison us, do we not die? and if you wrong us, shall we not revenge?
>
> —SHAKESPEARE, *The Merchant of Venice*

Structural emphasis. You discovered in studying Chapter 5 that one must consider the author's organization in order to find his meaning. The expert writer uses structural methods to emphasize his important ideas. In sentences, paragraphs, and in whole compositions you will find the most important ideas expressed in first and last positions. Consider the shades of meaning in the following sentence and its variations:

> When you have eliminated the impossible, whatever remains, however improbable, must be the truth.
>
> —ARTHUR CONAN DOYLE

> However improbable, the truth is whatever remains after you have eliminated the impossible.

> The truth is whatever remains after you have eliminated the impossible, no matter how improbable it is.

You will find that thoughts which are most fully developed by the author are usually his most important ideas, and you must find means for emphasizing them. You have already come to a realization that authors use repetition as a means of communicating their most important points. You will discover that within a sentence the most important thought-group is likely to be in the main clause rather than in a subordinate one. "I see all the new plays when I visit New York City." Changing the order of the clauses adds significance to the subordinate clause. "When I visit New York City, I see all the new plays."

In regard to sentence structure you will further discover that the usual word order in English is "subject—verb—object" and that when a good writer changes this order, he usually does so for the purpose of emphasizing those words out of order:

> Mine be a cot beside the hill;
> A beehive's hum shall soothe my ear;
> A willowy brook that turns a mill,
> With many a fall shall linger near.
>
> —SAMUEL ROGERS, *A Wish*

> To-morrow, and to-morrow, and to-morrow,
> Creeps in this petty pace from day to day
> To the last syllable of recorded time,
>
> —SHAKESPEARE, *Macbeth*

> How sharper than a serpent's tooth it is
> To have a thankless child!
>
> —SHAKESPEARE, *King Lear*

> Within him, as he hurled himself forward, was born a love, a despairing fondness for this flag which was near him.
>
> —STEPHEN CRANE, *The Red Badge of Courage*

Last, you will find, with a great deal of enthusiasm, that powerful writers emphasize by means of simple and concrete words—words that express the ideas so well that no other words can substitute for them. These are all structural and stylistic devices for emphasis. Watch for them.

A DEMONSTRATION OF THE PROCESS OF DETERMINING PHRASING AND EMPHASIS

Read the following selection, then study the analysis which follows.

THE CORVETTE CLAYMORE

from *Ninety-Three*

VICTOR HUGO

One of the carronades of the battery, a twenty-four pounder, had got loose.

This is perhaps the most formidable of ocean accidents. Nothing more terrible can happen to a ship of war at sea and under full sail.

A gun that breaks its moorings becomes suddenly some indescribable supernatural beast. It is a machine which transforms itself into a monster. This mass turns upon its wheels, has the rapid movements of a billiard-ball; rolls with the rolling, pitches with the pitching; goes, comes, pauses, seems to meditate; resumes its course, rushes along the ship from end to end like an arrow, circles about, springs aside, evades, roars, breaks, kills, exterminates. It is a battering-ram which assaults a wall at its own caprice. Moreover, the battering-ram is metal, the wall wood. It is the entrance of matter into liberty. One might say that this eternal slave avenges itself. It seems as if the power of evil hidden in what we call inanimate objects finds a vent and bursts suddenly out.

Analysis

The introduction for this material should set the scene for a short descriptive piece of fictional narration describing a terrifying experience aboard a sailing warship in the late eighteenth century. Such terms as *Corvette, carronade,* and *battery,* and the significance of the weight of the shot should be explained to most audiences of today.

One of the carronades of the battery, / a twenty-four pounder / had got loose.

This sentence has three thought-groups. Since the audience will now know that a carronade is a small cannon on wheels, it will be obvious that a carronade is to be found in the battery; thus, *of the battery* is not important enough to stand as an independent thought-group. *Carronades* is the new idea on which the mind focuses and therefore receives major emphasis. The second group, an appositive interjection, is not basic to the meaning of the sentence and yet it was so important to the writer that he interrupted the sentence to insert it. Therefore, it contains extremely significant information: the cannon is large enough to shoot a twenty-four pound ball, hence, a sizeable gun. The climactic interest of the sentence lies in the last word, which sets forth the action and problem of the incident.

This is perhaps the most formidable of ocean accidents.

The entire sentence constitutes one thought-group. *Formidable* is truly a formidable word, demanding much attention from the mind. It is the point of this sentence, expressing the seriousness of the situation. *Ocean* and *accidents* are both obvious by implication since the audience knows—and you do, too—that this scene takes place on a warship and that the carronade had broken loose. *Most* does not need much attention; in fact, if the reader centers on *most,* he will weaken the effect of *formidable.* Remember: emphasis is achieved by contrast in techniques. If you try to achieve too much emphasis, you will actually achieve less. Use emphasis sparingly, and make it count where it is truly needed!

> Nothing more terrible can happen to a ship of war / at sea / and under full sail.

The first thought-group is a long one. Any effort to break it up into shorter thought-units will lead to confused meanings. At *sea* and *and under full sail* delineate the separate conditions under which the accident occurs; the mind will dwell upon each condition. Which of the first three words will be emphasized? *Nothing* says nothing; the mind cannot center here. *More* will be centered if *terrible* is regarded as an echo of *formidable;* however, *terrible* seems to add new significance and should probably be the center of the first thought-group. Obvious by implication are *happen* and *ship of war.*

> A gun that breaks its moorings / becomes suddenly / some indescribable / supernatural / beast.

The first group merely repeats a condition already known to both reader and audience. *Moorings* is the center only because it is the most interesting word in the group. The remainder of the sentence is really one thought-group, but the mind will find the concepts expressed by *suddenly, indescribable, supernatural,* and *beast* so interesting that it will make each a thought-unit unto itself. Climactic interest will cause *beast* to be the most important concept of the sentence, therefore receiving the greatest emphasis.

> It is a machine which transforms itself into a monster.

While it might be argued that *machine* is obvious by implication, it can also be pointed out that a machine which becomes a monster is interesting. The mind will center on this comparison. The act of transforming itself is also significant. One cannot give equal emphasis to all four words; thus, individual readers are destined to vary in their interpretation of the sentence.

> This mass turns upon its wheels, / has the rapid movements of a billiard ball; / rolls with the rolling; / pitches with the pitching; / goes, / comes, / pauses, / seems to meditate; / resumes its course, / rushes along the ship from end to end like an arrow, / circles about, / springs aside, / evades, / roars, / breaks, / kills, / exterminates.

This is a sentence of activity; hence, the verbs assume the major role together with a couple of action adjectives. Each action becomes a thought which will occupy the mind of the effective reader. *End to end* is, of course, a contrast indicating the extent of the gun's mad flight. Which group is most important? Interest increases climactically as does the terror until *exterminates,* which is far more interesting than even *kills.*

> It is a battering-ram / which assaults a wall / at its own caprice.

The first group, a metaphor, draws forth a new image. *Assaults a wall* is implied by *battering-ram,* thus will be given little, if any, emphasis. *Caprice* is interesting; therefore, a thought-center.

> Moreover, the battering-ram is metal, / the wall wood.

Two different comparisons exist here. The contrast of *metal* and *wood* is the new concept, though, and therefore of greater importance.

> It is the entrance of matter into liberty.

One thought-group. *Matter* is implied. *Liberty* is the new idea.

> One might say that this eternal slave / avenges itself.

Two thought-groups. Interesting new ideas.

> It seems as if the power of evil / hidden in what we call inanimate objects / finds a vent / and bursts suddenly out.

Do you agree with the phrasing and emphasis indicated here? Now, turn to Exercise 4 at the end of this chapter which continues with this same selection of literature and the same problems in reading.

Summary

To be effective in communicating meaning audibly, you must be able to read aloud in thought-groups, which carry meaning, rather than in mere words, which are often meaningless when they stand alone. You must also be able to recognize and emphasize those words which carry the meaning and to de-emphasize those words which serve only as connective tissue.

This chapter has set forth the basic principles of audible communication. The chapters which follow will endeavor to show how these principles may be implemented. Chapter 8 will show you how you can deal with thought-groups through the use of the speaker's chief mark of punctuation—the pause. Chapters 8, 9, 10, and 11 will reveal how you can emphasize by means of changes in time, loudness, pitch, and quality.

Exercises

1. Copy five of the following quotations and, using virgules (/), indicate the thought-groups:

a. All religion, all life, all art, all expression come down to this: to the effort of the human soul to break through its barrier of loneliness, of intolerable loneliness, and make some contact with another seeking soul, or with what all souls seek, which is (by any name) God.—DON MARQUIS

b. Strange, when you come to think of it, that of all the countless folk who have lived before our time on this planet not one is known in history or in legend as having died of laughter.—SIR MAX BEERBOHM

c. The chess-board is the world, the pieces are the phenomena of the universe, the rules of the game are what we call the laws of Nature. The player on the other side is hidden from us. We know that his play is always fair, just, and patient. But also we know, to our cost, that he never overlooks a mistake, or makes the smallest allowance for ignorance.—THOMAS HENRY HUXLEY

d. Pride is an established conviction of one's own paramount worth in some particular respect; while vanity is the desire of rousing such a conviction in others. Pride works from within; it is the direct appreciation of oneself. Vanity is the desire to arrive at this appreciation indirectly, from without.—ARTHUR SCHOPENHAUER

e. Young men think old men are fools; but old men know young men are fools.—GEORGE CHAPMAN

f. To live content with small means; to seek elegance rather than luxury, and refinement rather than fashion; to be worthy, not respectable, and wealthy, not rich; to study hard, think quietly, talk gently, act frankly; to listen to stars and birds, to babes and sages, with open heart; to bear all cheerfully, do all bravely, await occasions, hurry never. In a word, to let the spiritual, unbidden and unconscious, grow up through the common. This is to be my symphony.—WILLIAM HENRY CHANNING

g. Be not angry that you cannot make others as you wish them to be, since you cannot make yourself as you wish to be.—THOMAS À KEMPIS

h. No house should ever be *on* any hill or on anything. It should be *of* the hill, belonging to it, so hill and house could live together each the happier for the other.—FRANK LLOYD WRIGHT

i. Romantic plays with happy endings are almost of necessity inferior in artistic value to true tragedies. Not, one would hope, simply because they end happily; happiness in itself is certainly not less beautiful than grief; but because a tragedy in its great moments can generally afford to be sincere, while romantic plays live in an atmosphere of ingenuity and make-believe.—GILBERT MURRAY

j. It is not only what we have inherited from our fathers that exists again in us, but all sorts of old dead ideas and all kinds of old dead beliefs. . . . They are not actually alive in us; but there they are dormant, all the same, and we can never be rid of them. Whenever I take up a newspaper and read it, I fancy I see ghosts creeping between the lines. There must be ghosts all over the world.—HENRIK IBSEN

k. But the artist appeals to that part of our being which is not dependent on wisdom; to that in us which is a gift and not an acquisition—and, therefore, more permanently enduring. He speaks to our capacity for delight and wonder, to the sense of mystery surrounding our lives: to our sense of pity, and beauty, and pain. —JOSEPH CONRAD

2. Copy five other quotations and underline the important words which will be emphasized. Underline twice the thought-centers, the words which will receive greatest emphasis to communicate the particular meaning you intend. Be ready to read them aloud in class as you have marked them.

3. In the above quotations, find examples of: echoes, implications, repetitions for emphasis, contrasts, comparisons, parallels, causal and conditional relationships, climaxes, and instances of structural emphasis. Be ready to read them aloud in class.

4. The following paragraphs continue the Victor Hugo selection considered on pages 191–94. In the first part to follow the authors have marked for phrasing and centering, but they have deliberately marked several phrases and centers *incorrectly*. Make a list of those instances with which you quarrel and check the list with your instructor's opinion. In the remainder of the quotation, which is not marked, copy the material and mark for phrasing and centering. Compare your work with that of a classmate.

> It has an air of having <u>lost</u> patience, / of seeking some <u>fierce</u>, / <u>obscure</u> <u>retribution</u>;/ nothing <u>more</u> inexorable than this <u>rage</u> of the inanimate./ The mad <u>mass</u> has the <u>bound</u> of a <u>panther</u>,/ the <u>weight</u> of the <u>elephant</u>,/ the <u>agility</u> of the <u>mouse</u>,/ the <u>obstinacy</u> of the <u>axe</u>,/ the <u>unexpectedness</u> of the <u>wave</u>,/ the <u>rapidity</u> of <u>lightning</u>,/ the <u>deafness</u> of the <u>tomb</u>./ It <u>weighs</u> <u>ten</u> thousand pounds,/ and it rebounds like a child's <u>ball</u>./ Its <u>flight</u> is a <u>wild</u> <u>whirl</u> / <u>abruptly</u> cut at right <u>angles</u>./ What <u>is</u> to <u>be</u> <u>done</u>?/ <u>How</u> to end this?/ A <u>tempest</u> <u>ceases</u>,/ a <u>cyclone</u> <u>passes</u>,/ a <u>wind</u> <u>falls</u>,/ a <u>broken</u> mast is <u>replaced</u>,/ a <u>leak</u> is <u>stopped</u>,/ a <u>fire</u> <u>dies</u> <u>out</u>;/ but how to control <u>this</u> enormous brute <u>of</u> bronze?/ In <u>what</u> way can one <u>attack</u> it?/
>
> You can make a mastiff hear reason, astound a bull, fascinate a boa, frighten a tiger, soften a lion; but there is no resource with that monster, a cannon let loose. You cannot kill it—it is dead; at the

same time it lives. It lives with a sinister life bestowed on it by Infinity.

The planks beneath it give it play. It is moved by the ship, which is moved by the sea, which is moved by the wind. This destroyer is a plaything. The ship, the waves, the blasts, all aid it; hence its frightful vitality. How to assail this fury of complication? How to fetter this monstrous mechanism for wrecking a ship? How foresee its comings and goings, its returns, its stops, its shocks? Any one of these blows upon the sides may stave out the vessel. How divine its awful gyrations! One has to deal with a projectile which thinks, seems to possess ideas, and which changes its direction at each instant. How stop the course of something which must be avoided? The horrible cannon flings itself about, advances, recoils, strikes to the right, strikes to the left, flees, passes, disconcerts, ambushes, breaks down obstacles, crushes men like flies. The great danger of the situation is in the mobility of its base. How combat an inclined plane which has caprices? The ship has, so to speak, lightning imprisoned in its womb which seeks to escape; it is like thunder rolling above an earthquake.

5. Read the following paragraph. Determine the attitude of the writer, and then decide which words must be emphasized. If you enjoy the selection, read it to some of your friends or relatives, or possibly to your class.

THE CHROMATIC FAMILY[1]

PHILIP HAMBURGER

A friend of mine who owns a color-television set went out of town for a couple of weeks recently and left me the key to his apartment. "Use the set any time you want, old man. There's plenty of beer in the icebox," he said, just before leaving. "You may have a bit of trouble with the Convergence dial, and some of the purples run to green, but if worst comes to worst, you can always switch to black-and-white." A week ago Wednesday night, just before ten; I went over to his place to try to catch the C.B.S. color production of George S. Kaufman's and Edna Ferber's "The Royal Family," starring Helen Hayes, Claudette Colbert, Charles Coburn, and Fredric March. I had no trouble finding my friend's set. It's *big* (I had the impression that it was several stories high), resembling an upended trailer. I opened the doors of the cabinet and faced a terrifying array of dials—Tuning, Contrast, Chroma, Color, Background, V Hold, H Hold, Convergence, and Focus. Promptly at ten, I turned on the set, twisted Color, and

[1] This article was originally published in *The New Yorker*.

waited. In came the first act of "The Royal Family," in blue—a lovely, dark, rich, midnight blue. I could see a butler wearing a short dark-blue jacket, and a maid wearing a blue uniform. The maid was fussing over a vase, arranging some blue roses. Charles Coburn appeared, blue as the Mediterranean. I crouched on the floor (several of the dials are on the lower part of the set) and turned Convergence. Mr. Coburn became a bright magenta—so bright, in fact, that I was afraid he was suffering some sort of stroke. I turned Chroma, and Coburn turned green. The roses turned green, too. Claudette Colbert showed up, in purple. Helen Hayes, who was playing the role of Fanny Cavendish (the Grand Old Lady of the American Stage), hobbled down a staircase. She was dead white, with blue around the edges, except for the tip of her nose, which was yellow. The roses were now yellow. I turned Background, and Coburn went white as a sheet, while Miss Hayes blossomed forth with a case of measles. Fredric March entered, wearing a stunning green raccoon coat. At last, by turning Contrast, Chroma, Convergence, Focus, and Background in furious succession, I began to perceive a semblance of rational color—roses were red, violets were blue, Kaufman was funny, and Ferber, too.

6. The selections which follow range from the humorous to the serious, from a poem for children to selections for the most mature person. Choose one which pleases you and study it thoroughly, as you have the quotations and selections above, with particular reference to the thought-group, emphasis, and subordination. Remember that the purpose of such study is to improve the *oral* reading; therefore you should study with the purpose of eventually reading the selection to an audience.

THE MAN IN THE ONION BED

JOHN CIARDI

I met a man in an onion bed.
He was crying so hard his eyes were red.
And the tears ran off the end of his nose
As he ate his way down the onion rows.

He ate and he cried, but for all his tears
He sang: "Sweet onions, oh my dears!
I love you, I do, and you love me,
But you make me as sad as a man can be."

"Why are you crying," I asked. And he
Stopped his singing and looked at me.

"I love my onions, I do," he said,
"And I hate to pull them out of bed.
And wouldn't it make *you* want to weep
To eat them up while they're still asleep?"

"Then why don't you wake them?"
"Ah," he said,
"Onions are best when they're still in bed!"
And he cried and he ate and he ate and he cried
Till row by row and side to side
He ate till there were no more, then sat
And started to cry again for that.

He cried till his coat and shoes were wet.
For all I know, he is crying yet.

THE RED-HAIRED MAN'S WIFE

JAMES STEPHENS

I have taken that vow—
  And you were my friend
But yesterday—now
  All that's at an end,
And you are my husband, and claim me, and I must depend.

Yesterday I was free,
  Now you, as I stand,
Walk over to me
  And take hold of my hand.
You look at my lips, your eyes are too bold, your smile is too bland.

My old name is lost,
  My distinction of race:
Now the line has been crossed,
  Must I step to your pace?
Must I walk as you list, and obey and smile up in your face?

All the white and the red
  Of my cheeks you have won;
All the hair of my head,
  And my feet, tho' they run,
Are yours, and you own me and end me just as I begun.

Must I bow when you speak,
  Be silent and hear,
Inclining my cheek
  And incredulous ear
To your voice, and command, and behest, hold your lightest wish dear?

I am woman, but still
  Am alive, and can feel
Every intimate thrill
  That is woe or is weal.
I, aloof, and divided, apart, standing far, can I kneel?

If not, I shall know,
  I shall surely find out,
And your world will throw
  In disaster and rout;
I am woman and glory and beauty, I mystery, terror, and doubt.

I am separate still,
  I am I and not you:
And my mind and my will,
  As in secret they grew,
Still are secret, unreached and untouched and not subject to you.

from THE RIVALS

RICHARD BRINSLEY SHERIDAN

MRS. MALAPROP. There, Sir Anthony, there sits the deliberate simpleton who wants to disgrace her family, and lavish herself on a fellow not worth a shilling.

LYDIA LANGUISH. Madam, I thought you once—

MRS. MAL. You thought, miss! I don't know any business you have to think at all—thought does not become a young woman. But the point we would request of you is, that you will promise to forget this fellow—to illiterate him, I say, quite from your memory.

LYD. Ah, madam! our memories are independent of our wills. It is not so easy to forget.

MRS. MAL. But I say it is, miss; there is nothing on earth so easy as to forget, if a person chooses to set about it. I'm sure I have as much forgot your poor dear uncle as if he had never existed—and I thought it my duty so to do; and let me tell you, Lydia, these violent memories don't become a young woman.

SIR ANTHONY ABSOLUTE. Why sure she won't pretend to remember what she's ordered not!—ay, this comes of her reading!

LYD. What crime, madam, have I committed, to be treated thus?

MRS. MAL. Now don't attempt to extirpate yourself from the matter; you know I have proof controvertible of it.—But tell me, will you promise to do as you're bid? Will you take a husband of your friends' choosing?

LYD. Madam, I must tell you plainly, that had I no preference for any one else, the choice you have made would be my aversion.

MRS. MAL. What business have you, miss, with preference and aversion? They don't become a young woman; and you ought to know, that as both always wear off, 'tis safest in matrimony to begin with a little aversion. I am sure I hated your poor dear uncle before marriage as if he'd been a blackamoor—and yet, miss, you are sensible what a wife I made!—and when it pleased Heaven to release me from him, 'tis unknown what tears I shed! But suppose we were going to give you another choice, will you promise us to give up this Beverley?

LYD. Could I belie my thoughts so far as to give that promise, my actions would certainly as far belie my words.

MRS. MAL. Take yourself to your room. You are fit company for nothing but your own ill-humours.

LYD. Willingly, ma'am—I cannot change for the worse. (*Exit.*)

MRS. MAL. There's a little intricate hussy for you!

SIR ANTH. It is not to be wondered at, ma'am,—all this is the natural consequence of teaching girls to read. Had I a thousand daughters, by Heaven! I'd as soon have them taught the black art as their alphabet!

MRS. MAL. Nay, nay, Sir Anthony, you are an absolute misanthropy.

SIR ANTH. In my way hither, Mrs. Malaprop, I observed your niece's maid coming forth from a circulating library!—She had a book in each hand—they were half-bound volumes, with marble covers!—From that moment I guessed how full of duty I should see her mistress!

MRS. MAL. Those are vile places, indeed!

SIR ANTH. Madam, a circulating library in a town is as an evergreen tree of diabolical knowledge! It blossoms through the year!—and depend on it, Mrs. Malaprop, that they who are so fond of handling the leaves, will long for the fruit at last.

MRS. MAL. Fy, fy, Sir Anthony, you surely speak laconically.

SIR ANTH. Why, Mrs. Malaprop, in moderation now, what would you have a woman know?

MRS. MAL. Observe me, Sir Anthony. I would by no means wish a daughter of mine to be a progeny of learning; I don't think so much learning becomes a young woman; for instance, I would never let her meddle with Greek, or Hebrew, or algebra, or simony, or fluxions, or paradoxes, or such inflammatory branches of learning—neither would it be necessary for her to handle any of your mathematical, astronomical, diabolical instruments.—But, Sir Anthony, I would send her, at nine years old, to a boarding-school, in order to let her learn a little ingenuity and artifice. Then, sir, she should have a supercilious knowledge in accounts;—and as she grew up, I would have her instructed in geometry, that she might know something of the contagious countries;—but above all, Sir Anthony, she should be mistress of orthodoxy, that she might not mis-spell, and mis-pronounce words so shamefully as girls usually do; and likewise that she might reprehend the true meaning of what she is saying. This, Sir Anthony, is what I would have a woman know;—and I don't think there is a superstitious article in it.

SIR ANTH. Well, well, Mrs. Malaprop, I will dispute the point no further with you; though I must confess that you are a truly moderate and polite arguer, for almost every third word you say is on my side of the question.

ULYSSES

ALFRED, LORD TENNYSON

It little profits that an idle king,
By this still hearth, among these barren crags,
Match'd with an aged wife, I mete and dole
Unequal laws unto a savage race,
That hoard, and sleep, and feed, and know not me.
I cannot rest from travel: I will drink
Life to the lees: all times I have enjoy'd
Greatly, have suffer'd greatly, both with those
That loved me, and alone; on shore, and when
Thro' scudding drifts the rainy Hyades
Vext the dim sea: I am become a name;
For always roaming with a hungry heart
Much have I seen and known; cities of men
And manners, climates, councils, governments,
Myself not least, but honour'd of them all;
And drunk delight of battle with my peers,
Far on the ringing plains of windy Troy.
I am a part of all that I have met;
Yet all experience is an arch wherethro'
Gleams that untravell'd world, whose margin fades

For ever and for ever when I move.
How dull it is to pause, to make an end,
To rust unburnish'd, not to shine in use!
As tho' to breathe were life. Life piled on life
Were all too little, and of one to me
Little remains: but every hour is saved
From that eternal silence, something more,
A bringer of new things; and vile it were
For some three suns to store and hoard myself,
And this gray spirit yearning in desire
To follow knowledge like a sinking star,
Beyond the utmost bound of human thought.
This is my son, mine own Telemachus,
To whom I leave the sceptre and the isle—
Well-loved of me, discerning to fulfil
This labour, by slow prudence to make mild
A rugged people, and thro' soft degrees
Subdue them to the useful and the good.
Most blameless is he, centred in the sphere
Of common duties, decent not to fail
In offices of tenderness, and pay
Meet adoration to my household gods,
When I am gone. He works his work, I mine.
There lies the port; the vessel puffs her sail:
There gloom the dark broad seas. My mariners,
Souls that have toil'd, and wrought, and thought with me—
That ever with a frolic welcome took
The thunder and the sunshine, and opposed
Free hearts, free foreheads—you and I are old;
Old age hath yet his honour and his toil;
Death closes all: but something ere the end,
Some work of noble note, may yet be done,
Not unbecoming men that strove with Gods.
The lights begin to twinkle from the rocks:
The long day wanes: the slow moon climbs: the deep
Moans round with many voices. Come, my friends,
'Tis not too late to seek a newer world.
Push off, and sitting well in order smite
The sounding furrows; for my purpose holds
To sail beyond the sunset, and the baths
Of all the western stars, until I die.
It may be that the gulfs will wash us down:
It may be we shall touch the Happy Isles,

And see the great Achilles, whom we knew.
Tho' much is taken, much abides; and tho'
We are not now that strength which in old days
Moved earth and heaven; that which we are, we are;
One equal temper of heroic hearts,
Made weak by time and fate, but strong in will
To strive, to seek, to find, and not to yield.

LET ME LIVE OUT MY YEARS

JOHN G. NEIHARDT

Let me live out my years in heat of blood!
Let me die drunken with the dreamer's wine!
Let me not see this soul-house built of mud
Go toppling to the dust—a vacant shrine.
Let me go quickly, like a candle light
Snuffed out just at the heyday of its glow.
Give me high noon—and let it then be night!
Thus would I go.
And grant that when I face the grisly Thing,
My song may trumpet down the grey Perhaps.
O let me be a tune-swept fiddle string
That feels the Master-Melody—and snaps!

Suggested Readings

Clark, S. H., and Maud May Babcock. *Interpretation of the Printed Page*. Englewood Cliffs, N.J.: Prentice-Hall, 1946, Chapter I, "The Speech Unit—Grouping," Chapter II, "The Speech Paragraph—Group Sequence," Chapter III, "Group Value," Chapter IV, "The Important Idea."

Lowrey, Sara, and Gertrude E. Johnson. *Interpretative Reading*. (Revised edition) New York: Appleton-Century-Crofts, 1953, Chapter V, "Structure in Interpretative Reading."

Lynch, Gladys E., and Harold C. Crain. *Projects in Oral Interpretation*. New York: Holt, 1959, pp. 30–43, 89–100.

Smith, Joseph F., and James R. Linn. *Skill in Reading Aloud*. New York: Harper, 1960, Chapter IV, "The Bare Essentials: Clear Expression."

Tassin, Algernon. *The Oral Study of Literature*. New York: Crofts, 1947, Lesson I, "Assertion and Implication," Lesson II, "Emphasis," Lesson III, "Three Kinds of Emphasis," Lesson IV, "Expressed Antithesis or Contrast."

Winans, James A. *Speech-Making*. New York: Appleton-Century, 1938, Chapter XX, "Further Study of Delivery."

8

AUDIBLE COMMUNICATION THROUGH TIME

In the preceding chapter we discussed the general uses of sound and silence in the audible phase of interpretative reading. Both sound and silence are chiefly characterized by time. Within a framework of silence, the organist paints a musical picture with sound. As long as he keeps his finger upon a key, the organ produces a tone. One continuous tone, however, does not communicate. Other sounds and silences must be incorporated to produce music. So it is with the interpretative reader. A sound in itself does not produce meaning or feeling; sounds and silences, properly arranged, do. Since the lives of sounds and silences are measured in time, time becomes one of the major considerations of the reader.

When speaking of time, we refer to four aspects: the use of silence, the rate of speaking, the length of sound, and the more or less regular recurrence of accents. These we call pause, rate, duration, and rhythm. We shall consider each in this chapter.

PAUSE

A pause is, of course, the absence of sound, but no one should assume that a pause is also the absence of meaning. Do not confuse a pause and a hesitation. A hesitation is accidental, "dead" silence, which communicates nothing. A pause is purposeful, "live" silence, which is charged with meaning. A good pause anticipates, reinforces, emphasizes, and thrusts home meaning. During the pause, both the reader and the listener think, feel, experience, and appreciate.

Separating thought-groups with pauses. To demonstrate for your own satisfaction that judicious use of the pause is essential to effective communication, read the following passage aloud to a friend. Read it rapidly, straight through, with absolutely no pauses. Then ask your friend how many of the ideas he has received. If you do not study it beforehand, it is probable that neither he nor you will get much meaning from it.

> The true rule in determining to embrace or reject anything is not whether it have any evil in it but whether it have more of evil than of good there are few things wholly evil or wholly good almost everything especially of government policy is an inseparable compound of the two so that our best judgment of the preponderance between them is continually demanded.

Now read the same paragraph as it is printed below, pausing wherever there is a virgule. Pause long enough to think through the ideas you are reading. Then see how many of the ideas your listener has absorbed. Also, see how much you, yourself, have gained from this reading.

> The true rule / in determining to embrace or reject anything, / is not whether it have any evil in it, / but whether it have more of evil than of good. / There are few things wholly evil / or wholly good. / Almost everything, / especially of government policy, / is an inseparable compound of the two, / so that our best judgment of the preponderance between them / is continually demanded.
>
> —ABRAHAM LINCOLN

It should be clear at this point that pauses do help in communicating meaning. Pauses must, however, be put into the right places; one does not pause just anywhere. You have probably already reached the conclusion that pauses most commonly fall *between* thought-groups, and you are correct in that assumption. When the reader pauses elsewhere, he does so purposely to anticipate, emphasize, experience, or appreciate an idea. If he merely hesitates within a thought-group, he will destroy meaning. Consider our example from the preceding chapter illustrating the thought-group and notice the effect on it if we break up the thoughts by placing pauses in the wrong places:

> The little brown Cocker / Spaniel from across / the street ran / up to me wiggled / all over licked / his chops and whined for / affection.

Now contrast that effect with the one obtained by placing the pauses only between thought-groups:

> The little brown Cocker Spaniel from across the street / ran up to me / wiggled all over / licked his chops / and whined for affection.

Punctuating with pauses. Why does the pause assist in communicating meaning? It is the major punctuation mark of oral communication. The writer may have his commas and periods, his interrogation and exclamation points, his colons and semicolons, his hyphens and his dashes, but he wishes that he had the pause in place of all of them! The pause, used by one who has mastered it, is far superior in indicating relationships of phrases, in emphasizing, and in building suspense, than any technique at the disposal of the writer. Since the pause is strictly a vocal skill, an attempt to write "(pause)" wherever a vocal pause would occur in a piece of literature would not be a successful device for the writer, and yet the writer must often wish he could do just that. Equally ridiculous is Victor Borge's comedy routine in which he attempts to reproduce written punctuation vocally by means of a different comic sound for each mark of punctuation. Borge's act is funny simply because it is preposterous. The pause, used with appropriate inflections of the voice, is far more effective than any audible commas, periods, or question marks could be.

Written punctuation versus oral punctuation. Do not make the mistake of assuming that written punctuation determines the interpreter's oral punctuation. It is true that you often pause where a writer has placed a period or a comma, but you will not always do so. What, then, is the purpose of written punctuation? To aid you—or any silent reader—in getting the meaning. In considering the following examples you will see that written punctuation dictates meaning. By changing the punctuation, you may be able to make them communicate still other meanings.

A. The professor says the student is stupid.
a. "The professor," says the student, "is stupid."

B. That that is is that that is not is not.
b. That that is, is; that that is not, is not.

C. Who says Jack is not generous he is always fond of giving and cares not for receiving what why advice.
c. Who says Jack is not generous? He is always fond of giving, and cares not for receiving—what?—why, advice.—BENJAMIN FRANKLIN

D. Men are conservatives when they are least vigorous or when they are most luxurious they are conservatives after dinner or before taking their rest when they are sick or aged in the morning or when their intellect or their conscience have been aroused when they hear music or when they read poetry they are radicals.
d. Men are conservatives when they are least vigorous, or when they are most luxurious. They are conservatives after dinner, or before taking their rest; when they are sick, or aged: in the morning, or when their intellect or their conscience have been aroused, when they hear music, or when they read poetry, they are radicals. —RALPH WALDO EMERSON

Just as the writer uses punctuation to communicate meaning to the eye, so the oral interpreter uses pauses to indicate significance to his listeners' ears. Written punctuation—let us repeat—does not determine oral punctuation; it does indicate meaning. From the meanings obtained, the reader then constructs his own oral punctuation to relay those meanings to a listener. Most beginners have the mistaken notion that a comma, for instance, always demands a pause, but only the uninitiated would pause at all these commas:

> Three cheers for the Red, White, and Blue!
>
> They know, and will, therefore, say, that kings are the servants, not proprietors of the people.
>
> —BENJAMIN FRANKLIN
>
> Who, then, art thou, vain dust and ashes! by whatever name thou art called, whether a king, a bishop, a church or a State, or anything else, that obtrudest thine insignificance between the soul of man and his Maker?
>
> —THOMAS PAINE

Sometimes, the emotional state of the speaker will cause him to "telescope" thought-groups, not pausing at all. He might even have to gasp for breath in the middle of a thought-group. Consider, for example, a scene in a play where a boy rushes into a farm kitchen, yelling:

> Maw, come, quick! The barn's on fire! Where's Paw? We've got to get the tractor, cows, and horses out! Somebody call the fire department!

It would be fortunate for the interpreter if there were concrete rules for the placing of pauses. It is always easy to live by rules. It is more difficult to use our heads and say to ourselves: "The sense of this passage demands that we pause here—and not there—to communicate this meaning to our listeners." Few rules are available to us as readers. We can say, however, that *generally* periods, question marks, exclamation points, colons, semicolons, and dashes are used where the sense alone demands that we pause, for these marks are usually placed at the end of rather complete ideas. The consequent pauses will be relatively long ones. We may or may not need to pause where the writer has placed commas. We usually pause many more times than there are marks of written punctuation.

The student of interpretative reading is often uncertain when to pause. As a rank beginner he seldom pauses. He accepts a long sentence as one thought-group and tries to read it without a break. Of course, a long sentence usually consists of several thought-groups expressing a complete idea. Each group has a center to be emphasized. When the reader reads with insufficient centering and oral punctuation, listeners are not likely to comprehend fully. Once the neophyte is instructed in the importance of pausing sufficiently between important thought-groups, a process called "phrasing,"—he often goes to the other extreme and reads in very short thought-groups, focusing on too many centers and pausing entirely too often. He also may make another error and emphasize the wrong thought-centers and misplace his phrasing, breaking up logical thought-groups with ill-placed pauses. In underphrasing the reader throws a mass of sounds at his listeners, sounds which are not separated into easily absorbed thought-units. In overphrasing the reader irritates his listeners by giving them too little information at a time, snatches of ideas with little relationship to each other. In misplaced phrasing the reader either communicates distorted ideas or no ideas at all.

Phrasing and pausing. There are two remedies for the beginner's problems in phrasing. One is "Think!" Think the thoughts of the author (as you have determined them) as you read aloud, and your phrasing will improve. If you fail to focus on thought-centers and to pause sufficiently, you are probably not thinking enough. Only by having a full realization of the meaning as you read aloud can you hope to emphasize the proper centers and pause meaningfully!

In the preceding chapter we found that a sentence could be divided into thought-groups as follows:

> One hot day / in December / I had been standing / perfectly still / for a few minutes / among the dry weeds / when a slight rustling sound / came from near my feet / and glancing down / I saw / the head and neck of a large black serpent / moving slowly / past me.

Where would you pause in reading that sentence? Certainly not between all thought-groups! Different readers might pause intelligently in many different places, depending on the particular shade of meaning they wish to convey. Phrasing, of course, bears a direct relationship to focusing attention upon (emphasizing) the thought-centers. Consider the effects of pausing in the following examples and decide what the thought-centers in each case would be. Read each aloud.

> 1. One hot day / in December / I had been standing perfectly still / for a few minutes among the dry weeds / when a slight rustling sound came from near my feet / and glancing down I saw the head and neck of a large black serpent / moving slowly past me.
>
> 2. One hot day in December / I had been standing perfectly still / for a few minutes among the dry weeds / when a slight rustling sound / came from near my feet / and glancing down / I saw the head and neck of a large black serpent / moving slowly / past me.
>
> 3. One hot day in December / I had been standing perfectly still for a few minutes / among the dry weeds / when a slight rustling sound came from near my feet / and glancing down I saw the head and neck of a large black serpent / moving slowly past me.
>
> 4. One hot day in December I had been standing perfectly still for a few minutes among the dry weeds / when a slight rustling sound came from near my feet / and glancing down / I saw the head and neck of a large black serpent / moving slowly past me.
>
> 5. One hot day in December / I had been standing perfectly still for a few minutes among the dry weeds / when a slight rustling sound came from near my feet / and glancing down / I saw the head and neck of a large black serpent / moving slowly past me.

The second remedy for poor phrasing is to keep in mind the following principles governing phrasing and pausing. Either shortening your phrases (which also means centering oftener) or lengthening your pauses enables the listener to grasp more easily the meaning of your reading. Do one or both of these things when: (1) the material is complex, abstract, or serious; (2) the audience is not well equipped to perceive the ideas in your material; (3) the audience is large or the acoustical situation poor; and (4) when the occasion is formal or serious.

When your reading material is difficult, shorten your phrases and lengthen your pauses. Your listener cannot relisten as the silent reader can reread when he fails to comprehend. Give your listener frequent enough and long enough pauses to permit him to understand. Give yourself sufficient pauses, too. When the material is complex, you also need time to think. If the material is light and simple, you can cope with longer thought-groups and shorter pauses. But if the selection is complex, abstract, serious, or thoughtful, or if it contains many important details, or if the vocabulary of the author is unusual or elevated in style, you must read in short phrases, centering more often, in order that you and your audience may have sufficient opportunity to think through the ideas as they are brought to light by your reading. Let us hasten to caution you thus: when you shorten your thought-groups for clarity in reading, you will never just arbitrarily stick in additional pauses. Shortening thought-groups means shortening the *extent* of the thought to be dealt with as a unit; it does not mean destroying thoughts by "bull-in-the-china-shop" pauses, which are illogically placed.

A study of the following examples should demonstrate the point. In reading the following passage from *The Adventures of Tom Sawyer,* which is very simple narration of concrete, specific images, you will not have to pause very often in order to communicate the scene to your listeners.

> By this time he was far down Meadow Lane, and the bell for school to "take up" tinkled faintly upon his ear. He sobbed, now, to think he should never, never hear that old familiar sound any more—it was very hard, but it was forced on him; since he was driven out into the cold world, he must submit—but he forgave them. Then the sobs came thick and fast.
>
> Just at this point he met his soul's sworn comrade, Joe Harper—hard-eyed, and with evidently a great and dismal purpose in his heart. Plainly here were "two souls with but a single thought." Tom, wiping his eyes with his sleeve, began to blubber out something about a resolution to escape from hard usage and lack of sympathy at home by roaming abroad into the great world never to return; and ended by hoping Joe would not forget him.
>
> But it transpired that this was a request which Joe had just been going to make of Tom, and had come to hunt him up for that purpose. His mother had whipped him for drinking some cream which he had never tasted and knew nothing about; it was plain that she was tired of him and wished him to go; if she felt that way, there was nothing for him to do but succumb; he hoped she would be happy, and never

regret having driven her poor boy out into the unfeeling world to suffer and die.

As the two boys walked sorrowing along, they made a new compact to stand by each other and be brothers and never separate till death relieved them of their troubles. Then they began to lay their plans. Joe was for being a hermit, and living on crusts in a remote cave, and dying, some time, of cold and want and grief; but after listening to Tom, he conceded that there were some conspicuous advantages about a life of crime, and so he consented to be a pirate.

—MARK TWAIN, *The Adventures of Tom Sawyer*

On the contrary, in reading the following sentences expressing abstract thought you will have to use frequent pauses and longer pauses in order to assimilate the thought-groups yourself, and in order to communicate them successfully.

So art, whether it be painting or sculpture, poetry or music, has no other object than to brush aside the utilitarian symbols, the conventional and socially accepted generalities, in short, everything that veils reality from us, in order to bring us face to face with reality itself. It is from a misunderstanding on this point that the dispute between realism and idealism in art has arisen. Art is certainly only a more direct vision of reality.

—HENRI BERGSON

Study the above examples thoroughly, determining, in each case, where you pause. Read them aloud.

The capabilities of the audience also determine the frequency of pausing done by the interpreter. If the listeners are well-equipped to comprehend the ideas expressed by the writer, the reader will not have to pause so often or so long as he will when the listeners do not have the educational or cultural background or the maturity necessary to enable them to understand the ideas readily. The more common ground you and your listeners have in relation to the subject, the fewer and shorter pauses you will need. Conversely, when your community of reference is small, more pauses and longer pauses will be required for effective communication. Let us consider an example. Suppose a philosopher were to read a scholarly paper of his own to a group of his colleagues. Pauses would be relatively few and short, for reader and audience would be able to think together rather rapidly. On the other hand, if the philosopher were to read the same paper to his beginning class in philosophy, he would necessarily have to read in shorter thought-groups, emphasizing more thought-centers, pausing frequently and longer to enable his students to absorb one idea at a time. This requirement is, of course, no reflection on the intelligence of the students; rather it is an illustration of a reader and his listeners having a less extensive common background for understanding. Teachers should always keep this fact in mind when reading or speaking to their students; and parents, too, when reading or speaking to their children. Because we are usually familiar with the material which we read aloud, we tend to think too little while reading; therefore, we read too rapidly for our listeners, who must have time to think the ideas through for the first time. Take your time. If you fill pauses with thought, you will rarely read too rapidly for your listeners.

The size of the audience and the general acoustical situation have a definite effect on the way in which the reader phrases and pauses. A small audience in an intimate situation is able to follow an oral reading relatively well. On the other hand, a large audience requires more time to think over the ideas expressed in the spoken thought-groups. In a poor acoustical situation, the reader faces the simple problem of making himself heard. If he makes his phrases too long, or reads too rapidly, sounds may "pile up" in reverberation, making succeeding sounds unintelligible. Deliberate pausing will assist in the distinct projection of thought-groups to their destination. This principle will be apparent to you if you will apply it to speaking situations in which you have participated, either as a speaker or as a listener. In a classroom or intimate meeting room, the speaker has little trouble in making himself heard, but in a large assembly hall, such as at a national political convention where acoustics are liable to be poor, he finds that he must go slower, speaking in shorter phrases, emphasizing more thought-centers, pausing longer. Particularly is this principle true for the speaker who uses a public address system. Such systems usually produce loud sounds which rumble about in a large hall and require time to die out. Only when one series of sounds has ceased reverberating should another series be started on its way. The reader, the public speaker, and the actor all have to learn how to make themselves heard under a great variety of acoustical conditions.

Last, the nature of the occasion will affect your phrasing. We need say little about this matter, for you are well aware that formal or solemn occasions require greater dignity and usually a slower rate than do light or frivolous occasions. Let your own common sense direct your phrasing.

Emphasizing with pauses. The pause is a vital technique for emphasizing important ideas. You can emphasize by pausing before, after, or both before and after, an important word or phrase. For examples, we can again use Hudson's sentence about the serpent. Several possibilities for emphasizing by pausing present themselves. What would be the effect of pausing in each of the following instances? (The marks represent pauses for emphasis; the pauses for phrasal breaks are *not* indicated.)

> One hot day in / December / I had been standing perfectly still / for a few minutes among the dry weeds when a slight / rustling sound came from near my feet, and glancing down I saw / the head and neck / of a large / black / serpent / moving / slowly / past me.

Of course, no one would pause for emphasis in all the places indicated, but each might well be used to emphasize a particular thought or shade of thought.

The pause before is often called the pause for suspense, effect, or anticipation. It says to the listener: "This next word is particularly important"; or "This is going to be the main point of this story"; or "Here's the joke!" Deprived of the pause for suspense, our favorite comedians would be without one of their most effective comic techniques. It is the prime element of the actor's art of timing. The chief element of comedy is surprise or incongruity; the pause of anticipation before the point of a story or joke or "punch line" makes it even more surprising, therefore funny. It need not be a long pause.

A comedian told this story, using his sense of timing to make it funny to his audience. He placed a very short, but decisive, pause in the place indicated. Speaking of his experiences in television, he said:

> Television is having a profound effect upon our lives. Some people think that all the effects are bad. You know, mystery stories, cowboy stories, space stories, crime, violence, too much commercialism. Well, I don't think television's so bad—certainly not for the kids. They're getting wonderful lessons in honesty. Why, my neighbor's ten-year-old daughter heard her little brother tell a lie the other day. And do you know what she did? She ran home to her mother and said: "Mommy, Johnny just told a / *commercial!*"

Breathing during pauses. By this time, you are pròbably persuaded that the uses of the pause are worth the interpretative reader's efforts to learn them. One more point needs to be made in behalf of the pause. It seems obvious to everyone that the reader inhales air during pauses, but the beginning reader often wonders "Which pauses?" Perhaps an analogy will help us arrive at a satisfactory conclusion about when to inhale while reading aloud.

When you take an auto trip, you are likely to start out with a plentiful supply of gasoline in the tank. If you are wise, you stop for refueling at some convenient time before the tank becomes empty. Now exactly the same principle applies to reading aloud. You never let your breath supply run out; you always stop at a convenient place and refuel. The convenient place is always between thought-groups, not in the middle of a thought-group. The convenient time is always during a pause long enough for you to inhale without interrupting communication of meaning or feeling. The further apart the groups are in meaning (frequently evidenced by such punctuation as periods, exclamation and interrogation marks, colons, semicolons, and dashes), the better the place for you to breathe. These will be the longer pauses. But you do not have to wait for the end of a sentence in order to take in air, as you might think. If you are able to inhale quickly and silently—usually through the mouth—you may breathe during a shorter pause, provided you do not interfere with the meaning.

Examples of pausing. Now that we have considered the pause in various functions, let us look at some transcriptions of readings by well-known interpreters, and compare the way in which they paused while reading the same selection. Norman Corwin, best known as a writer of exceptionally fine radio dramas, John Gielgud, the British actor, and Alexander Scourby, the American actor, have recorded their readings of Shelley's poem, "Ozymandias." We have indicated short pauses with one vertical mark and long ones with two vertical marks. Analyze and compare these versions. Which do you prefer? Try reading them aloud as they are marked. If you have access to these recordings, be sure to listen to them. How would *you* read this poem?

NORMAN CORWIN'S PAUSES:

I met a traveller / from an antique land
Who said: // Two vast and trunkless legs of stone
Stand in the desert. // Near them, / on the sand, /
Half sunk, / a shattered visage lies, / whose frown, /
And wrinkled lip, / and sneer of cold command,
Tell / that its sculptor well those passions read
Which yet survive, stamped on these lifeless things,
The hand that mocked them, / and the heart that fed: /
And on the pedestal / these words appear: //
"My name is Ozymandias, king of kings: /
Look on my works, ye Mighty, / and despair!" //
Nothing / beside / remains. // Round the decay
Of that colossal wreck, boundless and bare, /
The lone and level sands / stretch far away.

JOHN GIELGUD'S PAUSES:

I met a traveller from an antique land
Who said: // Two vast and trunkless legs of stone
Stand in the desert. // Near them, on the sand, /
Half sunk, / a shattered visage lies, / whose frown,
And wrinkled lip, and sneer of cold command, /

Tell that its sculptor / well those passions read /
Which yet survive, / stamped on these lifeless things, /
The hand that mocked them, / and the heart that fed: //
And on the pedestal / these words appear: //
"My name is Ozymandias, / king of kings: //
Look on my works, ye Mighty, / and despair!" //
Nothing beside remains. // Round the decay
Of that colossal wreck, / boundless and bare, /
The lone and level sands / stretch / far away.

Alexander Scourby's Pauses:

I met a traveller from an antique land
Who said: Two vast and trunkless legs of stone
Stand in the desert. // Near them, on the sand, /
Half sunk, / a shattered visage lies, whose frown,
And wrinkled lip, and sneer of cold command, /
Tell that its sculptor well those passions read
Which yet survive, / stamped on these lifeless things, /
The hand that mocked them / and the heart that fed: //
And on the pedestal / these words appear: //
"My name is Ozymandias, / king of kings: /
Look on my works, ye Mighty, and despair!" //
Nothing beside remains. // Round the decay
Of that colossal wreck, / boundless and bare, /
The lone and level sands stretch far away.

These markings are, of course, disputable. They were made by a class in interpretative reading and are the result of several critical listenings to, and lengthy discussions of, the recordings. Although there was some disagreement as to the existence of some of the pauses or the length of others, these markings represent the majority opinion. They are, admittedly, an oversimplification of the pausing done by the readers. Mere marks on paper cannot, of course, indicate the expressiveness of well-executed pauses, nor can they adequately indicate length of the pauses. But, by studying the marks, we can detect certain interesting similarities and differences in the readers' placement of the pause. What conclusions can you reach for the following questions?

1. Can you see any value in pausing, as Corwin did, in the first line?

2. Would you agree with Scourby that there is no need for a pause until the middle of the third line?

3. Why do all three readers have long pauses after the following words: *desert, appear, despair,* and *remains?*

4. The differences in the placement of pauses in the long sentence in

lines 3 to 11 are striking. Read the sentence aloud each of the three ways. In which places would *you* use pauses to fit your interpretation? Evaluate the logic of the phrasing of each of the professionals in reading this sentence.

5. Do you agree with Corwin's method of breaking up the short sentence "Nothing beside remains," with short pauses?

6. Do you approve of Gielgud's method of setting off "stretch" with short pauses? Does it aid in communicating the mood of desolation?

7. After listening to the recordings, which reader would you say used pauses best to contribute to poetic rhythm?

Several of the best actors have recorded Hamlet's famous soliloquy, "To be, or not to be." Among them are the British actors—all well known in America—Maurice Evans, Laurence Olivier, and John Gielgud. Below are transcriptions of the first portion of the soliloquy showing the placement of pauses by the three actors. Listen to the recordings if you possibly can, but by all means study these transcriptions, reading aloud to determine effectiveness of pausing.

JOHN GIELGUD'S PAUSES:

Note: Mr. Gielgud's stage production of *Hamlet* revealed the actor as one of the great Hamlets of the modern theater.

To be, // or not to be: // that is the question: //
Whether 'tis nobler in the mind / to suffer
The slings and arrows of outrageous fortune, /
Or to take arms against a sea of troubles,
And by opposing end them? // To die: // to sleep; //
No more; // and by a sleep to say we end
The heart-ache and the thousand natural shocks
That flesh is heir to, / 'tis a consummation
Devoutly to be wish'd. // To die, to sleep; //
To sleep: perchance to dream: ay, there's the rub; //
For in that sleep of death what dreams may come
When we have shuffled off this mortal coil, /
Must give us pause:

MAURICE EVANS' PAUSES:

Note: Mr. Evans has portrayed Hamlet in both a full-length (uncut) production and in a modern streamlined version of the play for men of the armed forces.

To be, or not to be: // that is the question: //
Whether 'tis nobler in the mind to suffer

The slings and arrows of outrageous fortune, /
Or to take arms against a sea of troubles,
And by opposing / end them? // To die: // to sleep; /
No more; // and by a sleep to say we end
The heart-ache and the thousand natural shocks
That flesh is heir to, // 'tis a consummation
Devoutly to be wish'd. // To die, // to sleep; //
To sleep: / perchance to dream: // ay, there's the rub; /
For in that sleep of death what dreams may come
When we have shuffled off this mortal coil, /
Must give us pause:

LAURENCE OLIVIER'S PAUSES:

Note: The recording was made from the soundtrack of Mr. Olivier's film, *Hamlet;* consequently, some of the pauses are quite long, perhaps longer than they would have been had he been reading the speech in a recording studio. Some of the pauses in this recording are filled with pertinent sound effects and music.

To be, // or not to be: // that is the question: ///
Whether 'tis nobler in the mind / to suffer
The slings and arrows of outrageous fortune, /
Or to take arms against a sea of troubles, //
And by opposing // end them? // To die: / to sleep;
No more; / and by a sleep to say we end
The heart-ache / and the thousand natural shocks
That flesh is heir to, // 'tis a consummation
Devoutly to be wish'd. / To die, / to sleep; //
To sleep: // perchance to dream: // ay, there's the rub; //
For in that sleep of death what dreams may come
When we have shuffled off this mortal coil, /
Must give us pause:

We need not try to establish the superiority of any of these readings; all are expert. Restricting ourselves to a consideration of pause placement, we can note that

1. Pauses were placed in twenty different locations. Olivier used nineteen of them; Evans, sixteen; Gielgud, fourteen.

2. The three actors paused in eleven identical places:

Line	*Location*
1	after *not to be;* end of line
3	end of line
5	after *end them;* after *To die*

Line	*Location*
6	after *No more*
8	after *heir to*
9	after *wish'd;* end of line
10	end of line
12	end of line

3. The actors differed in the use of pauses in nine places. Study these spots in detail to determine different meanings or different shades of meaning possibly communicated by the pauses. Of course, only by listening to the recordings can you determine this positively, for interpretation depends upon many variables besides the pause.

Line	*Location*
1	after first two words
2	after *mind*
4	end of line (Only Olivier used this one.)
5	after *opposing;* end of line
7	after *heart-ache* (Only Olivier used this one.)
9	after *to die;*
10	after *sleep;* after *dream*

As to length of pause, the three actors used about the same number of comparatively long pauses. Olivier used the greatest number of short pauses; Gielgud, the fewest.

Would you conclude from your study of this comparison and from listening to the records that these readings are significantly different in meaning?

RATE

Factors controlling rate. The second element of time which we must consider is rate or speed of utterance. Rate is to some extent dependent on the personality of the individual reader. We all have our normal, or habitual, rates of speaking. Some of us naturally talk slowly or deliberately. Others talk rapidly most of the time. We are accustomed to such individual differences. Radio and television audiences have had both deliberate speakers and rapid speakers among their favorite announcers, commentators, and comedians.

Certain practical considerations inherent in the reading situation also determine rate—the mood of the speaker, and the nature of the audience and the occasion. We know that when we are nervous or excited, we tend to speak faster. Many a radio or television speaker has carefully timed his talk, only to find—to his amazement—that under pressure of producing the program, he has finished ahead of time. He simply talked faster than he planned because he was excited. The beginning reader does the same: he tends to read much too rapidly. He races through thought-groups, sentences, and paragraphs, unaware that he has lost his audience. We have already seen how the relationships between the complexity of the material and the nature of the audience, and also the nature of the occasion and the acoustical situation determine the length of thought-groups and the number and length of pauses; so do they also determine how fast a reader can effectively utter sounds and yet communicate.

Another element which determines rate of utterance is the emotional content of the material. An exciting story, or one with lots of action, is likely to be read at a comparatively rapid rate, while a somber, serious selection will need to be read at a slow rate. Light, gay verses with little seriousness of purpose, such as these limericks, will be read rather rapidly:

There was an old man from Peru
Who dreamed he was eating his shoe.
    He woke in a fright
    In the middle of the night
And found it was perfectly true.

—ANONYMOUS

There was a young fellow named Hall,
Who fell in the spring in the fall;
    'Twould have been a sad thing
    If he'd died in the spring,
But he didn't—he died in the fall.

—ANONYMOUS

On the other hand, literature as seriously contemplative as these lines of Walt Whitman's deserves more time:

A noiseless patient spider,
I mark'd where on a little promontory it stood isolated,
Mark'd how to explore the vacant vast surrounding,
It launched forth filament, filament, filament, out of itself,
Ever unreeling them, ever tirelessly speeding them.

And you O my soul where you stand,
Surrounded, detached, in measureless oceans of space,
Ceaselessly musing, venturing, throwing, seeking the spheres to connect them,
Till the bridge you will need be form'd, till the ductile anchor hold,
Till the gossamer thread you fling catch somewhere, O my soul.

— *A Noiseless Patient Spider*

The reader, therefore, needs to be able to adjust his normal rate to a variety of possible circumstances related to the occasion, the audience, and the intellectual and emotional requirements of the material. Furthermore, he must be sensitive to the changes of rate demanded *within* a particular selection, as we shall see presently.

Examples of rate usage. By listening analytically to recordings of professional readers, we can study the uses of rate by those who should be able to utilize it best. We listened to fifty-five recordings of poetry by nineteen different readers, timed them, counted the words in the selections, and computed the rates in words-per-minute. A table listing these readings appears at the end of this chapter, on pages 237–38. Each rate is calculated from the reading of an entire poem and thus is affected by the time spent in pausing. While this rather simple approach to the study of rate may not be scientifically sophisticated, it suffices to indicate that good readers do use variation of rate as a technique.

The rates of reading varied from very slow, 91 words-per-minute for Carl Sandburg reading his own poem "Grass," to very fast, 210 words-per-minute for Edith Evans reading Carroll's nonsensical "Father William." Thus, the extremes represent a difference of 119 words-per-minute, quite a difference, indeed!

An individual reader uses a wide range of rates in reading a variety of materials. Edith Evans read "Father William" at an extremely fast rate, as we have just noted, but she read "She Walks in Beauty" quite slowly, at a rate of only 106. John Gielgud read "That time of year" at only 118, but "So We'll Go No More A-Roving" at a fast 171. Basil Rathbone, normally a fast reader, varied from 123 for "How do I love thee," to 193 for "Invictus." Claire Bloom, like Gielgud, chose a slow rate—116—for "That time of year" but read "It was a lover and his lass," a light-hearted lyric, at 147. John Neville did not limit himself to his slow rate of 100, which he used for the Milton poem, but read more rapidly—145—for "The Passionate Shepherd to His Mistress." Accomplished readers, therefore, recognize, at least subconsciously, that different pieces of literature require different time treatments in interpretation. We recommend that you examine the selections just mentioned to appreciate how their emotional contents dictate the appropriate reading rates.

No one can establish iron-clad rules as to specific rates for specific selections or emotional contents, however. For example, we see on the table that "She Walks in Beauty" received four different rates on these recordings: Evans, 106; Power, 109; Portman, 138; and Corwin, 150. A study of the poem should lead us to believe that it should be read at a predominantly slow rate. A study of these recordings might reveal that some are more effective than others, but, of course, we must acknowledge that factors other than rate may also make one reading better than another. Corwin's rate of 150 would seem to indicate that he did not make much use of rate to communicate the quiet beauty of the poem, although he *may* have used other techniques effectively. On the other hand, anyone who listens to the two recordings of Dylan Thomas's "Do Not Go Gentle into That Good Night" will adjudge the poet's own recording to be considerably superior to the one by Norman Rose, with the use of rate playing a significant role in this superiority. Thomas took the time to think, feel, and experience; Rose only skimmed the surface—the words. One might also contend, with some justification, that Rathbone's rapid 161 helps to keep his reading of "Ode to the West Wind" from being as effective as Gielgud's, which is rendered at only 122 words-per-minute. One might feel that Neville's 108 for "When, in disgrace with fortune" is irritatingly slow and Rathbone's 152, superficially rapid.

Some interesting agreements in rate appear on the table: the almost identical slow rates for Bloom and Gielgud in reading a Shakespearian sonnet; the similar middle-range rates for Portman and Scourby in reading Wordsworth's "Upon Westminster Bridge"; and the fast rates of Johnson and Evans in reading "Father William."

The average rate for the fifty readings was 140 words-per-minute. For ten sonnets, the average was 125; for eighteen serious, contemplative poems (other than the sonnets), the average was 134; for nineteen light, cheerful verses, the average was 154. One might draw some general conclusions from these averages if one also recognizes that the readers used a *range* of rates for each type of literature.

Study the table on pages 237–38 to learn about the uses of rate. If you are fortunate enough to be able to listen to some of the recordings, you can study the actual readings and perhaps compare them with other recordings, professional or amateur, of the same materials. Rate is worth studying; the ability to vary the rate to suit the material is worth cultivating.

Not only do accomplished interpreters vary their rates from selection to selection, but they also vary their rates to communicate the changing emotional tensions *within* a selection. John Gielgud read the first stanza of Kingsley's "Young and Old" at a rate of 184, but he slowed to 128 for the second stanza. Read the poem to determine why:

YOUNG AND OLD

CHARLES KINGSLEY

When all the world is young, lad,
  And all the trees are green;
And every goose a swan, lad,
  And every lass a queen;
Then hey for boot and horse, lad,
  And round the world away;
Young blood must have its course, lad,
  And every dog his day.

When all the world is old, lad,
  And all the trees are brown;
And all the sport is stale, lad,
  And all the wheels run down;
Creep home, and take your place there,
  The spent and maimed among:
God grant you find one face there,
  You loved when all was young.

Example of rate variety. In the previous exercise you saw that John Gielgud changed his rate for the second part of Kingsley's poem "Young and Old." Your attention was also called to the fact that the rates were determined by the relationship between the total number of words in a selection and the total time consumed in reading it. Such computation does not indicate the changes of rates used by a reader within the reading. The following example should demonstrate clearly that the good reader is sensitive to the emotional content of literature and consequently varies his rate—almost automatically—to communicate the changing emotional tensions in a selection.

Alexander Scourby read Alfred Noyes's poem "The Highwayman" at an over-all rate of 159 words-per-minute. During his reading he varied his rate often. Since we cannot catalogue all instances, a few will suffice for illustration of the principle. On the copy of the poem which follows are indicated the individual stanza rates, which vary from 142 to 221, and a few cases of changing rates within stanzas, specifically Stanzas III, VI, X, and XIII. The figures will be truly significant to you only if you make a thorough study of the poem and try to determine Scourby's reasons for changing his rate as he did. His is not the only way to read the poem: other good readings would differ from his. Yours might, too, but his way is worthy of careful analysis. To guide you in your analysis, the following questions are provided:

1. Why does Scourby read Stanza II (Rate: 221) so much faster than he does Stanza I (Rate: 155)?

2. Why does he read the first line and a half of Stanza III at the rapid rate of 300, then suddenly cut his rate in half for the rest of the stanza?

3. Scourby pauses for one second between Stanzas I and II and between Stanzas II and III. He pauses two seconds between Stanzas III and IV. Why? Why does he have no significant pause between Stanzas IV and V?

4. Why does he use a fast rate (205) on Stanza V?

5. What emotion expressed in the first portion of Stanza VI brings about the fast rate of 222? Why does the reader slow down to a rate of 180 for the last part of the stanza?

6. Why does Scourby speed up (Rate: 223) on the last portion of Stanza X? The rate on the first part was only 156.

7. Why does he read Stanza XII (Rate: 205) so much faster than Stanza XI (Rate: 162)?

8. Why does he use such a dramatic difference in rates in the two portions of Stanza XIII (225, 138)? What happens in line three to cause a slowing down?

9. Would you read Stanza XV at a relatively rapid rate to suggest the mad riding of the highwayman? Scourby chose to read it slowly (Rate: 142), with many pauses and much intensity.

10. Scourby has his longest between-stanzas' pause (three seconds) before Stanza XVI. Why?

THE HIGHWAYMAN

ALFRED NOYES

PART ONE

I. The wind was a torrent of darkness among the gusty trees,
(Rate: The moon was a ghostly galleon tossed upon cloudy seas,
155) The road was a ribbon of moonlight over the purple moor,
And the highwayman came riding—
        Riding—riding—
The highwayman came riding, up to the old inn-door.

II. He'd a French cocked-hat on his forehead, a bunch of lace
(Rate: at his chin,
221) A coat of the claret velvet, and breeches of brown doe-skin;

They fitted with never a wrinkle: his boots were up to the thigh!
And he rode with a jewelled twinkle,
His pistol butts a-twinkle,
His rapier hilt a-twinkle, under the jewelled sky.

III. (Rate: 183)
Over the cobbles he clattered and clashed in the dark inn-yard,
(Rate: 300)
And he tapped with his whip on the shutters, | but all was locked and barred;
He whistled a tune to the window, and who should be waiting there
But the landlord's black-eyed daughter,
Bess, the landlord's daughter,
(Rate: 150)
Plaiting a dark red love-knot into her long black hair. |

IV. (Rate: 155)
And dark in the dark old inn-yard a stable-wicket creaked
Where Tim, the ostler, listened; his face was white and peaked;
His eyes were hollows of madness, his hair like mouldy hay,
But he loved the landlord's daughter,
The landlord's red-lipped daughter;
Dumb as a dog he listened, and he heard the robber say—

V. (Rate: 205)
"One kiss, my bonny sweetheart, I'm after a prize tonight,
But I shall be back with the yellow gold before the morning light;
Yet, if they press me sharply, and harry me through the day,
Then look for me by moonlight,
Watch for me by moonlight,
I'll come to thee by moonlight, though hell should bar the way."

VI. (Rate: 191)
He rose upright in the stirrups; he scarce could reach her hand,
But she loosened her hair i' the casement! His face burnt like a brand
As the black cascade of perfume came tumbling over his
(Rate: 222)
breast; |
And he kissed its waves in the moonlight,

(Oh, sweet black waves in the moonlight!)
Then he tugged at his reins in the moonlight, and galloped
(Rate: 180) |
away to the West. |

PART TWO

VII. He did not come in the dawning; he did not come at noon;
(Rate: And out o' the tawny sunset, before the rise o' the moon,
165) When the road was a gipsy's ribbon, looping the purple moor,
A red-coat troop came marching—
Marching—marching—
King George's men came marching, up to the old inn-door.

VIII. They said no word to the landlord, they drank his ale instead,
(Rate: But they gagged his daughter and bound her to the foot of her narrow bed;
183) Two of them knelt at her casement, with muskets at their side!
There was death at every window;
And hell at one dark window;
For Bess could see, through her casement, the road that *he* would ride.

IX. They had tied her up to attention, with many a sniggering jest;
(Rate: They had bound a musket beside her, with the barrel beneath her breast!
171) "Now keep good watch!" and they kissed her. She heard the dead man say—
Look for me by moonlight;
Watch for me by moonlight;
I'll come to thee by moonlight, though hell should bar the way!

X. She twisted her hands behind her; but all the knots held good!
(Rate: She writhed her hands till her fingers were wet with sweat and blood!
169) They stretched and strained in the darkness, and the hours
(Rate: 156) |
crawled by like years, |
Till, now, on the stroke of midnight,

Cold on the stroke of midnight,
The tip of one finger touched it! The trigger at least was
(Rate: 223) |
hers! |

XI. (Rate: 162)
The tip of one finger touched it; she strove no more for the rest!
Up, she stood up to attention, with the barrel beneath her breast,
She would not risk their hearing; she would not strive again;
For the road lay bare in the moonlight;
Blank and bare in the moonlight;
And the blood of her veins in the moonlight throbbed to her love's refrain.

XII. (Rate: 205)
Tlot-tlot, tlot-tlot! Had they heard it? The horse-hoofs ringing clear;
Tlot-tlot, tlot-tlot, in the distance? Were they deaf that they did not hear?
Down the ribbon of moonlight, over the brow of the hill,
The highwayman came riding,
Riding, riding!
The red-coats looked to their priming! She stood up, straight and still!

XIII. (Rate: 171)
Tlot-tlot, in the frosty silence! *Tlot-tlot,* in the echoing night!
Nearer he came and nearer! Her face was like a light!
(Rate: 225) |
Her eyes grew wide for a moment; | she drew one last deep breath,
Then her finger moved in the moonlight,
Her musket shattered the moonlight,
Shattered her breast in the moonlight and warned him—with
(Rate: 138) |
her death. |

XIV. (Rate: 162)
He turned; he spurred him Westward; he did not know who stood
Bowed, with her head o'er the musket, drenched with her own red blood!
Not till the dawn he heard it, his face grew gray to hear
How Bess, the landlord's daughter,

The landlord's black-eyed daughter,
Had watched for her love in the moonlight, and died in the darkness there.

XV. (Rate: 142)
Back, he spurred like a madman, shrieking a curse to the sky,
With the white road smoking behind him, and his rapier brandished high!
Blood-red were his spurs i' the golden noon; wine-red was his velvet coat,
When they shot him down on the highway,
Down like a dog on the highway,
And he lay in his blood on the highway, with a bunch of lace at his throat.

. . .

XVI. (Rate: 154)
And still of a winter's night, they say, when the wind is in the trees,
When the moon is a ghostly galleon tossed upon cloudy seas,
When the road is a ribbon of moonlight over the purple moor,
A highwayman comes riding—
Riding—riding—
A highwayman comes riding up to the old inn-door.

XVII. (Rate: 161)
Over the cobbles he clatters and clangs in the dark inn-yard;
And taps with his whip on the shutters, but all is locked and barred;
He whistles a tune to the window, and who should be waiting there
But the landlord's black-eyed daughter,
Bess, the landlord's daughter,
Plaiting a dark red love-knot into her long black hair.

Summary on rate. Determining the exact rate for a reading is important only to illustrate how good readers use rate. We should note here that although readers differ in the rates they employ for reading the same selection, they usually vary their rates to suit the type of material. They use rate to help communicate the content of the literature.

Rate is a fundamental and interesting aspect of oral reading. You should learn to do the following:

1. Control your rate of reading so that you do not, under pressure, read too rapidly for your listeners to comprehend your reading.

2. Develop the ability to read at a variety of speeds.

3. Study the material you choose to read, and read it at a rate that is appropriate to the intellectual and emotional content. This principle means that you will alter your rate within a selection as the ideas and emotions change.

DURATION

The third aspect of time is duration, or length of sound. Some of our speech sounds are normally short; some, normally long. Although little research has yet been done on sound lengths in American speech, we can observe that the consonants p [p], b [b], t [t], and d [d], for example, are relatively short sounds. They are called plosives, and their lives end with their explosion from our lips and tongue; we cannot prolong them in utterance. We can also see that the consonants m [m], n[n], ng [ŋ], and l [l] are relatively long sounds. They are called continuants, for they can be prolonged indefinitely by the speaker. Thus, we can conclude that in our speech, normally some sounds are long, some short. It is also true that in our speaking, we deliberately make the same sounds sometimes long, sometimes short. In some foreign languages the length given a vowel in a word may actually determine the meaning of the word. Such is not the case in English, where the vowel length does not often affect the specific denotation.

We must, however, learn to determine the effect that sound length has upon meaning and feeling. We often use duration as a means for emphasizing. When we stress a syllable or word—in addition to using other vocal techniques yet to be considered—we usually extend the length of the sound. Thus duration is a means of communicating intellectual significance. Duration is also a valuable tool of the speaker for achieving emotional effects. As speakers and readers, we may wish to stretch or compress a word in order to give it a wanted emotional impact. Consider the following list of words. None of them is long in terms of number of letters. But if you will look at them intently, speaking them while letting your mind focus upon the feeling that is likely to go along with each, you will discover that subjectively, at least, some of them are long and some of them are short in terms of sound: *short, long, fast, slow, walk, stroll, hop, crawl, sit, lounge, peppy, lazy, flip, rumble.*

Duration is significant to the oral interpreter also because sounds are often symbolic of sense. We know, for example, that words containing the short i [ɪ] often suggest smallness, e.g., *bib, bit, chip, dim, fib, fig, fin, nit, pin, pip, sip, skip, slim, snip, tip,* and *tit.* We know also that words beginning with fl [fl] sometimes suggest moving light, as in *flame, flare, flash,* and *flicker;* sometimes, flatness, as in *flake, flat, float, flock, flotilla, flood, floor, flounder,* and *flow;* sometimes, quick movement, as in *flag, flail, flap, flaunt, flay, flee, fleet, flick, fling, flip, flit, flog, flop, flounce, flourish, fluent, flurry,* and *flutter*. We know that words beginning with gl [gl] often suggest light, e.g., *glamor, glance, glare, glass, glaucous, glaze, gleam, glimmer, glimpse, glint, glisten, glister, gloaming,* and *gloss*. We know that words ending in er [ɚ] often suggest repetition, e.g., *bicker, chatter, flicker, flutter, glimmer,* and *sputter*. We know that words, by their sounds, often suggest a state of mind or behavior or appearance, e.g., *droopy, gloomy, grisly, grumble, happy, lovely, merry, morbid,* and *sluttish*. Duration is especially important in the case of onomatopoetic words, in which the sound of the word is a direct imitation of the sense of the word, such as: *bang, crash, cuckoo, fluffy, hiss, hush, moan, murmur, pingpong, roar, rustle,* and *sock*.[1]

The sensitive interpreter is aware of sound lengths and treats them appropriately, for proper use of duration is one of the most effective techniques at the disposal of the reader for communicating emotion. Command of duration is usually a late accomplishment in the training of the oral interpreter, but you should begin acquiring skill in using it as soon as possible. Learn to appreciate the "taste" or flavor of words. Enjoy words for their sound as well as for the images they suggest.

Look again at "Ozymandias," which we used for an example a few pages back. The words containing long sounds, which might well be extended when read, are underscored:

I met a traveller from an antique land
Who said: Two vast and trunkless legs of stone
Stand in the desert. Near them, on the sand,
Half sunk, a shattered visage lies, whose frown,
And wrinkled lip, and sneer of cold command,
Tell that its sculptor well those passions read
Which yet survive, stamped on these lifeless things,
The hand that mocked them, and the heart that fed:
And on the pedestal these words appear:
"My name is Ozymandias, king of kings:
Look on my works, ye Mighty, and despair!"
Nothing beside remains. Round the decay
Of that colossal wreck, boundless and bare,
The lone and level sands stretch far away.

Notice that in the first part of the poem, most of the sounds are short, yet there are several long sounds to dwell upon in the last lines to picture the desolateness of the desert scene. We cannot indicate on paper how long a reader dwells on a sound, but if you can, listen to Corwin's, Gielgud's, and Scourby's recordings of "Ozymandias" to see which does the best job of

[1] See pages 410–11 for a more complete consideration of onomatopoeia in poetry and verse.

using duration of sound to communicate the emotional significance of Shelley's sonnet.

The good writer uses words not only for their meaning values, but also for their sound values. In order to read well, you should study the effects of word sounds in establishing the emotional spirit of the literature. Try yourself on the following selections. You should not have much trouble in deciding how to deal with each in respect to duration of sounds.

Similar remarks to those made in the first poem are made almost any date-night in college men's rooms! What is the attitude of the speaker? Is he serious? Although the language is a bit different from ours today, the minimum of long sounds and maximum of short sounds seem fitting to the "Encouragements" offered the poor lover.

ENCOURAGEMENTS TO A LOVER

SIR JOHN SUCKLING

Why so pale and wan, fond lover?
    Prithee, why so pale?
Will, when looking well can't move her,
    Looking ill prevail?
    Prithee, why so pale?

Why so dull and mute, young sinner?
    Prithee, why so mute?
Will, when speaking well can't win her,
    Saying nothing do't?
    Prithee, why so mute?

Quit, quit, for shame! This will not move,
    This cannot take her:
If of herself she will not love,
    Nothing can make her:
    The devil take her!

The following poem can be interpreted many different ways, and you will be interested in reading several interpretations rather amusingly presented in Theodore Morrison's story, "Dover Beach Revisited," published in *Harper's Magazine,* February 1940. You should study the poem thoroughly and do some background reading about the author and the period in which he lived, but from merely reading the poem—and being sensitive to the sounds—you can come close to determining the mood. What is it?

DOVER BEACH

MATTHEW ARNOLD

The sea is calm to-night.
The tide is full, the moon lies fair
Upon the straits;—on the French coast the light
Gleams and is gone; the cliffs of England stand,
Glimmering and vast, out in the tranquil bay.
Come to the window, sweet is the night-air!
Only, from the long line of spray
Where the sea meets the moon-blanch'd land,
Listen! you hear the grating roar
Of pebbles which the waves draw back, and fling,
At their return, up the high strand,
Begin, and cease, and then again begin,
With tremulous cadence slow, and bring
The eternal note of sadness in.
Sophocles long ago
Heard it on the Ægæan, and it brought
Into his mind the turbid ebb and flow
Of human misery; we
Find also in the sound a thought,
Hearing it by this distant northern sea.

The Sea of Faith
Was once, too, at the full, and round earth's shore
Lay like the folds of a bright girdle furl'd.
But now I only hear
Its melancholy, long, withdrawing roar,
Retreating, to the breath
Of the night-wind, down the vast edges drear
And naked shingles of the world.

Ah, love, let us be true
To one another! for the world, which seems
To lie before us like a land of dreams,
So various, so beautiful, so new,
Hath really neither joy, nor love, nor light,
Nor certitude, nor peace, nor help for pain;
And we are here as on a darkling plain
Swept with confused alarms of struggle and flight
Where ignorant armies clash by night.

You have probably already picked certain words which through the length of their sounds picture the apparent tranquility and beauty of the scene. In the first few lines, you found *calm, full, moon, fair, gleams, gone, glimmering, vast,* and *tranquil,* as deserving more than passing attention from the oral reader. When speaking them take time to *savor* them. Prolong the sounds. You will find that there is a real pleasure in savoring beautiful words. If you will prolong the sounds in such words as *sweet, long, line, spray,* and *moon-blanch'd* you will discover that you have learned a new technique—and a very effective one at that—for emphasizing. Such emphasis is far more penetrating than any force you may apply through mere loudness. Practice reading "Dover Beach" aloud, quietly getting your emphasis chiefly through duration.

RHYTHM [2]

Rhythm in literature is a more or less regular recurrence of some elements: a word, a phrase, an idea, a vocal accent, a pause, a sound, or a grammatical construction. We are accustomed to this recurrence in the alternate heavy and light beats in music. Our love for rhythm seems to be innate: witness the responses of a toddling youngster to the music of a brass band! Children love to beat on toy drums, tin cans, or even the side of a house. They stamp their feet, chant nursery rimes or nonsense syllables, not unlike the cultural dances of primitive peoples. As we grow more civilized, we learn to restrain our responses to rhythm, to some extent, but our love for rhythm—nay, our dependence upon rhythm—is still present. We live in rhythms; yes, we are governed by rhythm; and we would not be without rhythm!

Physiologically, we are rhythmical. We eat regularly, eliminate regularly, breathe regularly, sleep regularly, play regularly—if we value our health. Emotionally, we are rhythmical, too, for psychologists say that all of us feel alternate periods of relative depression and exhilaration. Intellectually we are rhythmical as well. Following periods of concentration, we must have periods of relaxation.

Persons in different walks of life live in different rhythms. A college student may live a very rhythmical life. For five days a week, thirty-six weeks in the year, his life is governed by a veritable metronome—the campus clock tower or master-clock. His day is composed of alternate periods of classes and intermissions. Three meals a day establish another rhythm in his day. Regular evening study or a date may furnish another recurring element. After five days of this regularity, he has two different kinds of days. Saturdays may be spent primarily in work, study, or play. Sundays are even more different, with church in the morning, library study in the afternoon, a date at night, and so on. You may find it interesting to plot the rhythms in your daily activities for a month, and you are quite likely to be surprised at how

[2] See pages 413–19 for a treatment of rhythm in relation to verse.

regular you are in your living. You will notice, of course, certain irregularities, such as an occasional week-end or holiday trip, but if you were to plot your activities during your four-year residence in college, you would discover, even more to your amazement, that there is a great regularity to even the irregularities. You might conclude from this study of your rhythms that regular rhythm is the sustenance of your life, but that it is the regular irregularities which add spice to life. Keep these principles in mind as we now consider rhythm in literature.

Literary rhythm can be extremely regular, as in:

Mary had a little lamb. 9.5
Its fleece was white as snow.
And everywhere that Mary went
That lamb was sure to go.

In this nursery rime, we find a regular alternation of heavy and light beats, which is called *meter*. Meter may be somewhat more varied and complex than that, however:

The wind was a torrent of darkness among the gusty trees,
The moon was a ghostly galleon tossed upon cloudy seas, 4
The road was a ribbon of moonlight over the purple moor,
And the highwayman came riding—
    Riding—riding—
The highwayman came riding, up to the old inn-door.

—ALFRED NOYES, *The Highwayman*

"The Highwayman" is a very rhythmical poem, and yet the irregularities in it are delightful to the ear. But some poetry, called *vers libre,* or free verse, has such an irregular rhythm that it is said to have no meter:

DEATH SNIPS PROUD MEN

CARL SANDBURG

Death is stronger than all the governments because the governments are men and men die and then death laughs: Now you see 'em, now you don't.

Death is stronger than all proud men and so death snips proud men on the nose, throws a pair of dice and says: Read 'em and weep.

Death sends a radiogram every day: When I want you I'll drop in—and then one day he comes with a master-key and lets himself in and says: We'll go now.

Death is a nurse mother with big arms: 'Twon't hurt you at all; it's your time now; you just need a long sleep, child; what have you had anyhow better than sleep?

Since there is no meter in Sandburg's poem, look for all the recurring elements (words, ideas, structure, etc.) to determine how rhythm is achieved. Rhythm is not limited to poetry; it is also found in prose. We find it in the parallel structure and other recurrences in this oration by one of America's greatest orators:

AT THE TOMB OF NAPOLEON

ROBERT INGERSOLL

A little while ago, I stood by the grave of the old Napoleon—a magnificent tomb of gilt and gold, fit almost for a dead deity—and gazed upon the sarcophagus of rare and nameless marble, where rest at last the ashes of that restless man. I leaned over the balustrade and thought about the career of the greatest soldier of the modern world.

I saw him walking upon the banks of the Seine, contemplating suicide. I saw him at Toulon—I saw him putting down the mob in the streets of Paris—I saw him at the head of the army of Italy—I saw him crossing the bridge of Lodi with the tri-color in his hand—I saw him in Egypt in the shadows of the Pyramids—I saw him conquer the Alps and mingle the eagles of France with the eagles of the crags. I saw him at Marengo—at Ulm and Austerlitz. I saw him in Russia, where the infantry of the snow and the cavalry of the wild

> blasts scattered his legions like winter's withered leaves. I saw him at Leipsic in defeat and disaster—driven by a million bayonets back upon Paris—clutched like a wild beast—banished to Elba. I saw him escape and retake an empire by the force of his genius. I saw him upon the frightful field of Waterloo, where Chance and Fate combined to wreck the fortunes of their former king. And I saw him at St. Helena, with his hands crossed behind him, gazing out upon the sad and solemn sea. I thought of the orphans and widows he had made—of the tears that had been shed for his glory, and of the only woman who ever loved him, pushed from his heart by the cold hand of ambition. And I said I would rather have been a French peasant and worn wooden shoes. I would rather have lived in a hut with a vine growing over the door, and the grapes growing purple in the kisses of the autumn sun. I would rather have been that poor peasant with my loving wife by my side, knitting as the day died out of the sky—with my children upon my knees and their arms about me—I would rather have been that man and gone down to the tongueless silence of the dreamless dust, than to have been that imperial impersonation of force and murder, known as "Napoleon the Great."

These examples should indicate to you that rhythm exists in literature in a very regular form, called meter, but also in looser, more flowing cadences. As interpreters we must be sensitive to the presence of rhythms.

Summary

Because sound and silence, the materials of oral interpretation, are measured in time, time becomes a major consideration in interpretative reading. We should consider four aspects of time: pause, rate of utterance, duration, and rhythm. Pause, which is silence charged with meaning, aids in communicating meaning, for it is the major punctuation mark of the speaker. Pauses separate thought-groups, emphasize, and provide times for thinking and breathing. Pauses are determined by the meaning and the complexity of the material, the capabilities of the audience, the acoustical situation, and the formality of the occasion. Rate of utterance is determined by the personality of the speaker, conditions of the reading situation, and the content of the material. We must learn to read at different rates appropriate to the material and resist the impulse to read too fast. Command of duration of sound is a definite technical asset to us in communicating mood and beauty of expression and in emphasizing. Rhythm, which is a fundamental aspect of our lives, is also found in good writing of all types. We delight in rhythms, particularly those which contain irregularities.

Exercises

1. With the aid of the table which follows, listen to some of the recordings and write a short paper presenting your observations concerning the use of rate (effective and not effective) by the readers involved. (Those marked with an asterisk are quoted in this textbook.)

READER	POET	POEM	RATE (*words per minute*)
Carl Sandburg	Sandburg	*Grass	91
John Neville	Milton	On His Blindness	100
Geraldine Brooks	E. B. White	Disturbers of the Peace	104
Dorothy Parker	Parker	One Perfect Rose	104
Edith Evans	Byron	She Walks in Beauty	106
John Neville	Shakespeare	*When, in disgrace	108
Tyrone Power	Byron	She Walks in Beauty	109
Norman Corwin	Milton	On His Blindness	109
Dylan Thomas	Thomas	Do Not Go Gentle	110
Dylan Thomas	Thomas	*In My Craft or Sullen Art	116
Claire Bloom	Shakespeare	That time of year	116
John Gielgud	Shakespeare	That time of year	118
Carl Sandburg	Sandburg	*Prayers of Steel	120
John Gielgud	Shelley	Ode to the West Wind	122
Basil Rathbone	E. B. Browning	*How do I love thee?	123
Dylan Thomas	Thomas	Poem in October	124
John Gielgud	Eliot	*Journey of the Magi	127
Geraldine Brooks	E. B. White	Springtime Crosstown Episode	132
John Neville	Wordsworth	*The World Is Too Much With Us	136
Eric Portman	Byron	She Walks in Beauty	138
Alexander Scourby	Yeats	The Lake Isle of Innisfree	138
Alexander Scourby	Milton	On His Blindness	138
Alexander Scourby	Gilbert	*To the Terrestrial Globe	139
Dorothy Parker	Parker	Parable for a Certain Virgin	139
Eric Portman	Wordsworth	Upon Westminster Bridge	139
Geraldine Brooks	Parker	Love Song	140
Robert Frost	Frost	*Stopping by Woods	144
Alexander Scourby	Wordsworth	Upon Westminster Bridge	145

READER	POET	POEM	RATE (*words per minute*)
John Neville	Marlowe	The Passionate Shepherd	145
Claire Bloom	Shakespeare	It was a lover and his lass	147
Dorothy Parker	Parker	The Red Dress	149
Alexander Scourby	Suckling	*Why so Pale and Wan	149
Alexander Scourby	R. Browning	*My Last Duchess	149
Norman Rose	Thomas	Do Not Go Gentle	150
Norman Corwin	Byron	She Walks in Beauty	150
Raymond E. Johnson	Lear	The Owl and the Pussy Cat	151
Basil Rathbone	Shakespeare	*When, in disgrace	152
Norman Rose	E. B. White	Village Revisited	153
Arnold Moss	Goldsmith	*Elegy on the Death of a Mad Dog	153
Edith Everett	E. B. Browning	*How do I love thee?	155
Alexander Scourby	Noyes	*The Highwayman	159
John Gielgud	C. Rossetti	A Birthday	159
Basil Rathbone	Shelley	Ode to the West Wind	161
Robert Frost	Frost	*Birches	169
John Gielgud	Byron	So We'll Go No More A-Roving	171
Raymond E. Johnson	Carroll	Father William	173
Alexander Scourby	Daly	Between Two Loves	174
Ogden Nash	Nash	Allow Me, Madam	190
Norman Rose	Nash	Lines to a World-Famous Poet	203
Edith Evans	Carroll	Father William	210

2. If you have access to a tape recorder and a stop watch, time recordings of your own readings of various types of literature and compute your rates to determine if you make use of variety of rate in reading aloud.

3. The following selection is an example of succinct expository prose. In it, a British scientist has stated a case so simply that "anyone can understand it." Furthermore, he has written interestingly. Think it through aloud, studying your natural inclinations to pause. Notice when pauses fall at written punctuation marks and when they do not. Notice how you break up sentences into thought-groups. Notice, also, how you pause to think and to emphasize.

LIFE ON MARS

from *A Guide to Mars*

PATRICK MOORE

Long before the term "science fiction" became part of our language, and when the only interplanetary stories widely read were those of Jules Verne and H. G. Wells, Mars was considered to be the likely abode of intelligent beings. There were sound reasons for such a belief only sixty or seventy years ago. Up to 1892 the dark areas were thought to be seas (for some reason, Liais' original suggestion of 1878 did not attract much attention), and it was also believed that the Martian air was fairly rich in both oxygen and water-vapour.

Wells set the fashion in his famous novel, *The War of the Worlds,* in which inhuman, all-conquering Martians descended upon the Earth and almost wrecked it before they were destroyed by terrestrial germs unknown upon their own planet. Like most of his subsequent imitators, Wells made his Martians thoroughly evil. Actually, this is illogical; the creatures of the Red World, if they existed, would hardly be both intelligent and evil. They would probably have reached a stage beyond our own condition of collective insanity, and the very last thing they would be likely to do would be to visit us equipped with heat-throwers, ray-guns and other impedimenta which belong more properly to boys' "comic" papers. The fondness for picturing them as bloodthirsty monsters is a relic from the days when astrology was rife and Mars a planet of ill omen.

Occasionally, there have been reports that the Martians have actually arrived. In 1938, a misleading broadcast of Wells' story started a panic in the United States, when thousands of people mistook it for an actual news bulletin; in 1950, a Russian "scientist" announced that the tremendous object that landed in Siberia in 1908 was not a meteorite, as was generally supposed, but a Martian spaceship that had met with disaster; and more recently (September, 1954) there has been an announcement that a certain Cedric Allingham has met and talked with a man from Mars who paid him a literal "flying visit" in a Saucer. We need waste little time over this sort of thing. Yet how can we be sure that there are in reality no men upon our brother world?

To begin with, it is quite definite that there are no living Martians built upon our own pattern. To stress this it is necessary to say something about the way in which a man breathes.

Oxygen is the vital gas; wartime flyers will remember the danger of going up much above 12,000 feet without proper breathing masks. When oxygen is drawn in from the air, coupled of course with nitrogen (we can neglect the tiny amounts of other gases such as argon), it mixes with carbon dioxide and water vapour produced inside the body to produce a certain pressure inside the lung. The human mechanism is adjusted so that the gas pressure inside the lung is always about the same, whatever the gas may be. If we breathe in less oxygen, more carbon dioxide and water vapour will be produced from inside the body to maintain the normal lung pressure. If we continue taking in less and less oxygen there will come a point at which most of the mixture inside the lung is made up of irrespirable carbon dioxide and water vapour, so that unconsciousness follows. The critical point at which no outside oxygen at all could be taken in occurs at about 56,000 feet above the Earth, though, of course, the oxygen would have become insufficient for respiration well below this height.

The atmospheric pressure on the surface of Mars is equal to that at about 55,000 feet above the Earth. Even if the Martian air consisted of pure oxygen, therefore, we should be unable to breathe it. But the air is not pure oxygen—it is practically pure nitrogen; and clearly it could not be of the slightest use to us. This has been emphasized by the eminent German scientist, Dr. Hubertus Strughold, in a recent book which should be read by everyone interested in the subject of Mars.

Earth-type animals being out of the question, what about non-terrestrial beings? Could they have lungs adapted to the peculiar Martian conditions?

We know a great deal about the structure of matter. There are 92 naturally-occurring types of atoms (a few more have been made artificially in recent years), and all material, whether on Earth or anywhere else in the universe, is made up of various combinations of these 92 fundamental "elements." Only two of them, carbon and silicon, have the ability to build up the large, complex atom-groups of "molecules" necessary to form living cells. Carbon is by far the better builder, and so far as we can make out every living creature must be carbon-based. There is no possible chance of our finding a Martian whose body is based upon some other element—gold, for instance—since other atoms are quite unable to link up in the way that carbon does.

We must be careful to distinguish between superficial and fundamental differences. The Earth swarms with all sorts of creatures, and at first sight there is not much resemblance between a camel and a penguin, for example. The camel would soon die if taken to the

Antarctic, while the penguin would be equally unhappy in the Sahara. Yet both are carbon-based, and both need an atmosphere rich in oxygen.

We must therefore dismiss all the fantastic creatures conjured up by the story-tellers. The only loophole for the Martians is to suppose that our spectroscopic measurements are wrong, and that there is, after all, just enough oxygen to support creatures with lungs specially adapted to utilize every scrap of it. This seems improbable, to put it mildly.

When we turn to plant life, the situation is brighter; and as we have seen, it is almost certain that extensive vegetation does exist on Mars.

Plants on Earth are vital to our existence. They take in carbon dioxide from the atmosphere, and use their green colouring matter or "chlorophyll" to combine it with moisture to form living matter, emitting the surplus oxygen in a pure form. This is fortunate for us; animals breathe in oxygen and expel carbon dioxide, so that the plants counteract the harm we do, preventing the atmosphere from becoming too rich in irrespirable carbon dioxide. The key to the whole process of photosynthesis, as it is termed, is the green chlorophyll. If we could discover traces of chlorophyll on Mars, one problem at least would be cleared up once and for all.

Spectroscopic research carried out by the Russian scientist Professor G. A. Tikhoff indicates that the dark areas do indeed show traces of chlorophyll. Up to now Tikhoff's results have not been confirmed this side of the Iron Curtain, and must thus be treated with reserve, but they sound reasonable enough. It is true that certain lowly plants known to us do maintain themselves by a process rather different from that of ordinary photosynthesis, but there seems no reason to manufacture difficulties.

When we come to consider the precise form of the Martian plants, we are reduced to little more than mere guesswork. Tikhoff believes that they absorb the warming red and yellow rays from the Sun and reflect the blue and green, which accounts well for the characteristic hue of the dark areas; we can also assume that the lack of suitable atmosphere rules out any such advanced forms as trees, bushes or even highly-developed flowers. Moss is more likely, but perhaps the best guess is that the Martian plants are similar to those strange and amazingly hardy organisms, the lichens.

To sum up: there is no reason to suppose that low forms of vegetation may not exist on Mars, while there is a great deal of evidence that they do. On the other hand, the thin, oxygen-poor atmosphere is certainly unable to support either animals or men. The fascinating

Martian forests, with their gay red flowers and towering trees, do not exist outside the story-books: and the brilliant, evil beings of the Red Planet are no more real than the shadowy gods of Ancient Olympus.

4. "A Poe-'m of Passion" is, of course, a parody and is just for fun. Since it is light material, the over-all rate would be comparatively rapid, but a sudden slowing down and pausing in crucial places will help communicate some very funny spots.

A POE-'M OF PASSION

C. F. LUMMIS

It was many and many a year ago,
  On an island near the sea,
That a maiden lived whom you mightn't know
  By the name of Cannibalee;
And this maiden she lived with no other thought
  Than a passionate fondness for me.

I was a child, and she was a child—
  Tho' her tastes were adult Feejee—
But she loved with a love that was more than love,
  My yearning Cannibalee;
With a love that could take me roast or fried
  Or raw, as the case might be.

And that is the reason that long ago,
  In that island near the sea,
I had to turn the tables and eat
  My ardent Cannibalee—
Not really because I was fond of her,
  But to check her fondness for me.

But the stars never rise but I think of the size
  Of my hot-potted Cannibalee,
And the moon never stares but it brings me nightmares
  Of my spare-rib Cannibalee;
And all the night-tide she is restless inside,
  Is my still indigestible dinner-belle bride,
In her pallid tomb, which is Me,
  In her solemn sepulcher, Me.

5. "O What Is That Sound" has an interesting rhythmic structure, a question and an answer in each stanza and a regular repetition of words and rimes. In this ballad structure, tension is slowly built up to a tremendous and dramatic climax. If you have a chance to listen to the recordings of this poem by Geraldine Brooks and the poet himself, you will find them radically different and worthy of analytic comparison.

O WHAT IS THAT SOUND

W. H. AUDEN

O what is that sound which so thrills the ear
    Down in the valley drumming, drumming?
Only the scarlet soldiers, dear,
    The soldiers coming.

O what is that light I see flashing so clear
    Over the distance brightly, brightly?
Only the sun on their weapons, dear,
    As they step lightly.

O what are they doing with all that gear,
    What are they doing this morning, this morning?
Only their usual manoeuvres, dear,
    Or perhaps a warning.

O why have they left the road down there,
    Why are they suddenly wheeling, wheeling?
Perhaps a change in their orders, dear.
    Why are you kneeling?

O haven't they stopped for the doctor's care,
    Haven't they reined their horses, their horses?
Why, they are none of them wounded, dear,
    None of these forces.

O is it the parson they want, with white hair,
    Is it the parson, is it, is it?
No, they are passing his gateway, dear,
    Without a visit.

O it must be the farmer who lives so near.
    It must be the farmer so cunning, so cunning?

They have passed the farmyard already, dear,
    And now they are running.

O where are you going? Stay with me here!
    Were the vows you swore deceiving, deceiving?
No, I promised to love you, dear,
    But I must be leaving.

O it's broken the lock and splintered the door,
    O it's the gate where they're turning, turning;
Their boots are heavy on the floor
    And their eyes are burning.

6. Read "The Harlot's House" aloud, noting the mechanical rhythm and the purposeful monotony of the three-line stanzas. Notice how the last line, departing from metrical form by having only six syllables rather than eight, must receive careful treatment by the interpreter. How would you handle it?

THE HARLOT'S HOUSE

OSCAR WILDE

We caught the tread of dancing feet,
We loitered down the moonlit street,
And stopped beneath the harlot's house.

Inside, above the din and fray,
We heard the loud musicians play
The "Treues Liebes Herz" of Strauss.

Like strange mechanical grotesques,
Making fantastic arabesques,
The shadows raced across the blind.

We watched the ghostly dancers spin
To sound of horn and violin,
Like black leaves wheeling in the wind.

Like wire-pulled automatons,
Slim silhouetted skeletons
Went sidling through the slow quadrille.

They took each other by the hand,
And danced a stately saraband;
Their laughter echoed thin and shrill.

Sometimes a clockwork puppet pressed
A phantom lover to her breast,
Sometimes they seemed to try to sing.

Sometimes a horrible marionette
Came out, and smoked its cigarette
Upon the steps like a live thing.

Then, turning to my love, I said,
"The dead are dancing with the dead,
The dust is whirling with the dust."

But she—she heard the violin,
And left my side and entered in:
Love passed into the house of lust.

Then suddenly the tune went false,
The dancers wearied of the waltz,
The shadows ceased to wheel and whirl

And down the long and silent street,
The dawn, with silver-sandaled feet,
Crept like a frightened girl.

7. When prose is beautiful, as it is in this passage from Lawrence Durrell's *Clea,* it becomes rhythmical. What rhythmical elements can you find? While studying it, also be on the lookout for instances in which duration must be used for effective interpretation.

from CLEA

LAWRENCE DURRELL

It was still dark when we lay up outside the invisible harbour with its remembered outworks of forts and anti-submarine nets. I tried to paint the outlines on the darkness with my mind. The boom was raised only at dawn each day. An all-obliterating darkness reigned. Somewhere ahead of us lay the invisible coast of Africa, with its "kiss of thorns" as the Arabs say. It was intolerable to be so aware of them, the towers and minarets of the city, and yet to be unable to will them to appear. I could not see my own fingers before my face. The sea had become a vast empty ante-room, a hollow bubble of blackness.

Then suddenly there passed a sudden breath, a whiff like a wind passing across a bed of embers, and the nearer distance glowed pink as a sea-shell, deepening gradually into the rose-richness of a flower. A faint and terrible moaning came out across the water towards us, pulsing like the wing-beats of some fearful prehistoric bird—sirens which howled as the damned must howl in limbo. One's nerves were shaken like the branches of a tree. And as if in response to this sound lights began to prick out everywhere, sporadically at first, then in ribbons, bands, squares of crystal. The harbour suddenly outlined itself with complete clarity upon the dark panels of heaven, while long white fingers of powder-white light began to stalk about the sky in ungainly fashion, as if they were the legs of some awkward insect struggling to gain a purchase on the slippery black. A dense stream of coloured rockets now began to mount from the haze among the battleships, emptying on the sky their brilliant clusters of stars and diamonds and smashed pearl snuff-boxes with a marvellous prodigality. The air shook in strokes. Clouds of pink and yellow dust arose with the maroons to shine upon the greasy buttocks of the barrage balloons which were flying everywhere. The very sea seemed to tremble. I had had no idea that we were so near, or that the city could be so beautiful in the mere saturnalia of a war. It had begun to swell up, to expand like some mystical rose of the darkness, and the bombardment kept it company, overflowing the mind. To our surprise we found ourselves shouting at each other. We were staring at the burning embers of Augustine's Carthage, I thought to myself, we were observing the fall of city man.

It was as beautiful as it was stupefying. In the top left-hand corner of the tableau the searchlights had begun to congregate, quivering and sliding in their ungainly fashion, like daddy-long-legs. They intersected and collided feverishly, and it was clear that some signal had reached them which told of the struggles of some trapped insect on the outer cobweb of darkness. Again and again they crossed, probed, merged, divided. Then at last we saw what they were bracketing: six tiny silver moths moving down the skylanes with what seemed unbearable slowness. The sky had gone mad around them yet they still moved with this fatal languor; and languidly too curled the curving strings of hot diamonds which spouted up from the ships, or the rank lacklustre sniffs of cloudy shrapnel which marked their progress.

And deafening as was the roaring which now filled our ears it was possible to isolate many of the separate sounds which orchestrated the bombardment. The crackle of shards which fell back like a hailstorm upon the corrugated roofs of the waterside cafes: the scratchy mechanical voices of ships' signallers repeating, in the voices of ventriloquists' dummies, semi-intelligible phrases which sounded like "Three o'clock red, Three o'clock red". Strangely too, there was music somewhere at the heart of all the hubbub, jagged quartertones which stabbed; then, too, the foundering roar of buildings falling. Patches of light which disappeared and left an aperture of darkness at which a dirty yellow flame might come and lap like a thirsty animal. Nearer at hand (the water smacked the echo out) we could hear the rich harvest of spent cannon-shells pouring upon the decks from the Chicago Pianos: an almost continuous splashing of golden metal tumbling from the breeches of the skypointed guns.

So it went on, feasting the eye yet making the vertebrae quail before the whirlwind of meaningless power it disclosed. I had not realised the impersonality of war before. There was no room for human beings or thought of them under this vast umbrella of coloured death. Each drawn breath had become only a temporary refuge.

Then, almost as suddenly as it had started, the spectacle died away. The harbour vanished with theatrical suddenness, the string of precious stones was turned off, the sky emptied, the silence drenched us, only to be broken once more by that famished crying of the sirens which drilled at the nerves. And then, nothing—a nothingness weighing tons of darkness out of which grew the smaller and more familiar sounds of water licking at the gunwales. A faint shore-wind crept out to invest us with the alluvial smells of an invisible estuary. Was it only in my imagination that I heard from far away the sounds of wild-fowl on the lake?

We waited thus for a long time in great indecision; but meanwhile from the east the dawn had begun to overtake the sky, the city and desert. Human voices, weighted like lead, came softly out, stirring curiosity and compassion. Children's voices—and in the west a sputum-coloured meniscus on the horizon. We yawned, it was cold. Shivering, we turned to one another, feeling suddenly orphaned in this benighted world between light and darkness.

But gradually it grew up from the eastern marches, this familiar dawn, the first overflow of citron and rose which would set the dead waters of Mareotis a-glitter; and fine as a hair, yet so indistinct that one had to stop breathing to verify it, I heard (or thought I heard) the first call to prayer from some as yet invisible minaret.

Were there, then, still gods left to invoke? And even as the question entered my mind I saw, shooting from the harbour-mouth, the three small fishing-boats—sails of rust, liver and blue plum. They heeled upon a freshet and stooped across our bows like hawks. We could hear the rataplan of water lapping their prows. The small figures, balanced like riders, hailed us in Arabic to tell us that the boom was up, that we might enter harbour.

8. What words would you savor (dwell upon, using duration of sound) in reading this poem. Why? If possible, contrast your work with John Gielgud's recording of the poem.

PRELUDES

T. S. ELIOT

(I) The winter evening settles down
With smell of steaks in passageways.
Six o'clock.
The burnt-out ends of smoky days.
And now a gusty shower wraps
The grimy scraps
Of withered leaves about your feet
And newspapers from vacant lots;
The showers beat
On broken blinds and chimney-pots,
And at the corner of the street
A lonely cab-horse steams and stamps.
And then the lighting of the lamps.

(II) The morning comes to consciousness
Of faint stale smells of beer
From the sawdust-trampled street
With all its muddy feet that press
To early coffee-stands.
With the other masquerades
That time resumes,
One thinks of all the hands
That are raising dingy shades
In a thousand furnished rooms.

(III) You tossed a blanket from the bed,
You lay upon your back, and waited;
You dozed, and watched the night revealing
The thousand sordid images
Of which your soul was constituted;

They flickered against the ceiling.
And when all the world came back
And the light crept up between the shutters
And you heard the sparrows in the gutters,
You had such a vision of the street
As the street hardly understands;
Sitting along the bed's edge, where
You curled the papers from your hair,
Or clasped the yellow soles of feet
In the palms of both soiled hands.

(IV) His soul stretched tight across the skies
That fade behind a city block,
Or trampled by insistent feet
At four and five and six o'clock;
And short square fingers stuffing pipes,
And evening newspapers, and eyes
Assured of certain certainties,
The conscience of a blackened street
Impatient to assume the world.
I am moved by fancies that are curled
Around these images, and cling:
The notion of some infinitely gentle
Infinitely suffering thing.

Wipe your hand across your mouth, and laugh;
The worlds revolve like ancient women
Gathering fuel in vacant lots.

9. Repeat Exercise 8 with the following poem. If possible, listen to the poet's own recording of this poem. Thomas, probably better than any other reader, made maximum use of duration.

IN MY CRAFT OR SULLEN ART

DYLAN THOMAS

In my craft or sullen art
Exercised in the still night
When only the moon rages
And the lovers lie abed
With all their griefs in their arms,
I labour by singing light

Not for ambition or bread
Or the strut and trade of charms
On the ivory stages
But for the common wages
Of their most secret heart.
Not for the proud man apart
From the raging moon I write
On these spindrift pages
Not for the towering dead
With their nightingales and psalms
But for the lovers, their arms
Round the griefs of the ages,
Who pay no praise or wages
Nor heed my craft or art.

10. Find all examples you can of onomatopoeia and other significant sound values in the following poem.

A GOOD NIGHT

WILLIAM CARLOS WILLIAMS

Go to sleep—though of course you will not—
to tideless waves thundering slantwise against
strong embankments, rattle and swish of spray
dashed thirty feet high, caught by the lake wind,
scattered and strewn broadcast in over the steady
car rails! Sleep, sleep! Gulls' cries in a wind-gust
broken by the wind; calculating wings set above
the field of waves breaking.
Go to sleep to the lunge between foam-crests,
refuse churned in the recoil. Food! Food!
Offal! Offal! that holds them in the air, wave-white
for the one purpose, feather upon feather, the wild
chill in their eyes, the hoarseness in their voices—
sleep, sleep . . .

Gentlefooted crowds are treading out your lullaby.
Their arms nudge, they brush shoulders,
hitch this way then that, mass and surge at the crossings—
lullaby, lullaby! The wild-fowl police whistles,
the enraged roar of the traffic, machine shrieks:

it is all to put you to sleep,
to soften your limbs in relaxed postures,
and that your head slip sidewise, and your hair loosen
and fall over your eyes and over your mouth,
brushing your lips wistfully that you may dream,
sleep and dream—

A black fungus springs out about lonely church doors—
sleep, sleep. The Night, coming down upon
the wet boulevard, would start you awake with his
message, to have in at your window. Pay no
heed to him. He storms at your sill with
cooings, with gesticulations, curses!
You will not let him in. He would keep you from sleeping.
He would have you sit under your desk lamp
brooding, pondering; he would have you
slide out the drawer, take up the ornamented dagger
and handle it. It is late, it is nineteen-nineteen—
go to sleep, his cries are a lullaby;
his jabbering is a sleep-well-my-baby; he is
a crackbrained messenger.

The maid waking you in the morning
when you are up and dressing,
the rustle of your clothes as you raise them—
it is the same tune.
At table the cold, greenish, split grapefruit, its juice
on the tongue, the clink of the spoon in
your coffee, the toast odors say it over and over.

The open street-door lets in the breath of
the morning wind from over the lake.
The bus coming to a halt grinds from its sullen brakes—
lullaby, lullaby. The crackle of a newspaper,
the movement of the troubled coat beside you—
sleep, sleep, sleep, sleep . . .
It is the sting of snow, the burning liquor of
the moonlight, the rush of rain in the gutters packed
with dead leaves: go to sleep, go to sleep.
And the night passes—and never passes—

11. Look for examples of onomatopoeia in other selections in this book.
12. Analyze the uses of time by professional readers who have made

recordings. If possible, compare two different readings of the same piece of literature, as we have done in this chapter.

13. Select three distinctly different types of literature in respect to their demands for rate and time yourself in reading them, to see whether you have adequate variety of rate.

14. Try reading the same selection in a variety of acoustical situations, such as a radio studio, a small classroom, a large classroom, an auditorium, outdoors, and in various places using a public address system. Study the demands made by each situation upon your phrasing and pausing.

15. Study several selections in this book and select one which demands a slow rate, one which requires a fast rate, and one which calls for several different rates. Be able to justify your conclusions.

16. Enlist the cooperation of three or four other students from your class in conducting an experiment. All of you should agree upon one short prose or poetic selection to read. Study it and practice reading it. Separately, record your readings. Then, compare your interpretations as to rate, use of pauses, and emphasis of thought-centers.

Suggested Readings

Rosenthal, M. L., and A. J. M. Smith. *Exploring Poetry.* New York: Macmillan, 1955, "Sound and Sense" (see Index).

Stageberg, Norman E., and Wallace L. Anderson. *Poetry as Experience.* New York: American Book, 1952, Chapter VI, "Sound Symbolism."

Woolbert, Charles H., and Severina E. Nelson. *The Art of Interpretative Speech.* (4th edition) New York: Appleton-Century-Crofts, 1956, Chapter 9, "Vocal Tempo."

9

AUDIBLE COMMUNICATION THROUGH LOUDNESS

Here are six common English words with their pronunciations. In each case the standard spelling is followed by the diacritical markings from *Webster's Third New International Dictionary of the English Language Unabridged* and the phonetic symbols from Kenyon and Knott's *A Pronouncing Dictionary of American English*. Read the words aloud clearly pronouncing each several times.

livelihood, /'līvlēˌhu̇d/['laɪvlɪˌhʊd]
indent, /ən'dent/[ɪn'dɛnt]
grimy, /grīmē/['graɪmɪ]
fanatic, /fə'nɑd ik/[fə'nætɪk]
cohesion, /kō'hēzhən/[ko'hiʒən]
chiropractor, /kīrəˌprɑktə(r)/['kaɪrəˌpræktɚ]

Which syllable of *livelihood* was said with the most force? Which syllable of *grimy?* Reread all six words and you will find that normally the accented syllable is the one spoken with the greatest degree of loudness, the highest pitch, and the longest duration.

Of course, sound must have loudness, pitch, and duration to be recognized as sound, but from our experiment in pronunciation we see that variation in these respects is inherent in the nature of intelligible speech. Such variation is not confined simply to the presence and the absence of accent. *Indent* and *grimy* have two levels of loudness and pitch, but *chiropractor* has at least three such levels: *chi* carries the primary accent, *prac* carries the secondary accent, and the remaining two syllables are unaccented. Long acquaintance with English pronunciation enables us to employ unconsciously many different degrees of loudness, pitch, and duration. Therefore, we say that these factors are two of the major variables in spoken language and of the utmost importance in expressing meaning.

THE NECESSITY FOR LOUDNESS

Perhaps you have attended an amateur play where you had great difficulty hearing the actors' lines. You may have strained your ears and still found the words unintelligible. This kind of experience can provide a most frustrating evening. You will agree that loudness sufficient for audibility is the first requirement for the success of any oral expression. It must be heard and understood. Nothing else matters if speech is not heard. Careful timing, dramatic pauses, meaningful inflections, and artistic quality are all wasted when loudness is inadequate. If you have ever seen a silent movie or a television program without the audio in which the actors mouthed and gesticulated in an elegant and realistic fashion while you wondered what it was all about, you know how pathetic and even ludicrous it can be for an audience to *watch* the speech arts at work and not be able to *hear* them. Spoken language must be heard to be understood.

Apparently, however, there are people who have not grasped this obvious fact. Teachers and students are all too familiar with the person who participates in discussion or rises publicly to speak or read in a tiny, mousy voice that almost no one can hear. Usually such a person is mildly offended when it is suggested that he repeat what he has said. Sometimes a girl protests that she cannot speak any louder, yet she can easily be heard in halls, on the athletic field, or at a party. She somehow seems to feel that in a formal situation it is the essence of propriety to speak so quietly that she simply cannot be heard. If you have been guilty of this kind of speaking or reading, decide finally that far from being genteel or proper, speech which is too quiet is useless. While there is normally no occasion to shout, there is every occasion to be heard.

THE NATURE OF LOUDNESS

The speech scientist tells us that loudness is that quality of sound responsible for the impact upon the ear. Perhaps we might call it the inherent weight of sound. The same sound has different degrees of loudness when heard at ten feet from its source and at forty feet. The degree of loudness is also determined by the amount of force exerted on the vibrator, which in the case of voice is the vocal folds. Thus, a sound may be very *intense* at the point of origin because a great deal of *force* has been exerted to produce it. At that point it may be heard as a very *loud* sound, but at some distance it will be less loud although no less intense. *Loudness* refers to the effect upon a listener. *Force* is merely the motivating element responsible for the sound. *Intensity* is descriptive of the physical nature of the sound wave.

VARIATION IN LOUDNESS FOR MEANING

Not only is loudness necessary for simple audibility, but variation in loudness is essential to the communication of meaning. This fact was evident in our reading of the six words at the beginning of this chapter. Try to read them again with exactly the same amount of loudness on every syllable:

livelihood, indent, grimy, fanatic,
cohesion, chiropractor

If you have been successful in using a monoloudness, you have probably made these familiar words almost meaningless and unrecognizable.

In Chapter 4 you experimented with the sentence, "I am going to Chicago" and discovered that it could be made to convey many different meanings. By slightly increasing your loudness on a single different word each time, you were able to express five different meanings. Of course, you made changes in other vocal variables too, but loudness is the element under consideration here. Now try the same experiment with a more complicated sentence. Employing the greatest degree of loudness on a different word each time, see how many meanings you can convey with this sentence:

> The great convenience of masterpieces is that they are so astonishingly lucid.—MATTHEW ARNOLD

You will be able to increase the number of meanings by stressing more than one word at a time.

When you have satisfied yourself that several meanings are possible, read the sentence once more with one consistent, unchanging level of loudness.

> *The great convenience of masterpieces is that they are so astonishingly lucid.*

It is not likely that any clear meaning will be conveyed. This last reading is not the kind you expect from the mature person. For effective reading it is essential to vary the application of force. This fact the clever radio or television news reporter learns early in his career. Although he maintains a basic level of volume, he sometimes conveys the meaning he wishes by the simple expedient of appropriately varying the loudness. Of course, he is not likely to use this technique in isolation. Sometimes, unfortunately, he will deliberately editorialize without adding or subtracting from the words that come in over the press wires. If you will read aloud the following news item and stress those words underlined, you will see that a minor distortion is easily achieved. Of course, variation of loudness is only one of the means of emphasis.

> The United States government wound up the fiscal year nine million dollars in the red. One reason for the deficit was a carry-over of bills incurred by the Democratic administration. Others were disappointing tax collections and the inability of the Republicans to achieve all of their promised economies. The administration remains confident that despite a tradition of expensive government the margin of deficit will be further reduced.

Now read this version remembering again to stress the underlined words.

> The United States government wound up the fiscal year nine million dollars in the red. One reason for the deficit was a carry-over of bills incurred by the Democratic administration. Others were disappointing tax collections and the inability of the Republicans to achieve all of their promised economies. The administration remains confident that despite a tradition of expensive government the margin of deficit will be further reduced.

Can you tell which is more favorable to the Republicans and which to the Democrats?

Loudness is only one of the speech variables. Practically speaking we almost never vary the loudness alone to express different meanings. Instead we combine changes in time, quality, and visible action as well as pitch and loudness. The techniques of variability are not used in isolation, but we must study them in isolation for the sake of clarity.

VARIATION IN LOUDNESS FOR RHYTHM

Varying degrees of loudness are also required for rhythm of language. Copy this limerick and mark the accents, as we have done in the first line:

There wás an old mán of Taréntum,
Who gnashed his false teeth till he bent 'em.
When they asked him the cost
Of what he had lost,
He replied, "I can't say, for I rent 'em."

Read the limerick aloud, employing the accents you have marked, and you will see that they are achieved primarily by increased loudness and higher pitch. This change of loudness for rhythm is not confined to light verse, or serious, either, for that matter. Copy this sentence and mark the accents.

> Is life so dear, or peace so sweet, as to be purchased at the price of chains and slavery?—PATRICK HENRY

Rhythm in prose, like rhythm in verse, may be expressed largely through accents of loudness, although it is also achieved through pauses, repetitions of words, and other devices.

Having observed that loudness is necessary for audibility, that it must be varied to transmit the sense the speaker intends, and that it is used to reveal the rhythm of both verse and prose, we are ready to study *how* you can *produce* adequate loudness and *control* its application.

ABDOMINAL CONTROL OF BREATHING

To the speech correction clinic of a large university a few years ago came a young man whom we shall call Dick. He was referred to the clinic by his teacher of public speaking because of a very weak voice. The cause was thought to be spastic paralysis incurred many years before. Dick was now an obviously healthy young man. His paralysis had so challenged his courage that he had become an all-round athlete, excelling in swimming, tennis, and other sports. Yet when he faced his public speaking class, he seemed unable to make himself heard. Furthermore, he became so frightened that speaking made him actually ill. After hearing Dick speak, studying his breathing, and observing his tension, the clinicians decided that Dick's spasticity was completely irrelevant and that apparently his whole trouble resulted from inadequate breathing.

Dick was a chest breather. Somewhere he had learned to breathe unnaturally. Perhaps a misinformed teacher had urged him to throw back his shoulders and expand his chest, to breathe deeply, all the while holding in his abdomen in the manner of a military caricature. In other words, he tried to increase his chest capacity simply by expanding the rib cage.

The cage itself, however, is relatively rigid, and its expansion alone does not provide maximum room for inhalation. Inhalation requires that the chest cavity be enlarged to produce a partial vacuum, and the only way to achieve the necessary room is to expand the chest cavity downward as well as from front to back and side to side. The floor of that cavity is largely muscular and separates the chest from the vital organs in the abdomen. The contraction of the diaphragm, a dome-shaped structure, enlarges the room for the lungs by pushing the contents of the abdomen downward and outward. When the diaphragm is relaxed, the return of the abdominal organs to their normal position provides sufficient pressure for effortless exhalation. On the other hand, controlled exhalation, as in speech, requires the contraction of the muscles of the abdominal cavity. As they force the abdominal organs inward and upward, the chest cavity is made smaller, and air is forcefully exhaled from the lungs.

During his many sessions in the clinic Dick relearned the method of breathing he had naturally practiced as a baby. He lay on his back with a book resting on his abdomen just below the bottom ribs and watched it rise and fall. The strokes or movements of the diaphragm caused the abdominal wall in front, on the sides, and in the back to move outward every time he inhaled. As Dick stood facing a clinician, he felt that same movement on the clinician's body and tried to reproduce it in his own. With abdominal control of breathing he slowly acquired a much greater lung capacity. He engaged in regular practice periods of extended phonation of vowel sounds. Eventually he was able to produce continuous sound twice as long as when he had first come to the clinic.

The next step was to employ his increased lung capacity and control of exhalation in making a broken vowel sound. For example, he practiced saying "ah, ah, ah" as many times as he could with one breath. Each syllable of sound employed a partial contraction of the abdominal muscles. When he added a consonant like "p" or "b" in front of the vowel, even more careful muscular control was needed. Of course, it was a long step to transfer such techniques of breathing to the normal speech processes, but Dick was eventually able to return to his public speaking class and to employ far more force in speaking than ever before. More remarkable, however, was the way in which stage fright diminished. Since he no longer depended on a rigid and straining chest to produce his power, the tensions in his chest and throat were largely relieved. The larger and more capable muscles of the abdomen did the work while the throat area relaxed to produce full and resonant tones. Dick's pitch was noticeably lower, and the quality of his voice much more pleasant. He could speak at great length with little fatigue and no loss of force.

Although your speaking and breathing habits are probably much better than Dick's, you may still be trying to breathe with too little action of the diaphragm and abdomen. If you are a singer, ask your vocal teacher; if you are an athlete, ask your coach. Either one will assure you that abdominal breathing promotes vocal and bodily relaxation, provides more oxygen for the blood stream, makes for better control of exhalation, and permits greater and more sustained use of force.

The first six steps in the following formula will help you to discover whether you have adequate breathing habits, and the remaining five will enable you to make more use of abdominal breathing.

1. To observe genuine abdominal breathing, lie on your back and hold your chest high with a book resting just below the sternum or breastbone. Watch the book rise and fall as you breathe. In order to increase the "feel" of such breathing, increase the number of books.

2. Remaining on your back and removing the books, place your hand just below the sternum or breastbone and feel the movement of the abdominal wall as you breathe. Then stand, put your hand in the same spot, and see if you continue to breathe in the same way.

3. Pant in quick breaths with the mouth open. You should be able to feel vigorous abdominal thrusts.

4. Inhale all the breath you can hold and then blow it out in a long whistle. As you reach the end of the whistle, prolong it by pressing with both hands against the abdomen just below the ribs. With proper breathing you should be able to whistle for fifteen or twenty seconds.

5. If you would like to see a mechanical illustration of abdominal breathing, study the action of a hand-operated bicycle or automobile tire pump. Hold the pump upside down so that you can visualize the force of the abdominal muscles pushing the air out of the lungs from below.

6. Using abdominal breathing, practice the extended phonation of some vowel sound for as long as one breath will permit. You ought to be able to hold the tone for twenty to thirty seconds. If you are unable to sustain it this long, practice the exercise repeatedly over a period of several days until you have substantially increased your time. Learn not to waste your breath on too rapid exhalation.

7. Instead of holding the same sound, try a succession of different vowel sounds with only one breath, beginning each one separately from the previous sound. You should be able to make twenty or thirty different sounds with one breath. Again it may be necessary to practice repeatedly for several days.

8. With short quick strokes of the diaphragm and abdominal muscles phonate a series of separate vowel sounds, each with a separate breath. Be sure you can feel the breathing action with one hand on the front of your body just below the sternum.

9. Now do the same exercise beginning each phonation with the sound of a consonant such as p, b, k, g, t, d, s, or sh. Try them all and try them often, making sure you employ abdominal action.

10. Practice reading the following lines, holding the longer vowel sounds and clearly articulating the consonants. Speak with enough volume for a large room.

a. We want a basket! We want a basket!
b. Go team go! Go team go!
c. Yu, rah, rah, Statesville College! Yu, rah, rah, Statesville College!
d. Boomlay, boomlay, boomlay, boom!
e. Mumbo Jumbo will hoodoo you.
f. Mark Twain! (Find out what it means!)
g. On your mark, get set, go!
h. Help! Thief!
i. Run! Run! Lions!

USING LOUDNESS TO CONVEY SENSE

Assuming now that you are able to employ sufficient loudness to be heard, we shall study the use of loudness to convey sense. Speak into the microphone of a recording machine and watch the "eye" to see the little fan in it become smaller every time the loudness increases. The thought-centers will be mechanically indicated every time normal speech is recorded. You may observe this same phenomenon in the action of the volume hand on the control board of a public address system or radio studio. The hand will swing farthest to the right on the thought-centers as normal speech is directed into the microphone.

Perhaps you have heard the efforts of a child who is just beginning to read. Because he does not distinguish thought-centers, he is inclined to stroke all syllables with the same amount of force, much like a beginning typist stroking all keys with equal force. Such reading is often almost unintelligible. Just as the skilled typist uses less force on the comma and period keys, the child ultimately learns to use less force on the less important words and syllables and more on the more important.

This process of emphasizing the significant and de-emphasizing the insignificant you must now learn to perfect. In order that you may save the time necessary to get acquainted with a new selection, turn back to Chapter 5 and reread aloud "Create Great Peace." After you have reviewed thought-centers in the poem, emphasize them by increasing the loudness as you say the significant words. In the first line the words "end war" will be spoken somewhat louder than the rest. In the second line "great" will receive the emphasis. In the third the loudness will increase with "all." Go on through the whole poem and apply this same principle of pointing up thought-centers by means of increased loudness. You will want to emphasize primary thought-centers more than the secondary ones. You will discover that as ideas vary greatly in importance, so the level of loudness will vary too.

The following sentences will give you an opportunity to practice the principles we have been learning. Determine the thought-centers in each. Then read aloud the sentences increasing your loudness in different degrees to point up those thought-centers.

1. Peace is rarely denied to the peaceful.—SCHILLER

2. If nobody loves you, be sure it is your own fault.—PHILIP DODDRIDGE

3. A new commandment I give unto you, that you love one another.—JESUS

4. I believe Plato and Socrates. I believe in Jesus Christ.—SAMUEL TAYLOR COLERIDGE

5. Some books are to be tasted; others swallowed; and some few to be chewed and digested.—FRANCIS BACON

6. There is only one virtue, pugnacity; only one vice, pacifism. That is an essential condition of war.—GEORGE BERNARD SHAW

When you have had the foregoing practice in the use of loudness to point up the relative significance of ideas, you are ready to attempt the same task in an extended piece of literature. To make the experience an interesting one, you may use the following excerpt from a letter by Robert Browning written shortly after the death of his wife. The romance of Robert and Elizabeth Barrett Browning has been immortalized in Virginia Woolf's *Flush: A Biography* and in Elizabeth's own love lyrics published under the title, *Sonnets from the Portuguese.* If you do not know the story of their love, find out something about it before you read this selection. Be sure to read Elizabeth's "How do I love thee?" in Chapter 3. Now carry out all of the steps in finding the meaning (Chapter 5) and then try to read aloud the following lines taking special care to distinguish the relative importance of ideas by means of varying the loudness. Of course, you will use changes in time, quality, visible action, and pitch as well.

from LETTER TO MISS HAWORTH

ROBERT BROWNING

. . . The main comfort is that she suffered very little pain, none beside that ordinarily attending the simple attacks of cold and cough she was subject to—had no presentiment of the result whatever, and was consequently spared the misery of knowing she was about to leave us; she was smilingly assuring me she was "better," "quite comfortable"—if I would but "come to bed," to within a few minutes of the last. I think I foreboded evil at Rome, certainly from the beginning of the week's illness—but when I reasoned about it, there was no justifying fear—she said on the last evening, "It is merely the old attack, not so severe a one as that of two years ago—there is no doubt I shall soon recover," and we talked over plans for the summer, and next year. I sent the servants away and her maid to bed—so little reason for disquietude did there seem. Through the night she slept heavily, and brokenly—that was the bad sign—but then she would sit up, take her medicine, say unrepeatable things to me and sleep again. At four o'clock there were symptoms that alarmed me; I called the maid and sent for the doctor. She smiled as I proposed to bathe her feet, "Well, you *are* determined to make an exaggerated case of it!" Then came what my heart will keep till I see her again and longer—the most perfect expression of her love to me within my whole knowledge of her. Always smiling, happily, and with a face like a girl's—and in a few minutes she died in my arms; her head on my cheek. These incidents so sustain me that I tell them to her beloved ones as their right: there was no lingering, nor acute pain, nor consciousness of separation, but God took her to himself as you would lift a sleeping child from a dark, uneasy bed into your arms and the light. Thank God. . . .

TOUCH

When this principle of varying the loudness according to the sense is applied to extended phrases, sentences, paragraphs, or even to whole selections, it is called *touch*. We read, "The rattling old Ford galloped by" with a different touch—that is, with a different over-all use of loudness—than we use on, "Slowly and silently the funeral procession wound by." Another instance of how touch differs may be seen in the following poem and an excerpt from a speech.

WHO LOVES THE RAIN

FRANCES SHAW

Who loves the rain
And loves his home,
And looks on life with quiet eyes,
Him will I follow through the storm;
And at his hearth-fire keep me warm;
Nor heaven nor hell shall that soul surprise,
Who loves the rain,
And loves his home,
And looks on life with quiet eyes.

Come then; let us to the task, to the battle, to the toil. . . . We shall fight on the beaches, we shall fight on the landing grounds, we shall fight in the fields and in the streets, we shall fight in the hills; we shall never surrender.—WINSTON CHURCHILL

Obviously the quiet and philosophic poem requires a different touch from Sir Winston's ringing oratory. To distinguish among the various kinds of touch is, however, extremely difficult, for touch is determined by at least three unmeasurable and intangible factors: the highly personalized nature of meaning, the reader's habits and capacities of speech, and his willingness to express meaning without inhibition. On the other hand, different kinds of literature do suggest decidedly different kinds of touch.

We speak of three kinds of touch or attack: *gentle, conversational,* and *forceful*. These terms are by no means descriptive of all the possibilities in touch, but we use them for the sake of major distinctions. Each will be best understood if illustrated.

The calm, soothing, and lullaby-like nature of the following poem suggests the use of *gentle* touch. Avoid any decided change in loudness, pitch, or timing.

FOUR LITTLE FOXES

LEW SARETT

Speak gently, Spring, and make no sudden sound;
For in my windy valley yesterday I found
New-born foxes squirming on the ground—
Speak gently.

Walk softly, March, forbear the bitter blow;
Her feet within a trap, her blood upon the snow,
The four little foxes saw their mother go—
Walk softly.

Go lightly, Spring—oh, give them no alarm;
When I covered them with boughs to shelter them from harm,
The thin blue foxes suckled at my arm—
Go lightly.

Step softly, March, with your rampant hurricane;
Nuzzling one another, and whimpering with pain,
The new little foxes are shivering in the rain—
Step softly.

The *conversational* touch is that which we normally employ with the simplest and most direct conversation. The following quotation from a charming and witty personal essay is a good example of the kind of literature which you will want to read with a *conversational* touch.

When you read, make the selection sound as if someone is talking directly and sincerely but not dramatically. You will employ much variety of loudness. To put it briefly, you will be *conversational.*

from FRESHMAN ADVISER

GEORGE BOAS

We are sitting pencil in hand, surrounded by college catalogues, rules and regulations, directories, handbooks, mimeographed slips with last-minute changes of courses on them, folders with big cards for the student records, pads with two carbons on which to write out schedules. We are all washed and clean, fresh from a summer in which we were supposed to rest and which we spent making enough money to fill out the gap between our salaries and a living wage. We are all resigned to the winter that is before us. . . . We smile . . . and sigh at the mass of paper. . . .

You know, of course, that anger or excitement often prompts you to employ more loudness and to employ it more abruptly than normally. In this quotation from one of our very best murder stories the nobleman Macduff is rousing the slumbering household to announce that the king has been killed in his sleep. If you are to convey the meaning, you will have to fill your lungs to capacity and say the words with quick, heavy strokes of the abdominal muscles. Probably you will want to use the most climactic intensity near the end of the third line and again in the last three lines. We call this a *forceful* touch.

Awake! Awake!
Ring the alarum-bell:—murder and treason!
Banquo and Donalbain! Malcolm! awake!
Shake off this downy sleep, death's counterfeit,
And look on death itself! up, up, and see
The great doom's image! Malcolm! Banquo!
As from your graves rise up, and walk like sprites,
To countenance this horror!

—SHAKESPEARE, *Macbeth*

As you become more skilled in reading, you will realize that instead of employing only three kinds of touch you can use many different degrees of each and probably other quite different touches as well. Your employment of touch will become a matter of simply adapting the application of force to the nature of what you are reading.

PROJECTION

Now that we have discussed loudness at length, we turn to an important technique known as *projection*. If you hold up before an audience a small glass slide which is meant for projection upon a screen, its detail will be almost indistinguishable because the size is inadequate. If, on the other hand, you place the slide in a projector and throw the image on a screen, everyone in the room will be able to appreciate the color, form, and detail, for the size is now adequate. Projection in public speaking or reading is much the same. It is enlargement of the normal characteristics of conversational speech. It will appear as natural and be as meaningful in the back row of the auditorium as in the front row.

Projection is enlargement of *all* the aspects of visible and audible speech. Visibly, facial expression and bodily action are more obvious. The small sneer easily seen at a distance of a few feet becomes a larger one. A slight movement of the head may become a movement of the entire body. Audibly, all vocal techniques are enlarged. Loudness is increased without the strain and distortion of a shout. The speaker may exert more force upon the breath stream, but he also achieves vocal projection by means of increased resonance: he opens his mouth more and relaxes the pharyngeal walls so that the resonating cavities reinforce the vocal tones. The result is improved vocal quality as well as increased audibility. In addition, the speaker slows his rate of utterance and uses long, well-placed pauses following the most important words or thoughts. He increases the duration of words, especially those deserving emphasis. He extends the range of pitch employed. His inflectional patterns are more pronounced. His speech melody is enhanced and is therefore more expressive. Indeed, the whole process of visible and audible communication is *enlarged.*

Never forget that you must adjust both the visible and the audible aspects of utterance to the circumstances of the speaking situation.

Summary

Loudness is necessary for audibility. Furthermore, a variety of loudness must be employed to convey meaning and to express the rhythms inherent in language. If you are to employ loudness effectively, you should use abdominal breathing. Focus attention upon thought-centers by modification of the vocal variables, including loudness. Use the appropriate touch for the selection being read. Strive to project, which is to enlarge all the aspects of utterance.

Exercises

1. Reading to children is excellent practice in developing effective use of touch. Practice reading the following selections to youngsters.

THE DUEL

EUGENE FIELD

The gingham dog and the calico cat
Side by side on the table sat;
'T was half-past twelve, and (what do you think!)
Nor one nor t' other had slept a wink!
    The old Dutch clock and the Chinese plate

Appeared to know as sure as fate
There was going to be a terrible spat.
(I wasn't there; I simply state
What was told to me by the Chinese plate!)

The gingham dog went "bow-wow-wow!"
And the calico cat replied "me-ow!"
The air was littered, an hour or so,
With bits of gingham and calico,
While the old Dutch clock in the chimney-place
Up with its hands before its face,
For it always dreaded a family row!
(Now mind: I'm only telling you
What the old Dutch clock declares is true!)

The Chinese plate looked very blue,
And wailed, "Oh, dear! what shall we do!"
But the gingham dog and the calico cat
Wallowed this way and tumbled that,
Employing every tooth and claw
In the awfulest way you ever saw—
And, oh! how the gingham and calico flew!
(Don't fancy I exaggerate—
I got my news from the Chinese plate!)

Next morning, where the two had sat
They found no trace of dog or cat;
And some folks think unto this day
That burglars stole that pair away!
But the truth about the cat and pup
Is this: they ate each other up!
Now what do you really think of that!
The old Dutch clock it told me so,
And that is how I came to know.)

THE PLAINT OF THE CAMEL

GUY WETMORE CARRYL

"Canary-birds feed on sugar and seed,
Parrots have crackers to crunch;
And, as for the poodles, they tell me the noodles
Have chickens and cream for their lunch.

But there's never a question
About MY digestion—
ANYTHING does for me!

"Cats, you're aware, can repose in a chair,
Chickens can roost upon rails;
Puppies are able to sleep in a stable,
And oysters can slumber in pails.
But no one supposes
A poor Camel dozes—
ANY PLACE does for me!

"Lambs are enclosed where it's never exposed,
Coops are constructed for hens;
Kittens are treated to houses well heated,
And pigs are protected by pens.
But a Camel comes handy
Wherever it's sandy—
ANYWHERE does for me!

"People would laugh if you rode a giraffe,
Or mounted the back of an ox;
It's nobody's habit to ride on a rabbit,
Or try to bestraddle a fox.
But as for a Camel, he's
Ridden by families—
ANY LOAD does for me!

"A snake is as round as a hole in the ground,
And weasels are wavy and sleek;
And no alligator could ever be straighter
Than lizards that live in a creek.
But a Camel's all lumpy
And bumpy and humpy—
ANY SHAPE does for me!"

THE LITTLE TURTLE

VACHEL LINDSAY

There was a little turtle.
He lived in a box.

He swam in a puddle.
He climbed on the rocks.

He snapped at a mosquito.
He snapped at a flea.
He snapped at a minnow.
And he snapped at me.

He caught the mosquito.
He caught the flea.
He caught the minnow.
But he didn't catch me.

2. Practice reading the following selections with appropriate vocal touch. Strive for great variety of loudness. Remember that touch, like any other technique of expression, is a *communicative* device: it must help to convey meaning and it must not distract.

JIM BLUDSO

JOHN HAY

Wall, no! I can't tell whar he lives,
Because he don't live, you see;
Leastways, he's got out of the habit
Of livin' like you and me.
Whar have you been for the last three year
That you haven't heard folks tell
How Jimmy Bludso passed in his checks,
The night of the *Prairie Belle?*

He weren't no saint,—them engineers
Is all pretty much alike,—
One wife in Natchez-under-the-Hill
And another one here, in Pike;
A keerless man in his talk was Jim,
And an awkward hand in a row,
But he never flunked, and he never lied,—
I recken he never knowed how.

And this was all the religion he had,—
To treat his engine well;

Never be passed on the river;
    To mind the pilot's bell;
And if ever the *Prairie Belle* took fire—
    A thousand times he swore
He'd hold her nozzle agin the bank
    Till the last soul got ashore.

All boats has their day on the Mississip,
    And her day come at last—
The *Movastar* was a better boat,
    But the *Belle* she wouldn't be passed.
And so she come tearin' along that night—
    The oldest craft on the line—
With a nigger squat on her safety valve,
    And her furnace crammed, rosin and pine.

The fire bust out as she clared the bar,
    And burnt a hole in the night,
And quick as a flash she turned, and made
    For that willer-bank on the right.
There was runnin' and cursin', but Jim yelled out,
    Over all the infernal roar,
"I'll hold her nozzle agin the bank
    Till the last galoot's ashore."

Through the hot, black breath of the burnin' boat
    Jim Bludso's voice was heard,
And they all had trust in his cussedness,
    And knowed he would keep his word.
And, sure's you're born, they all got off
    Afore the smokestacks fell,—
And Bludso's ghost went up alone
    In the smoke of the *Prairie Belle*.

He weren't no saint—but at jedgment
    I'd run my chance with Jim,
'Longside of some pious gentlemen
    That wouldn't shook hands with him.
He seen his duty, a dead-sure thing—
    And went for it thar and then;
And Christ ain't a goin' to be too hard
    On a man that died for men.

SONNET

WILLIAM SHAKESPEARE

When to the sessions of sweet silent thought
I summon up remembrance of things past,
I sigh the lack of many a thing I sought,
And with old woes new wail my dear time's waste;
Then can I drown an eye, unused to flow,
For precious friends hid in death's dateless night,
And weep afresh love's long-since-cancell'd woe,
And moan the expense of many a vanish'd sight.
Then can I grieve at grievances foregone,
And heavily from woe to woe tell o'er
The sad account of fore-bemoanéd moan,
Which I new pay as if not paid before.
    But if the while I think on thee, dear Friend,
    All losses are restored, and sorrows end.

WAR IS KIND

STEPHEN CRANE

Do not weep, maiden, for war is kind.
Because your lover threw wild hands toward the sky
And the affrighted steed ran on alone,
Do not weep.
War is kind.

Hoarse, booming drums of the regiment,
Little souls who thirst for fight,
These men were born to drill and die.
The unexplained glory flies above them,
Great is the battle-god, and his kingdom—
A field where a thousand corpses lie.

Do not weep, babe, for war is kind.
Because your father tumbled in the yellow trenches
Raged at his breast, gulped and died,
Do not weep.
War is kind.

Swift-blazing flag of the regiment,
Eagle with crest of red and gold,
These men were born to drill and die.
Point for them the virtue of slaughter,
Make plain to them the excellence of killing,
And a field where a thousand corpses lie.

Mother whose heart hung humble as a button
On the bright splendid shroud of your son,
Do not weep.
War is kind.

from NATIVE SON

RICHARD WRIGHT

"There he is again, Bigger!" the woman screamed, and the tiny one-room apartment galvanized into violent action. A chair toppled as the woman, half-dressed and in her stocking feet, scrambled breathlessly upon the bed. Her two sons, barefoot, stood tense and motionless, their eyes searching anxiously under the bed and chairs. The girl ran into a corner, half-stooped and gathered the hem of her slip into both of her hands and held it tightly over her knees.

"Oh! Oh!" she wailed.

"There he goes!"

The woman pointed a shaking finger. Her eyes were round with fascinated horror.

"Where?"

"I don't see 'im!"

"Bigger, he's behind the trunk!" the girl whimpered.

"Vera!" the woman screamed. "Get up here on the bed! Don't let that thing *bite* you!"

Frantically, Vera climbed upon the bed and the woman caught hold of her. With their arms entwined about each other, the black mother and the brown daughter gazed open-mouthed at the trunk in the corner.

Bigger looked round the room wildly, then darted to a curtain and swept it aside and grabbed two heavy iron skillets from a wall above a gas stove. He whirled and called softly to his brother, his eyes glued to the trunk.

"Buddy!"

"Yeah?"

"Here; take this skillet."

"O.K."

"Now, get over by the door!"

"O.K."

Buddy crouched by the door and held the iron skillet by its handle, his arm flexed and poised. Save for the quick, deep breathing of the four people, the room was quiet. Bigger crept on tiptoe toward the trunk with the skillet clutched stiffly in his hand, his eyes dancing and watching every inch of the wooden floor in front of him. He paused and, without moving an eye or muscle, called:

"Buddy!"

"Hunh?"

"Put that box in front of the hole so he can't get out!"

"O.K."

Buddy ran to a wooden box and shoved it quickly in front of a gaping hole in the molding and then backed again to the door, holding the skillet ready. Bigger eased to the trunk and peered behind it cautiously. He saw nothing. Carefully, he stuck out his bare foot and pushed the trunk a few inches.

"There he is!" the mother screamed again.

A huge black rat squealed and leaped at Bigger's trouser-leg and snagged it in his teeth, hanging on.

"Goddam!" Bigger whispered fiercely, whirling and kicking out his leg with all the strength of his body. The force of his movement shook the rat loose and it sailed through the air and struck a wall. Instantly, it rolled over and leaped again. Bigger dodged and the rat landed against a table leg. With clenched teeth, Bigger held the skillet; he was afraid to hurl it, fearing that he might miss. The rat squeaked and turned and ran in a narrow circle, looking for a place to hide; it leaped again past Bigger and scurried on dry rasping feet to one side of the box and then to the other, searching for the hole. Then it turned and reared upon its hind legs.

"Hit 'im, Bigger!" Buddy shouted.

"Kill 'im!" the woman screamed.

The rat's belly pulsed with fear. Bigger advanced a step and the rat emitted a long thin song of defiance, its black beady eyes glittering, its tiny forefeet pawing the air restlessly. Bigger swung the skillet; it skidded over the floor, missing the rat, and clattered to a stop against a wall.

"Goddam!"

The rat leaped. Bigger sprang to one side. The rat stopped under a chair and let out a furious screak. Bigger moved slowly backward toward the door.

"Gimme that skillet, Buddy," he asked quietly, not taking his eyes from the rat.

Buddy extended his hand. Bigger caught the skillet and lifted it high in the air. The rat scuttled across the floor and stopped again at the box and searched quickly for the hole; then it reared once more and bared long yellow fangs, piping shrilly, belly quivering.

Bigger aimed and let the skillet fly with a heavy grunt. There was a shattering of wood as the box caved in. The woman screamed and hid her face in her hands. Bigger tiptoed forward and peered.

"I got 'im," he muttered, his clenched teeth bared in a smile. "By God, I got 'im."

THE LAUGHERS

LOUIS UNTERMEYER

SPRING!
And her hidden bugles up the street.
Spring—and the sweet
Laughter of winds at the crossing;
Laughter of birds and a fountain tossing
Its hair in abandoned ecstasies.
Laughter of trees.
Laughter of shop-girls that giggle and blush;
Laugh of the tug-boat's impertinent fife.
Laughter followed by a trembling hush—
Laughter of love, scarce whispered aloud.
Then, stilled by no sacredness or strife,
Laughter that leaps from the crowd:
Seizing the world in a rush.
Laughter of life . . .

Earth takes deep breaths like a man who had feared he might smother,
Filling his lungs before bursting into a shout . . .
Windows are opened—curtains flying out;
Over the wash-lines women call to each other.
And, under the calling, there surges, too clearly to doubt,
Spring, with the noises
Of shrill, little voices;
Joining in "Tag" and the furious chase
Of "I-spy," "Red Rover" and "Prisoner's Base";
Of the roller-skates whir at the sidewalk's slope,
Of boys playing marbles and girls skipping rope.
And there, down the avenue, behold,
The first true herald of the Spring—
The hand-organ gasping and wheezily murmuring

Its tunes ten-years old . . .
And the music, trivial and tawdry, has freshness and magical swing
And over and under it,
During and after—
The laughter
Of Spring!

And lifted still
With the common thrill,
With the throbbing air, the tingling vapor,
That rose like strong and mingled wines,
I turned to my paper,
And read these lines:

Now that the Spring is here,
The war enters its bloodiest phase . . .
The men are impatient . . .
Bad roads, storms and the rigors of the winter
Have held back the contending armies . . .
But the recruits have arrived,
And are waiting only the first days of warm weather . . .
There will be terrible fighting along the whole line—
Now that Spring has come.

I put the paper down . . .
Something struck out the sun—something unseen;
Something arose like a dark wave to drown
The golden streets with a sickly green.
Something polluted the blossoming day
With the touch of decay.
The music thinned and died;
People seemed hollow-eyed.
Even the faces of children, where gaiety lingers,
Sagged and drooped like banners about to be furled—
And Silence laid its bony fingers
On the lips of the world . . .
A grisly quiet with the power to choke;
A quiet that only one thing broke;
One thing alone rose up thereafter . . .
Laughter!
Laughter of streams running red.
Laughter of evil things in the night;
Vultures carousing over the dead;
Laughter of ghouls.
Chuckling of idiots, cursed with sight.

Laughter of dark and horrible pools.
Scream of the bullet's rattling mirth,
Sweeping the earth.
Laugh of the cannon's poisonous breath . . .
And over the shouts and the wreckage and crumbling
The raucous and rumbling
Laughter of death.
Death that arises to sing,—
Hailing the Spring.

3. Practice reading the following selections with adequate projection for a large room and audience.

from SINNERS IN THE HANDS OF AN ANGRY GOD

JONATHAN EDWARDS

O sinner! Consider the fearful danger you are in. 'Tis a great furnace of wrath, a wide and bottomless pit, full of the fire of wrath, that you are held over in the hand of that God whose wrath is provoked and incensed as much against you as against many of the damned in hell. You hang by a slender thread, with the flames of divine wrath flashing about it, and ready every moment to singe it and burn it asunder; and you have no interest in any Mediator, and nothing to lay hold of to save yourself, nothing to keep off the flames of wrath, nothing of your own, nothing that you ever have done, nothing that you can do, to induce God to spare you one moment. . . .

Therefore, let every one that is out of Christ now awake and fly from the wrath to come. The wrath of Almighty God is now undoubtedly hanging over a great part of his congregation. Let every one fly out of Sodom. "Haste and escape for your lives, look not behind you, escape to the mountain, lest ye be consumed."

FAREWELL TO SPRINGFIELD NEIGHBORS UPON LEAVING FOR WASHINGTON, FEBRUARY 11, 1861

ABRAHAM LINCOLN

My Friends: No one, not in my situation, can appreciate my feeling of sadness at this parting. To this place, and the kindness of these people, I owe everything. Here I have lived a quarter of a century, and have passed from a young to an old man. Here my children have been born, and one is buried. I now leave, not knowing when or whether ever I may return, with a task before me greater than that which rested upon Washington. Without the assistance of that Divine Being who ever attended him, I cannot succeed. With that assistance, I cannot fail. Trusting in Him who can go with me, and remain with you, and be everywhere for good, let us confidently hope that all will yet be well. To His care commending you, as I hope in your prayers you will commend me, I bid you an affectionate farewell.

TO F________S S. O________D

EDGAR ALLAN POE

Thou wouldst be loved?—then let thy heart
  From its present pathway part not!
Being everything which now thou art,
  Be nothing which thou art not.
So with the world thy gentle ways,
  Thy grace, thy more than beauty,
Shall be an endless theme of praise,
  And love—a simple duty.

TO ________.

EDGAR ALLAN POE

I heed not that my earthly lot
  Hath little of Earth in it,
That years of love have been forgot
  In the hatred of a minute:
I mourn not that the desolate
  Are happier, sweet, than I,
But that you sorrow for my fate
  Who am a passer-by.

PORTRAIT OF A GIRL WITH A COMIC BOOK

PHYLLIS McGINLEY

Thirteen's no age at all. Thirteen is nothing.
It is not wit, or powder on the face,

Or Wednesday matinees, or misses' clothing,
Or intellect, or grace.
Twelve has its tribal customs. But thirteen
Is neither boys in battered cars nor dolls,
Not *Sara Crewe,* or movie magazine,
Or pennants on the walls.
Thirteen keeps diaries and tropical fish
(A month, at most); scorns jumpropes in the spring;
Could not, would fortune grant it, name its wish;
Wants nothing, everything;
Has secrets from itself, friends it despises;
Admits none to the terrors that it feels;
Owns half a hundred masks but no disguises;
And walks upon its heels.

Thirteen's anomalous—not that, not this:
Not folded bud, or wave that laps a shore,
Or moth proverbial from the chrysalis.
Is the one age defeats the metaphor.
Is not a town, like childhood, strongly walled
But easily surrounded; is no city.
Nor, quitted once, can it be quite recalled—
Not even with pity.

Suggested Readings

Bacon, Wallace A., and Robert S. Breen. *Literature as Experience.* New York: McGraw-Hill, 1959, pp. 289–91, "Breathing and Speech."

Kenyon, John Samuel. *American Pronunciation.* Ann Arbor, Mich.: George Wahr Publishing Co., 1950, pp. 24–32, "Phonetic Symbols."

Lee, Charlotte I. *Oral Interpretation.* (2nd edition) Boston: Houghton Mifflin, 1959, pp. 108–22, breathing, loudness, and projection.

Parrish, Wayland Maxfield. *Reading Aloud.* (3rd edition) New York: Ronald Press, 1953, pp. 130–38, breathing.

10

AUDIBLE COMMUNICATION THROUGH PITCH

As observed in the previous chapter, when syllables are stressed and words are emphasized, loudness is usually increased, duration usually extended, and pitch usually raised.

VARIATION IN PITCH

The variation of vocal pitch is one of the chief means by which we communicate meaning. It is employed by most of the animal world, where the higher ranges of pitch usually indicate fear or excitement and the lower ones composure and sometimes aggressiveness. Human beings of all ages use this same basic method of communicating meaning by varying vocal pitch. Every family with a baby can distinguish among wordless sounds which denote hunger, fear, pain, anger, contentment, and pleasure. In each case the primary difference is one of pitch. Adults employ pitch levels in a multitude of ways. We have already observed the role of pitch in accents upon syllables. Such pitch variation is also used in inflections of single words, where it often means the difference between a statement of fact and a question. In the same way it is employed in sentences. Here, however, we often adapt the level of pitch to the over-all meaning of the sentence. For example, the quiet restrained "I hate you" suggests a pitch level which is different from that of the carefree invitation "Let's go to the ball game." The same distinction applies to whole paragraphs or even more extended speech: obviously you would employ a lower level of pitch in reading the following passage from Henry Van Dyke's *The Other Wise Man* than you would in reading the succeeding one from Mark Twain's *The Adventures of Huckleberry Finn*. Read each of them aloud.

from THE OTHER WISE MAN

HENRY VAN DYKE

So I saw the other wise man again and again, traveling from place to place, and searching among the people of the dispersion, with whom the little family from Bethlehem might, perhaps, have found a refuge. He passed through countries where famine lay heavy upon the land and the poor were crying for bread. He made his dwelling in plague-stricken cities where the sick were languishing in the bitter companionship of helpless misery. He visited the oppressed and the afflicted in the gloom of subterranean prisons, and the crowded wretchedness of slave-markets, and the weary toil of galley-ships. In all this populous and intricate world of anguish, though he found none to worship, he found many to help. He fed the hungry, and clothed the naked, and healed the sick, and comforted the captive; and his years went by more swiftly than the weaver's shuttle that flashes back and forth through the loom while the web grows and the invisible pattern is completed.

It seemed almost as if he had forgotten his quest. But once I saw him for a moment as he stood alone at sunrise, waiting at the gate of a Roman prison. He had taken from a secret resting-place in his bosom the pearl, the last of his jewels. As he looked at it, a mellower lustre, a soft and iridescent light, full of shifting gleams of azure and rose, trembled upon its surface. It seemed to have absorbed some reflection of the colors of the lost sapphire and ruby. So the profound, secret purpose of a noble life draws into itself the memories of past joy and past sorrow. All that has helped it, all that has hindered it, is transfused by a subtle magic into its very essence. It becomes more luminous and precious the longer it is carried close to the warmth of the beating heart.

from THE ADVENTURES OF HUCKLEBERRY FINN

MARK TWAIN

It was a real bully circus. It was the splendidest sight that ever was when they all come riding in, two and two, a gentleman and lady, side by side, the men just in their drawers and undershirts, and no shoes nor stirrups, and resting their hands on their thighs easy and comfortable—there must 'a' been twenty of them—and every lady with a lovely complexion and perfectly beautiful, and looking just like a gang of real sure-enough queens and dressed in clothes that cost millions of dollars, and just littered with diamonds. It was a powerful fine sight; I never seen anything so lovely. And then one by one they got up and stood, and went a-weaving round the ring so gentle and wavy and graceful, the men looking ever so tall and airy and straight, with their heads bobbing and skimming along, away up there under the-tent-roof, and every lady's rose-leafy dress flapping soft and silky round her hips, and she looking like the most loveliest parasol.

And then faster and faster they went, all of them dancing, first one foot out in the air and then the other, the horses leaning more and more, and the ringmaster going round and round the center pole, cracking his whip and shouting "Hi!—hi!" and the clown cracking jokes behind him; and by and by all hands dropped the reins, and every lady put her knuckles on her hips and every gentleman folded his arms, and then how the horses did lean over and hump themselves! And so one after the other they all skipped off into the ring, and made the sweetest bow I ever see, and then scampered out, and everybody clapped their hands and went just wild.

In addition to reading each of these two passages in a different general level of pitch, you have probably distinguished them in another way. In order to express the excitement inherent in *Huckleberry Finn,* you have probably employed a greater range of pitch in reading it. Such variation of pitch to convey meaning is a normal part of oral expression.

ORIGINS OF VOCAL PITCH

When you have become conscious of using different levels of pitch for different kinds of material, one of the questions you ultimately ask is, "How does it happen that my voice is higher (or lower) than my neighbor's?" Like most of the aspects of personality, voice is derived basically from the two sources of heredity and environment.

The habitual level at which you speak is largely determined by your physical inheritance. The vocal mechanism dictated by the germ cells has set up pitch limits below and above which you cannot go. Place your finger on the point of your Adam's apple. Slide your finger upward slightly until you find the little groove just above. This marks the top of the *larynx,* often erroneously called the voice box. The larynx houses two muscular bands, which apparently were originally employed only as a valve in the breath stream. If you will again place your hands under the seat of your chair and try to lift both the chair and yourself, you will notice that you close this valve when you make a major bodily effort. Most animals, however, have learned to control the *glottis* or opening in the valve to produce voice. The length and thickness of these muscular bands, which we call the *vocal cords* or *folds,* limit the pitches at which they can vibrate in the breath stream. In this regard the vocal folds are analogous to the strings of a violin: the larger or longer the string, the lower the pitch. You know that as you shorten the vibrating length of the violin string by placing your finger nearer the bridge a higher note is produced. You cannot, however, make a lower note than the size and length of the string permit. So it is that the thickness and length of your vocal folds set up broad limits for the pitches you can produce: the longer and heavier your vocal bands, the lower the possible pitch of your voice. On the other hand, we must recognize that few people employ the full range of their pitch possibilities. Therefore, you may be reasonably sure that you can learn to raise or lower your pitch beyond its habitual limits.

Another factor in the determination of the pitch at which you normally speak is your environment. If you live in an atmosphere of composure, quite probably your normal pitch will be lower than it would be if you were surrounded by excitement. Excitement produces tension; tension raises pitch. Even more influential than such environment is the pitch level employed by people with whom you associate. As a general rule we tend to copy the speech of other members of the family or of intimate friends. Girls often approximate the pitch of their mothers and boys of their fathers. This tendency to imitate means that your pitch may or may not be a natural one within the limits your vocal mechanism has set for you.

A final factor in the determination of your pitch is your personality. Of

I

One of the greatest joys that we can experience is that feeling which results from the combination of <u>Spring</u> + <u>Childhood</u>.

After those months + months of being caged inside houses and schools + stuffy cars + buses, <u>Spring</u> frees our bodies ~~and minds~~. We run wildly thru grassy meadows on farms or thru blossoming parks in the city. We feel the wetness of rain as we're caught in a sudden thunderstorm. We run to play soft ball + marbles with friends down the block, or we tumble in the grass — jealously watching the birds + butterflies fly + flit overhead in the blue sky.

course, personality itself is the product of heredity and environment, but your attitudes, tensions, and even health may cause you to use a characteristic pitch level. In this sense pitch is often an indicator of the inner man.

OPTIMUM PITCH

Since these two factors of heredity and environment determine the pitch you normally use, you may wonder whether that pitch is the best one for you. There is no positive way of answering this question, for actually the limits are broad and indefinite. There are, however, a few simple procedures you might try in order to ascertain your *optimum pitch.* One way is to sing to the highest and lowest limits you can comfortably reach, find those limits on the keys of the piano, and then locate the middle of this range. Generally speaking your optimum pitch should be about two notes below this middle point. Another way is to sing down the scale to the lowest note you can easily reach. Then sing up again five notes to reach the optimum. An even simpler method is to produce an easy, open-mouthed "ah-h-h-h." This tone is usually the optimum one for your voice. We suggest that you try all three of these methods. See if you arrive at the same pitch every time. Almost certainly you will be able to approximate your optimum pitch level, the one to which you should return most often in speaking. If it is different from the normal level at which you speak, we suggest you try to make the necessary change. There are three big advantages in doing so: first, the use of your optimum pitch results in maximum ease of speech; second, it permits maximum flexibility above and below; and third, it usually results in a more pleasant voice.

PITCH FAULTS

Although you may have achieved your optimum pitch in speaking or reading, your effective use of voice may still be hampered by one or more pitch faults. The most serious of these is a monopitch. A lack of variety in pitch results in inattention and boredom. Very few people speak in one constant pitch, for the nature of English pronunciation requires some variety: remember that "grimy" and "indent" have two pitch levels. To speak with no pitch variety is at best to sound as silly as some comedians; at worst it is to be almost completely unintelligible. Many persons, however, are handicapped by a monotonous range of only two or three half-notes. Such speech is only a little more expressive than an absolute monopitch.

Almost as serious as a lack of pitch variety is the employment of a pitch pattern. Perhaps you hear such patterns most often in church when the minister reads scripture. These lines from the fourteenth chapter of John are marked to illustrate a common pattern. This mark (/) means a rising pitch and this (\) a falling one. Try reading aloud this passage in the pattern indicated.

> Let not your heart be troubled: ye believe in God, believe also in me. In my Father's house are many mansions: if it were not so, I would have told you. I go to prepare a place for you. And if I go and prepare a place for you, I will come again, and receive you unto myself; that where I am, there ye may be also.

Pitch patterns are not confined to the pulpit. A few old-time politicians still use them. Sometimes we speak of "Wigwam oratory," referring to the speaking style which was so common a half century ago at the political conventions held in the Wigwam in Chicago. Occasionally you still hear political figures in today's conventions and elsewhere speak in a repetitious pattern of pitches that could be plotted on a musical scale.

Surely if the utterance of ideas is to be meaningful such a pitch pattern must be avoided. Far from adding to communication, such regular repetition of pitch levels lulls the unsuspecting listener into slumber. The pattern usually results from failure to experience the thoughts as the words are being uttered. Reading is thus sound without sense. Rethink your material. Discipline yourself to think as you speak.

While a monopitch or a repetitious pattern causes dullness, the overemployment of pitch variety may just as definitely detract from the communication of the meaning. Probably you are familiar with the caricature of the elocutionist who so nimbly trips up and down the scale in a fantastic display of versatility that the listener sits in rapt admiration of his skill but never of his ideas. Such a reader apparently believes that if a little is good a great deal is better. We deplore such overuse of pitch variety as much as underuse. The employment of pitch should aid and never hinder communication.

VOCAL MELODY

For interesting speaking or reading, the speech melody or arrangement of pitch changes should be smooth and rhythmical, involving as much variation as is necessary for maximum communication of meaning. Listening to speech melody should be both a meaningful and a pleasant experience, unless of course full awareness of meaning is actually implemented by unpleasant listening: the paragraph from *Spark of Life* found later in this chapter is perhaps properly unpleasant to the ear. The melody will focus attention upon meaning, upon the pronounced changes of thought and the delicate nuances as well. Normally it will never call attention to itself alone. Perhaps we can emphasize this point by noting the dramatic exception. A few poems can be most effectively read by employing a melody which the listener is sure to notice for its own sake. Examples are Lindsay's "The Congo" and Lanier's "The Song of the Chatahoochee." Actually these may be considered full-length examples of onomatopoeia: the utterance must sound like the subject matter. However, even these do not demonstrate a dominance of sound over sense. Melody is always properly an implemeting device. Sense dominates.

Vocal melody is an elusive but nevertheless significant index of a person's inner feelings. It suggests the degree to which a reader has achieved identification with his meaning. It reveals comprehension and sincerity. It may also reveal lack of understanding and insincerity. Thus, melody is the reason that the single most important factor in effective reading or speaking is vivid awareness of meaning at the moment of utterance. You cannot depend on hiding your lack of understanding or your insincerity. Vocal melody provides a ready index to what is going on in the speaker's mind. That melody involves the pitch devices called *key, step,* and *inflection.*

MAINTAINING A KEY

The word *key* indicates the general level of tone in an extended section of speech. It may be higher or lower than your optimum pitch and will be determined by the emotion you wish to convey. For example, the despair and tragedy of the following lines seem to suggest that you read them in about as low a key as you can comfortably employ. Try to do so.

from SPARK OF LIFE

ERICH MARIA REMARQUE

> Skeleton 509 slowly raised its skull and opened its eyes. It did not know whether it had been unconscious or merely asleep. By now there was hardly any difference between the one and the other; hunger and exhaustion had long ago seen to that. Both were a sinking into boggy depths, from which there seemed to be no more rising to the surface.

When you have read the lines in a very low key, experiment with other keys and finally return to the lowest. Probably such a key will contribute to an appreciation of the emotion for both the listener and the reader.

The next paragraph expresses insane excitement and rage. You will need to read it in a higher key than the first and quite probably a higher key than your optimum one.

from THE CASK OF AMONTILLADO

EDGAR ALLAN POE

A succession of loud and shrill screams, bursting suddenly from the throat of the chained form, seemed to thrust me violently back. For a brief moment I hesitated, I trembled. Unsheathing my rapier, I began to grope with it about the recess; but the thought of an instant reassured me. I placed my hand upon the solid fabric of the catacombs, and felt satisfied. I reapproached the wall; I replied to the yells of him who clamoured. I re-echoed, I aided, I surpassed them in volume and in strength. I did this, and the clamourer grew still.

Once more you will find it interesting to read the paragraph in different keys to discover that the highest is actually the most appropriate.

To generalize about the choice of key in speaking or reading, it may be said that the three main levels have different broad uses. Usually the higher keys are used to express excitement, fear, rage, delight, and the other emotions characterized by great tension. The medium key (analogous to the optimum pitch discussed earlier) is commonly employed to suggest sincerity and calmness. The lower keys may be used to mean tragedy, worship, repressed hate, and despair. These three designations are not hard and fast rules but rather the broadest of generalities: there are many exceptions. Keys do overlap. You cannot catalogue the qualities of voice and say that if you speak in such and such a pitch you will express a specific emotion. The dividing line, for example, between fear, which we tend to express in the highest key, and tragedy, for which we use the lowest, is slight and indefinite at best.

VARYING THE KEY

Quite often the appropriate key for reading a piece of literature changes from one section of the piece to another. This change is especially important in reading drama or a story with dialogue. The following selection is a famous humorist's account of some of his college experiences. The stars (*) indicate some of the places where you may want to change key in reading it aloud. First study it silently and then read it orally. Make an effort to change to a different appropriate key each time you come to a star. Perhaps you will find other places to change key. Do not hesitate to make the changes very obvious. They will add to the humor. Remember to be faithful to the author's intention as you see it.

from UNIVERSITY DAYS

JAMES THURBER

I passed all the other courses that I took at my University, but I could never pass botany. This was because all botany students had to spend several hours a week in a laboratory looking through a microscope at plant cells, and I could never see through a microscope. I never once saw a cell through a microscope. This used to enrage my instructor. He would wander around the laboratory pleased with the progress all the students were making in drawing the involved and, so I am told, interesting structure of flower cells, until he came to me. I would just be standing there. *"I can't see anything," *I would say. He would begin patiently enough, explaining how anybody can see through a microscope, but he would always end up in a fury, claiming that I *could too see through a microscope but just pretended that I couldn't. *"It takes away from the beauty of flowers anyway," *I used to tell him. *"We are not concerned with beauty in this course," *he would say. *"We are concerned solely with what I may call the *mechanics* of flars." *"Well," *I'd say, *"I can't see anything." *"Try it just once again," *he'd say, and I would put my eye to the microscope and see nothing at all, except now and again a nebulous milky substance—a phenomenon of maladjustment. You were supposed to see a vivid, restless clockwork of sharply defined plant cells. *"I see what looks like a lot of milk," *I would tell him. This, he claimed, was the result of my not having adjusted the microscope properly, so he would readjust it for me, or rather, for himself. And I would look again and see milk.

I finally took a deferred pass, as they called it, and waited a year and tried again. (You had to pass one of the biological sciences or you couldn't graduate.) The professor had come back from vacation brown as a berry, bright-eyed, and eager to explain cell-structure again to his classes. *"Well," *he said to me, cheerily, when we met in the first laboratory hour of the semester, *"We're going to see cells this time, aren't we?" *"Yes, sir," *I said. Students to right of me and to left of me and in front of me were seeing cells; what's more, they were quietly drawing pictures of them in their notebooks. Of course, I didn't see anything.

*"We'll try it," *the professor said to me, grimly, *"with every

adjustment of the microscope known to man. As God is my witness, I'll arrange this glass so that you see cells through it or I'll give up teaching. In twenty-two years of botany, I—" *He cut off abruptly, for he was beginning to quiver all over, like Lionel Barrymore, and he genuinely wished to hold on to his temper; his scenes with me had taken a great deal out of him.

*So we tried it with every adjustment of the microscope known to man. With only one of them did I see anything but blackness or the familiar lacteal opacity, *and that time I saw, to my pleasure and amazement, a variegated constellation of flecks, specks, and dots. These I hastily drew. The instructor, noting my activity, came back from an adjoining desk, a smile on his lips and his eyebrows high in hope. He looked at my cell drawing. *"What's that?" *he demanded, with a hint of a squeal in his voice. *"That's what I saw," *I said. *"You didn't, you didn't, you *didn't!*" *he screamed, losing control of his temper instantly, and he bent over and squinted into the microscope. His head snapped up. *"That's your eye!" *he shouted. *"You've fixed the lens so that it reflects! You've drawn your eye!"

STEP

The vocal *step* in speaking or reading is most obviously illustrated by a similar practice in singing. In this bit of music there are pitch changes be-

tween words and sometimes between syllables. This same phenomenon occurs in normal speech and is called the vocal step. Just as there are such changes of pitch in singing without a change of key, so there are steps in speech without a change of key.

While your musical steps are dictated by the score, your steps in speaking and reading are determined entirely by your understanding of the meaning. Different people repeat the age-old crucial declaration, "I love you," in a variety of steps. Here are three of them. See if you can read the words aloud with the steps indicated.

    love
I   you.

I
    love you.

you.
I love

Shortly we shall see how "I love you" can be made more meaningful with the use of pitch slides, or inflections. Practice reading the following lines with the steps indicated.

God
in
His curse
May heaven you.

Praise Praise the Lord
the
Lord! from the heavens.

Praise
him
in
the
heights!

After you have copied the following poem in the manner in which the above lines are arranged, practice reading it with the steps which you have indicated to be appropriate.

THE DUCK

OGDEN NASH

Behold the duck.
It does not cluck.
A cluck it lacks.
It quacks.
It is especially fond
Of a puddle or pond.
When it dines or sups,
It bottoms ups.

Almost all intelligible speech employs pitch steps. The only exception is that speech in which monotony is deliberately sought. Sometimes the purpose of such monotony is humor, and sometimes it is the communication of the idea of sameness as in these lines from "The Rime of the Ancient Mariner" by Coleridge:

> Alone, alone, all, all alone,
> Alone on a wide, wide sea!

For normal communicative reading you must be able to use pitch steps.

INFLECTION

Inflection is the process of changing pitch within a syllable. Someone has called it bending pitch to make the sense. It is certainly the most versatile and the most difficult of all the pitch devices used to convey meaning. The word "yes" may be used to demonstrate the most common inflectional patterns.

upward inflection—yes (/)

downward inflection—yes (\)

varieties of the circumflex—yes (∧)

yes (∨)

By means of the upward inflection you say "Yes" and mean "What?" By means of the downward inflection you say "Yes" and express an affirmation. Using the first circumflex you may convey the meaning "I *certainly* do!" By inverting the circumflex you may mean "I'm thinking about what you said and you *may* be right although I'm *not sure*." Depending on the length of the word and the complexity of the meaning intended, you may repeat these patterns or you may alter them by beginning or ending the pitch at a different level or by modifying the amount of pitch change. Experiment with the word "Oh-h-h" to see how many different meaningful patterns of inflection you can produce.

In Chapter 4 we found we could convey an almost infinite number of meanings with the words, "I am going to Chicago." Many of those meanings were expressed primarily through inflections. Using the following sentence see how many meanings you can express through differing inflections. Remember that you have at least four inflectional patterns which you can use on each word. Then, of course, you can employ those patterns on the individual words in different combinations with other words. You should be able

No one else dares to love you because	I love you!	(A strong assertion.)
How do I feel about you?	Why, I love you.	(A simple assertion.)
I mean it!	I love you!	(A strong assertion.)
I don't hate you.	I love you.	(An intellectual distinction.)
I don't hate you.	I love you.	(But you burn me up sometimes!)
Quit pestering me! All right, I'll say it once and for all.	I love you.	(Now, let me alone!)

Summary

Vocal pitch is the chief means of communicating meaning. Your pitch is determined primarily by heredity, environment, and personality. Your normal pitch may not be your optimum one. If you can achieve an optimum pitch, it will result in greater ease, flexibility, and pleasantness of speech. Monotony, pattern, and overinflection are the major pitch faults. Vocal melody should normally be smooth and rhythmical and should communicate. Such melody involves the use of key, step, and inflection. It is characteristic of good oral reading in the same way it is characteristic of good conversation.

Exercises

1. Experiment in conveying different meanings by reading the following selections aloud with different uses of inflection, step, and key.

THERE WAS A CHILD WENT FORTH

WALT WHITMAN

There was a child went forth every day;
And the first object he look'd upon, that object he became;
And that object became part of him for the day or a certain part of the day,

Or for many years or stretching cycles of years.
The early lilacs became part of this child,
And grass and white and red morning-glories, and white and red clover, and the song of the phoebe-bird,
And the Third-month lambs and the sow's pink-faint litter, and the mare's foal, and the cow's calf,
And the noisy brood of the barn-yard or by the mire of the pond-side,
And the fish suspending themselves so curiously below there—and the beautiful curious liquid,
And the water-plants with their graceful flat heads—all became part of him.

The field-sprouts of Fourth-month and Fifth-month became part of him;
Winter-grain sprouts and those of the light-yellow corn, and the esculent roots of the garden,
And the apple-trees cover'd with blossoms and the fruit afterward, and wood-berries, and the commonest weeds by the road;
And the old drunkard staggering home from the outhouse of the tavern whence he had lately risen,
And the school mistress that pass'd on her way to the school,
And the friendly boys that pass'd, and the quarrelsome boys,
And the tidy and fresh-cheek'd girls,—and the barefoot negro boy and girl,
And all the changes of city and country wherever he went.

His own parents, he that had father'd him and she that had conceiv'd him in her womb and birth'd him,
They gave this child more of themselves than that;
They gave him afterward every day, they became part of him.

The mother at home, quietly placing the dishes on the supper-table,
The mother with mild words, clean her cap and gown, a wholesome odor falling off her person and clothes as she walks by;
The father, strong, self-sufficient, manly, mean, anger'd, unjust,
The blow, the quick loud word, the tight bargain, the crafty lure,
The family usages, the language, the company, the furniture, the yearning and swelling heart,
Affection that will not be gainsay'd, the sense of what is real, the thought if after all it should prove unreal,
The doubts of day-time and the doubts of night-time, the curious whether and how,
Whether that which appears so is so, or is it all flashes and specks?
Men and women crowding fast in the streets, if they are not flashes and specks what are they?
The streets themselves and the façades of houses, and goods in the windows,

Vehicles, teams, the heavy-plank'd wharves, the huge crossing at the ferries,
The village on the highland seen from afar at sunset, the river between,
Shadows, aureola and mist, the light falling on roofs and gables of white or brown two miles off,
The schooner near by sleepily dropping down the tide, the little boat slack-tow'd astern,
The hurrying tumbling waves, quick-broken crests, slapping,
The strata of color'd clouds, the long bar of maroon-tint, away solitary by itself, the spread of purity it lies motionless in,
The horizon's edge, the flying sea-crow, the fragrance of salt marsh and shore mud,
These became part of that child who went forth every day, and who now goes, and will always go forth every day.

I SAW IN LOUISIANA A LIVE-OAK GROWING

WALT WHITMAN

I saw in Louisiana a live-oak growing,
All alone stood it and the moss hung down from the branches,
Without any companion it grew there uttering joyous leaves of dark green,
And its look, rude, unbending, lusty, made me think of myself,
But I wonder'd how it could utter joyous leaves standing alone there without its friend near, for I knew I could not,
And I broke off a twig with a certain number of leaves upon it, and twined around it a little moss,
And brought it away, and I have placed it in sight in my room,
It is not needed to remind me as of my own dear friends,
(For I believe lately I think of little else than of them,)
Yet it remains to me a curious token, it makes me think of manly love;
For all that, and though the live-oak glistens there in Louisiana solitary in a wide flat space,
Uttering joyous leaves all its life without a friend a lover near,
I know very well I could not.

COUNTRY CLUB SUNDAY

PHYLLIS McGINLEY

It is a beauteous morning, calm and free.
    The fairways sparkle. Gleam the shaven grasses.
Mirth fills the locker rooms and, hastily,
    Stewards fetch ice, fresh towels, and extra glasses.

On terraces the sandaled women freshen
Their lipstick; gather to gossip, poised and cool;
And the shrill adolescent takes possession,
Plunging and splashing, of the swimming pool.

It is a beauteous morn, opinion grants,
Nothing remains of last night's Summer Formal
Save palms and streamers and the wifely glance,
Directed with more watchfulness than normal,
At listless mate who tugs his necktie loose,
Moans, shuns the light, and gulps tomato juice.

2. Read the following selections, pointing up thought-centers by means of pitch variations.

EACH IN HIS OWN TONGUE

WILLIAM HERBERT CARRUTH

A fire-mist and a planet,
A crystal and a cell,
A jelly-fish and a saurian,
And caves where the cave-men dwell;
Then a sense of law and beauty
And a face turned from the clod,—
Some call it Evolution,
And others call it God.

A haze on the far horizon,
The infinite, tender sky,
The ripe, rich tint of the cornfields,
And the wild geese sailing high;
And all over upland and lowland,
The charm of the golden-rod—
Some of us call it Autumn,
And others call it God.

Like tides on a crescent sea-beach,
When the moon is new and thin,
Into our hearts high yearnings
Come welling and surging in;
Come from the mystic ocean
Whose rim no foot has trod,—

Some of us call it Longing,
    And others call it God.

A picket frozen on duty,
    A mother starved for her brood,
Socrates drinking the hemlock,
    And Jesus on the rood;
And millions who, humble and nameless,
    The straight, hard pathway plod,—
Some call it Consecration,
    And others call it God.

I HEAR AMERICA SINGING

WALT WHITMAN

I hear America singing, the varied carols I hear,
Those of mechanics, each one singing his as it should be blithe and strong,
The carpenter singing his as he measures his plank or beam,
The mason singing his as he makes ready for work, or leaves off work,
The boatman singing what belongs to him in his boat, the deckhand singing on the steamboat deck,
The shoemaker singing as he sits on his bench, the hatter singing as he stands,
The wood-cutter's song, the plowboy's on his way in the morning, or at noon intermission or at sundown,
The delicious singing of the mother, or of the young wife at work, or of the girl sewing or washing,
Each singing what belongs to him or her and to none else,
The day what belongs to the day—at night the party of young fellows, robust, friendly,
Singing with open mouths their strong melodious songs.

CAROL: NEW STYLE

STEPHEN VINCENT BENÉT

If Jesus Christ *should come again,*
On Christmas day, on Christmas day,
To bother the minds of gentlemen
On Christmas day in the morning?

The first one said as he passed by,
As he passed by, as he passed by,

"I see three thieves a-hanging high,
This Christmas day in the morning."

The second one said, "What sinful men!
What sinful men, what sinful men!
Hanging is too good for them,
On Christmas day in the morning."

The third one said, "Oh stay your word!
Stay your word, oh stay your word!
Do you not see that one's the Lord,
This Christmas day in the morning?

"I know him by his weary head,
His weary head, his weary head."
Whereat they all fell sore adread,
That Christmas day in the morning.

"How sad this is we all avow,
Yes, indeed, we all avow!
But what shall we do about it now,
On Christmas day in the morning?"

PRIMUS
"I'll run away as fast as I may,
As fast as I may, as fast as I may,
And pretend I haven't been out all day,
On Christmas day in the morning."

SECUNDUS
"I'll buy Him a shroud that's spick and span,
Spick and span, spick and span,
For I was always a generous man,
On Christmas day in the morning."

TERTIUS
"But what if we should cut Him down,
Cut Him down, cut Him down?"

SECUNDUS ET PRIMUS
"You fool, do you want to arouse the town,
On Christmas day in the morning?"

"My speech was rash," the third one said,
The third one said, the third one said,
"We're surer of God when we know He's dead,
On any day in the morning."

They knelt in the snow and prayed and bowed,
Prayed and bowed, prayed and bowed,
And the dead thieves laughed out loud
On Christmas day in the morning.

As Jesus Christ was hanging high,
Hanging high, hanging high,
He saw three Christians, passing by,
On Christmas day in the morning.

HISTORY REPEATS ITSELF

MARK TWAIN

The following I find in a Sandwich Island paper which some friend has sent me from that tranquil far-off retreat. The coincidence between my own experience and that here set down by the late Mr. Benton is so remarkable that I cannot forbear publishing and commenting upon the paragraph. The Sandwich Island paper says:

"How touching is this tribute of the late Hon. T. H. Benton to his mother's influence:—'My mother asked me never to use tobacco; I have never touched it from that time to the present day. She asked me not to gamble, and I have never gambled. I cannot tell who is losing in games that are being played. She admonished me, too, against liquor-drinking, and whatever capacity for endurance I have at present, and whatever usefulness I may have attained through life, I attribute to having complied with her pious and correct wishes. When I was seven years of age she asked me not to drink, and then I made a resolution of total abstinence; and that I have adhered to it through all time I owe to my mother.' "

I never saw anything so curious. It is almost an exact epitome of my own moral career—after simply substituting a grandmother for a mother. How well I remember my grandmother's asking me not to use tobacco, good old soul. She said, "You're at it again, are you, you whelp? Now don't ever let me catch you chewing tobacco before breakfast again, or I lay I'll blacksnake you within an inch of your life!" I have never touched it at that hour of the morning from that time to the present day.

She asked me not to gamble. She whispered and said, "Put up those wicked cards this minute!—two pair and a jack, you numbskull, and the other fellow's got a flush!"

I never have gambled from that day to this—never once—without a "cold deck" in my pocket. I cannot even tell who is going to lose in games that are being played unless I deal myself.

When I was two years of age she asked me not to drink, and then I made a resolution of total abstinence. That I have adhered to it and enjoyed the beneficent effects of it through all, I owe to my grandmother. I have never drunk a drop from that day to this of any kind of water.

3. The following story is remarkable for its subtle overtones of meaning. Read it carefully. Notice the genial mood of the opening description. Observe how rising tension is created. The line "There's always been a lottery" may reveal the central social criticism of the story. Perhaps you can find in Miss Jackson's story some implications for our modern society. As you learn to read it aloud, make special use of touch, key, inflection, and step to convey a maximum of meaning.

THE LOTTERY

SHIRLEY JACKSON

The morning of June 27th was clear and sunny, with the fresh warmth of a full summer day; the flowers were blossoming profusely and the grass was richly green. The people of the village began to gather in the square, between the post office and the bank, around ten o'clock; in some towns there were so many people that the lottery took two days and had to be started on June 26th, but in this village, where there were only about three hundred people, the whole lottery took less than two hours, so it could begin at ten o'clock in the morning and still be through in time to allow the villagers to get home for noon dinner.

The children assembled first, of course. School was recently over for the summer, and the feeling of liberty sat uneasily on most of them; they tended to gather together quietly for a while before they broke into boisterous play, and their talk was still of the classroom and the teacher, of books and reprimands. Bobby Martin had already stuffed his pockets full of stones, and the other boys soon followed his example, selecting the smoothest and roundest stones; Bobby and Harry Jones and Dickie Delacroix—the villagers pronounced this name "Dellacroy"—eventually made a great pile of stones in one corner of the square and guarded it against the raids of the other boys. The girls stood aside, talking among themselves, looking over their shoulders at the boys, and the very small children rolled in the dust or clung to the hands of their older brothers or sisters.

Soon the men began to gather, surveying their own children, speaking of planting and rain, tractors and taxes. They stood together, away from the pile of stones in the corner, and their jokes were quiet and they smiled rather than laughed. The women, wearing faded house dresses and sweaters, came shortly after their menfolk. They greeted one another and exchanged bits of gossip as they went to join their husbands. Soon the women, standing by their husbands, began to call to their children, and the children came reluctantly, having to be called four or five times. Bobby Martin ducked under his mother's grasping hand and ran, laughing, back to the pile of stones. His father spoke up sharply, and Bobby came quickly and took his place between his father and his oldest brother.

The lottery was conducted—as were the square dances, the teenage club, the Hallowe'en program—by Mr. Summers, who had time and energy to devote to civic activities. He was a round-faced, jovial man and he ran the coal business, and people were sorry for him, because he had no children and his wife was a scold. When he arrived in the square, carrying the black wooden box, there was a murmur of conversation among the villagers, and he waved and called, "Little late today, folks." The postmaster, Mr. Graves, followed him, carrying a three-legged stool, and the stool was put in the center of the square and Mr. Summers set the black box down on it. The villagers kept their distance, leaving a space between themselves and the stool, and when Mr. Summers said, "Some of you fellows want to give me a hand?" there was a hesitation before two men, Mr. Martin and his oldest son, Baxter, came forward to hold the box steady on the stool while Mr. Summers stirred up the papers inside it.

The original paraphernalia for the lottery had been lost long ago, and the black box now resting on the stool had been put into use even before Old Man Warner, the oldest man in town, was born. Mr. Summers spoke frequently to the villagers about making a new box, but no one liked to upset even as much tradition as was represented by the black box. There was a story that the present box had been made with some pieces of the box that had preceded it, the one that had been constructed when the first people settled down to make a village here. Every year, after the lottery, Mr. Summers began talking again about a new box, but every year the subject was allowed to fade off without anything's being done. The black box grew shabbier each year; by now it was no longer completely black but splintered badly along one side to show the original wood color, and in some places faded or stained.

Mr. Martin and his oldest son, Baxter, held the black box securely on the stool until Mr. Summers had stirred the papers thoroughly with his hand. Because so much of the ritual had been forgotten or discarded, Mr. Summers had been successful in having slips of paper substituted for the chips of wood that had been used for generations. Chips of wood, Mr. Summers had argued, had been all very well when the village was tiny, but now that the population was more than three hundred and likely to keep on growing, it was necessary to use something that would fit more easily into the black box. The night before the lottery, Mr. Summers and Mr. Graves made up slips of paper and put them in the box, and it was then taken to the safe of Mr. Summers' coal company and locked up until Mr. Summers was ready to take it to the square next morning. The rest of the year, the box was put away, sometimes one place, sometimes another; it had spent one year in Mr. Graves's barn and another year underfoot in the post office, and sometimes it was set on a shelf in the Martin grocery and left there.

There was a great deal of fussing to be done before Mr. Summers declared the lottery open. There were the lists to make up—of heads of families, heads of households in each family, members of each household in each family. There was the proper swearing-in of Mr. Summers by the postmaster, as the official of the lottery; at one time, some people remembered, there had been a recital of some sort, performed by the official of the lottery, a perfunctory, tuneless chant that had been rattled off duly each year; some people believed that the official of the lottery used to stand just so when he said or sang it, others believed that he was supposed to walk among the people, but years and years ago this part of the ritual had been allowed to lapse. There had been, also, a ritual salute, which the official of the lottery had to use in addressing each person who came up to draw from the box, but this also had changed with time, until now it was felt necessary only for the official to speak to each person approaching. Mr. Summers was very good at all this; in his clean white shirt and blue jeans, with one hand resting carelessly on the black box, he seemed very proper and important as he talked interminably to Mr. Graves and the Martins.

Just as Mr. Summers finally left off talking and turned to the assembled villagers, Mrs. Hutchinson came hurriedly along the path to the square, her sweater thrown over her shoulders, and slid into place in the back of the crowd. "Clean forgot what day it was," she said to Mrs. Delacroix, who stood next to her, and they both laughed softly. "Thought my old man was out back stacking wood," Mrs. Hutchinson went on, "and then I looked out the window and the kids was gone, and then I remembered it was the twenty-seventh and came a-running." She dried her hands on her apron, and Mrs. Delacroix said, "You're in time, though. They'll still talking away up there."

Mrs. Hutchinson craned her neck to see through the crowd and found her husband and children standing near the front. She tapped Mrs. Delacroix on the arm as a farewell and began to make her way through the crowd. The people separated good-humoredly to let her through; two or three people said, in voices just loud enough to be heard across the crowd, "Here comes your Missus, Hutchinson," and "Bill, she made it after all." Mrs. Hutchinson reached her husband, and Mr. Summers, who had been waiting, said cheerfully, "Thought we were going to have to get on without you, Tessie." Mrs. Hutchinson said, grinning, "Wouldn't have me leave m'dishes in the sink, now, would you, Joe?" and soft laughter ran through the crowd as the people stirred back into position after Mrs. Hutchinson's arrival.

"Well, now," Mr. Summers said soberly, "guess we better get started, get this over with, so's we can go back to work. Anybody ain't here?"

"Dunbar," several people said. "Dunbar, Dunbar."

Mr. Summers consulted his list. "Clyde Dunbar," he said. "That's right. He's broke his leg, hasn't he? Who's drawing for him?"

"Me, I guess," a woman said, and Mr. Summers turned to look at her. "Wife draws for her husband," Mr. Summers said. "Don't you have a grown boy to do it for you, Janey?" Although Mr. Summers and everyone else in the village knew the answer perfectly well, it was the business of the official of the lottery to ask such questions formally. Mr. Summers waited with an expression of polite interest while Mrs. Dunbar answered.

"Horace's not but sixteen yet," Mrs. Dunbar said regretfully. "Guess I gotta fill in for the old man this year."

"Right," Mr. Summers said. He made a note on the list he was holding. Then he asked, "Watson boy drawing this year?"

A tall boy in the crowd raised his hand. "Here," he said. "I'm drawing for m'mother and me." He blinked his eyes nervously and ducked his head as several voices in the crowd said things like "Good fellow, Jack," and "Glad to see your mother's got a man to do it."

"Well," Mr. Summers said, "guess that's everyone. Old Man Warner make it?"

"Here," a voice said, and Mr. Summers nodded.

A sudden hush fell on the crowd as Mr. Summers cleared his throat and looked at the list. "All ready?" he called. "Now, I'll read the names—heads of families first—and the men come up and take a paper out of the box. Keep the paper folded in your hand without looking at it until everyone has had a turn. Everything clear?"

The people had done it so many times that they only half listened to the directions; most of them were quiet, wetting their lips, not looking around. Then Mr. Summers raised one hand high and said, "Adams." A man disengaged himself from the crowd and came forward. "Hi, Steve," Mr. Summers said, and Mr. Adams said, "Hi, Joe." They grinned at one another humorlessly and nervously. Then Mr. Adams reached into the black box and took out a folded paper. He held it firmly by one corner as he turned and went hastily back to his place in the crowd, where he stood a little apart from his family, not looking down at his hand.

"Allen," Mr. Summers said. "Anderson. . . . Bentham."

"Seems like there's no time at all between lotteries any more," Mrs. Delacroix said to Mrs. Graves in the back row. "Seems like we got through with the last one only last week."

"Time sure goes fast," Mrs. Graves said.

"Clark. . . . Delacroix."

"There goes my old man," Mrs. Delacroix said. She held her breath while her husband went forward.

"Dunbar," Mr. Summers said, and Mrs. Dunbar went steadily to the box while one of the women said, "Go on, Janey," and another said, "There she goes."

"We're next," Mrs. Graves said. She watched while Mr. Graves came around from the side of the box, greeted Mr. Summers gravely, and selected a slip of paper from the box. By now, all through the crowd there were men holding the small folded papers in their large hands, turning them over and over nervously. Mrs. Dunbar and her two sons stood together, Mrs. Dunbar holding the slip of paper.

"Harburt. . . . Hutchinson."

"Get up there, Bill," Mrs. Hutchinson said, and the people near her laughed.

"Jones."

"They do say," Mr. Adams said to Old Man Warner, who stood next to him, "that over in the north village they're talking of giving up the lottery."

Old Man Warner snorted. "Pack of crazy fools," he said. "Listening to the young folks, nothing's good enough for *them.* Next thing you know, they'll be wanting to go back to living in caves, nobody work any more, live *that* way for a while. Used to be a saying about

'Lottery in June, corn be heavy soon.' First thing you know, we'd all be eating stewed chickweed and acorns. There's *always* been a lottery," he added petulantly. "Bad enough to see young Joe Summers up there joking with everybody."

"Some places have already quit lotteries," Mrs. Adams said.

"Nothing but trouble in *that,*" Old Man Warner said stoutly. "Pack of young fools."

"Martin." And Bobby Martin watched his father go forward. "Overdyke. . . . Percy."

"I wish they'd hurry," Mrs. Dunbar said to her oldest son. "I wish they'd hurry."

"They're almost through," her son said.

"You get ready to run tell Dad," Mrs. Dunbar said.

Mr. Summers called his own name and then stepped forward precisely and selected a slip from the box. Then he called, "Warner."

"Seventy-seventh year I been in the lottery," Old Man Warner said as he went through the crowd. "Seventy-seventh time."

"Watson." The tall boy came awkwardly through the crowd. Someone said, "Don't be nervous, Jack," and Mr. Summers said, "Take your time, son."

"Zanini."

After that there was a long pause, a breathless pause, until Mr. Summers, holding his slip of paper in the air, said, "All right, fellows." For a minute, no one moved, and then all the slips of paper were opened. Suddenly, all the women began to speak at once, saying, "Who is it?," "Who's got it," "Is it the Dunbars?," "Is it the Watsons?" Then the voices began to say, "It's Hutchinson. It's Bill." "Bill Hutchinson's got it."

"Go tell your father," Mrs. Dunbar said to her older son.

People began to look around to see the Hutchinsons. Bill Hutchinson was standing quiet, staring down at the paper in his hand. Suddenly, Tessie Hutchinson shouted to Mr. Summers, "You didn't give him time enough to take any paper he wanted. I saw you. It wasn't fair!"

"Be a good sport, Tessie," Mrs. Delacroix called, and Mrs. Graves said, "All of us took the same chance."

"Shut up, Tessie," Bill Hutchinson said.

"Well, everyone," Mr. Summers said, "that was done pretty fast, and now we've got to be hurrying a little more to get done in time." He consulted his next list. "Bill" he said, "you draw for the Hutchinson family. You got any other households in the Hutchinsons?"

"There's Don and Eva," Mrs. Hutchinson yelled. "Make *them* take their chance!"

"Daughters draw with their husbands' families, Tessie," Mr. Summers said gently. "You know that as well as anyone else."

"It wasn't *fair,*" Tessie said.

"I guess not, Joe," Bill Hutchinson said regretfully. "My daughter draws with her husband's family, that's only fair. And I've got no other family except the kids."

"Then, as far as drawing for families is concerned, it's you," Mr. Summers said in explanation, "and as far as drawing for households is concerned, that's you, too. Right?"

"Right," Bill Hutchinson said.

"How many kids, Bill?" Mr. Summers asked formally.

"Three," Bill Hutchinson said. "There's Bill, Jr., and Nancy, and little Dave. And Tessie and me."

"All right, then," Mr. Summers said. "Harry, you got their tickets back?"

Mr. Graves nodded and held up the slips of paper. "Put them in the box, then," Mr. Summers directed. "Take Bill's and put it in."

"I think we ought to start over," Mrs. Hutchinson said, as quietly as she could. "I tell you it wasn't *fair*. You didn't give him time enough to choose. *Every*body saw that."

Mr. Graves had selected the five slips and put them in the box, and he dropped all the papers but those onto the ground, where the breeze caught them and lifted them off.

"Listen, everybody," Mrs. Hutchinson was saying to the people around her.

"Ready, Bill?" Mr. Summers asked, and Bill Hutchinson, with one quick glance around at his wife and children, nodded.

"Remember," Mr. Summers said, "take the slips and keep them folded until each person has taken one. Harry, you help little Dave." Mr. Graves took the hand of the little boy, who came willingly with him up to the box. "Take a paper out of the box, Davy," Mr. Summers said. Davy put his hand into the box and laughed. "Take just *one* paper," Mr. Summers said. "Harry, you hold it for him." Mr. Graves took the child's hand and removed the folded paper from the tight fist and held it while little Dave stood next to him and looked up at him wonderingly.

"Nancy next," Mr. Summers said. Nancy was twelve, and her school friends breathed heavily as she went forward, switching her skirt, and took a slip daintily from the box. "Bill, Jr.," Mr. Summers said, and Billy, his face red and his feet overlarge, nearly knocked the box over as he got a paper out. "Tessie," Mr. Summers said. She hesitated for a minute, looking around defiantly, and then she set her lips and went up to the box. She snatched a paper out and held it behind her.

"Bill," Mr. Summers said, and Bill Hutchinson reached into the box and felt around, bringing his hand out at last with the slip of paper in it.

The crowd was quiet. A girl whispered, "I hope it's not Nancy," and the sound of the whisper reached the edges of the crowd.

"It's not the way it used to be," Old Man Warner said clearly. "People ain't the way they used to be."

"All right," Mr. Summers said. "Open the papers. Harry, you open little Dave's."

Mr. Graves opened the slip of paper and there was a general sigh through the crowd as he held it up and everyone could see that it was blank. Nancy and Bill, Jr., opened theirs at the same time, and both beamed and laughed, turning around to the crowd and holding their slips of paper above their heads.

"Tessie," Mr. Summers said. There was a pause, and then Mr. Summers looked at Bill Hutchinson, and Bill unfolded his paper and showed it. It was blank.

"It's Tessie," Mr. Summers said, and his voice was hushed. "Show us her paper, Bill."

Bill Hutchinson went over to his wife and forced the slip of paper out of her hand. It had a black spot on it, the black spot Mr. Summers had made the night before with the heavy pencil in the coal-company office. Bill Hutchinson held it up, and there was a stir in the crowd.

"All right, folks," Mr. Summers said. "Let's finish quickly."

Although the villagers had forgotten the ritual and lost the original black box, they still remembered to use stones. The pile of stones the boys had made earlier was ready; there were stones on the ground with the blowing scraps of paper that had come out of the box. Mrs. Delacroix selected a stone so large she had to pick it up with both hands and turned to Mrs. Dunbar. "Come on," she said. "Hurry up."

Mrs. Dunbar had small stones in both hands, and she said, gasping for breath, "I can't run at all. You'll have to go ahead and I'll catch up with you."

The children had stones already, and someone gave little Davy Hutchinson a few pebbles.

Tessie Hutchinson was in the center of a cleared space by now, and she held her hands out desperately as the villagers moved in on her. "It isn't fair," she said. A stone hit her on the side of the head.

Old Man Warner was saying, "Come on, come on, everyone."

Steve Adams was in the front of the crowd of villagers, with Mrs. Graves beside him.

"It isn't fair, it isn't right," Mrs. Hutchinson screamed, and then they were upon her.

4. The absence of conventional punctuation and the typographical isolation of word groups in "Epistle to Be Left in the Earth" by Archibald MacLeish on page 352 suggest great freedom of interpretation for the reader. Carefully determine what you think the selection means from word group to word group, and then attempt to communicate that meaning with all its fine distinctions. Make effective use of key, inflections, and steps.

Suggested Readings

Lee, Charlotte I. *Oral Interpretation.* (2nd edition) Boston: Houghton Mifflin, 1959, pp. 123–6, pitch.

Mouat, Lawrence H. *Reading Literature Aloud.* New York: Oxford, 1962, pp. 20–5, "Pitch."

11

AUDIBLE COMMUNICATION THROUGH QUALITY

If a musician in the next room were to produce the same pitch on a violin, saxophone, trombone, and clarinet in succession, you would have no difficulty in distinguishing the instruments. You know that each has a characteristic sound. If two of your friends in the same room were to sing the same note, you would have little difficulty in telling one voice from the other. Finally, if two friends in the other room were to utter a sentence in the same key, volume, and tempo, you could easily tell which voice was which. In each instance the sound is distinguished by a characteristic *quality,* which you have no trouble in recognizing. You may, however, have difficulty in explaining the difference you can so easily hear, for quality is the most elusive aspect of voice and the most difficult to improve.

THE USES OF QUALITY

No other aspect of voice can so subtly and effectively communicate an emotional experience. Your attitudes toward yourself, toward the idea you are expressing, and toward your listeners are normally quite obvious in the quality of your voice. For this reason, few persons, except perhaps the best actors, can convincingly pretend an attitude. The voice belies the words. Vocal quality is also the primary source of the beauty of language. Not even the finest line of poetry can be beautiful to the ear if the voice used in reading it is harsh and unpleasant. In addition to conveying emotion and making language beautiful, vocal quality is important in securing and focusing listener attention. A speaker is simply more "listenable" when his vocal quality is pleasing and varied. It was this listenable quality which characterized the speaking of Franklin D. Roosevelt. The recordings of Dylan Thomas and Alexander Scourby are also distinguished by an especially effective quality of voice. Arrange, if possible, to hear one of their records and recognize for yourself that the quality is primarily responsible for your careful listening.

THE NATURE OF VOCAL TONE

In order to understand vocal quality and to consider the improvement of your own, you should first understand the nature of vocal tone. It is produced when the breath stream causes the vocal folds to vibrate and they in turn set the molecules of air in motion. Tone as perceived by the listener is the interpretation of these vibrations after they impinge upon his eardrum.

Many vibrators, such as violin strings and the vocal folds, are able to carry on several modes of vibration simultaneously. The total result is a *tone complex.* It consists of the lowest audible pitch, called the *fundamental,* and additional frequencies produced as the vibrating body divides into halves, thirds, fourths, fifths, etc. These additional frequencies sounding above and simultaneously with the fundamental pitch are called *overtones.* The halves involve vibration at twice the frequency of the whole vibrator, and produce a pitch one octave higher than the fundamental; the fourths, two octaves higher; and so forth. The tone complex is heard by the ear as a single pitch.

The fundamental, or the lowest frequency, is the one you hear most clearly and by which you identify the pitch because it has the greatest amplitude. If we could remove all overtones and retain only the fundamental, we would be unable to distinguish the tones of the violin, saxophone, trombone, clarinet, and the human voice—provided, of course, that the same fundamental were being produced in each case. When we say that middle C on a perfectly tuned piano has 261.626 vibrations per second, we mean that the fundamental of that pitch has that many vibrations in one second. We know, however, that a violin and a trumpet or often two pianos differ in the quality of middle C. The reason is simple: each produces a different set of overtones simultaneously with the fundamental.

QUALITY IN VOICE

In the human voice, quality is determined by the purity of the vocal tone in the sense that it is produced without extraneous speech noises and by the pattern of overtones—their relative volumes and their harmony. This pattern of overtones results in part from the physical nature of the larynx and vocal folds, which the person has inherited. The overtones those folds can be made to produce in any given position are determined by their own peculiar physical make-up. The limits of vocal quality are "built in" the individual. One can, however, improve his vocal quality by improving his resonance, as we shall see in the next section of this chapter.

Other factors also help to determine the pattern of overtones in your speech. The ability to hear pleasing tones and to distinguish them from less pleasing ones is such a factor. Perhaps an "ear for sound" is also inherited: certainly such a condition as "tone deafness" seems to be innate. But for most of us the ability to recognize pleasing vocal quality depends on acquaintance with such quality in vocal or instrumental music or in speech. Mere recognition of pleasing quality must be accompanied by the ability to so approximate the vocal folds and adjust their tension as to produce the most pleasing tones possible.

Unfortunately these factors are to a great extent outside your conscious control in so far as the limits of a speech class are concerned. You can do very little about the length, size, and contour of your vocal folds and about your ear for the quality of different sounds.

On the other hand, you can make the most of the opportunity to begin the practice which will eventually effect great improvement in the pattern of overtones in your speech. During your course in oral interpretation try to become aware of pleasing voice. It is an asset well worth your cultivation. In order to begin to improve your own pattern of overtones, develop a maximum relaxation of the throat in speech. Effective resonance is your goal.

RESONANCE

The second and more obvious aspect of quality in sound is resonance. The notes of some musical instruments differ in quality primarily because of resonance. It is the length and shape of the air column rather than the nature of the mouthpiece which is mainly responsible for the difference in the quality of the trumpet and the trombone. So it is also that the saxophone and clarinet produce different qualities because of different resonance chambers. Likewise, your voice and that of your neighbor differ in quality because of different resonating chambers and different employment of them.

What is this remarkable aspect of the production of sound which we call resonance? Perhaps it can best be explained by illustrations. Borrow from your speech, music, or physics instructor a tuning fork. Remove the fork from its sounding box and strike it hard enough to produce a loud tone. While the fork is still making sound, apply the shank to the top of a table or desk. The whole surface will pulsate, and the sound can be heard throughout a large room. The vibrations are transmitted directly to the sounding board in a process called *forced vibration*. The resonance of forced vibration is non-selective and merely amplifies the sound.

Sympathetic vibration can be demonstrated by sitting at the piano, depressing the "loud" pedal so that all strings are free to vibrate, and then singing various tones up and down the scale. Soon you will produce a tone that will easily set up audible sympathetic vibration in one of the strings. You have struck a pitch that corresponds to that of the string, and the sound waves have set the string in vibration.

So-called cavity resonance is in reality merely another manifestation of sympathetic vibration, but a slight distinction is possible. Cavity resonance is the concentration and reflection of sound waves. Take up the tuning fork again. Let's assume for convenience that it represents middle C. This time we will use a collection of bottles and jars of various shapes and sizes. If the collection is extensive, you will find at least one bottle or jar which will greatly amplify the tone when the vibrating fork is held over the opening. Now take a large jar with a relatively small opening, and, as you hold the vibrating fork over the opening, slowly pour water into the jar. As the volume of the open cavity in the jar diminishes, you will find a size that corresponds to the pitch of the fork.

If you had another fork that vibrated at twice the frequency of the first, you would have to use much more water to reduce the size of the resonance cavity. The smaller cavity resonates the higher pitch. This principle is illustrated in the various resonating cavities of the marimba: long brass tubes for low tones, small and short ones for the high. Thus we are speaking of tuned resonance. It is selective.

Resonance in general is both amplification and the mechanism by which a given combination of partials is selected for emphasis and subordination to transmit a given quality. It emphasizes some overtones and subordinates others. Those frequencies to which the resonator is "in tune" pass freely;

those to which the resonator is not "in tune" do not. It is selective transmission. The selectivity of the resonator is determined by its size, mass, and texture: the resonance capacity of either a surface or cavity resonator may be either variable or fixed.

VOCAL RESONANCE

To discover how resonance is employed in voice, produce a sustained monotone with your own vocal folds, and, without interrupting the flow of sound or changing the pitch, alter the sound to produce the following long vowel sounds.

e [i]
a [e]
o [o]
u [u]

The difference you hear in these four sounds is one of resonance.

You may feel this resonance in your speech by applying your finger tips to certain parts of your body. Repeat aloud the first few words of the Gettysburg Address while you touch your forehead. Do the same thing as you place your finger tips to the bridge of your nose, your teeth, your Adam's apple, and finally your ribs. The vibration you feel is resonance.

According to *Webster's Third New International Dictionary,* resonance is "the intensification and enrichment of a musical tone by supplementary vibration." Such intensification or amplification takes place in the air within cavities and on hard and soft surfaces. In the case of the tuning fork resonance takes place in the box, its hollow interior and its walls. When the vibrating fork is held over the partially filled glass of water, resonance occurs in the column of air and in the walls of the glass. In the human voice resonance occurs theoretically in every cavity and surface of the body. Practically speaking, resonance takes place in the cavities and bones of the head, in the mouth, in the throat or pharynx, in their respective walls, and in the chest cavity and walls.

In the proper production of speech sounds resonance plays a major role. In the formation of all vowel and diphthong sounds the tongue and the palate serve to modify the shape and size of the oral resonance chamber. Diphthongs are combinations of two vowel sounds pronounced consecutively without a break in phonation. The so-called long "i" [aɪ] as in "ice" is such a sound.

Resonance is not, however, confined to the formation of vowels and diphthongs. It is employed in the making of all voiced sounds, including the vocal consonants: b [b], m [m], w [w], v [v], th [ð], z [z], d [d], n [n], r [r], l [l], zh [ʒ], j [dʒ], y [j], g [g], ng [ŋ]. In these sounds the role of resonance is primarily one of simple amplification.

Furthermore, all voiced sounds employ other kinds of resonance as well. This resonance is largely beyond conscious control and occurs in the lower pharynx, the larynx itself, and the remaining cavities and surfaces of the head, throat, and chest.

In order to complete the picture of vocal resonance we must mention an additional specialized form without which normal speech is impossible. The consonants m [m], n [n], and ng [ŋ] are resonated in the nasal cavity. In fact, the major difference between the *m* and the *b*, the *n* and the *d*, and the *ng* and the *g*, is that the former in each instance is resonated nasally. If you will pronounce "come" and "cub," you will see that the same mouth positions are employed except that in "come" the passageway between the mouth and nose is kept open while in "cub" it is closed. Try the same experiment and you will recognize the same difference between "bun" and "bud" and "rang" and "rag." When this normal *nasal* resonance is not present for these consonants and their neighboring vowels, we speak of *denasal* speech. When you have a severe cold in your head, so that the nasal passages are blocked, your sentence "I am not going to come again" becomes "I ab dot goig to cub agaid." Usually the correction of such speech, whether it results from a cold infection or some more serious structural malformation, is achieved only through the removal of the blockage.

NASALITY

While we have spoken favorably of nasal resonance and have observed that without it speech is abnormal, we must hasten to observe that it can be, and often is, overdone. To "talk through your nose," as we say, is to overuse nasal resonance. Such speech is readily recognizable to the listener, but many of us have habitual nasality ourselves and often are not aware of it. Nasality is monotonous and unpleasant to the listener. You may discover whether you are guilty of such nasality by doing the following simple experiment. With thumb and forefinger pinch the bridge of your nose about where the supports of eyeglasses ordinarily rest. Now feel the resonance as you say the following sentence: "My nasal resonance is usually adequate." While speaking the first three words, you should feel much more vibration than during the last three. If you feel much vibration during all of the sentence, you may be sure that you employ an excessive amount of nasal resonance.

Nasality results from failure to reduce the opening between the mouth and the nasal cavity when making sounds other than m [m], n [n], and ng [ŋ]. In normal speech, except the formation of the three sounds just mentioned, the soft palate and the uvula rise and meet the back wall of the throat, which comes forward, almost to close off the nasal passages. When this closure is not adequate, the voice is nasal. Usually the condition can be corrected with persistent practice in the acceptable formation of sounds. Sometimes, however, structural difficulties must have the care of a surgeon. If you discover that you have a nasal voice and if you can consciously reduce the nasality, you may be assured that persistent practice will result in diminishing it appreciably.

VOCAL RESONANCE FOR PROJECTION

In Chapter 9 it was observed that speaking and reading require *projection* or enlargement of tone and that one of the results of its achievement is loudness. Obviously you can enlarge the sound of the tuning fork by striking it with more force, but you can also enlarge it by attaching the sounding box. Increasing the resonance of any sound results in its greater projection. With the trumpet mouthpiece alone you can produce any pitch you desire, but when you also use the rest of the instrument you are able to project the tone by increasing the resonance.

So it is that vocal tones can be projected. Open your mouth and throat in a huge yawn to produce greater relaxation, greater resonance, and greater projection. If you relax your mouth, throat, and chest structures to provide a maximum opportunity for resonance, and if you employ a limited but not offensive degree of nasal resonance, coupled with adequate breath support, your speech tones will have an optimum projection.

VOCAL RESONANCE FOR BEAUTY OF SPEECH

Not only does resonance contribute to projection, but it also enriches speech by amplifying harmonious overtones so that the resultant sound is more pleasing to the ear. In your reading it is often therefore desirable to use a maximum of resonance not only for projection but also for beauty. A pleasing voice, like pleasing personal appearance, is an asset in communication, especially when the ideas being expressed or the phrases being uttered are in themselves beautiful.

KINDS OF VOCAL QUALITY AND THEIR USES

Just as different pitches of voice tend to suggest certain attitudes or emotions to the listener, so do certain kinds of vocal quality. In the days of the elocutionist the student made a catalogue of these vocal qualities and learned to apply them on demand. We know today that any classification of vocal qualities is about the least scientific aspect of voice work because the significance of quality depends upon the subjective reaction of the listener. Who can say how another will react to the taste of okra? Who can say that a certain vocal quality will positively produce a certain reaction in a listener? Therefore, we no longer believe that vocal qualities can be adequately categorized and used upon demand. Nevertheless, it is helpful for the student to learn to employ a variety of qualities.

You will be interested in the following qualities of voice and the possible opportunities to use them. Since only the terms breathy, throaty, hollow, nasal, and denasal can be described with acoustical or anatomical accuracy, you must regard the rest as much less definite descriptive words.

Breathy. In the employment of this kind of vocal quality, the vocal folds fail to approximate along their entire length, and so there is a mixture of vibrating and nonvibrating air. The stage whisper is an extreme of this quality inasmuch as it involves a great amount of nonvibrating air and a small amount of phonation.

Sometimes a *breathy* quality is used to express a confidential manner. It is also employed to communicate fear, surprise, or even horror. In reading Poe's "The Cask of Amontillado" you might want in some places to use such a vocal quality. After the vengeful Montressor has entombed Fortunato alive in a remote recess of the catacombs, the victim suddenly sheds his drunkenness and in mortal terror calls, *For the love of God, Montressor!* This line might require a *breathy* quality. The gentle touch recommended in the reading of "Four Little Foxes" by Lew Sarett might well involve some *breathy* quality in such lines as *Speak gently, Walk softly, Go lightly,* and *Step softly.* Look back at the poem in Chapter 9 and see if you think this is true.

Throaty. When the breath stream is forced roughly between tense vocal folds and through a tense pharynx, the result is a rasping quality we call *throaty* or guttural. It is frequently expressive of coarseness, crudity, or roughness. Occasionally you find a brutish, Frankensteinian character who will be best expressed with this quality. For example, if you were reading a cutting from Shakespeare's *The Tempest,* including the following lines by Caliban, the savage and deformed slave, you might speak with a *throaty* quality:

As wicked dew as e'er my mother brush'd
With raven's feather from unwholesome fen,
Drop on you both! a south-west blow on ye,
And blister you all o'er.

You might use a little less of much the same quality in reading the following speech of Captain Keeney in Eugene O'Neill's *Ile:*

> Hell! I got to git the ile, I tell you . . .
> I got to get me the ile! I got to git it
> in spite of all hell, and I ain't agoin' home
> till I do git it!

To a much more limited degree you might use some *throaty* quality in these lines from "The Man with the Hoe" by Edwin Markham.

> Down all the caverns of Hell to their last gulf
> There is no shape more terrible than this—

Frequently an isolated word or phrase will be best expressed with a touch of *throaty* quality. Because of sound combinations and connotations, some words require a bit of this quality for normal utterance. Practice the following as examples: *gruesome, gruff, grumble, awful, horror.*

Hollow. When you have a maximum of pharyngeal resonance you can produce a *hollow,* barrel-sounding quality. Sometimes we call it a funereal tone. It often suggests remoteness or morbidity. It is sometimes called sepulchral. Readers and actors use it for such characters as the ghost in *Hamlet* and Marley's ghost in *A Christmas Carol* by Charles Dickens. Some readers make limited use of this quality in the following lines from "Break, Break, Break" by Alfred, Lord Tennyson.

> Break, break, break,
> On thy cold gray stones, O Sea!
> And I would that my tongue could utter
> The thoughts that arise in me.

"The Laughers" by Louis Untermeyer, which is included in the exercises at the end of the previous chapter, may in places need some *hollow* quality for full communication. Look up these lines in that poem and see if you agree.

> A grisly quiet with the power to choke;
> A quiet that only one thing broke;
> One thing alone rose up thereafter. . . .
> Laughter.

Nasal. The twangy sound produced by too much *nasal* resonance often expresses ignorance or rusticity and is frequently used to suggest a humorous response. The whine, which may indicate an ingratiating attitude, is nasality coupled with slow rate of utterance and prolonged duration of sounds. The *nasal* quality should be used with great discretion.

Denasal. Earlier in this chapter we recognized that the absence of nasal resonance, especially on m [m], n [n], and ng [ŋ], produces a *denasal* quality. This quality is, of course, most immediately suggestive of some nasal stoppage but is sometimes used to indicate stupidity. It may be useful for humor but even for that purpose should very seldom be employed.

Oral. When resonance is held to a bare minimum and is kept largely in the mouth, the result is a relatively weak, confined quality which we call *oral.* When the speaker or reader wishes to convey quietness, gentleness, weakness, fatigue, illness, or age, this quality may be an effective one to use. It is frequently employed when circumstances permit doing so without loss of audibility. Try reading the following poem with an *oral* quality.

I'M NOBODY

EMILY DICKINSON

I'm nobody! Who are you?
Are you nobody, too?
Then there's a pair of us—don't tell!
They'd banish us, you know.

How dreary to be somebody!
How public like a frog
To tell your name the livelong day
To an admiring bog!

Falsetto. Etymologically, this word may be translated as "little false voice." The *falsetto* is thin, shrill, and unnaturally high. It is uttered with the glottis completely closed at the front.

The *falsetto* is sometimes employed for broad comic effect. In serious reading or speaking it occasionally characterizes great wonder or surprise. Some of the wide variety of voice necessary in the reading of Vachel Lindsay's "The Congo," which is partially quoted in Chapter 14, may be achieved by the occasional use of the *falsetto.* It is also sometimes used to a very limited extent in distinguishing voices in comic dialogue.

Tremulous. Voice in which the force and resonance are uncertainly maintained in a wavering pattern is generally designated as *tremulous.* It seems to suggest extreme uncertainty, perhaps great pain or great age. It may sometimes be used in those portions of dialogue which are meant to communicate these conditions. Used discretely it may sometimes be meaningful in the reading of delicate verse. When used generously it results in melodrama.

Full. If both the volume and the resonance of the normal tone are increased, a speaker or reader may produce a so-called *full* quality. This quality is often thought to be suggestive of dignity and confidence but may easily degenerate into the melodramatic. When we speak disparagingly of "ministerial tone," this quality is usually what we mean. The *full* quality is frequently necessary, but its excessive use is to be carefully avoided.

Normal. The quality of voice which one uses most often is referred to as the *normal* and should involve all the resonators. It is the quality of good conversational speech.

Other words we could use to describe vocal quality are *sharp, metallic, harsh, bored, tired,* and *passionate,* to mention only a few. However, these may well refer only to special uses of those vocal qualities already described: for example, the *breathy* quality may communicate passion. You may go on to add other descriptive or functional terms to the list. It is interesting to speak a few lines in a particular quality of voice and to see if others can recognize the quality and its significance. Do not be disappointed if you have only a little success: it takes a great deal of skill deliberately to assume a meaningful vocal quality, and, furthermore, you can almost never be positive that the listener will respond to your speech as you intend.

ONE PRINCIPLE FOR VOCAL QUALITY

You can experiment with vocal quality and learn to improve it, as you will be asked to do in the exercises at the end of this chapter, but your effective employment of quality in speaking and reading depends primarily on one simple principle: *to feel like is to sound like.* The teacher of acting speaks of *kinesthetic* tone. He tells the player that any particular word, "rose" for example, lacks real significance until its utterance gives some intimation of the speaker's feelings toward the entity being named. His feelings involve an inclination to do something about the entity—to seek it, to avoid it, to foster it, to sense it more fully, or to eliminate it from his mind. Whatever mental, emotional, and bodily activity is implicit in the speaker as he says the word is reflected in the quality of the sound of the word. Thus it is that whatever imagery is being experienced by the speaker will be shown in the quality of his voice. If you feel scared, you will sound scared. If you wish to convey fright in reading, you must recall the image of fear. To convey anger in reading, you must recall the image of anger. So it is with any emotion: first feel it, and then you can express it—provided, of course, you have the faculty for doing so.

Because of the principle *to feel like is to sound like,* vocal quality must ever spring from within the reader. Quality should always result from intellectual and emotional stimulation. To impose a specific quality is to create the artificiality we deplore in the elocutionist and the "ham." Furthermore, the imposition of vocal quality without comprehension inevitably calls attention to the vocal technique and not to the meaning.

When you read aloud to others, adjust all of your body tensions to the nature of the meaning being expressed. Feel the meaning with all of yourself, down to your finger tips. When you have succeeded in doing so, your most suitable vocal quality is most likely to ensue.

Summary

Effective vocal quality, though easy to recognize, is difficult to achieve. It is important for the communication of meaning and for beauty of utterance. It is conducive to good listening. Quality results from the pattern of overtones and the employment of resonance. With careful listening and practice you can improve both. Differences in quality suggest different attitudes and emotions, but you must sense emotional meaning in order to achieve appropriate vocal quality.

Exercises

1. Read aloud the following words, holding the nasals for full resonance:

rang	tongue	win	mass	hymn
sang	clung	bone	main	rhyme
bang	ran	cone	made	time
ring	ban	flown	dam	dime
sing	tan	grown	clam	home
bing	man	prone	bam	roam
thing	den	throne	gleam	loam
song	hen	run	cream	gloom
bong	men	stun	team	bloom
thong	sin	spun	dim	tomb
sung	bin	mad	limb	thumb
bung	tin	mat	grim	some

2. You will notice that the following poem is subtitled, "The Power of Music," for this is its theme. In a broader sense, however, it demonstrates

that differing sounds can excite different emotional responses. (a) Study the poem to determine what are the different emotions of Alexander which are played upon in each stanza. (b) Practice reading the poem with such changes in vocal quality as you think most effectively convey the varying emotional content. Remember to use the steps for finding the meaning.

ALEXANDER'S FEAST; OR, THE POWER OF MUSIC

JOHN DRYDEN

I

'T was at the royal feast, for Persia won
By Philip's warlike son:
Aloft in awful state
The god-like hero sate
On his imperial throne:
His valiant peers were placed around,
Their brows with roses and with myrtles bound;
(So should desert in arms be crowned.)
The lovely Thais, by his side,
Sate like a blooming Eastern bride
In flow'r of youth and beauty's pride.
Happy, happy, happy pair!
None but the brave,
None but the brave,
None but the brave deserves the fair.

Chorus: Happy, happy, happy pair!
None but the brave,
None but the brave,
None but the brave deserves the fair.

II

Timotheus, placed on high
Amid the tuneful choir,
With flying fingers touch'd the lyre:
The trembling notes ascend the sky,
And heav'nly joys inspire.
The song began from Jove,
Who left his blissful seats above,
(Such is the pow'r of mighty love.)
A dragon's fiery form belied the god:
Sublime on radiant spires he rode,
When he to fair Olympia pressed:

And while he sought her snowy breast:
Then round her slender waist he curled,
And stamped an image of himself, a sov'reign of the world.
—The list'ning crowd admire the lofty sound;
"A present deity!" they shout around;
"A present deity!" the vaulted roofs rebound:
With ravished ears
The monarch hears,
Assumes the god;
Affects to nod
And seems to shake the spheres.

Chorus: *With ravished ears*
The monarch hears,
Assumes the god:
Affects to nod
And seems to shake the spheres.

III

The praise of Bacchus then the sweet musician sung,
Of Bacchus ever fair and ever young:
The jolly god in triumph comes;
Sound the trumpets, beat the drums!
Flushed with a purple grace
He shows his honest face:
Now give the hautboys breath; he comes, he comes.
Bacchus, ever fair and young,
Drinking joys did first ordain;
Bacchus' blessings are a treasure,
Drinking is the soldier's pleasure:
Rich the treasure,
Sweet the pleasure,
Sweet is pleasure after pain.

Chorus: *Bacchus' blessings are a treasure,*
Drinking is the soldier's pleasure:
Rich the treasure,
Sweet the pleasure,
Sweet is pleasure after pain.

IV

Soothed with the sound, the king grew vain;
Fought all his battles o'er again,

And thrice he routed all his foes, and thrice he slew the slain!
The master saw the madness rise;
His glowing cheeks, his ardent eyes;
And, while he heav'n and earth defied,
Changed his hand, and check'd his pride.
He chose a mournful Muse
Soft pity to infuse:
He sung Darius, great and good;
By too severe a fate,
Fallen, fallen, fallen, fallen,
Fallen from his high estate,
And welt'ring in his blood;
Deserted, at his utmost need,
By those his former bounty fed;
On the bare earth exposed he lies,
With not a friend to close his eyes.
With downcast looks the joyless victor sate,
Revolving in his alter'd soul
The various turns of chance below;
And, now and then, a sigh he stole;
And tears began to flow.

Chorus: Revolving in his alter'd soul
The various turns of chance below;
And, now and then, a sigh he stole;
And tears began to flow.

V

The mighty master smiled to see
That love was in the next degree;
'Twas but a kindred sound to move,
For pity melts the mind to love.
Softly sweet, in Lydian measures,
Soon he soothed his soul to pleasures.
"War," he sung, "is toil and trouble;
Honour, but an empty bubble;
Never ending, still beginning,
Fighting still, and still destroying:
If the world be worth thy winning,
Think, O think it worth enjoying;
Lovely Thais sits beside thee,
Take the good the gods provide thee."
The many rend the skies with loud applause;

So Love was crowned, but Music won the cause.
The prince, unable to conceal his pain,
    Gazed on the fair
    Who caused his care,
And sighed and looked, sighed and looked,
Sighed and looked, and sighed again:
At length, with love and wine at once oppressed,
The vanquished victor sunk upon her breast.

Chorus: The prince, unable to conceal his pain,
    Gazed on the fair
    Who caused his care,
And sighed and looked, sighed and looked,
Sighed and looked, and sighed again:
At length, with love and wine at once oppressed,
The vanquished victor sunk upon her breast.

VI

Now strike the golden lyre again:
A louder yet, and yet a louder strain.
Break his bands of sleep asunder,
And rouse him, like a rattling peal of thunder.
    Hark, hark, the horrid sound
        Has raised up his head:
        As awaked from the dead,
    And amazed, he stares around.
"Revenge, revenge!" Timotheus cries,
    "See the Furies arise!
    "See the snakes that they rear
    How they hiss in their hair,
And the sparkles that flash from their eyes!
    Behold a ghastly band,
    Each a torch in his hand!
Those are Grecian ghosts, that in battle were slain
    And unburied remain
    Inglorious on the plain:
    Give the vengeance due
    To the valiant crew!
Behold how they toss their torches on high,
    How they point to the Persian abodes,
And glitt'ring temples of their hostile gods!"
The princes applaud, with a furious joy:
And the King seized a flambeau with zeal to destroy;

Thais led the way,
To light him to his prey,
And, like another Helen, fired another Troy.

Chorus: And the King seized a flambeau with zeal to destroy;
Thais led the way
To light him to his prey,
And, like another Helen, fired another Troy!

VII

Thus, long ago,
Ere heaving bellows learned to blow,
While organs yet were mute;
Timotheus, to his breathing flute,
And sounding lyre,
Could swell the soul to rage, or kindle soft desire.
At last, divine Cecilia came,
Inventress of the vocal frame;
The sweet enthusiast, from her sacred store,
Enlarged the former narrow bounds,
And added length to solemn sounds,
With Nature's mother wit, and arts unknown before.
Let old Timotheus yield the prize,
Or both divide the crown;
He raised a mortal to the skies,
She drew an angel down.

Grand Chorus: At last, divine Cecilia came,
Inventress of the vocal frame;
The sweet enthusiast, from her sacred store,
Enlarged the former narrow bounds
And added length to solemn sounds,
With Nature's mother wit, and arts unknown before.
Let old Timotheus yield the prize,
Or both divide the crown;
He raised a mortal to the skies,
She drew an angel down.

3. In the chapters on loudness and pitch you were warned to avoid the "ministerial" pattern which is so often imposed on Bible reading. In this present chapter you learned that the "ministerial" tone is also undesirable. Practice reading the following story using loudness, pitch, time, and quality

to achieve a maximum communication of meaning. First, of course, be sure you are fully aware of the meaning. Listen to the Charles Laughton record before you read. Count and identify the many voice qualities he uses.

THE FIERY FURNACE

from *The Bible, King James Version*

DANIEL 3:1–30

1 Nebuchadnezzar the king made an image of gold, whose height was three-score cubits, and the breadth thereof six cubits: he set it up in the plain of Dura, in the province of Babylon.

2 Then Nebuchadnezzar the king sent to gather together the princes, the governors, and the captains, the judges, the treasurers, the counsellors, the sheriffs, and all the rulers of the provinces, to come to the dedication of the image which Nebuchadnezzar the king had set up.

3 Then the princes, the governors, and captains, the judges, the treasurers, the counsellors, the sheriffs, and all the rulers of the provinces, were gathered together unto the dedication of the image that Nebuchadnezzar had set up, and they stood before the image that Nebuchadnezzar had set up.

4 Then an herald cried aloud, To you it is commanded, O people, nations, and languages,

5 That at what time ye hear the sound of the cornet, flute, harp, sackbut, psaltery, dulcimer, and all kinds of musick, ye fall down and worship the golden image that Nebuchadnezzar the king hath set up:

6 And whoso falleth not down and worshippeth shall the same hour be cast into the midst of a burning fiery furnace.

7 Therefore at that time, when all the people heard the sound of the cornet, flute, harp, sackbut, psaltery, and all kinds of musick, all the people, the nations, and the languages fell down and worshipped the golden image that Nebuchadnezzar the king had set up.

8 Wherefore at that time certain Chaldeans came near, and accused the Jews.

9 They spake and said to the king Nebuchadnezzar, O king, live for ever.

10 Thou, O king, hast made a decree, that every man that shall hear the sound of the cornet, flute, harp, sackbut, psaltery, and dulcimer, and all kinds of musick, shall fall down and worship the golden image:

11 And whoso falleth not down and worshippeth, that he should be cast into the midst of a burning fiery furnace.

12 There are certain Jews whom thou hast set over the affairs

of the province of Babylon, Shadrach, Meshach, and Abednego; these men, O king, have not regarded thee: they serve not thy gods, nor worship the golden image which thou hast set up.

13 Then Nebuchadnezzar in his rage and fury commanded to bring Shadrach, Meshach, and Abednego. Then they brought these men before the king.

14 Nebuchadnezzar spake and said unto them, Is it true, O Shadrach, Meshach, and Abednego, do not ye serve my gods, nor worship the golden image which I have set up?

15 Now if ye be ready that at what time ye hear the sound of the cornet, flute, harp, sackbut, psaltery, and dulcimer, and all kinds of musick, ye fall down and worship the image which I have made; well: but if ye worship not, ye shall be cast the same hour into the midst of a burning fiery furnace; and who is that God that shall deliver you out of my hands?

16 Shadrach, Meshach, and Abednego, answered and said to the king, O Nebuchadnezzar, we are not careful to answer thee in this matter.

17 If it be so, our God whom we serve is able to deliver us from the burning fiery furnace, and he will deliver us out of thine hand, O king.

18 But if not, be it known unto thee, O king, that we will not serve thy gods, nor worship the golden image which thou hast set up.

19 Then was Nebuchadnezzar full of fury, and the form of his visage was changed against Shadrach, Meshach, and Abednego: therefore he spake, and commanded that they should heat the furnace seven times more than it was wont to be heated.

20 And he commanded the most mighty men that were in his army to bind Shadrach, Meshach, and Abednego, and to cast them into the burning fiery furnace.

21 Then these men were bound in their coats, their hosen, and their hats, and their other garments, and were cast into the midst of the burning fiery furnace.

22 Therefore because the king's commandment was urgent, and the furnace exceeding hot, the flame of the fire slew those men that took up Shadrach, Meshach, and Abednego.

23 And these three men, Shadrach, Meshach, and Abednego, fell down bound into the midst of the burning fiery furnace.

24 Then Nebuchadnezzar the king was astonished, and rose up in haste, and spake, and said unto his counsellors, Did not we cast three men bound into the midst of the fire? They answered and said unto the king, True, O king.

25 He answered and said, Lo, I see four men loose, walking in

the midst of the fire, and they have no hurt; and the form of the fourth is like the Son of God.

26 Then Nebuchadnezzar came near to the mouth of the burning fiery furnace, and spake, and said, Shadrach, Meshach, and Abednego, ye servants of the most high God, come forth, and come hither. Then Shadrach, Meshach, and Abednego, came forth of the midst of the fire.

27 And the princes, governors, and captains, and the king's counsellors, being gathered together, saw these men, upon whose bodies the fire had no power, nor was an hair of their head singed, neither were their coats changed, nor the smell of fire had passed on them.

28 Then Nebuchadnezzar spake, and said, Blessed be the God of Shadrach, Meshach, and Abednego, who hath sent his angel, and delivered his servants that trusted in him, and have changed the king's word, and yielded their bodies, that they might not serve nor worship any god, except their own God.

29 Therefore I make a decree, That every people, nation, and language, which speak anything amiss against the God of Shadrach, Meshach, and Abednego, shall be cut in pieces, and their houses shall be made a dunghill: because there is no other God that can deliver after this sort.

30 Then the king promoted Shadrach, Meshach, and Abednego, in the province of Babylon.

4. This excerpt from a famous play requires many changes in vocal quality in order to express the meaning. The character whose lines we are quoting is valiant and romantic in the extreme, but he is desperately sensitive about the length of his enormous nose. Read the play to appreciate fully Cyrano's personality. Listen to José Ferrer's recording if possible. Practice reading aloud the "Nose Speech" with such vocal qualities as best express the meaning: Cyrano is telling a fool how he might have been clever in insulting his nose.

from CYRANO DE BERGERAC

EDMOND ROSTAND

(translated by Brian Hooker)

CYRANO:

Ah, no, young sir!
You are too simple. Why, you might have said—
Oh, a great many things! Mon dieu, why waste

Your opportunity? For example, thus:—
[*Aggressive*] I, sir, if that nose were mine,
I'd have it amputated—on the spot!
[*Friendly*] How do you drink with such a nose?
You ought to have a cup made specially.
[*Descriptive*] 'Tis a rock—a crag—a cape—
A cape? say rather, a peninsula!
[*Inquisitive*] What is that receptacle—
A razor-case or a portfolio?
[*Kindly*] Ah, do you love the little birds
So much that when they come and sing to you,
You give them this to perch on? [*Insolent*]
Sir, when you smoke, the neighbors must suppose
Your chimney is on fire. [*Cautious*] Take care—
A weight like that might make you topheavy.
[*Thoughtful*] Somebody fetch my parasol—
Those delicate colors fade so in the sun!
[*Pedantic*] Does not Aristophanes
Mention a mythologic monster called
Hippocampelephantocamelos?
Surely we have here the original!
[*Familiar*] Well, old torchlight! Hang your hat
Over that chandelier—it hurts my eyes.
[*Eloquent*] When it blows, the typhoon howls,
And the clouds darken. [*Dramatic*] When it bleeds—
The Red Sea! [*Enterprising*] What a sign
For some perfumer! [*Lyric*] Hark—the horn
Of Roland calls to summon Charlemagne!—
[*Simple*] When do they unveil the monument?
[*Respectful*] Sir, I recognize in you
A man of parts, a man of prominence—
[*Rustic*] Hey? What? Call that a nose? Na, na—
I be no fool like what you think I be—
That there's a blue cucumber! [*Military*]
Point against cavalry! [*Practical*] Why not
A lottery with this for the grand prize?
Or—parodying Faustus in the play—
"Was this the nose that launched a thousand ships
And burned the topless towers of Ilium?"
These, my dear sir, are things you might have said
Had you some tinge of letters, or of wit
To color your discourse. But wit,—not so,
You never had an atom—and of letters,

You need but three to write you down—an Ass.
Moreover,—if you had the invention, here
Before these folk to make a jest of me—
Be sure you would not then articulate
The twentieth part of half a syllable
Of the beginning! For I say these things
Lightly enough myself, about myself,
But I allow none else to utter them.

5. The cuttings from *The Human Comedy* by William Saroyan in Chapter 2, "The Highwayman" by Alfred Noyes in Chapter 8, "The Laughers" by Louis Untermeyer in Chapter 9, "How to Tell a Major Poet from a Minor Poet" by E. B. White in Chapter 13, and the portion of "The Congo" by Vachel Lindsay in the poetry recital in Chapter 14 all require a variety of vocal qualities. Study and then experiment with some of them.

6. Study the following selections and practice reading them with appropriate vocal quality. You will probably discover that each requires its own characteristic quality. In at least one of them you will find it effective to employ different qualities in different sections.

from THE BALLAD OF READING GAOL

OSCAR WILDE

In Reading gaol by Reading town
    There is a pit of shame,
And in it lies a wretched man
    Eaten by teeth of flame,
In a burning winding-sheet he lies,
    And his grave has got no name.

And there, till Christ call forth the dead,
    In silence let him lie:
No need to waste the foolish tear,
    Or heave the windy sigh:
The man had killed the thing he loved,
    And so he had to die.

And all men kill the thing they love,
    By all let this be heard,
Some do it with a bitter look,
    Some with a flattering word,
The coward does it with a kiss,
    The brave man with a sword!

THE CLEAN PLATTER

OGDEN NASH

Some painters paint the sapphire sea,
And some the fathering storm.
Others portray young lambs at play,
But most, the female form.
'Twas trite in that primeval dawn
When painting got its start,
That a lady with her garments on
Is Life, but is she Art?
By undraped nymphs
I am not wooed;
I'd rather painters painted food.

Food,
Yes, food,
Just any old kind of food.
Pooh for the cook,
And pooh for the price!
Some of it's nicer, but all of it's nice.
Pheasant is pleasant, of course,
And terrapin, too, is tasty,
Lobster I freely endorse,
In pâté or patty or pasty.
But there's nothing the matter with butter,
And nothing the matter with jam,
And the warmest of greetings I utter
To the ham and yam and clam.
For they're food,
All food
And I think very highly of food.
Though I am broody at times
When bothered by rhymes,
I brood
On food.

Food,
Just food,
Just any old kind of food.
Let it be sour
Or let it be sweet,

As long as you're sure it is something to eat.
Go purloin a sirloin, my pet,
If you'd win a devotion incredible;
And asparagus tips vinaigrette,
Or anything else that is edible.
Bring salad or sausage or scrapple,
A berry or even a beet,
Bring an oyster, an egg, or an apple,
As long as it's something to eat.
For it's food,
It's food;
Never mind what kind of food.
Through thick and through thin
I am constantly in
The mood
For food.

Some singers sing of ladies' eyes,
And some of ladies' lips,
Refined ones praise their ladylike ways,
And coarse ones hymn their hips.
The Oxford Book of English Verse
Is lush with lyrics tender;
A poet, I guess, is more or less,
Preoccupied with gender.
Yet I, though custom call me crude,
Prefer to sing in praise of food.

THE BELLS

EDGAR ALLAN POE

Hear the sledges with the bells,
Silver bells!
What a world of merriment their melody foretells!
How they tinkle, tinkle, tinkle,
In the icy air of night!
While the stars, that oversprinkle
All the heavens, seem to twinkle
With a crystalline delight;
Keeping time, time, time,
In a sort of Runic rime,
To the tintinnabulation that so musically wells

From the bells, bells, bells, bells,
Bells, bells, bells—
From the jingling and the tinkling of the bells.

Hear the mellow wedding bells,
Golden bells!
What a world of happiness their harmony foretells!
Through the balmy air of night
How they ring out their delight!
From the molten-golden notes,
And all in tune,
What a liquid ditty floats
To the turtle-dove that listens, while she gloats
On the moon!
Oh, from out the sounding cells,
What a gush of euphony voluminously wells!
How it swells!
How it dwells
On the Future! how it tells
Of the rapture that impels
To the swinging and the ringing
Of the bells, bells, bells,
Of the bells, bells, bells, bells,
To the riming and the chiming of the bells!

Hear the loud alarum bells,
Brazen bells!
What a tale of terror, now, their turbulency tells!
In the startled ear of night
How they scream out their affright!
Too much horrified to speak,
They can only shriek, shriek,
Out of tune,
In a clamorous appealing to the mercy of the fire,
In a mad expostulation with the deaf and frantic fire,
Leaping higher, higher, higher,
With a desperate desire,
And a resolute endeavor
Now—now to sit or never,
By the side of the pale-faced moon.
Oh, the bells, bells, bells!
What a tale their terror tells
Of Despair!

How they clang, and clash, and roar!
What a horror they outpour
On the bosom of the palpitating air!
Yet the ear it fully knows,
By the twanging
And the clanging,
How the danger ebbs and flows;
Yet the ear distinctly tells,
In the jangling
And the wrangling,
How the danger sinks and swells—
By the sinking or the swelling in the anger of the bells,
Of the bells,
Of the bells, bells, bells, bells,
Bells, bells, bells—
In the clamor and the clangor of the bells!

Hear the tolling of the bells,
Iron bells!
What a world of solemn thought their monody compels!
In the silence of the night
How we shiver with affright
At the melancholy menace of their tone!
For every sound that floats
From the rust within their throats
Is a groan.
And the people—ah, the people,
They that dwell up in the steeple,
All alone,
And who tolling, tolling, tolling
In that muffled monotone,
Feel a glory in so rolling
On the human heart a stone—
They are neither man nor woman—
They are neither brute nor human—
They are Ghouls:
And their king it is who tolls;
And he rolls, rolls, rolls,
Rolls
A paean from the bells,
And his merry bosom swells
With the paean of the bells,
And he dances, and he yells:

Keeping time, time, time,
In a sort of Runic rime,
To the paean of the bells,
Of the bells:
Keeping time, time, time,
In a sort of Runic rime,
To the throbbing of the bells,
Of the bells, bells, bells—
To the sobbing of the bells;
Keeping time, time, time,
As he knells, knells, knells,
In a happy Runic rime,
To the rolling of the bells,
Of the bells, bells, bells:
To the tolling of the bells,
Of the bells, bells, bells, bells,
Bells, bells, bells—
To the moaning and the groaning of the bells.

FOUR POEMS

STEPHEN CRANE

I

In the desert
I saw a creature, naked, bestial,
Who, squatting upon the ground,
Held his heart in his hands,
And ate of it.
I said, 'Is it good, friend?'
'It is bitter—bitter,' he answered;
'But I like it
Because it is bitter,
And because it is my heart.'

II

Once there came a man
Who said,
'Range me all men of the world in rows.'
And instantly
There was terrific clamour among the people
Against being ranged in rows.
There was a loud quarrel, world-wide.

It endured for ages;
And blood was shed
By those who would not stand in rows,
And by those who pined to stand in rows.
Eventually, the man went to death, weeping.
And those who stayed in bloody scuffle
Knew not the great simplicity.

III

A man said to the universe:
'Sir, I exist!'
'However,' replied the universe,
'The fact has not created in me
A sense of obligation.'

IV

A man adrift on a slim spar
A horizon smaller than the rim of a bottle
Tented waves rearing lashy dark points
The near whine of froth in circles.
God is cold.

The incessant raise and swing of the sea
And growl after growl of crest
The sinkings, green, seething, endless
The upheaval half-completed.
God is cold.

The seas are in the hollow of The Hand;
Oceans may be turned to a spray
Raining down through the stars
Because of a gesture of pity toward a babe.
Oceans may become grey ashes,
Die with a long moan and a roar
Amid the tumult of the fishes
And the cries of the ships,
Because The Hand beckons the mice.
A horizon smaller than a doomed assassin's cap,
Inky, surging tumults
A reeling, drunken sky and no sky
A pale hand sliding from a polished spar.
God is cold.

The puff of a coat imprisoning air:
A face kissing the water-death
A weary slow sway of a lost hand
And the sea, the moving sea, the sea.
God is cold.

7. The following short story is a vivid satirical commentary on commercialization of sentimentality. Perhaps you would call it melodrama: while it is to be read as if serious, the listener must always remember that it is ridiculous. Constant attention to both vocal quality and inflections will serve to depict the significance to the listener.

A DEATH IN THE STADIUM

ROBERT NATHAN

My friend approached me with these words: "How are you?" Before I could reply, he exclaimed: "I am on my way to attend the public death of Principus, the great actor, at the stadium. Come, we will go together, for it is sure to be an interesting spectacle." And he added: "He was the greatest actor in the world."

I turned and went with him, for I had heard of this affair. Indeed, it seemed as if the whole city were hurrying in that direction; nevertheless, we managed to squeeze ourselves into the subway. As we jogged slowly up-town, with many stops and waits, my friend told me a little more about Principus, whose death was convulsing the entire nation. "He was a great hero. Now he is dying; with a showman's instinct, and also in order to provide for his family, he has determined to die in public, comforted during his last moments by the groans of his admirers."

It was a peaceful evening; the roof-tops of the city towered upward into the sky stained by the sunset and lighted by a few pale stars. The great actor lay dying in a field ordinarily given over to prize-fights or baseball, and rented for this occasion; the seats which rose in concrete tiers all about him were entirely filled, while crowds of men and women at the gates gazed with gloomy interest at the ushers, who gazed back at them with a lofty expression.

After some delay, due to the crowds, we bought our tickets, and also two small straw mats to sit on, and ascended to our seats. Next to us sat an Englishman, an acquaintance of my friend's. "How do you do?" he said; "this is extraordinary."

The death-bed was in the center of the field, under a bright light, and surrounded by doctors, nurses, reporters, and newspaper photographers. We were a little late; when we arrived, the mayor had already been there: assisted by the doctors, he had given Principus the first injection of strychnine, after which he had retired amid applause. Thereafter the dying man had received visits from the Fire Commissioner, a committee from the Actor's Equity, three State Senators, and a Mr. Cohen, of Hollywood. The President of the United States had been invited, and had sent a small cake.

The audience gazed at the dying man with anxious enthusiasm. Now and then a sigh, like a gust of wind on a hill, rippled up and down the aisles where venders of lemonade, peanuts, sausages, and pennants moved about, calling their wares. On the pennants, which were arranged with black mourning borders, were printed the names of the most important plays in which Principus had taken the part of hero. Spectators bought their favorites, and waved them at the dying man.

"Ah!" they cried. "Oh!"

"Principus."

"Don't let them kill you."

And they shouted advice, interspersed with jeers at the doctors.

Suddenly, in the row in front of us, a man stood up, and turned around to glare at me. "I am a friend of his," he exclaimed with energy. "I am also a member of the Rotary Club of Syracuse, N.Y. Who are you pushing?"

"Nobody," I answered firmly; and after some hesitation he sat down again.

The Englishman gave me a gloomy glance. "The trouble with America," he said, "is that you do nothing original. This reminds me of the ancient festivals at Rome under Diocletian. You are always borrowing something. Why don't you strike out for yourself?"

He had hardly finished speaking when a woman rose in her seat in a far corner of the stadium, gave a scream and fell forward on her face. At once there was a rush for her, she was lifted up, examined by some police matrons, photographed, and her name and address taken; after which she was carried out, with an expression of satisfaction on her face. A moment later, in another part of the great circle, another woman repeated this performance. She also was photographed and carried out, looking very pleased. As a result of this incident, all over the stadium women rose screaming, and fell in various attitudes, some with their noses pointed to the sky, others on their stomachs. These, however, were left where they fell, and presently got up again and sat down, waving their flags.

"You Americans," said the Briton, "you are like everybody else.

Why should I watch this sort of thing, which was done very much better by the Druids in England centuries ago?" And leaning forward with a strained expression, he shouted: "Look here, are you going to die, or not?"

The sick actor lay gazing at his public with weary eyes. In the bright light above his bed, he looked pale and thin; I wondered how it felt to die. The doctors moved anxiously about the bedside, conferring with the nurses and with each other; but they did not seem to agree with each other, or to notice the cheers with which the audience greeted each bulletin, regardless of its content.

An hour later extras were for sale in the aisles. "Woman Swoons at Principus Death," shouted the newsboys. "All about the big death." These editions already had photographs of the first woman to faint, whose pet name was Pinky. The Englishman bought one.

"We also," he observed, "have women in England."

"They have also been known to faint."

The man in front of us looked back at him angrily. "This is the largest death," he said, "there has ever been."

"It is a triumph," agreed my friend.

All at once a hush fell upon the stadium. All eyes were directed at the doctors; huddled around the bedside of the dying actor, they made it plain by their expressions that a crisis had arrived. The audience held its breath; the lemonade venders were silent. At last the head doctor stepped back, and held up his hand. Pale, but with a noble look, he exclaimed: "He will live."

A few cheers broke out, but they were immediately drowned in a storm of hisses. Men and women rose to their feet; flags were waved, peanuts, sausages, and pop bottles were hurled at the doctors and at the dying man. "We want to see him die," shouted the crowds who had bought tickets for this event. Led by the two women who had been photographed, they broke into jeers and catcalls.

"Cowards," they shrieked; "idiots."

"Let us have some new doctors."

The dying man raised himself warily; he seemed to be searching for the sky, already dark with night. His eyes scanned with amazement the stormy sea of faces around him and above him. The desire of so many people for his death descended upon him in an overwhelming compulsion, fell upon him in an irresistible wave; with a sigh he lay down and died. At once flashlights went off, a procession was formed with Pinky at the head, and pieces of the bed were broken off for souvenirs. Several men threw their hats into the air; and an old woman who happened to fall down in the excitement, was trampled upon.

"We also die in England," said the Englishman bitterly. "Can't you be original?"

And he went home, first stopping to buy a small piece of cotton cloth from the death-sheet of Principus, the world's greatest lover.

Suggested Readings

Lee, Charlotte I. *Oral Interpretation.* (2nd edition) Boston: Houghton Mifflin, 1959, pp. 126–9, quality.

Mouat, Lawrence H. *Reading Literature Aloud.* New York: Oxford, 1962, pp. 25–9, "Quality."

Parrish, Wayland Maxfield. *Reading Aloud.* (3rd edition) New York: Ronald Press, 1953, pp. 143–5, resonance.

Part IV

INTENSIFYING THE MEANING

12

INTENSIFYING MEANING THROUGH CONCENTRATION

We have studied the fundamental techniques of interpretative reading—for selecting materials, for finding and expressing meaning. Before considering some specialized means for handling specific forms of literature, we should discuss one of the most important problems of the art: the problem of intensifying meaning, of reading dynamically, of lending impact to our act of communication. A reader may try to carry out most of the techniques discussed previously and still not communicate effectively, for lack of the most important technique: concentration. No matter how superb the reader's mastery of phrasing, emphasis, and gesture, he will not communicate vital experiences to his listeners unless he has these experiences, himself, while reading. Vivid experiencing of content at the moment of utterance is the life blood of the oral interpretation of literature.

You will recall that in Chapters 4 and 5 we found that because meaning is the response of a person to symbols, the interpretative reader has a tremendous creative part to play in the use of his imagination and his entire background of actual and vicarious experience. In Chapter 5 we considered many steps for finding meaning, which are procedures for studying the selection and its author and for probing one's own responses. Effective interpretation can result only from both scholarly and personal research. The former is necessary for intelligent, ethical, legitimate interpretation; the latter is essential for dynamic interpretation and communication. No two readers will ever read anything the same way because they will always have different experiences with what they read. This is not unethical; it is unavoidable and necessary. Each reader must find meanings of his own in what he reads, and, the more intense these meanings are, the more dynamic the oral reading of them will be. Never feel that you are a mere mechanism for reproducing someone else's experiences. Your function is to communicate experiences that an author has stimulated in *you*. You will wish to communicate them as vividly as you possibly can.

As we sit in our room reading a favorite story, novel, or poem, it is relatively easy to think and feel as the author wishes us to. While standing before an audience, reading the same material aloud, it is somewhat more difficult to experience a full appreciation of the selection. To do so, we must learn to concentrate, for strong concentration on our part intensifies meaning for our listeners.

Concentration can be learned by directed and assiduous practice. Let us use an example to see how it is done. Notice that we do not contend that the interpreter learns to concentrate by simply saying to himself: "Now, concentrate on this!" Proper concentration is effected by occupying the mind on *each passing thought, feeling, and image.*

In Herman Wouk's excellent, best-selling novel, *The Caine Mutiny,* is a scene in which three young men, striving to make good in a naval cadet school during World War II, are learning to disassemble and reassemble Springfield rifles. The men are in their room on the tenth floor of a building in New York City.

> Willie wrestled vainly with the bolt for a while and panted, "They should have bilged me on lordosis. It would have been more dignified. I'll be out of this Navy tomorrow—*Get* in there, lousy damn spring—" He had never touched a gun before. The potential deadliness of it meant nothing to him. It was simply a troublesome assignment: a knotty page of Beethoven, an overdue book report on *Clarissa Harlowe.*
>
> "Jam the butt of that bolt in your stomach, see?" said Keefer. "Then press the spring down with both hands."

Anyone who has had a similar experience in the army can immediately sympathize with Willie's plight. But if the reader has had no direct experience with a rifle, he can recall any personal frustrating experience in which he has been forced to learn something entirely foreign to his past experience and to learn it under pressure of time. Wouk has already drawn such a comparison in Willie's life. Willie must learn to strip the rifle by the next morning or suffer unpleasant consequences: discharge from the Navy. College students face the same crisis when they must learn a very difficult principle the night before a final examination.

As we read this passage, we therefore sense Willie's almost panic-stricken frustration. We are relieved, though, when we read these words:

> Willie obeyed. The spring yielded slowly. The end of it sank at last into the rim. "It works! Thanks, Rollo—"

We are disturbed again when:

> At that moment the spring, still unsecured, escaped between his fingers and leaped from the bolt. It soared across the room. The window was conveniently open. The spring sailed out into the night.
>
> His roommates stared at him in horror. "That's bad, isn't it?" quavered Willie.
>
> "Anything happens to your rifle, boy—that does it," said the Southerner, walking to the window.

We feel despair for Willie as we recall the almost inhuman lack of sympathy for human error in the armed services. We are excited by the hero's problem, and we rush on to find out what he is going to do.

> "I'll run downstairs," Willie said.

Here is a glimmer of hope—that Willie can recover the lost piece.

> "What, during study hour? Twelve demerits!" Keggs said.

Despair again. Demerits are serious.

> "Come here, fella." Keefer pointed out through the window. The spring lay in a rain gutter at the edge of a steeply slanting copper-covered roof projection beneath the window. The tenth floor was set slightly back from the rest of the building.

The words force us to visualize the picture. We again have hope!

> "I can't get that," said Willie.

Frustrating despair, again.

> "You better, fella."

The forces of duty and necessity are speaking, forcing Willie to attempt the impossible.

> Keggs peered out. "You'd never make it. You'd fall off."
> "That's what I think," said Willie. He was not at all a daredevil. His mountain climbing had been done in plenty of stout company, and with much gulping horror. He hated high places and poor footing.

Willie's fears and tensions inhabit us.

> "Look fella, you want to stay in the Navy? Climb out there. Or d'you want me to do it?"

No one wishes to be a coward. Shame drives us to do what we are mortally afraid to do.

> Willie climbed out, clinging to the window frame. The wind moaned in the darkness. Broadway twinkled far, far below. The ledge seemed to drop away beneath his trembling legs. He stretched a hand vainly toward the spring, and gasped, "Need another couple of feet—"

If you are afraid of high places, Willie's plight catches you in the pit of the stomach. Painful muscular tensions grip you there. Listen to a movie audience gasp whenever a film camera peeks over the top ledge of a tall city building. By the process of empathy the audience is actually on that ledge! We are now projecting ourselves into the fictional person of Willie Keith.

> "If we only had a rope," said Keefer. "Look man. One of us gets out with you, see, and hangs onto the window. And you hang onto him. That does it."

Because of our own nature, we judge that Willie would gladly have climbed back into the room and given up, but Keefer's determined and daring efforts to help Willie force him into greater efforts to retrieve the lost spring.

> "Let's get it over with," said Keggs anxiously. "If he gets caught out there we all bilge." He sprang through the window, stood beside

> Willie, and gripped his hand. "Now get it." Willie let go of the window, and inched downward, clinging to Kegg's powerful grip. He teetered at the edge of the roof, the wind whipping his clothes. The spring was in easy reach. He grasped it and thrust it into a pocket.

Without waiting for the finish of the episode, we experience some relief, but the author has not finished with us!

> Ensign Acres might have picked a less awkward moment to make his study-hour round of the tenth floor, but he chose this one. He walked past the room, peeped in, stopped short, and roared, "Attention on deck! What the hell is going on here?"
>
> Keggs neighed in terror and let go of Willie's hand. Willie lunged and clutched him around the knees. The two midshipmen swayed back and forth on the ledge, not far from death. But Keggs' urge to live was slightly stronger than his fear of ensigns. He reared backward and fell into the room on his head, hauling Willie through the window on top of him.

Terror and relief! A parade of images, ideas, and strong emotions, each of which must register in the mind and body of the oral interpreter while in action.

You may have appreciated—experienced!—the above scene from Wouk's novel, but your oral reading of it to others will not be effective unless you intensify the meaning by abandoning yourself to the purposes of communication by concentrating upon re-experiencing all that you felt originally. When your fear of high places returns during the reading, your body tenses, your voice automatically becomes constricted by fear, and your rate of speaking is increased. You are concentrating: you are intensifying your communication by reliving. If this seems preposterous to you, just picture the opposite situation. Suppose that you were to stand casually leaning against a table, perhaps one hand in your pocket, reading in a relaxed, resonant voice quality, and at a slow rate. Could your reading be effective?

To say "Concentrate!" is perhaps futile. To say "Experience!" is probably better advice, for it demands that the reader re-experience what he felt, saw, and thought when he first read the selection to himself. In fact, new experiences may also present themselves during the reading. The interpretative reader first reads, then he studies and practices. But study and practice are not just concerned with the ideas to emphasize. Study and practice consist of studying and practicing one's own responses to a particular literary work. The interpreter asks himself: "How does this selection make me feel?" "What past experiences come to mind?" "What effect is this writing having upon my established beliefs and opinions?" "What emotions are stirred up within me?" In addition, the interpreter studies his own mental and physical responses to literary suggestion. When he reads aloud he reproduces the same impression within himself as he reads, and he so absorbs his being in what he is reading that again the same images file before his mind's eye, the same emotions affect him, and the same muscular reactions flow through his body.

We need only listen to others read to know that the human mind must be active in communication, for we can hear the active and concentrating mind speaking, and we can also recognize its absence when that mind has wandered away from the context. Teachers of speech often surprise a student reader by announcing that the reader's mind has wandered from the material, or by accurately determining that the reader does not know the meaning of a particular word, or by disclosing by means of probing questions that the material means little or nothing to the reader because he has little, or no, similar background experience. Although the student may think the teacher psychic, the explanation is quite simple: teachers are not mind readers; any listener can tell when a reading becomes drab and mechanical. When it does, the reader's mind is simply not concentrating. When listeners' minds wander, they do so—often—because the reader's mind has wandered, too.

To assure that you will read dynamically, do the following:

1. Choose to read literary materials that are meaningful to *you,* in which you can participate because you have the interest and background of actual and/or vicarious experience essential to real understanding and appreciation.

2. Choose to read literary materials that are so worthy of your time and effort that they will grow on you rather than pall on you. Worthless materials quickly grow tiresome because repeated experiences with them offer nothing new. Good literature offers new experiences with each reading. Effective reading results from extensive practice, but practice is deadly if the material is dull.

3. Experience and re-experience literary content actively each time you read the selection. Automatic utterance of words cannot be effective communication. Automatic utterance of words in practice cannot be effective preparation for communication. The reader who admits he has grown tired of his material is bringing nothing *to* the symbols. The reader must concentrate upon thinking each thought completely, visualizing each image thoroughly, and recreating the image of each attitude and emotion intensely each time he reads aloud.

Exercises

1. Nearly all boys get into fist fights, and these fights are frequently more fun than fury. If you have had such a fight, you will perhaps relive it as you read this selection by Dylan Thomas.

from *THE FIGHT*

DYLAN THOMAS

I was standing at the end of the lower playground and annoying Mr Samuels, who lived in the house just below the high railings. Mr Samuels complained once a week that boys from the school threw apples and stones and balls through his bedroom window. He sat in a deck chair in a small square of trim garden and tried to read the newspaper. I was only a few yards from him. I was staring him out. He pretended not to notice me, but I knew he knew I was standing there rudely and quietly. Every now and then he peeped at me from behind his newspaper, saw me still and serious and alone, with my eyes on his. As soon as he lost his temper I was going to go home. Already I was late for dinner. I had almost beaten him, the newspaper was trembling, he was breathing heavily, when a strange boy, whom I had not heard approach, pushed me down the bank.

I threw a stone at his face. He took off his spectacles, put them in his coat pocket, took off his coat, hung it neatly on the railings, and attacked. Turning round as we wrestled on the top of the bank, I saw that Mr Samuels had folded his newspaper on the deck chair and was standing up to watch us. It was a mistake to turn round. The strange boy rabbit-punched me twice. Mr Samuels hopped with excitement as I fell against the railings. I was down in the dust, hot and scratched and biting, then up and dancing, and I butted the boy in the belly and we tumbled in a heap. I saw through a closing eye that his nose was bleeding. I hit his nose. He tore at my collar and spun me round by the hair.

'Come on! come on!' I heard Mr Samuels cry.

We both turned towards him. He was shaking his fists and dodging about in the garden. He stopped then, and coughed, and set his panama straight, and avoided our eyes, and turned his back and walked slowly to the deck chair.

We both threw gravel at him.

'I'll give him "Come on!"' the boy said, as we ran along the playground away from the shouts of Mr Samuels and down the steps on to the hill.

We walked home together. I admired his bloody nose. He said that my eye was like a poached egg, only black.

'I've never seen such a lot of blood,' I said.

He said I had the best black eye in Wales, perhaps it was the best black eye in Europe; he bet Tunney never had a black eye like that.

'And there's blood all over your shirt.'

'Sometimes I bleed in dollops,' he said.

On Walter's Road we passed a group of high school girls, and I cocked my cap and hoped my eye was as big as a bluebag, and he walked with his coat flung open to show the bloodstains.

I was a hooligan all during dinner, and a bully, and as bad as a boy from the Sandbanks, and I should have more respect, and I sat silently, like Tunney, over the sago pudding. That afternoon I went to school with an eye-shade on. If I had had a black silk sling I would have been as gay and desperate as the wounded captain in the book that my sister used to read, and that I read under the bed-clothes at night, secretly with a flash-lamp.

On the road, a boy from an inferior school, where the parents did not have to pay anything, called me 'One eye!' in a harsh, adult voice. I took no notice, but walked along whistling, my good eye on the summer clouds, sailing, beyond insult, above Terrace Road.

The mathematics master said: 'I see that Mr Thomas at the back of the class has been straining his eyesight. But it isn't over his home-work, is it, gentlemen?'

Gilbert Rees, next to me, laughed loudest.

'I'll break your leg after school!' I said.

He'd hobble, howling, up to the head master's study. A deep hush in the school. A message on a plate brought by the porter. 'The head master's compliments, sir, and will you come at once?' 'How did you happen to break this boy's leg?' 'Oh! damn and bottom, the agony!' cried Gilbert Rees. 'Just a little twist,' I would say. 'I don't know my own strength. I apologize. But there's nothing to worry about. Let me set the leg, sir.' A rapid manipulation, the click of a bone. 'Doctor Thomas, sir, at your service.' Mrs Rees was on her knees. 'How can I thank you?' 'It's nothing at all, dear lady. Wash his ears every morning. Throw away his rulers. Pour his red and green inks down the sink.'

2. Have you ever been thrilled by music? Have you, when singing with others—perhaps in church or around a campfire—had an experience like this one?

EVERYONE SANG

SIEGFRIED SASSOON

Everyone suddenly burst out singing;
And I was filled with such delight

As prisoned birds must find in freedom
Winging wildly across the white
Orchards and dark green field; on; on; and out of sight.
Everyone's voice was suddenly lifted,
And beauty came like the setting sun.
My heart was shaken with tears, and horror
Drifted away. . . . O, but everyone
Was a bird; and the song was wordless; the singing will never be done.

3. If you have fought in the front lines, you will be able to re-experience while reading the following poem. If you have not had first-hand war experiences, what vicarious ones enable you to participate?

BREAKFAST

WILFRID GIBSON

We ate our breakfast lying on our backs
Because the shells were screeching overhead.
I bet a rasher to a loaf of bread
That Hull United would beat Halifax
When Jimmy Stainthorpe played full-back instead
Of Billy Bradford. Ginger raised his head
And cursed, and took the bet, and dropt back dead.
Because the shells were screeching overhead.

4. We all wonder about the future of the planet Earth and mankind. Can you apply your previous thoughts on this subject to the following poem?

EPISTLE TO BE LEFT IN THE EARTH

ARCHIBALD MACLEISH

. . . It is colder now
there are many stars
we are drifting
North by the Great Bear
the leaves are falling
The water is stone in the scooped rocks
to southward
Red sun gray air
the crows are

Slow on their crooked wings
                    the jays have left us
Long since we passed the flares of Orion
Each man believes in his heart he will die
Many have written last thoughts and last letters
None know if our deaths are now or forever
None know if this wandering earth will be found
We lie down and the snow covers our garments
I pray you
        you (if any open this writing)
Make in your mouths the words that were our names
I will tell you all we have learned
                        I will tell you everything
The earth is round
            there are springs under the orchards
The loam cuts with a blunt knife
                        beware of
Elms in thunder
            the lights in the sky are stars
We think they do not see
                    we think also
The trees do not know nor the leaves of the grasses
                                    hear us
The birds too are ignorant
                    Do not listen
Do not stand at dark in the open windows
We before you have heard this
                        they are voices
They are not words at all but the wind rising
Also none among us has seen God
(. . . We have thought often
The flaws of sun in the late and driving weather
Pointed to one tree but it was not so)
As for the nights I warn you the nights are dangerous
The wind changes at night and the dreams come

It is very cold
            there are strange stars near Arcturus

Voices are crying an unknown name in the sky

5. To read the following poem effectively the interpreter must re-experience a child's thrill in ghosts, goblins, and Hallowe'en. The mood is a

combination of the eerie and the playful. Notice how Cummings has helped the oral reader by indicating phrasing through word spacing and line arrangement.

HIST WHIST

E. E. CUMMINGS

hist whist
little ghostthings
tip-toe
twinkle-toe

little twitchy
witches and tingling
goblins
hob-a-nob hob-a-nob

little hoppy happy
toad in tweeds
tweeds
little itchy mousies

with scuttling
eyes rustle and run and
hidehidehide
whisk

whisk look out for the old woman
with the wart on her nose
what she'll do to yer
nobody knows

for she knows the devil ooch
the devil ouch
the devil
ach the great

green
dancing
devil
devil

devil
devil

wheeEEE

6. If you have actually climbed birch trees in your childhood, you will be able to re-experience that pleasure while reading the following poem. If you have not, you may still be able to appreciate "Birches" by using your imagination. What experiences have you had which enable you to feel the elation of the poem as he swings through the air? What other images does the poet use which enable you to experience what he wishes you to?

BIRCHES

ROBERT FROST

When I see birches bend to left and right
Across the lines of straighter darker trees,
I like to think some boy's been swinging them.
But swinging doesn't bend them down to stay.
Ice-storms do that. Often you must have seen them
Loaded with ice a sunny winter morning
After a rain. They click upon themselves
As the breeze rises, and turn many-colored
As the stir cracks and crazes their enamel.
Soon the sun's warmth makes them shed crystal shells
Shattering and avalanching on the snow-crust—
Such heaps of broken glass to sweep away
You'd think the inner dome of heaven had fallen.
They are dragged to the withered bracken by the load,
And they seem not to break; though once they are bowed
So low for long, they never right themselves:
You may see their trunks arching in the woods
Years afterwards, trailing their leaves on the ground
Like girls on hands and knees that throw their hair
Before them over their heads to dry in the sun.
But I was going to say when Truth broke in
With all her matter-of-fact about the ice-storm
I should prefer to have some boy bend them
As he went out and in to fetch the cows—
Some boy too far from town to learn baseball,
Whose only play was what he found himself,
Summer or winter, and could play alone.
One by one he subdued his father's trees

By riding them down over and over again
Until he took the stiffness out of them,
And not one but hung limp, not one was left
For him to conquer. He learned all there was
To learn about not launching out too soon
And so not carrying the tree away
Clear to the ground. He always kept his poise
To the top branches, climbing carefully
With the same pains you use to fill a cup
Up to the brim, and even above the brim.
Then he flung outward, feet first, with a swish,
Kicking his way down through the air to the ground.
So was I once myself a swinger of birches.
And so I dream of going back to be.
It's when I'm weary of considerations,
And life is too much like a pathless wood
Where your face burns and tickles with the cobwebs
Broken across it, and one eye is weeping
From a twig's having lashed across it open.
I'd like to get away from earth awhile
And then come back to it and begin over.
May no fate willfully misunderstand me
And half grant what I wish and snatch me away
Not to return. Earth's the right place for love:
I don't know where it's likely to go better.
I'd like to go by climbing a birch tree,
And climb black branches up a snow-white trunk
Toward heaven, till the tree could bear no more,
But dipped its top and set me down again.
That would be good both going and coming back.
One could do worse than be a swinger of birches.

7. Depending on your past experience, you may or may not agree with the following criticism of our age. Read it. Think it through. How does it affect your emotions? If you are not in agreement with the author, you will probably not communicate his ideas effectively. If you do agree with him, you will re-experience appropriately when you read the poem aloud.

THE WORLD

LAWRENCE FERLINGHETTI

The world is a beautiful place
                                        to be born into

if you don't mind happiness
not always being
so very much fun
if you don't mind a touch of hell
now and then
just when everything is fine
because even in heaven
they don't sing
all the time

The world is a beautiful place
to be born into
if you don't mind some people dying
all the time
or maybe only starving
some of the time
which isn't half so bad
if it isn't you

Oh the world is a beautiful place
to be born into
if you don't much mind
a few dead minds
in the higher places
or a bomb or two
now and then
in your upturned faces
or such other improprieties
as our Name Brand society
is prey to
with its men of distinction
and its men of extinction
and its priests
and other patrolmen
and its various segregations
and congressional investigations
and other constipations
that our fool flesh
is heir to

Yes the world is the best place of all
for a lot of such things as
making the fun scene
and making the love scene
and making the sad scene
and singing low songs and having inspirations

and walking around
looking at everything
and smelling flowers
and goosing statues
and even thinking
and kissing people and
making babies and wearing pants
and waving hats and
dancing
and going swimming in rivers
on picnics
in the middle of the summer
and just generally
'living it up'

Yes
but then right in the middle of it
comes the smiling

mortician

8. If you are deeply fascinated by trains, you should have no difficulty in absorbing yourself in the following poem. Within the extraordinary rhythm of the poem, carefully try to experience each image.

THE EXPRESS

STEPHEN SPENDER

After the first powerful plain manifesto
The black statement of pistons, without more fuss
But gliding like a queen, she leaves the station.
Without bowing and with restrained unconcern
She passes the houses which humbly crowd outside,
The gasworks and at last the heavy page
Of death, printed by gravestones in the cemetery.
Beyond the town there lies the open country
Where, gathering speed, she acquires mystery,
The luminous self-possession of ships on ocean.
It is now she begins to sing—at first quite low
Then loud, and at last with a jazzy madness—
The song of her whistle screaming at curves,
Of deafening tunnels, brakes, innumerable bolts.
And always light, aerial, underneath

Goes the elate metre of her wheels.
Steaming through metal landscape on her lines
She plunges new eras of wild happiness
Where speed throws up strange shapes, broad curves
And parallels clean like the steel of guns.
At last, further than Edinburgh or Rome,
Beyond the crest of the world, she reaches night
Where only a low streamline brightness
Of phosphorus on the tossing hills is white.
Ah, like a comet through flame she moves entranced
Wrapt in her music no bird song, no, nor bough
Breaking with honey buds, shall ever equal.

9. Ours is called the "Atomic Age." Before the birth of the atom bomb, Stephen Vincent Benét wrote "Nightmare at Noon." A short description of one student's reading of it appeared in Chapter 1. What does Benét's "Nightmare" do to you? Is it as appropriate and timely today as it was in 1940?

NIGHTMARE AT NOON

STEPHEN VINCENT BENÉT

There are no trenches dug in the park, not yet.
There are no soldiers falling out of the sky.
It's a fine, clear day, in the park. It is bright and hot.
The trees are in full, green, summer-heavy leaf.
An airplane drones overhead but no one's afraid.
There's no reason to be afraid, in a fine, big city
That was not built for a war. There is time and time.

There was time in Norway and time, and the thing fell.
When they woke, they saw the planes with the black crosses.
When they woke, they heard the guns rolling in the street.
They could not believe, at first. It was hard to believe.
They had been friendly and thriving and inventive.
They had had good arts, decent living, peace for years.
Those were not enough, it seems.
There were people there who wrote books and painted pictures,
Worked, came home tired, liked to be let alone.
They made fun of the strut and the stamp and the strained salute,
They made fun of the would-be Caesars who howl and foam.
That was not enough, it seems. It was not enough.
When they woke, they saw the planes with the black crosses.

There is grass in the park. There are children on the long meadow
Watched by some hot, peaceful nuns. Where the ducks are fed
There are black children and white and the anxious teachers
Who keep counting them like chickens. It's quite a job
To take so many school-kids out to the park,
But when they've eaten their picnic, they'll go home.
(And they could have better homes, in a rich city.)
But they won't be sent to Kansas or Michigan
At twenty-four hours' notice,
Dazed, bewildered, clutching their broken toys,
Hundreds on hundreds filling the blacked-out trains.
Just to keep them safe, just so they may live not die.
Just so there's one chance that they may not die but live.
That does not enter our thoughts. There is plenty of time.

In Holland, one hears, some children were less lucky.
It was hard to send them anywhere in Holland.
It is a small country, you see. The thing happened quickly.
The bombs from the sky are quite indifferent to children.
The machine-gunners do not distinguish. In Rotterdam
One quarter of the city was blown to bits.
That included, naturally, ordinary buildings
With the usual furnishings, such as cats and children.
It was an old, peaceful city, Rotterdam,
Clean, tidy, full of flowers.
But that was not enough, it seems.
It was not enough to keep all the children safe.
It was ended in a week, and the freedom ended.

There is no air-raid siren yet, in the park.
All the glass still stands, in the windows around the park.
The man on the bench is reading a Yiddish paper.
He will not be shot because of that, oddly enough.
He will not even be beaten or imprisoned.
Not yet, not yet.
You can be a Finn or a Dane and an American.
You can be German or French and an American,
Jew, Bohunk, Nigger, Mick—all the dirty names
We call each other—and yet American.
We've stuck to that quite a while.
Go into Joe's Diner and try to tell the truckers
You belong to a Master Race and you'll get a laugh.
What's that, brother? Double-talk?

I'm a stranger here myself but it's a free country.
It's a free country . . .
Oh yes, I know the faults and the other side,
The lyncher's rope, the bought justice, the wasted land,
The scale on the leaf, the borers in the corn,
The finks with their clubs, the grey sky of relief,
All the long shame of our hearts and the long disunion.
I am merely remarking—as a country, we try.
As a country, I think we try.

They tried in Spain but the tanks and the planes won out.
They fought very well and long.
They fought to be free but it seems that was not enough.
They did not have the equipment. So they lost.
They tried in Finland. The resistance was shrewd,
Skillful, intelligent, waged by a free folk.
They tried in Greece, and they threw them back for a while
By the soul and spirit and passion of common men.
Call the roll of fourteen nations. Call the roll
Of the blacked-out lands, the lands that used to be free.

But do not call it loud. There is plenty of time.
There is plenty of time, while the bombs on London fall
And turn the world to wind and water and fire.
There is time to sleep while the fire-bombs fall on London.
They are stubborn people in London.

We are slow to wake, good-natured as a country.
(It is our fault and our virtue.) We like to raise
A man to the highest power and then throw bricks at him.
We don't like war and we like to speak our minds.
We're used to speaking our minds.
There are certain words,
Our own and others', we're used to—words we've used,
Heard, had to recite, forgotten,
Rubbed shiny in the pocket, left home for keepsakes,
Inherited, stuck away in the back-drawer,
In the locked trunk, at the back of the quiet mind.
Liberty, equality, fraternity.
To none will we sell, refuse or deny, right or justice.
We hold these truths to be self-evident.

I am merely saying—what if these words pass?
What if they pass and are gone and are no more,

Eviscerated, blotted out of the world?
We're used to them, so used that we half-forget,
The way you forget the looks of your own house
And yet you can walk around it, in the darkness.
You can't put a price on sunlight or the air,
You can't put a price on these, so they must be easy.
They were bought with belief and passion, at great cost.
They were bought with the bitter and anonymous blood
Of farmers, teachers, shoemakers and fools
Who broke the old rule and the pride of kings.
And some never saw the end and many were weary,
Some doubtful, many confused.
They were bought by the ragged boys at Valmy mill,
The yokels at Lexington with the long light guns
And the dry, New England faces,
The iron barons, writing a charter out
For their own iron advantage, not the people,
And yet the people got it into their hands
And marked it with their own sweat.
It took long to buy these words.
It took a long time to buy them and much pain.

Thenceforward and forever free.
Thenceforward and forever free.
No man may be bound or fined or slain till he has been judged by his peers.
To form a more perfect Union.

The others have their words too, and strong words,
Strong as the tanks, explosive as the bombs.

The State is all, worship the State!
The Leader is all, worship the Leader!
Strength is all, worship strength!
Worship, bow down or die!

I shall go back through the park to my safe house,
This is not London or Paris.
This is the high, bright city, the lucky place,
The place that always had time.
The boys in their shirtsleeves here, the big, flowering girls,
The bicycle-riders, the kids with the model planes,
The lovers who lie on the grass, uncaring of eyes,
As if they lay on an island out of time,
The tough kids, squirting the water at the fountain,

Whistled at by the cop.
The dopes who write "Jimmy's a dope" on the tunnel walls.
These are all quite safe and nothing will happen to them.
Nothing will happen, of course.
Go tell Frank the Yanks aren't coming, in Union Square.
Go tell the new brokers' story about the President.
Whatever it is. That's going to help a lot.
There's time to drink your highball—plenty of time.
Go tell fire it only burns in another country,
Go tell the bombers this is the wrong address,
The hurricane to pass on the other side.
Go tell the earthquake it must not shake the ground.

The bell has rung in the night and the air quakes with it.

I shall not sleep tonight when I hear the plane.

1940.

10. The following verse is for women, or for parents of daughters. Young men will probably not have had the appropriate background experience to enable them to interpret the verse effectively.

GIRL'S-EYE VIEW OF RELATIVES

PHYLLIS McGINLEY

FIRST LESSON

The thing to remember about fathers is, they're men.
A girl has to keep it in mind.
They are dragon-seekers, bent on improbable rescues.
Scratch any father, you find
Someone chock-full of qualms and romantic terrors,
Believing change is a threat—
Like your first shoes with heels on, like your first bicycle
It took such months to get.

Walk in strange woods, they warn you about the snakes there.
Climb, and they fear you'll fall.
Books, angular boys, or swimming in deep water—
Fathers mistrust them all.
Men are the worriers. It is difficult for them
To learn what they must learn:
How you have a journey to take and very likely,
For a while, will not return.

Suggested Readings

Bowen, Elbert R. "Promoting Dynamic Interpretative Reading," *The Speech Teacher* (March 1958), 118–20.

Parrish, Wayland Maxfield. *Reading Aloud.* (3rd edition) New York: Ronald Press, 1953, Chapter IV, "Vividness," Chapter X, "Imagination."

Simon, Clarence T. "Appreciation in Reading." In *Studies in the Art of Interpretation* (Gertrude E. Johnson, ed.) New York: Appleton-Century-Crofts, 1940, pp. 18–28. The same article was originally published in the *Quarterly Journal of Speech* (April 1930), 185–93.

Smith, Joseph F., and James R. Linn. *Skill in Reading Aloud.* New York: Harper, 1960, Chapter V, "The Bare Essentials: Vivid Expression."

Suggested Readings

[illegible]

Part V

INTERPRETING THE BASIC FORMS OF LITERATURE

13

■ SUGGESTIONS ON THE INTERPRETATIVE READING OF PROSE

As oral readers we are most often concerned with the interpretation of prose, simply because it is the largest classification of literature. Prose is the common ingredient of lecture, sermon, after-dinner speech, short story, novel, biography, essay, newscast, and many more kinds of informal composition. It is that form of literature which does not employ the distinctive form of verse nor the dialogue structure of drama. In general the principles and practices we have studied in Chapters 1 through 12 are all relevant to the effective oral interpretation of prose. The purpose of this chapter is to stress those principles especially involved in the interpretative reading of prose.

ON READING ANY PROSE

Purpose. Full achievement of the author's *purpose* is our first consideration. Inasmuch as the purpose of any employment of language is communication, the most significant universal purpose of prose is *to obtain a response.* That universal purpose is implemented by one or more of these three specialized purposes: to inform, to persuade, and to entertain. Prose to inform is simply that which is intended to convey information: the anticipated response is comprehension. Prose to persuade is intended to stimulate thinking, to make a point of view convincing, to prompt to some action, or to inspire. Prose to entertain is meant to elicit vicarious participation in an emotional or intellectual experience. The most common emotional experiences resulting from such prose are humor and adventure, but there are many more. In many prose selections the author has combined and mingled these three purposes. Nevertheless, you must determine the author's specialized purpose at any particular point before you can hope to help him achieve it.

Imagery. The second general suggestion on the reading of prose concerns your recognition of *imagery.* In Chapter 5 we studied imagery in poems; however, what applies to imagery in poetry applies as well to imagery in prose. You must learn to sense the images whatever the form of literature may be. Read the following two sentences for an excellent illustration of imagery in prose.

> That was the day he'd first seen dead men wearing white ballet skirts and upturned shoes with pompons on them. The Turks had come steadily and lumpily and he had seen the skirted men running and the officers shooting into them and running then themselves and he and the British observer had run too until his lungs ached and his mouth was full of the taste of pennies and they stopped behind some rocks and there were the Turks coming as lumpily as ever.
>
> —ERNEST HEMINGWAY, *The Snows of Kilimanjaro*

Other impressive illustrations of imagery in prose occur in "Christmas Afternoon" by Robert Benchley in Chapter 3, the selection from *The Caine Mutiny* by Herman Wouk in Chapter 12, and the selection from *Clea* by Durrell in Chapter 8. Prose is not without images, and if you would read effectively you must *reflect* those images in your voice and body.

Rhythm. The third consideration is *prose rhythm.* Turn back to Chapter 8 and reread Robert Ingersoll's famous oration "At the Tomb of Napoleon."

You will see that the rhythm is effected by the use of parallel structure, that is, the repetition of "I saw him" and "I would rather have," and by the remarkably regular pattern of sound and silence called cadence. We speak of these as the *larger rhythms* of prose. The oral interpreter must recognize them in order to give them adequate but not excessive prominence as he reads the prose according to the author's apparent intention. To neglect these rhythms may be to obscure the author's style and drastically reduce the effectiveness of the selection.

The *lesser rhythms* of prose are those which correspond roughly to meter in poetry. Great prose is often characterized by a rhythm of stressed syllables at more or less regular intervals with varying numbers of unstressed syllables in between. The story of "The Fiery Furnace" quoted in Chapter 11 presents an outstanding illustration of this quality. Listen to Charles Laughton's recording and you cannot miss the rhythm. In rhythm the King James Version of the Bible is sometimes superior to the 1941 revision of the Latin Vulgate translation and to the Revised Standard Version. Compare these three quotations.

> Finally, brethren, whatsoever things are true, whatsoever things are honest, whatsoever things are just, whatsoever things are pure, whatsoever things are lovely, whatsoever things are of good report; if there be any virtue, and if there be any praise, think on these things.
>
> —*Philippians 4:8,* KING JAMES VERSION

> For the rest, brethren, whatever things are true, whatever honorable, whatever just, whatever holy, whatever lovable, whatever of good repute, if there be any virtue, if anything worthy of praise, think upon these things.
>
> —*Philippians 4:8,* CONFRATERNITY OF CHRISTIAN DOCTRINE VULGATE TRANSLATION

> Finally, brethren, whatever is true, whatever is honorable, whatever is just, whatever is pure, whatever is lovely, whatever is gracious, if there is any excellence, if there is anything worthy of praise, think about these things.
>
> —*Philippians 4:8,* REVISED STANDARD VERSION

The oral interpreter must recognize these lesser rhythms in order to give expression to the full beauty of the prose.

Cutting. Our fourth general consideration in the reading of prose is *cutting*. Unless you have elected to read a complete short story, essay, or speech, one of your most difficult problems may be to cut your selection. If it is a fragment of a much longer selection, make sure that it is a unit in itself or that you provide an introduction to give the context. On the other hand, if you decide you must retain the essential unity of the complete short story, for example, and yet reduce the length, you have a much more difficult problem. Generally in such an instance it is better to *cut whole segments* rather than to destroy the author's style by extracting sentences and phrases here and there. Of course, you must be sure to cut only those segments to which no later part of the selection refers. Nothing is so disturbing to the listener as to lose the train of thought because the reader has omitted essential portions of the text. Very infrequently you may be able to cut out a segment and replace it with a few of your own words to bridge the gap or supply the content which will be necessary later on. As a precaution in this kind of cutting, always review the whole selection to see whether any other portion is dependent on the part you anticipate leaving out.

One other kind of cutting is made feasible by the very nature of oral reading. Portions of the text such as "He said," "Raising her eyebrows she responded quickly," and others, the meaning of which you can supply with your visible action and voice, should be left out whenever possible. Save time, make your task easier, and communicate more effectively by supplying the meaning with your manner. Be careful, however, not to skeletonize your selection. In your cutting try to find the happy medium wherein you do not destroy the style nor handicap the author's effort to achieve his purpose.

Sight reading. The fifth general suggestion for the oral interpretation of prose is to *avoid sight reading*. Because we are more familiar with the structure of prose than that of poetry and drama, the temptation to read prose without preparation is correspondingly greater. While it may be necessary sometimes for the radio or television announcer or newscaster to read aloud copy he has never seen before, the practice is in general a most deplorable one. It usually means that if the reader becomes aware of the meaning at all, he does so only as soon as his listeners do, and possibly later. Consequently his "reading" is simply and unhappily a process of creating audible symbols to match the visible ones he sees on the page: interpretation of meaning may be nonexistent. To put the matter briefly, insofar as possible you should never read at sight publicly, whether the reading be simple or complex.

ON READING NARRATIVE PROSE

Climax. Narrative is normally the most appealing kind of prose because it employs action. That action usually involves one or more *climaxes*. The author builds these high points into his story to achieve a maximum degree of interest, and you must be aware of them in order to promote that interest. If you know where climaxes are, you can help with your voice and manner to achieve them.

Dialogue. Unlike the other forms of prose, narrative necessarily has characters. While those characters need not be people, they usually are, and more often than not they engage in *dialogue*. These simple techniques for the reading of dialogue should be helpful to you. First, *build* in your mind *an image* of the character who is speaking. Sometimes his appearance and personality are made clear in outright description: the author may tell you that he is tall, black-haired, coarse-featured, and crude. Not infrequently you may discover his personality in the role he plays in the story: his actions may speak louder than words. Occasionally you may find what a character is like from the attitudes of the other characters: they may tell you he is strong and courageous, or they may reveal his courage by appealing to him for strength. Last, but certainly not least, you may discover the make-up of a character by his own remarks: after all a man's speech is a primary indicator of his personality.

When you have built an image of the character whose lines you are going to read, your next task is to *distinguish* him in the minds of your listeners. Probably the simplest way to do this is *character placement*. Each time you read the lines of a certain character, turn your eyes and face just a little in a certain direction. If you have more than one character, give each a distinguishing placement. This method is quite practical for at least five characters. If you have more, you probably have too many; in fact, two or three are usually enough. The following character placements should meet your needs.

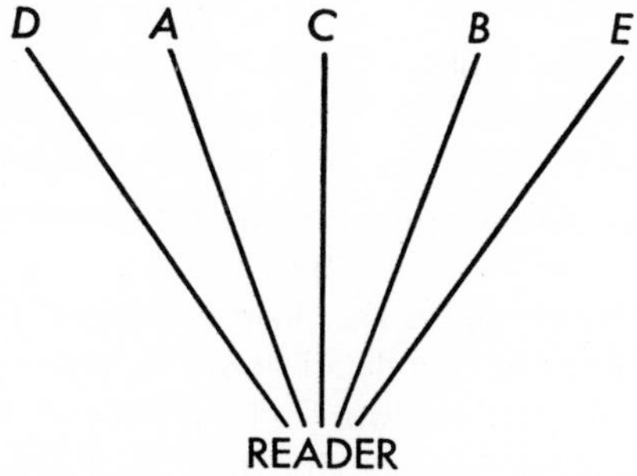

If you have only one character, place him at *A*, *B*, or *C*. If you have two, use *A* and *B*. If three, *A*, *B*, and *C*. If four, *A*, *B*, *C*, and *D* or *E*. If five, *A*, *B*, *C*, *D*, and *E*.

Additional means of distinguishing each individual character include assumption of his *attitude*, suggestion of his *visible action* and *mannerisms*, and the use of appropriate *speech habits*. No story would be interesting if its characters had strictly identical attitudes. You can help your listeners to keep the characters straight by assuming *A*'s *attitude* as you read his lines, *B*'s as you read his, and so on. Next, you may distinguish a character by means of *visible action*. If he is taller than the person to whom he is talking, he will look down slightly; or if he is shorter or is seated, he will look up. If he is apart from the other participants in the story and is talking to them across some distance, he will direct his gaze into the distance. If he is grouchy, he will scowl. If he is nervous, he will move much and rapidly. He may even have simple visible actions suggestive of distinguishing personal mannerisms. Of course the amount of such visible action will depend on the degree of impersonation your story requires. Always remember, however, to retain your own identity. Do not try to become the character. Finally, you may make one character different from others by the use of appropriate *speech habits*. His habitual pitch level, quality, volume, and rate may be peculiarly his own. In addition he may speak with a distinctive rhythm or inflection and thus employ a dialect. Sometimes, even without the specific indication of the author, you may use a very limited dialect in a characterization; always be sure, however, that the characterization is true to the author's intent as you have perceived it. Do not overuse dialect: usually only a suggestion of it is needed. Again, remember that you are not acting.

Although character interpretation and suggestion would seem to be the most difficult aspect of reading narrative prose, many readers do a worse job in trying to interpret the *continuity,* which is the part between the speeches of dialogue when the author is speaking in his own words. Normally continuity makes up the great bulk of narrative. All too often the inexperienced reader will race through the continuity in a meaningless monotone. His constant upward inflection is evidence of his lack of comprehension. He is only waiting for the next bit of dialogue so that he may "interpret" again. If he only knew the opportunities he is missing! As you read prose narrative, try to be vividly aware of meaning as you utter the words. Above all, try to sense the imagery. Narrative provides the opportunity for visualization, to "see" the characters participate in the events as they unfold. Imagine the detail of the room, know where the doors, windows, furniture, and participants are. Work out all of this detail ahead of time and then call to mind a full picture as you utter the words. By means of facial, eye, and body gestures suggest the scene and activity for your listeners. Only as *you* can "see" the story will *they* be able to "see" it too.

The following selection from a famous modern novel will give you an opportunity to try these suggestions for interpreting prose in general and narrative in particular. What is the author's purpose? What are the images? You should be able to sense literally dozens of them. Where are the points of highest interest? What are the distinguishing traits of each of the three characters? How can you most effectively suggest Mrs. Dalton as you read her many short speeches? Visualize the continuity, make it throb with fear and excitement.

from NATIVE SON

RICHARD WRIGHT

He lifted her and laid her on the bed. Something urged him to leave at once, but he leaned over her, excited, looking at her face in the dim light, not wanting to take his hands from her breasts. She tossed and mumbled sleepily. He tightened his fingers on her breasts kissing her again, feeling her move toward him. He was aware only of her body now; his lips trembled. Then he stiffened. The door behind him had creaked.

He turned and a hysterical terror seized him as though he were falling from a great height in a dream. A white blur was standing by the door, silent, ghostlike. It filled his eyes and gripped his body. It was Mrs. Dalton. He wanted to knock her out of his way and bolt from the room.

"Mary!" she spoke softly, questioningly.

Bigger held his breath. Mary mumbled again; he bent over her, his fists clenched in fear. He knew that Mrs. Dalton could not see him; but he knew that if Mary spoke she would come to the side of the bed and discover him, touch him. He waited tensely, afraid to move for fear of bumping into something in the dark and betraying his presence.

"Mary!"

He felt Mary trying to rise and quickly he pushed her head back to the pillow.

"She must be asleep," Mrs. Dalton mumbled.

He wanted to move from the bed, but was afraid he would stumble over something and Mrs. Dalton would hear him, would know that someone besides Mary was in the room. Frenzy dominated him. He held his hand over her mouth and his head was cocked at an angle that enabled him to see Mary and Mrs. Dalton by merely shifting his eyes. Mary mumbled and tried to rise again. Frantically, he caught a corner of the pillow and brought it to her lips. He had to stop her from mumbling, or he would be caught. Mrs. Dalton was moving slowly toward him and he grew tight and full, as though about to explode. Mary's fingernails tore at his hands and he caught the pillow and covered her entire face with it, firmly. Mary's body surged upward and he pushed downward upon the pillow with all of his weight, determined that she must not move or make any sound that would betray him. His eyes were filled with the white blur moving toward him in the shadows of the room. Again Mary's body heaved and he held the pillow in a grip that took all of his strength. For a long time he felt the sharp pain of her fingernails biting into his wrists. The white blur was still.

"Mary? Is that you?"

He clenched his teeth and held his breath, intimidated to the core by the awesome white blur floating toward him. His muscles flexed taut as steel and he pressed the pillow, feeling the bed give slowly, evenly, but silently. Then suddenly her fingernails did not bite into his wrists. Mary's fingers loosened. He did not feel her surging and heaving against him. Her body was still.

"Mary! Is that you?"

He could see Mrs. Dalton plainly now. As he took his hands from the pillow he heard a long slow sigh go up from the bed into the air of the darkened room, a sigh which afterwards, when he remembered it, seemed final, irrevocable.

"Mary! Are you ill?"

He stood up. With each of her movements toward the bed his body made a movement to match hers, away from her, his feet not lifting themselves from the floor, but sliding softly and silently over the smooth deep rug, his muscles flexed so taut they ached. Mrs. Dalton now stood over the bed. Her hands reached out and touched Mary.

"Mary! Are you asleep, I heard you moving about . . ."

Mrs. Dalton straightened suddenly and took a quick step back.

"You're dead drunk! You *stink* with whiskey!"

She stood silently in the hazy blue light, then she knelt at the side of the bed. Bigger heard her whispering. She's praying, he thought in amazement and the words echoed in his mind as though someone had spoken them aloud. Finally, Mrs. Dalton stood up and her face tilted to that upward angle at which she always held it. He waited, his teeth clamped, his fists clenched. She moved slowly toward the door; he could scarcely see her now. The door creaked; then silence.

He relaxed and sank to the floor, his breath going in a long gasp. He was weak and wet with sweat. He stayed crouched and bent, hearing the sound of his breathing filling the darkness. Gradually, the intensity of his sensations subsided and he was aware of the room. He felt that he had been in the grip of a weird spell and was now free. The fingertips of his right hand were pressed deeply into the soft fibers of the rug and his whole body vibrated from the wild pounding of his heart. He had to get out of the room, and quickly.

Suppose that had been Mr. Dalton? His escape had been narrow enough, as it was.

He stood and listened. Mrs. Dalton might be out there in the hallway. How could he get out of the room? He all but shuddered with the intensity of his loathing for this house and all it had made him feel since he had first come into it. He reached his hand behind him and touched the wall; he was glad to have something solid at his back. He looked at the shadowy bed and remembered Mary as some person he had not seen in a long time. She was still there. Had he hurt her? He went to the bed and stood over her; her face lay sideways on the pillow. His hand moved toward her, but stopped in mid-air. He blinked his eyes and stared at Mary's face; it was darker than when he had first bent over her. Her mouth was open and her eyes bulged glassily. Her bosom, her bosom, her—her bosom was not moving! He could not hear her breath coming and going now as he had when he had first brought her into the room! He bent and moved her head with his hand and found that she was relaxed and limp. He snatched his hand away. Thought and feeling were balked in him; there was something he was trying to tell himself, desperately, but could not. Then, convulsively, he sucked his breath in and huge words formed slowly, ringing in his ears: *She's dead* . . .

The reality of the room fell from him; the vast city of white people that sprawled outside took its place. She was dead and he had killed her. He was a murderer, a Negro murderer, a black murderer. He had killed a white woman.

ON READING EXPOSITORY PROSE

The reading of exposition involves a few special considerations. First, look to the *organization*. Analyze the whole selection; discover the over-all plan. Unless the structure is very simple, outline it on paper. Then examine each paragraph. Find out which is the topic sentence. If there is none, make one of your own in order that you may have the purpose of the paragraph in a few words. You will not read aloud your original topic sentence: it will merely help you to sense the total structure. Make certain that you see relationship of every sentence to the topic sentence. Then analyze each individual sentence: which parts are major and which minor; what relationship does each part have to some other part? Finally, you may have to analyze some troublesome words: do not miss a one. You must never attempt to read exposition without a thorough study of *relationships* and *meanings*.

It is quite easy to make your reading of exposition suffer from overemphasis. Much of the content is really subordinate: much of it is proof material intended to substantiate larger contentions. The subordinate parts must be given less emphasis than the larger ideas which they serve to prove. With faster rate, fewer and shorter pauses, and perhaps less volume, *subordinate the unimportant.*

Important as intellectual meaning may be, the expository prose you read is never without some *emotional significance,* though in pure exposition emotion is at a minimum. Still the words suggest *images* and the author has an *attitude.* These you must sense. In the following example of exposition, which is actually a satire upon exposition, you will find the author's attitude quite pronounced. Before reading the selection aloud, be sure that you know the attitude, that you have analyzed the relationships and meanings, and that you have distinguished the proof material and decided how to subordinate it.

HOW TO TELL A MAJOR POET FROM A MINOR POET[1]

E. B. WHITE

Among the thousands of letters which I received two years ago from people thanking me for my article "How to Drive the New Ford" were several containing the request that I "tell them how to distinguish a major poet from a minor poet." It is for these people that I have prepared the following article, knowing that only through one's ability to distinguish a major poet from a minor poet may one hope to improve one's appreciation of, or contempt for, poetry itself.

Take the first ten poets that come into your head—the list might run something like this: Robert Frost, Arthur Guiterman, Edgar Lee Masters, Dorothy Parker, Douglas Fairbanks, Jr., Stephen Vincent Benét, Edwin Arlington Robinson, Lorraine Fay, Berton Braley, Edna St. Vincent Millay. Can you tell, quickly and easily, which are major and which minor? Or suppose you were a hostess and a poet were to arrive unexpectedly at your party—could you introduce him properly: "This is Mr. Lutbeck, the major poet," or "This is Mr. Schenk, the minor poet"? More likely you would have to say merely, "This is Mr. Masefield, the poet"—an embarrassing situation for both poet and hostess alike.

All poetry falls into two classes: serious verse and light verse. Serious verse is verse written by a major poet; light verse is verse written by a minor poet. To distinguish the one from the other, one must have a sensitive ear and a lively imagination. Broadly

[1] First published in *The New Yorker* in 1930.

speaking, a major poet may be told from a minor poet in two ways: (1) by the character of the verse, (2) by the character of the poet. (Note: it is not always advisable to go into the character of the poet.)

As to the verse itself, let me state a few elementary rules. Any poem starting with "And when" is a serious poem written by a major poet. To illustrate—here are the first two lines of a serious poem easily distinguished by the "And when":

> And when, in earth's forgotten moment, I
> Unbound the cord to which the soul was bound. . .

Any poem, on the other hand, ending with "And how" comes under the head of light verse, written by a minor poet. Following are the *last* two lines of a "light" poem, instantly identifiable by the terminal phrase:

> Placing his lips against her brow
> He kissed her eyelids shut. And how.

All poems of the latter type are what I call "light by degrees"—that is, they bear evidences of having once been serious, but the last line has been altered. The above couplet, for example, was unquestionably part of a serious poem which the poet wrote in 1916 while at Dartmouth, and originally ended:

> Placing his lips against her brow
> He kissed her eyelids shut enow.

It took fourteen years of knocking around the world before he saw how the last line could be revised to make the poem suitable for publication.

While the subject matter of a poem does not always enable the reader to classify it, he can often pick up a strong clue. Suppose, for instance, you were to run across a poem beginning:

> When I went down to the corner grocer
> He asked would I like a bottle of Welch's
> grape juice
> And I said, "No, sir."

You will know that it is a minor poem because it deals with a trademarked product. If the poem continues in this vein:

"Then how would you like a package of Jello,
A can of Del Monte peaches, some Grape Nuts,
And a box of Rinso—
Or don't you thin' so?"

you may be reasonably sure not only that the verse is "light" verse but that the poet has established some good contacts and is getting along nicely.

And now we come to the use of the word "rue" as a noun. All poems containing the word "rue" as a noun are serious. This word, rhyming as it does with "you," "true," "parvenu," "emu," "cock-a-doodle-doo," and thousands of other words, and occupying as it does a distinguished place among nouns whose meaning is just a shade unclear to most people—this word, I say, is the sort without which a major poet could not struggle along. It is the hallmark of serious verse. No minor poet dares use it, because his very minority carries with it the obligation to be a little more explicit. There are times when he would like to use "rue," as, for instance, when he is composing a poem in the A. E. Housman manner:

When drums were heard in Pelham,
The soldier's eyes were blue,
But I came back through Scarsdale,
And oh the . . .

Here the poet would like to get in the word "rue" because it has the right sound, but he doesn't dare.

So much for the character of the verse. Here are a few general rules about the poets themselves. All poets who, when reading from their own works, experience a choked feeling, are major. For that matter, all poets who read from their own works are major, whether they choke or not. All women poets, dead or alive, who smoke cigars are major. All poets who have sold a sonnet for one hundred and twenty-five dollars to a magazine with a paid circulation of four hundred thousand are major. A sonnet is composed of fourteen lines; thus the payment in this case is eight dollars and ninety-three cents a line, which constitutes a poet's majority. (It also indicates that the editor has probably been swept off his feet.)

All poets whose work appears in "The Conning Tower" of the *World* are minor, because the *World* is printed on uncoated stock—which is offensive to major poets. All poets named Edna St. Vincent Millay are major.

All poets who submit their manuscripts through an agent are

major. These manuscripts are instantly recognized as serious verse. They come enclosed in a manila folder accompanied by a letter from the agent: "Dear Mr.———: Here is a new group of Miss McGroin's poems, called 'Seven Poems.' We think they are the most important she has done yet, and hope you will like them as much as we do." Such letters make it a comparatively simple matter for an editor to distinguish between serious and light verse, because of the word "important."

Incidentally, letters from poets who submit their work directly to a publication without the help of an agent are less indicative but are longer. Usually they are intimate, breezy affairs, that begin by referring to some previously rejected poem that the editor has forgotten about. They begin: "Dear Mr.———: Thanks so much for your friendly note. I have read over 'Invulnerable' and I think I see your point, although in line eight the word 'hernia' is, I insist, the only word to quite express the mood. At any rate, here are two new offerings. 'Thrush-Bound' and 'The Hill,' both of which are rather timely. I suppose you know that Vivien and I have rented the most amusing wee house near the outskirts of Sharon—it used to be a well house and the well still takes up most of the living room. We are as poor as church mice but Vivien says, etc., etc."

A poet who, in a roomful of people, is noticeably keeping at a little distance and "seeing into" things is a major poet. This poet commonly writes in unrhymed six-foot and seven-foot verse, beginning something like this:

When, once, finding myself alone in a gathering of people,
I stood, a little apart, and through the endless confusion of voices . . .

This is a major poem and you needn't give it a second thought.

There are many more ways of telling a major poet from a minor poet, but I think I have covered the principal ones. The truth is, it is fairly easy to tell the two types apart; it is only when one sets about trying to decide whether what they write is any good or not that the thing really becomes complicated.

ON READING DESCRIPTIVE PROSE

Pure descriptive prose is the least common of the three kinds. Description is usually employed as a subordinate form within narration or exposition. Whether it exists alone or is involved in one of the other forms, description is primarily dependent on *imagery*. Because many individual images are likely to be used, it is especially important for the reader to relate them to the *dominant mood* which the images are meant to implement. The specific is ever relevant to the dominant mood and should be consistent with it.

Read the following delightful cutting from a story in *The New Yorker* of September 19, 1953. The dominant mood is one of painful and yet pleasurable melancholy and reminiscence. Be sure that the images of the polar bear, the grizzlies, and the monkeys promote that larger mood and do not detract from it. Do not miss the farmer, Clancy, and a multitude of tiny images. Perhaps you would like to look up and read the whole story in *The New Yorker.*

from IN THE ZOO

JEAN STAFFORD

Keening harshly in his senility, the blind polar bear slowly and ceaselessly shakes his head in the stark heat of the July and mountain moon. His open eyes are blue. No one stops to look at him; an old farmer, in passing, sums up the old bear's situation by observing, with a ruthless chuckle, that he is a "back number." Patient and despairing, he sits on his yellowed haunches on the central rock of his pool, his huge toy paws wearing short boots of mud.

The grizzlies to the right of him, a conventional family of father and mother and two spring cubs, alternately play the clown and sleep. There is a blustery, scoundrelly, half-likable bravado in the manner of the black bear on the polar's left; his name, according to the legend on his cage, is Clancy, and he is a rough-and-tumble, brawling blowhard, thundering continually as he paces back and forth, or pauses to face his audience of children and mothers and release from his great, gray-tongued mouth a perfectly Vesuvian roar. If he were to be reincarnated in human form, he would be a man of action, possibly a football coach, probably a politician. One expects to see his black hat hanging from a branch of one of his trees; at any moment he will light a cigar.

The polar bear's next-door neighbors are not the only ones who offer so sharp and sad a contrast to him. Across a reach of scrappy grass and litter is the convocation of conceited monkeys, burrowing into each other's necks and chests for fleas, picking their noses with their long, black, finicky fingers, swinging by their gifted tails on the flying trapeze, screaming bloody murder. Even when they mourn—one would think the male orangutan was on the very brink of suicide—they are comedians; they only fake depression, for they are firmly secure in their rambunctious tribalism and in their appalling insight and contempt. Their flibbertigibbet gamboling is a sham, and, stealthily and shiftily, they are really watching the pitiful polar bear ("Back number," they quote the farmer. "That's *his* number all right," they snigger), and the windy black bear ("Life of the party. Gasbag. Low I.Q." they note scornfully on his dossier), and the stupid, bourgeois grizzlies ("It's feed the face and hit the sack for them," the monkeys say). And they are watching my sister and me, two middle-aged women, as we sit on a bench between the exhibits, eating popcorn, growing thirsty. We are thoughtful.

A chance remark of Daisy's a few minutes before has turned us to memory and meditation. "I don't know why," she said, "but that poor blind bear reminds me of Mr. Murphy." The name "Mr. Murphy" at once returned us both to childhood, and we were floated far and fast, our later lives diminished. So now we eat our popcorn in silence with the ritualistic appetite of childhood, which has little to do with hunger; it is not so much food as a sacrament, and in tribute to our sisterliness and our friendliness I break the silence to say that this is the best popcorn I have ever eaten in my life. The extravagance of my statement instantly makes me feel self-indulgent, and for some time I uneasily avoid looking at the blind bear. My sister does not agree or disagree; she simply says that popcorn is the only food she has ever really liked. For a long time, then, we eat without a word, but I know, because I know her well and know her similarity to me, that Daisy is thinking what I am thinking; both of us are mournfully remembering Mr. Murphy, who, at one time in our lives, was our only friend.

ON READING A SPEECH

Today the occasion to read an entire nonoriginal speech is less common than in former years. Public recital of memorable speeches is now confined to an occasional Independence Day program. However, many a public speaker frequently finds occasion to quote excerpts of speeches others have composed. In doing so, he should be aware that his basic goal is the same as in any oral interpretation: to make his understanding of the thoughts and feelings of the author come alive in the listener. Sometimes this purpose is augmented by the desire to communicate an appreciation of the speaker's skill. In any event, a *sense of purpose* is the first requirement for effective quotation of a speech someone else has written.

The second requirement derives from the peculiar opportunity the speaker has to make it appear that the thoughts are his own. While he may have a strong personal identification with the meaning of the quotation, he must retain in himself and in his listeners the *sense of sharing* what someone else has said. He can achieve this sense by means of a careful introduction which gives due credit to the author and also by the constant presence and employment of the manuscript. He will look at his copy somewhat more frequently and perhaps for longer periods of time than is the case in presenting his own remarks. Perhaps his gestures will be fewer and more covert than in his own speaking.

Because speeches are designed to be heard, the third requirement for effective quotation from them is that the reader must pay special attention to *oral obligations and opportunities*. Clarity and emphasis are of prime importance. He must recognize thought-centers, topic sentences, climaxes, and subordination; and by means of such vocal techniques as pauses, rate, duration, touch, inflection, step, and key he must communicate these aspects of meaning to his listeners.

While there is only limited occasion today to read a nonoriginal speech, there is frequent occasion to read your own. Although it is generally preferable to speak extemporaneously, the pressures of modern living often require the use of a manuscript: the news media want an exact copy, and the broadcaster demands precise timing.

Of course, the major difference between reading your own speech and one someone else has written is that rather than sharing another's ideas you are now expressing your own. It therefore follows that you will avoid calling attention to the existence of your copy. You will certainly not ask to be excused for reading the speech. Nor will you flourish the copy for all to see. Instead, you will assume an *extemporaneous manner,* reading with maximum *awareness of meaning* at the moment of utterance. No vocal or visible techniques can substitute for this.

As you can readily tell from the widespread use of the teleprompter, audiences prefer that the speaker use a maximum of *direct eye contact.* Indeed they want the speaker, even if he is using a manuscript, to look at them longer and more often than does the reader. When reading your own speech, look at the audience at least ninety per cent of the time. To do this, you must of course be so familiar with your copy that you can repeat a whole sentence or even a paragraph after only one glance at the manuscript.

Summary

All of the principles of oral interpretation in Chapters 1 through 12 apply in the interpretative reading of prose, but the following special emphases are in order.

1. When reading any prose, you should
    a. Determine the author's specialized purposes,

   b. Experience and reflect in your voice and body the author's use of imagery,
   c. Give adequate prominence to the author's use of literary rhythms,
   d. Make such cuttings as necessary without destroying the style or handicapping the author's purposes, and
   e. Avoid sight reading.
2. When reading narrative prose, you should
   a. Recognize the author's climaxes,
   b. Make the dialogue clear and interesting, and
   c. Carefully visualize the continuity.
3. When reading expository prose, you should
   a. Always make an especially thorough preliminary study of relationships and meanings, and
   b. Never neglect the emotional significance.
4. When reading descriptive prose, you should
   a. Take special care to sense the imagery, and
   b. Relate the individual images to the dominant mood.
5. When reading a nonoriginal speech, you should
   a. Maintain your sense of purpose in doing so,
   b. Remember that you are sharing what some else has said, and
   c. Pay special attention to oral obligations and opportunities.
6. When reading your own speech, you should
   a. Appear extemporaneous, and
   b. Use a maximum of direct eye contact with your audience.

A READING PROGRAM OF "ISLAND OF FEAR" [1]

Like millions of other readers, I am addicted to literary fantasies, including, of course, science fiction. While my addiction often results in a waste of time as I read worthless stories devoid of skill, it frequently rewards me with intriguing literary experiences: the downright impossible and ridiculous become real, vivid, and breathtaking.

The secret of this capacity to become at least momentarily believable often lies in the meticulous employment of realistic details and in the use of a frame of reference already somewhat familiar to the reader. The writer weaves his fascinating tapestry out of threads which seem individually genuine.

Such is the case in "Island of Fear," by William Sambrot. The central

[1] This sample program of reading a short story illustrates many of the problems faced by the interpreter in reading narrative prose. It includes a demonstration of how to cut a story which would otherwise be too long for the time allotment. The copy is heavily annotated to provide the student assistance in understanding the story and in actually reading it aloud.

figure of the story is a modern and apparently young man who has sufficient money and leisure to pursue an intense search for relics of the ancient past. You find him on an island in the Aegean Sea. It was in this ancient sea that Ulysses wandered for twenty years after the Trojan War, and it was here that he encountered the strange creatures about which you read as a child.[2]

ISLAND OF FEAR[3]

WILLIAM SAMBROT

Kyle Elliot[4] clutched the smooth tight-fitting stones of the high wall, unmindful of the fierce direct rays of the Aegean sun on his neck, staring, staring through a chink.

He'd come to this tiny island, dropped into the middle of the Aegean like a pebble on a vast blue shield,[5] just in the hope that something—something like what lay beyond that wall—might turn up. And it had.[6] It had.

Beyond,[7] in the garden behind the wall, was a fountain, plashing gently. And in the center of that fountain, two nudes, a mother and child.

A mother and child, marvelously intertwined, intricately wrought of some stone that almost might have been heliotrope, jasper or one of the other semi-precious chalcedonies[8]—although that would have been manifestly impossible.

[2] Please notice that the introduction attempts to achieve at least three purposes: to interest the listener, to assist him in understanding, and to give him some idea of what to look for. Incidentally, you must secure the copyright owner's permission for public reading.

[3] The complete story would require about twenty-eight minutes to read. The short version, employing the deletions indicated here, can be read in nineteen or twenty minutes. In your study of this program, first read the story in its entirety and then reread, leaving out the deletions.

[4] Because Mr. Elliot is not directly described or characterized by the author, you must picture him for yourself. His apparent financial circumstances, his interests, his actions, and his thoughts will give you many clues. We think he has an overpowering obsession for antiquities. He seems intelligent, educated, curious, and brave, perhaps foolhardy.

[5] Note the rich, romantic flavor which the author executes with a minimum of verbiage.

[6] Foreshadowing such as this seems a favorite device of the author. Upon reading the story aloud, you will want to recognize these shadows for what they are: seeds of suspense, as in this instance, and subtle hints that the listener may later remember as the events unfold.

[7] The next four paragraphs describe a lovely statue, intricate and beautiful in its detail, a supreme work of art. The description, typical of good writing, leaves much to the imagination: it is rich in suggestion. Give your imagination free reign so that you see infinitely more than a literal interpretation of the words would provide. You can further enhance the beauty of this portion by providing full utterance to the ear appeal of the lines, especially the cadences, the liquid consonants, and the syllables of inherently long duration.

[8] The three terms, "heliotrope," "jasper," and "chalcedonies," may be new to you. What are their meanings? Why "would that have been manifestly impossible?"

~~He took a small object like a pencil from his pocket and extended it. A miniature telescope. He gasped, looking once more through the chink.~~[9] Heavens, the detail of the woman! Head slightly turned, eyes just widening with the infinitesimal beginning of an expression of surprise[10] as she looked—at what? And half sliding, clutching with one hand at the smooth thigh, reaching mouth slightly rounded, plump other hand not quite touching the milk-swollen breast—the child.[11]

His professional eye moved over the figures, his mind racing, trying to place the sculptor, and failing. It was of no known period. It might have been done yesterday; it might be millenniums old. Only one thing was certain—no catalogue on earth listed it.[12]

Kyle had found this island by pure chance.[13] He'd taken passage on a decrepit Greek caïque[14] that plied the Aegean, nudging slowly and without schedule from island to island. From Lesbos to Chios to Samos, down through the myriad Cyclades, and so on about the fabled sea, touching the old, old lands where the gods had walked like men.[15] The islands where occasionally some treasure, long buried, came to light, and if it pleased Kyle's eyes, and money obtained it, then he would add it to his small collection. But only rarely did anything please Kyle. ~~Only rarely~~.[16]

~~The battered caïque's engine had quit in the midst of a small storm which drove them south and west. By the time the storm had cleared, the asthmatic old engine was back in shape, coughing along. There was no radio, but the captain was undisturbed. Who could get lost in the Aegean?~~[17]

They had been drifting along, a small water bug of a ship lost in the greenish-blue sea, when Kyle had seen the dim purple shadow that was a tiny island in the distance. The glasses brought the little blob of land closer and he sucked in his breath.[18] An incredible wall, cover-

[9] Deletions such as this remove small elements from the action of the story without diminishing the mood or handicapping the plot.

[10] The forepart of this sentence is rich in literary suggestion: visualize!

[11] Again, visualize!

[12] Here is an element essential to the story: it explains Collector Elliot's fascination.

[13] Now the author backtracks to explain how Elliot happened to be on the island looking through the chink in this strange wall: indeed, the next nineteen paragraphs are to be uttered while he remains fascinated with the sight of the statue.

[14] Consult the dictionary!

[15] Do not miss the romantic allusions. The author assumes they will be meaningful to you. Refresh your memory of them by referring to Bullfinch's *Mythology*.

[16] Here you learn more about the collector: discriminating and apparently wealthy enough to buy anything he wanted. Incidentally, we have deleted the last sentence of the paragraph and similar portions elsewhere because they are elements of emphasis in written style, which emphasis the oral reader will achieve with the vocal variables at his command.

[17] In the interest of brevity this paragraph has been omitted: the action herein does not seem essential to the plot. No later portion of the story depends on this for understanding.

[18] Here is the first element of mystery Kyle encountered in his adventure. It is another

ing a good quarter of the miniature island, leaped into view,[19] a great horseshoe of masonry that grew out of the sea, curved, embraced several acres of the land, then returned, sinking at last into the sea again, where white foam leaped high even as he watched.

He called the captain's attention to it. "There is a little island over there." [20] And the captain, grinning, had squinted in the direction of Kyle's pointing finger.

"There is a wall on it," Kyle said, and instantly the grin vanished from the captain's face; his head snapped around and he stared rigidly ahead, away from the island.[21]

"It is nothing," ~~the captain said harshly.~~[22] "Only a few goatherders live there. It has no name, even."

"There is a wall," ~~Kyle had said gently.~~ "Here"—handing him the glasses—"look."

"No." ~~The captain's head didn't move an iota.~~ His eyes remained straight ahead. "It is just another ruin. There is no harbor there; it is years since anyone has gone there. You would not like it. No electricity."

"I want to see the wall and what is behind it."

~~The captain flicked an eye at him. Kyle started. The eye seemed genuinely agitated.~~ "There is nothing behind it. It is a very old place and everything is long since gone."

"I want to see the wall," ~~Kyle said quietly.~~

They'd put him off, finally,[23] the little caïque pointing its grizzled snout to sea, its engine turning over just enough to keep it under way, its muted throbbing the only sound. They'd rowed him over in a dinghy,[24] and as he approached he'd noticed the strangely quiet single street of the village, the lone inn, the few dories with patched lateen sails, and on the low, worn-down hills the herds of drifting goats.

---

source of suspense for the reader. Strive to speak the lines with a suggestion of the awe and amazement Kyle must have experienced.

[19] Be sure you understand the arrangement of the wall.

[20] The first dialogue in the story. Remember that your manner of uttering Elliot's lines can help to communicate his personality. Perhaps his eager interest will be demonstrated with eyes and a gesture as well as with voice. We suggest you direct your eyes and face slightly to the right of center as you read Elliot's lines.

[21] The reason for the captain's response is a mystery at this point and is another source of suspense. The role of the narration here is to communicate both the nature of the captain's response and the storyteller's surprise and wonder.

[22] If you will direct the captain's lines slightly to the left of center, you will help the listeners to distinguish his words from those of Elliot. In addition, contrasting his harshness with the eagerness of Elliot will make the phrases such as, "the captain said harshly," unnecessary. In this instance and in most other cases we have omitted such phrases.

[23] There is a minor climax here, and the line should be spoken clearly and quietly.

[24] Here is the beginning of a new segment of the story. It provides an excellent opportunity for imagery.

~~Almost, he might have believed the captain; that here was an old tired island, forgotten, out of the mainstream of the brilliant civilization that had flowered in this sea—almost, until he remembered that wall. Walls are built to protect, to keep out or keep in. He meant to see what.~~

After he'd settled in the primitive little inn,[25] he'd immediately set out for the wall, surveying it from the low knoll, surprised again to note how much of this small island it encompassed.

He'd walked all around it,[26] hoping to find a gate or a break in the smooth, unscalable wall that towered up. There had been none. The grounds within sprawled on a sort of peninsula that jutted out to where rock, barnacled, fanged, resisted the restless surf.

And coming back along the great wall, utterly baffled, he'd heard the faint musical sound of water dropping within, and, ~~peering carefully at the wall,~~ had seen the small aperture, no bigger than a walnut, just above his head.

And looked through the aperture,[27] and so stood, dazed at so much beauty, staring at the woman and child, unable to tear away, knowing that here, at last, was the absolute perfection he'd sought throughout the world.

How was it that the catalogues failed to list this master work? [28] These things were impossibly hard to keep quiet. And yet, ~~not a whisper,~~ not a rumor had drifted from this island ~~to the others of what lay within those walls.~~ Here on this remote pinprick of land, ~~so insignificant as to go unnamed,~~ here behind a huge wall ~~which was itself a work of genius,~~ here was this magic mother and child glowing all unseen.

He stared, throat dry, heart pumping with the fierce exultation of the avid connoisseur who has found something truly great—and unknown. He must have it [29]—he would have it. ~~It wasn't listed, possibly—just possibly—its true worth was unknown. Perhaps the owner~~

[25] Because these three paragraphs which take Elliot from the ship, to the village, and to the wall have been reduced to two, you will want to speak somewhat more slowly than you would if all three were used. Surely several hours transpire.

[26] This paragraph, as well as the following one, also seems to require slow utterance: they say much in few words.

[27] Although the author has already told us what lies behind the wall, Elliot is now actually to see the statue for the first time: pause at this spot to make your listeners want to hear what is to follow.

[28] This paragraph and the next one too express the collector's wonder and ecstasy as he stares at this object which he feels he must have. You will read this portion well to the degree that you can vicariously experience his emotions.

[29] Apparently the summit of his appreciation, and incidentally the climax of another portion of the story, is the desire to acquire: perhaps you and your listeners can begin to sense here that Elliot's acquisitiveness will bring him only tragedy. Note that the succeeding lines, which have been deleted, reveal his sudden hope that he can get the statue for less than it is worth.

~~of this estate had inherited it, and it remained there, in the center of the gently falling water, unnoticed, unappreciated.~~

He reluctantly turned away from the chink in the wall [30] and walked slowly back toward the village, scuffling the deep, pale immemorial dust.[31] Greece. Cradle of western culture. He thought again of the exquisite perfection of the mother and child back there. The sculptor of that little group deserved to walk on Olympus. Who was it? [32]

Back in the village [33] he paused before the inn to take some of the dust off his shoes,[34] thinking again how oddly incurious, for Greeks,[35] these few villagers were.

~~"Permit me?"~~

A boy,[36] eyes snapping, popped out of the inn with a rag in one hand and some primitive shoe blacking in the other, and began cleaning Kyle's shoes.

Kyle sat down on a bench and examined the boy. He was about fifteen, wiry and strong, but small for his age. He might have, ~~in an earlier era,~~ been a model for one of Praxiteles' [37] masterpieces: the same perfectly molded head, the tight curls, two ringlets falling over the brows, like Pan's snubbed horns, the classic Grecian profile. But no, a ridged scar ran from the boy's nose to the corner of the upper lip, lifting it ever so slightly, revealing a glimmer of white teeth.

~~No, Praxiteles would never have used him for a model—unless, of course, he had a slightly flawed Pan in mind.~~

"Who owns the large estate beyond the village?" [38] ~~he asked in his excellent Greek.~~ The boy looked up quickly and it was as if a shutter came down over his dark eyes.[39] He shook his head.

[30] This is transition from his experience at the wall to his search for someone to help him secure the statue. Take your time!

[31] Although dust is normally insignificant, it is in this instance essential to subsequent action. It's foreshadowing. Make it clear without emphasis.

[32] Suspense again.

[33] Another segment of the plot: Elliot's search for assistance. Tension and interest are less again.

[34] "Immemorial dust" and essential to the plot!

[35] Your inflection will say, in effect, "Why should these Greeks be so different?" More suspense.

[36] The second major character in the story, an appealing lad and somehow pathetic too. His significance is not to be revealed for a time but he is extensively characterized now. Excellent visual imagery. Try to construct a detailed mental picture.

[37] Check on this allusion. Perhaps some readers would like to refer to it in the introduction.

[38] Elliot should be the same character who engaged in conversation with the captain earlier. Give him the same character placement. He looks down to the boy.

[39] The same inexplicable response the captain made! Your manner of utterance should reveal Elliot's mystification: an occasion perhaps for circumflex inflections.

"You must know it," ~~Kyle persisted.~~[40] "It covers the whole south end of this island. A big wall, very high, all the way to the water."

~~The boy shook his head stubbornly.~~[41] "It has always been there."

~~Kyle smiled at him. "Always is a long time," he said. "Perhaps your father might know?"~~[42]

"~~I am alone," the boy said with dignity.~~

"~~I'm sorry to hear that." Kyle studied the small, expert movement of the boy.~~ "You really don't know the name of the persons who live there?"

The boy muttered a single word.

"Gordon?"[43] ~~Kyle leaned forward.~~ "Did you say 'The Gordons'? Is it an English family that owns that property?" He felt the hope dying within.[44] If an English family owned it, the chances were slim indeed of obtaining that wonderful stone pair.

"They are not English,"[45] ~~the boy said.~~

"I'd like very much to see them."

"There is no way."

"I know there's no way from the island,"[46] ~~Kyle said,~~ "but I suppose they must have a dock or some facilities for landing from the sea?"

The boy shook his head, keeping his eyes down. Some of the villagers had stopped, and now were clustered about him, watching and listening quietly. Kyle knew his Greeks, a happy boisterous people, intolerably curious sometimes; full of advice, quick to give it. These peop.e merely stood, unsmiling, watching.[47]

The boy finished and Kyle flipped him a fifty-lepta coin.[48] ~~The~~

[40] He fears his search is to be thwarted, and so perhaps he will emphasize "must," "whole," "big," "very," and "all the way."

[41] Supply the action as you speak the line. Does not the boy's answer really say, "I refuse to tell you about the wall"?

[42] These lines which reveal that the boy is alone in the world are useful but probably not essential to the plot, and so we have omitted them, allowing Elliot's interrogation of the boy to proceed without interruption.

[43] The boy has been so reluctant to answer and so unclear that Elliot cannot be sure he has said, "Gordon." Probably these three questions are uttered rapidly and in quick succession. Elliot's anxiety is very evident in his manner of speaking.

[44] He senses that his acquisitiveness is about to be thwarted. The lines bespeak dejection, which perhaps you can express with downward inflections.

[45] This is an answer to only the last of Elliot's questions, but apparently the collector is unaware of the fact and assumes, as you will see in his reply, that the name is "Gordon," that the family is not English, and that he still has a chance to persuade them to part with the statue.

[46] The same persistence and emphasis he used in saying the boy must know the wall.

[47] More mystery. Why are these Greeks so different?

[48] What's a fifty-lepta coin? Apparently this action is to give the impression of removing the boy from the story.

boy caught it and smiled, a flawed masterpiece.

"That wall," [49] Kyle said to the spectators, singling out one old man,[50] "I am interested in meeting the people who own that property."

The old man muttered something and walked away.

Kyle mentally kicked himself for the psychological error. In Greece, money talks first. "I will pay fifty—one hundred drachmas," [51] he said loudly, "to anyone who will take me in his boat around to the seaward side of the wall."

It was a lot of money, he knew, to a poor people eking out a precarious existence on this rocky island, with their goats and scanty gardens. Most of them wouldn't see that much in a year's hard work. A lot of money [52]—but they looked at one another,[53] then turned and without a backward glance they walked away from him. All of them.

Throughout [54] the village he met the same mysterious refusal, as difficult to overcome as that enigmatic wall that embraced the end of the island. They refused even to mention the wall or what it contained, who built it, and when. It was as though it didn't exist for them.

At dusk he went back to the inn, ate *dolmadakis* [55]—minced meat, rice, egg and spices—surprisingly delicious; drank *retsina*, the resinated, astringent wine of the peasant; and wondered about the lovely mother and child, standing there behind that great wall with the purple night clothing them.[56] A vast surge of sadness, of longing for the statues swept over him.

What a rotten break! [57] He'd run into local taboos before. Most of them were the results of petty feuds, grudges going back to antiquity. They were cherished by the peasants, held tight, jealously guarded. What else was there of importance in their small lives? But this was something entirely different.

[49] A little subterfuge here: he makes no reference to the statue, which is his real object.

[50] The incident of the old man is being omitted, and so this remark and the next one are directed to the whole group of villagers.

[51] Find out what this is in American currency.

[52] The deletion results in condensation: a generous pause may make the lines more believable and heighten the contrast between the first clause and the second. Note that we have made one sentence where the author had three.

[53] Here's some effective though unconventional style. Beginning with "but" there are five groups of words which show the slow and complete rejection of Elliot: they can be read in steps of diminishing emphasis. Do some experimenting with the method of utterance.

[54] Another sizable portion of the story is being removed. Show the passage of time with a long pause.

[55] This deleted portion seems to lend authenticity; we will risk the loss.

[56] Imagery here for Elliot and for you.

[57] Again you must take your time where several lines are omitted.

He [58] was standing on the outskirts of the darkened village, gazing unhappily out to sea, when he heard a soft scuffling. He turned quickly. ~~A small boy was approaching~~. It was the shoeshine boy,[59] eyes gleaming in the starshine, shivering slightly,[60] though the night was balmy.

The boy clutched his arm. "~~The others—tonight,~~ I will take you in my boat," ~~he whispered.~~[61]

Kyle smiled, relief exploding within him.[62] Of course, he should have thought of the boy. A young fellow, ~~alone, without family,~~ could use a hundred drachmas, whatever the taboo.

"Thank you," ~~he said warmly.~~ "When can we leave?"

"Before the ebb tide—an hour before sunrise," ~~the boy said. "Only"—his teeth were chattering—~~"I will take you, but I will not come any closer than the outer rocks between the walls. From there, you must wait until the ebb tide and walk—and walk—" ~~He gasped, as though choking.~~[63]

~~"What are you afraid of?" Kyle said. "I'll take all the responsibility for trespassing, although I don't think—"~~

~~The boy clutched his arm. "The others—~~tonight, when you go back to the inn, you will not tell the others that I am rowing you there?"

"Not if you don't want me to."

"Please do not!" ~~he gasped.~~ "They would not like it if they knew—after, that I—" [64]

~~"I understand," Kyle said. "I won't tell anyone."~~

"An hour before sunrise," ~~the boy whispered.~~ "I will meet you at the wall where it goes into the water to the east." [65]

The stars were still glowing, but faintly, when Kyle met the boy,[66] a dim figure sitting in a small rowboat that bobbed up and down, scraping against the kelp and barnacles that grew from the base of the monolithic wall. ~~He realized suddenly that the boy must have rowed for hours to get the boat this far around the island. It had no sails.~~

He climbed in and they shoved off, the boy strangely silent. The sea was rough, a chill predawn wind blowing raggedly. The wall loomed up alongside, gigantic in the mist.

[58] There is a quality of reverie here.
[59] Both pleasure and surprise.
[60] Suspense again. We wonder why he shivers.
[61] Simply read the dialogue with a suggestion of a whisper.
[62] His relief will show in the manner in which you read this account of his response.
[63] Again we delete the unnecessary: say the line appropriately.
[64] Suspense!
[65] A long pause before you begin the last major section of the story.
[66] A fine opportunity for imagery.

"Who built this wall?" he asked, once they were out onto the pitching water, heading slowly around the first of a series of jagged, barnacled rocks, thrusting wetly above the rapidly ebbing tide.

"The old ones," the boy said. His teeth were-chattering, he kept his back steadfastly to the wall,[67] glancing only seaward to measure his progress. "It has always been there."

Always. ~~And yet,~~ studying the long sweep of the wall beginning to emerge in the first light, Kyle knew that it was very old. Very old. It might well date back to the beginning of Greek civilization.[68] And the statues—the mother and child. All of it an enigma ~~no greater than the fact that they were unknown to the outside world.~~

As they drew slowly around until he was able to see the ends of the thick walls rising out of the swirling, sucking sea,[69] he realized that most certainly he could not have been the first—not even one of the first hundred. This island was remote, not worth even being on a mail route, but surely, over the many, many years that wall had towered, it must have been visited by people as curious as he. Other collectors. And yet, not a rumor.[70]

The boat rasped up against an enormous black rock, its tip, white with bird droppings, startlingly luminous in the half light.[71] The boy shipped [72] his oars.

"I will come back here at the next tide," ~~he said, shaking as though with a fever.~~ "Will you pay me now?" [73]

"Of course." ~~Kyle took out his billfold.~~ "But aren't you at least going to take me farther in than this?"

"No," ~~the boy said shrilly.~~ "I cannot."

"How about the dock?" Kyle surveyed the considerable expanse of shallow, choppy surf between the rocks and the narrow sloping beach. "Why, there isn't a dock!"

There was nothing between the walls but sand, dotted with huge rocks, and inland, a tangled growth of underbrush with an occasional cypress rearing tall.

"I'll tell you what. I'll take the boat in and you wait here," ~~Kyle said.~~ "I won't be long. I just want to get a chance to meet whoever owns the place and arrange—"

"No!" [74] There was sharp panic in the boy's voice. "~~If you take the boat—~~" He half rose, leaning forward to shove off from the rock.

[67] Suspense! What would happen if he looked at the wall? This is foreshadowing.
[68] Foreshadowing, too.
[69] Imagery again! Perhaps a hint of disaster, too.
[70] Why? Suspense.
[71] More images—both audible and visual.
[72] Be sure you know the meaning of the word.
[73] Why should he be paid now? Foreshadowing of disaster for Elliot.
[74] The boy's reaction is violent. Your reading of this paragraph should reveal the climax when the boy sinks into the water.

At that instant a swell raised the boat, then dropped it suddenly out from under the boy. Overbalanced, he swayed, arms waving wildly, then went over backwards, hitting his head on the rock. He slipped under the water like a stone.

Kyle made a quick lunge, and missing, immediately dived out of the rowboat after him, rasping his chest on the barnacled shelf of rock a few feet beneath the boat.[75] He got ~~a good handful of the boy's shirt, but it tore like paper. He grabbed again, got~~ a firm grip on his hair and stroked for the surface. He held him easily, treading water, looking for the rowboat. It was gone, ~~kicked away by his powerful dive, perhaps behind one of the other rocks.~~ No time to waste looking for it now.

He swam to shore, pulling the boy easily.[76] ~~It was only a hundred yards or so to the smooth white beach, curving between the two arms of the wall that sloped out and down into the ocean. When he came out of the water the boy was coughing weakly, salt water dribbling from his nose.~~

~~Kyle~~ carried him well above the tide mark and sat him down on the sand. The boy opened his eyes and peered at him, puzzled.

"You'll be all right," ~~Kyle said~~. "I'd better get your boat before it drifts too far."

He walked back down to the surf line, kicked off his shoes and stroked off to where the boat rose and fell, nuzzling another of the large rocks that littered the space between the towering walls. He rowed the boat back, facing the sea and the swift-rising sun.[77] The wind had dropped to a whisper.

He beached the boat and gathered up his shoes. The boy was leaning against a rock, looking inland over his shoulder in an attitude of rigid watchfulness.[78]

"Feeling better now?" Kyle called cheerfully. ~~It occurred to him that their little mishap was an excellent excuse for being here, on property belonging to someone who obviously valued his privacy highly.~~

The boy didn't move.[79] He remained staring back into the tangle of trees, back to where the massive walls converged in the distance, stark, white, ancient.

Kyle touched him on the bare shoulder. He pulled his hand away,

[75] The excitement of the rescue should be revealed in the voice of the reader.

[76] Note that this period is removed and the sentence is completed in the next paragraph. The deletion should cause you to read the lines more slowly than you otherwise would.

[77] Why should the author note that Elliot faces the sea and sun as he rows back to the boy? Another bit of foreshadowing.

[78] The boy's "rigid watchfulness" constitutes foreshadowing, but it receives only a little attention in order that the climax can be saved for a few more seconds.

[79] You wonder why, and so the author builds suspense for the climax.

fists tightly clenched.[80] He looked at the sand. Here were the marks where the boy had risen, here the dragging footsteps where he'd come to lean against this rock. And here he still stood, glancing over his shoulder toward the trees, lips barely parted, a look of faint surprise just starting on his face.[81]

And there, coming out of the tangled trees, a delicate tracery of footsteps led toward this rock and behind.[82] Footsteps, slender, high-arched, as though a woman barefooted, scarcely touching the sand, had approached for just an instant. Looking at the strange footprints, Kyle understood completely [83] what he should have guessed when first he'd peered through that chink in the wall, gasping at the unimaginable perfection of the woman and her child.

Kyle knew intimately all the ancient fables of early Greece. And now, looking at the footprints in the sand, one of the most terrible leaped into his mind: the Gorgons.[84]

The Gorgons were three sisters, Medusa, Euryale and Stheno,[85] with snakes writhing where their hair should have been. Three creatures so awful to look upon, the legend said, that whosoever dared gaze upon them instantly turned to stone.

Kyle stood on the warm sand, with the gull cries, the restless Aegean sea sounds all about him, and he knew, at last, who the old ones were who'd built the wall; [86] why they'd built it to lead into the living waters—and whom—what—the walls were meant to contain.

Not an English family named the Gordons.[87] A much more ancient family, named—the Gorgons. Perseus had slain Medusa, but her two hideous sisters, Euryale and Stheno, were immortal.

Immortal.[88] Oh, God! It was impossible! A myth! [89] And yet—

His connoisseur's eyes,[90] even through the sweat of fear, noted the utter perfection of the small statue that leaned against the rock, head turned slightly, an expression of surprise on the face as it peered

[80] He begins to sense what has happened and seeks confirmation or denial in the circumstances.

[81] Remember the expression on the face of the woman in the statue.

[82] His awe, fear, and comprehension slowly grow.

[83] Now he knows, but the listener is kept wondering a bit longer. Indeed, Elliot's awareness only serves to enhance the suspense of the listener.

[84] Climax, unless listeners need the explanation of the next paragraph, as some will.

[85] Pronounce them accurately and confidently.

[86] Elliot prolongs the awful moment for several seconds and reviews its horrors.

[87] Both "Gordon's and "Gorgons" must be said very clearly in order that the audience will understand.

[88] Set off the word with a pause before and another after. Each of the following three exclamation marks calls for a meaningful pause too.

[89] He wants to deny the truth of what has happened—indeed, he does, but he rejects his own denial. Vocal contrast here.

[90] This paragraph describes beauty, and the manner of reading it must reveal the beauty of the lines. Even in the midst of tragedy, Elliot remains a lover of the beautiful.

over one shoulder in the direction of the trees. The two tight ringlets, like snubbed horns above the brow, the perfect molding of the head, the classic Grecian profile. Salt water still flecked the smoothly gleaming shoulders, still dripped from the torn shirt that flapped about the stone waist.

Pan in chalcedony.[91] But Pan had a flaw. From the nose to the corner of the upper lips ran a ridge, an onyx scar that lifted the edge of the onyx lip slightly, so that, faintly, a glimmer of onyx teeth showed. A flawed masterpiece.

He heard the rustle behind him,[92] as of robes, smelled an indescribable scent, heard a sound that could only have been a multiple hissing[93]—and though he knew he mustn't, he turned slowly. And looked.[94]

Suggested Readings

Boardman, Gail. *Oral Communication* of Literature. Englewood Cliffs, N.J.: Prentice-Hall, 1952, pp. 149–57, prose structure.

Lee, Charlotte I. *Oral Interpretation.* (2nd edition) Boston: Houghton Mifflin, 1959, Part Two, "The Interpretation of Prose."

Parrish, Wayland Maxfield. *Reading Aloud.* (3rd edition) New York: Ronald Press, 1953, Chapter XIII, "Prose Rhythm."

[91] Apparently the story is to be completed by tying in the earlier description of the boy with his appearance as a statue.

[92] This seems a kind of postscript, a surprise ending to a story which has already ended. The surprise of Elliot is reflected in the surprise of the reader.

[93] Images of repulsion: sense them.

[94] The ending should be read slowly. Retain the suspense to the very last word. It's a remarkable story that permits you to do this. We know what happens when he looks.

14

SUGGESTIONS ON THE INTERPRETATIVE READING OF POETRY AND VERSE

Students of literature agree that poetry, especially when in verse form, is the highest refinement of language—that actually it is communication at its best. However, if the opinions of these experts were weighed against those of the "solid citizens" of today, we would find the verdict on Shakespeare, Keats, Shelley, Whitman, Poe, Eliot, Frost, and other poets far less favorable. Most often, people say, "It's not for me!"

Why do so many of us care so little for the kind of writing loosely lumped as "poetry"? The *first* reason may be that we have usually looked at it rather than listened to it. The ancient, honorable art of the troubadour is almost lost in antiquity. We have come increasingly to regard poetry as material for silent reading. *Second,* we have spent interminable hours in

English classes in analyzing it rather than experiencing it. Too often our analysis has consisted only of marking the accented and unaccented syllables, dividing the lines into feet, ascertaining the rime scheme, and dissecting the verses mercilessly without enjoying the beauty or understanding the message. *Third,* we have with "pathetic reluctance" tackled the ancient vintage before enjoying the current. Our courses in literature have been so organized chronologically that those works most difficult to appreciate because of their background, allusions, and unfamiliar structure have been studied first, and we have been robbed of enthusiasm for poetry of today. *Fourth,* we have tried to delve into the obscure before learning to perceive the obvious. Unfortunately we have read Ogden Nash only after being forced to undergo Milton. This is not to say that Milton is any less significant and rewarding than the ages have proved him, but merely that the simple should precede the complex. One does not study algebra before arithmetic, nor an electric motor before the wheel and axle. The *fifth* reason that many of us care so little for poetry may be that we have foolishly allowed a few unsatisfactory experiences with verse to sour us on all poetry. We are like the man who rejects all vegetables because he has found one or two he did not like. Perhaps we have attempted to understand and appreciate a poem which was completely outside of our experience and so failed miserably. At any rate we may have judged all verse by the little we have not liked. Such a prejudice can shut the door against a whole world of experience, whether with vegetables or with verse. *Sixth,* perhaps we have associated poetry with hearts, flowers, and fleecy clouds rather than with the multiplicity which is life. Perhaps we have come to mark the poet for an impractical idealist completely divorced from the ordinary world. We say we are practical men and women and have no use for him.

Everyone of these reasons is unfortunate and fallacious. Each is based on a false premise. We shall approach our problem of the oral interpretation of poetry with the idea that as a form it contains the most meaningful, the most stimulating, and indeed the best of all literature—for such is really the case. If you need to be convinced of this fact, perhaps the following quotations will help.

SAMUEL TAYLOR COLERIDGE: Prose: words in their best order. Poetry: the best words in the best order.

MATTHEW ARNOLD: Poetry is simply the most beautiful, the most impressive, and the most effective mode of saying things.

CARL SANDBURG: Poetry is an art practiced with the terribly plastic material of human language.

Poetry is a series of explanations of life, fading off into horizons too swift for explanations.

Poetry is the capture of a picture, a song, or a flair, in a deliberate prism of words.

MICHAEL ROBERTS: If a piece of writing achieves something impossible for prose, you had better call it poetry.

LOUIS UNTERMEYER: It [poetry] is the height of literature, and its enjoyment is the greatest of literary joys.

If you have thought that you dislike verse, you may be especially interested in the following poem by Marianne Moore. She also has her reservations about poetry.

POETRY

MARIANNE MOORE

I, too, dislike it: there are things that are important beyond all this fiddle.
Reading it, however, with a perfect contempt for it, one
discovers in
it after all, a place for the genuine.
Hands that can grasp, eyes
that can dilate, hair that can rise
if it must, these things are important not because a

high-sounding interpretation can be put upon them but because they are
useful. When they become so derivative as to become
unintelligible,
the same thing may be said for all of us, that we
do not admire what
we cannot understand: the bat
holding on upside down or in quest of something to

eat, elephants pushing a wild horse taking a roll, a tireless
wolf under
a tree, the immovable critic twitching his skin like a
horse that feels a flea, the base-
ball fan, the statistician—
nor is it valid
to discriminate against 'business documents and
school-books'; all these phenomena are important. One
must make a distinction

however: when dragged into prominence by half poets,
the result is not poetry,
nor till the poets among us can be
'literalists of
the imagination'—above
insolence and triviality and can present
for inspection, 'imaginary gardens with real toads in them,'
shall we have
it. In the meantime, if you demand on the one hand,
the raw material of poetry in
all its rawness and
that which is on the other hand
genuine, you are interested in poetry.

POETRY-PROSE-VERSE

You have undoubtedly noticed that we have been speaking of both *poetry* and *verse,* which may seem to you to be the same thing. Most persons think they are identical, but they really are distinctly different entities. Poetry may occur in verse form but does not always do so. Poetry may exist outside of verse: for example, we can often find poetry in prose form. Verse may exist without any poetic value whatsoever. Some people think that poetry is the opposite of prose, but they are wrong: the true opposite of prose is verse. Poetry is not the opposite of anything.

Well, then, what is poetry? Judging from definitions we have just quoted from the poets, no one does a very satisfying job of clearing up this question. You will just have to accept the fact that this question, like so many facing the thinking human being, cannot be answered easily in a few concrete words. Poetry is an essence which defies a definitive explanation. We can, however, set down some of the characteristics of poetry. Poetry tends to be concentrated-condensed-squeezed; it says much in a few words. Poetry tends to be figurative and symbolic; it often speaks of matters other than those it seems to speak about. Poetry depends to a great extent on sound and is meant to be read aloud and heard; the words are important for their sound values as well as for their meanings. Poetry deals in strong imagery. Poetry is usually rhythmical. Poetry is nearly always emotional in impact. Poetry is — — —. Books on poetry list the attributes of poetry. Our purpose here is only to throw a shaft or two of light upon the subject. We invite you, however, to pursue it elsewhere.

What is prose? Simply the work-a-day form of language in which we normally speak and write: conversation, sermons, political speeches, radio and television commercials (except for those jingles!), letters, essays, narrative fiction, and so on. Sometimes, prose is touched by the poetic spirit. Sometimes the speaker or writer becomes inspired and his words become eloquent, rhythmical, figurative, "the best words in the best order"; and a phrase, sentence, or a longer passage suddenly becomes sheer poetry.

What is verse? Verse is a highly structured form of writing, tending to use lines of arbitrary length and number, a rather tight pattern of rhythm (usually in the form of meter), and often rime. Of course, there are different forms: regular rimed verse, blank verse, and free verse. The first contains all three elements: line form, meter, and rime. Blank verse uses a very regular metrical form but does not use rime. Free verse, containing no meter and no rime, may sometimes be so far from regular verse as to be hardly distinguishable from prose, and yet it still may be fine poetry.

Here are some examples of what we have been saying:

Poetry in verse form: Most of the verse quoted in this textbook. (We would be the first to admit that some of the verse we have quoted does not rise to the level of poetry, but that does not mean that it is unworthy. This would be especially true of light, or nonserious, verse.)

Poetry in prose form: The Gettysburg Address. Ingersoll's speech "At the Tomb of Napoleon," quoted on pages 235–36. The passage from Durrell's novel *Clea* on pages 245–48.

Nonpoetic verse: "April Fool's Day has passed, And you're the biggest fool at last." Most children's rimes. Most of Ogden Nash's verses. Most of Robert Service. "Elegy on the Death of a Mad Dog," pages 58–59.

In this chapter we are concerned with both poetry and verse. Since poetry most often occurs in verse form, it is appropriate that we discuss them together. We shall use the term *poem* to refer to verse that is poetic.

POETRY MUST COMMUNICATE

As an oral interpreter, you may be disturbed by the current fashion of expressionism in the arts. It is concerned with the "expression" of the artist's state of mind, thoughts, emotions, dreams, and the like by means of objects or words which have some public reference but are not necessarily interrelated. Expressionism, while originating in painting, has been utilized in prose, drama, and verse. Its defenders may say that true art is never a representation of nature. Many persons have come to feel that any art, poetry for example, is worthwhile only because it is "self-expression." What the poet is expressing does not matter. Whether it is worthy of being expressed is beside the point. Whether it is understood is completely irrelevant. Adoration for the cult of expressionism has gone so far that sometimes we are inclined to feel that a poem is good because we do not understand it or simply because it is peculiar.

As students of literature we must never assume that the obscure is necessarily profound nor that the ridiculous is somehow sublime. A monkey can make scratches on a canvas, an infant can beat indiscriminately on the keys of a piano, or a mad man rant and rave, but such "self-expression" is not necessarily art. Francis Henry Taylor, museum director and art critic, has said that art is the general communication of human experience and the human spirit. He calls the universality of its message and the instantaneousness of its appeal the two distinguishing characteristics of great art. The highest praise that can be offered an art is not that it is "original" and that few if any can understand it, but rather that it communicates. As observed in Chapter 4, meaning is response: to secure a response is to communicate. Theoretically, a poem may communicate either or both emotional and intellectual meaning, but *communicate it must*. Whatever the form may be, that form must promote communication. To the degree that the form obscures communication, any literature is poor. All aesthetic considerations depend on this fact.

Allen Tate in his book *On the Limits of Poetry* contends that a poem does not need to involve a communication of denotative meaning: it can communicate a progression of tension. This is to say that poetry can be an emotional experience in itself. When this is the case, meaning is clearly response, as was seen in Chapter 4.

If you have read a poem and received no meaning from it, one of three reasons may have been responsible: the poem may have had nothing to communicate, the poem's message may have been unduly obscured by its style, or your background may have been inadequate to permit you to understand the poem. If the poem has achieved recognition, you should make a real effort to understand it. If then you still find nothing in the poem, it is not suitable for your oral interpretation. Of course, no one can be expected to like or to understand all poetry, and it must be recognized that some modern verse is unduly obscure. At any rate, if a poem is not readily understood, it is in no case suitable for oral interpretation. This assertion does not imply that poetry should be as easy to understand as the comics. Nor does it suggest that you read infantile material: good poetry often requires study. Meet the poet more than halfway! However, a poem or a verse must communicate.

THE COMMUNICATIVE PURPOSE

Although all verses worth reading must communicate, poetry as a type of literature may embody a great variety of purpose—of author relationship to the meaning, of poetic techniques, and of structure. The purpose may be to tell a story, as is the case with Lowell's "The Courtin'," Bret Harte's "Plain Language from Truthful James," and the classic *Beowulf*. These are narrative poems. In some poems the purpose is to communicate the author's feeling, and these we call lyrics. Examples are manifold: "Barter" by Sara Teasdale in Chapter 5, "The Great Lover" by Rupert Brooke in Chapter 5, "How do I love thee?" by Elizabeth Barrett Browning in Chapter 3, and "God's World" by Edna St. Vincent Millay in this chapter, to mention only a few. Sometimes the purpose of poetry is to teach, and such poetry is called didactic. Alexander Pope's "An Essay on Criticism" and Robert Frost's "Mending Wall" are examples. Another purpose of verse is to reveal character. Examples are Frost's "Home Burial" and "The Witch of Coös," and Browning's "My Last Duchess." The last of the most common purposes of poetry is dramatic, and illustrations may be seen in dramatic monologues such as "My Last Duchess" and in a multitude of verse plays such as those of William Shakespeare, Christopher Fry, and T. S. Eliot. Many poetic writings combine two or more of these purposes.

AUTHOR'S RELATIONSHIP TO THE MEANING

Verse may also differ greatly in the author's relationship to the meaning. First, there are poems or parts of poems wherein the writer expresses personal attitudes or emotions which you can share. In these instances, your role is to experience these attitudes or emotions as if they were your own. For example, in the following poem you, the reader, should attempt to experience the dedication the author expresses.

PRAYERS OF STEEL

CARL SANDBURG

Lay me on an anvil, O God.
Beat me and hammer me into a crowbar.
Let me pry loose old walls.
Let me lift and loosen old foundations.
Lay me on an anvil, O God.
Beat me and hammer me into a steel spike.
Drive me into the girders that hold a
skyscraper together.
Take red-hot rivets and fasten me into the
central girders.

Let me be the great nail holding a skyscraper
through blue nights into white stars.

Similarly, in the next poem the poet herself is experiencing the emotion of the lines, and you the reader should try to do it too.

THE COIN

SARA TEASDALE

Into my heart's treasury
I slipped a coin
That time cannot take
Nor a thief purloin,—
Oh, better than the minting
Of a gold-crowned king
Is the safe-kept memory
Of a lovely thing.

Second, we often find poems in which the author expresses a meaning which is uniquely that of the *speaker,* whether that be the poet or another for whom he speaks. Into this meaning you can enter in only a limited or very general sense. You certainly cannot adore Robert Browning as Elizabeth did in her sonnet "How do I love thee?" in Chapter 3. To assume the role of the *speaker* and to address the lines to your audience would be to make them false. As you read the following illustrations, you will see that it would be ridiculous for you to assume a full identification of yourself with the meaning.

TO HELEN

EDGAR ALLAN POE

Helen, thy beauty is to me
Like those Nicean barks of yore,
That gently, o'er a perfumed sea,
The weary, wayworn wanderer bore
To his own native shore.

On desperate seas long wont to roam,
Thy hyacinth hair, thy classic face,
Thy Naiad airs have brought me home

To the glory that was Greece
And the grandeur that was Rome.

Lo! in yon brilliant window niche
How statuelike I see thee stand,
The agate lamp within thy hand!
Ah, Psyche, from the regions which
Are Holy Land!

GRASS

CARL SANDBURG

Pile the bodies high at Austerlitz and Waterloo.
Shovel them under and let me work—
I am the grass; I cover all.
And pile them high at Gettysburg
And pile them high at Ypres and Verdun.
Shovel them under and let me work.
Two years, ten years, and passengers ask the conductor:
What place is this?
Where are we now?

I am the grass.
Let me work.

Third, and perhaps as common as the poems wherein the author expresses his own emotions which you must try to share, are those in which he reports someone else's emotional experience with a particular attitude of his own. In these instances you the reader should make an effort to share the emotion being reported but to allow it to be dominated by the attitude of the author. For example, in "Mending Wall" by Robert Frost the poet repeatedly quotes the neighbor, *Good fences make good neighbors* and always does so with an attitude which says the neighbor is narrow-minded and mistaken. In the following poem various ideas and attitudes are reported, but each is dominated by the attitude of the poet. Ask yourself in every instance, "What does the poet think of this idea?"

END OF THE SEERS' CONVENTION

KENNETH FEARING

We were walking and talking on the roof of the world,
In an age that seemed, at that time, an extremely modern age

Considering a merger, last on the agenda, of the Seven Great Leagues that held the Seven True Keys to the Seven Ultimate Spheres of all moral, financial, and occult life.

"I foresee a day," said one of the delegates, an astro-analyst from Idaho, "when men will fly through the air, and talk across space;
They will sail in ships that float beneath the water;
They will emanate shadows of themselves upon a screen, and the shadows will move, and talk, and seem as though real."

"Very interesting, indeed," declared a Gypsy delegate.
"But I should like to ask, as a simple reader of tea-leaves and palms:
How does this combat the widespread and growing evil of the police?"

The astrologer shrugged, and an accidental meteor fell from his robes and smoldered on the floor.
"In addition," he said, "I foresee a war,
And a victory after that one, and after the victory, a war again."

"Trite," was the comment of a crystal-gazer from Miami Beach.
"Any damn fool, at any damn time, can visualize wars, and more wars, and famines and plagues.
The real question is: How to seize power from entrenched and organized men of Common Sense?"

"I foresee a day," said the Idaho astrologer, "when human beings will live on top of flag-poles,
And dance, at some profit, for weeks and months without any rest,
And some will die very happily of eating watermelons, and nails, and cherry pies."

"Why," said a bored numerologist, reaching for his hat, "can't these star-gazers keep their feet on the ground?"
"Even if it's true," said a Bombay illusionist, "it is not, like the rope-trick, altogether practical."

"And furthermore, and finally," shouted the astrologer, with comets and half-moons dropping from his pockets, and his agitated sleeves,
"I prophesy an age of triumph for laziness and sleep, and dreams and utter peace.
I can see couples walking through the public parks in love, and those who do not are wanted by the sheriff.
I can see men fishing beside quiet streams, and those who do not are pursued by collectors, and plastered with liens."

"This does not tell us how to fight against skepticism," muttered a puzzled
mesmerist, groping for the door.
"I think," agreed a lady who interpreted the cards, "we are all inclined to
accept too much on faith."

A sprinkling of rain, or dragon's blood,
Or a handful of cinders fell on the small, black umbrellas they raised against
the sky.

In this next poem the reader must determine what is the attitude of Hughes toward the mother's remarks.

MOTHER TO SON

LANGSTON HUGHES

Well, son, I'll tell you:
Life for me ain't been no crystal stair.
It's had tacks in it,
And splinters,
And boards torn up,
And places with no carpet on the floor—
Bare.
But all the time
I'se been a-climbin' on,
And reachin' landin's,
And turnin' corners,
And sometimes goin' in the dark
Where there ain't been no light.
So, boy, don't you turn back;
Don't you set down on the steps
'Cause you find it kinder hard.
Don't you fall now—
For I'se still goin', honey,
I'se still climbin',
And life for me ain't been no crystal stair.

The poems by Edgar Lee Masters in the sample program at the end of this chapter are excellent illustrations of this same practice of a writer reporting someone else's thoughts and feelings with a particular attitude of his own.

ELEMENTS OF POETRY

Poems also differ greatly in those elements which make them poetry. The amount and quality of imagery and symbolism may differ. Turn back to Chapter 5 if you wish to refresh yourself on this aspect of literature. Certainly an appreciation of images and symbols is necessary to effective oral reading of poetry.

Figures of speech. Images are sometimes expressed in what we call figures of speech. While it is important to be able to grasp the significance of a figure of speech rather than merely to call it by name, your attention should be directed to the major kinds of figures to be found in poetry.

The basis of the common figures of speech is comparison between two entities which are quite unlike in general but have some special point of resemblance. A *simile* is a comparison expressed by "like," "as," "such as," or some similar connecting word.

One by one, like leaves from a tree,
All my faiths have forsaken me.

—SARA TEASDALE, *Leaves*

As idle as a painted ship
    Upon a painted ocean . . .

—SAMUEL TAYLOR COLERIDGE,
The Rime of the Ancient Mariner

A *metaphor* is a comparison which is assumed or implied; the connecting word is omitted. An object is given the name of that with which it is compared.

My vigor is a new-minted penny,
Which I cast at your feet.

—AMY LOWELL, *A Lady*

Blossomed the lovely stars,
    the forget-me-nots of the angels.

—HENRY WADSWORTH LONGFELLOW, *Evangeline*

An *allegory* is a comparison extended to a considerable length, as in Spenser's *The Faerie Queene* and "The Chambered Nautilus" by Oliver Wendell Holmes. In *The Autocrat of the Breakfast Table,* in which the last-named poem was originally published, Dr. Holmes describes "the ship of pearl" as "a series of enlarging compartments successively dwelt in by the animal that inhabits the shell, which is built in a widening spiral." The last stanza of the poem reveals that the shell of the nautilus is compared with and is symbolic of a man's life.

THE CHAMBERED NAUTILUS

OLIVER WENDELL HOLMES

This is the ship of pearl, which, poets feign,
Sails the unshadowed main,—
The venturous bark that flings
On the sweet summer wind its purpled wings
In gulfs enchanted, where the Siren sings,
And coral reefs lie bare,
Where the cold sea-maids rise to sun their streaming hair.

Its webs of living gauze no more unfurl;
Wrecked is the ship of pearl!
And every chambered cell,
Where its dim dreaming life was wont to dwell,
As the frail tenant shaped his growing shell,
Before thee lies revealed,—
Its irised ceiling rent, its sunless crypt unsealed!

Year after year beheld the silent toil
That spread his lustrous coil;
Still, as the spiral grew,
He left the past year's dwelling for the new,
Stole with soft step its shining archway through,
Built up its idle door,
Stretched in his last-found home, and knew the old no more.

Thanks for the heavenly message brought by thee,
Child of the wandering sea,
Cast from her lap, forlorn!

From thy dead lips a clearer note is born
Than ever Triton blew from wreathed horn!
While on mine ear it rings,
Through the deep caves of thought I hear a voice
that sings:—

Build thee more stately mansions, O my soul,
As the swift seasons roll!
Leave thy low-vaulted past!
Let each new temple, nobler than the last,
Shut thee from heaven with a dome more vast,
Till thou at length art free,
Leaving thine outgrown shell by life's unresting sea!

An *apostrophe* is direct address to an object or an idea as if it were a person.

O Holy Night! from thee I learn to bear
What man has borne before.

—HENRY WADSWORTH LONGFELLOW,
Hymn to the Night

Personification is the comparison of an object, animal, or idea to a human being by giving it human qualities.

When duty whispers low, *Thou must,*
The youth replies, *I can.*

—RALPH WALDO EMERSON, *Voluntaries*

Hyperbole is obvious exaggeration to produce some definite effect such as impressiveness, terror, or humor.

Here once the embattled farmers stood
And fired the shot heard round the world.

—RALPH WALDO EMERSON, *The Concord Hymn*

Ten days and nights, with sleepless eye
I watched that wretched man,
And since, I never dare to write
As funny as I can.

—OLIVER WENDELL HOLMES,
The Height of the Ridiculous

Metonymy and *synecdoche* are two other figures of speech, but these two are not comparisons. Both are the employment of one word for another which it suggests. In *metonymy* the poet may employ the cause for the effect, the effect for the cause, the sign for what it signifies, or the container for what it contains: "Uncle Sam" or "Columbia" may suggest the United States, "table" may suggest food, or "purple and gold" may suggest a particular college. In *synecdoche* the poet employs the name of a part to represent the whole: a "sail" represents a ship, "heads" represents cattle, "noses" people, or "hands" workers. A careful distinction between metonymy and synecdoche is often difficult. In either case the figure is used to suggest certain characteristics which the author wishes to emphasize.

In reading a poem, indeed any literature, which employs figures of speech, the interpreter needs to be aware not only of the literal meaning implied but of the figurative as well. Furthermore, he needs to sense the special attributes involved in the figure which make it meaningful and significant. In Sara Teasdale's simile,

> One by one, like leaves from a tree,
> All my faiths have forsaken me.
>
> —*Leaves*

the reader should remember that leaves fall slowly, that they never return to their former places, and we associate the falling of leaves with sadness.

Sound devices. Poetry differs, too, in its employment of sound devices. Good poetry is an attempt to form a perfect union of sense and sound. This association is one of the main reasons a poem is communicative and satisfying. In order for this perfect union to be effected, a poem must be given voice: it must be read aloud, and the reader must give special attention to the formation and combination of sounds as the poet planned them.

Onomatopoeia or sound symbolism, already mentioned in Chapter 8, is the use of words whose sounds suggest their sense. It is natural correspondence between sound and sense. Simple examples are "buzz," "hiss," "clack," "bang," and "twitter." Onomatopoeia is employed in poetry in single words such as the above, in phrases, and in extended pieces such as "The Bells" by Poe in Chapter 11. The following are instances of onomatopoeia at its best:

> And thumping and plumping, and bumping and jumping,
> And dashing and flashing, and splashing and clashing,
>   And so never ending,
>   And always descending,
> Sounds and motions for ever and ever are blending,

All at once and all o'er,
With a mighty uproar,
And this way the water comes down at Lodore.

—ROBERT SOUTHEY, *How the Water Comes Down at Lodore*

—the wind that far away
Comes sighing o'er the healthy sea.

—EMILY FANE BRONTË, *The Sun Has Set*

And the plashing of waterdrops
In the marble fountain
Comes down the garden paths.

—AMY LOWELL, *Patterns*

Discover the instances of onomatopoeia in the poetry you are to read. Try fully to recognize the correspondence between sound and sense. Then when you read aloud, try to utter the words in such a way as to make the most of the sound values. In reading the last lines above, you would adjust rhythm, pitch, loudness, and quality so as to suggest the actual sound of water drops. Perhaps a warning is necessary: do not allow the way you read it to seem more important than what you read.

Alliteration is the device of beginning syllables in close succession with the same consonantal sound. It is a means to the musical quality in poetry, and quite often the reader will want to emphasize it—but never to the exclusion of the sense. Examples are quite common; here are a few.

The fair breeze blew, the white foam flew.
The furrow followed free.

—SAMUEL TAYLOR COLERIDGE,
The Rime of the Ancient Mariner

The moan of doves in immemorial elms,
And murmuring of innumerable bees.

—ALFRED, LORD TENNYSON, *The Princess*

Of course alliteration can readily be used for comic effect, as in the following.

With blade, with bloody blameful blade,
He bravely broached his boiling bloody breast.

—SHAKESPEARE, *A Midsummer Night's Dream*

Assonance is the repetition of vowel or diphthong sounds, especially in stressed syllables, as in *freedom, sleep, free.* These sounds are usually identical although they may be only similar. One of the purposes of assonance in poetry is to provide pleasure to the ear. The device may be used, however, for other purposes: it helps to fuse the poetic unit into an integrated whole; and it may serve to emphasize certain elements of meaning. The following examples may help you to identify assonance.

I arise from dreams of thee,
In the first sweet sleep of night.

—PERCY BYSSHE SHELLEY, *Lines to an Indian Air*

The viol, the violet, and the vine.

—EDGAR ALLAN POE, *The City in the Sea*

The curfew tolls the knell of parting day,
The lowing herd wind slowly o'er the lea.

—THOMAS GRAY,
Elegy Written in a Country Churchyard

It is probably unnecessary for the good oral reader to make a more thorough study of poetic sound devices. We could speak at length about direct repetition of words, phrases, clauses, or sentences; syzygy; and consonance. All involve the repetition of sounds to make a pattern impressive to the ear. Inasmuch as the poet has employed his skill to create sound devices, the reader must recognize the inherent values in sounds and use them to communicate as the poet intended.

These devices are used with great effectiveness in the following poem, which you may want to read aloud as a means of impressing yourself with the values of alliteration and assonance.

CHILL OF THE EVE

JAMES STEPHENS

A long green swell
Slopes soft to the sea;
And a far-off bell
Swings sweet to me;
As the grey
Chill day

Slips away
From the lea.

Spread cold and far,
Without one glow
From a mild pale star,
Is the sky's steel bow;
And the grey
Chill day
Slips away
Below.

Yon green tree grieves
To the air around;
And the whispering leaves
Have a lonely sound;
As the grey
Chill day
Slips away
From the ground.

And dark, more dark,
The shades settle down;
Far off is a spark
From the lamp-lit town;
And the grey
Chill day
Slips away
With a frown.

Another poetic element which differs widely from one poem to another is rhythm. Good poetry, whether in verse or prose form, is characterized by a kind of rhythm called *cadence*. Of course, poetry in verse form often employs metrical rhythm too, but meter is reserved for discussion later in this chapter. To put it quite simply, *cadence* is the flow of sound. More technically it is the pattern of sounds and silences. A complete unit of meaning is known as a *primary cadence*. The thought-groups we learned to recognize in Chapters 5 and 7 were usually primary cadences. They are not hard to distinguish and are essentially the same no matter who may be reading a particular poem. *Secondary cadences* are poetic lines and speech phrases within the lines. Of course the cadence of the line itself is obvious, but the cadences of the lesser phrases are often a matter of individual interpretation. For purposes of illustration the cadences have been marked in the following poems as they might be interpreted. Two lines (//) indicate the end of a primary cadence, one (/) a secondary cadence.

A WORD

EMILY DICKINSON

A word is dead /
When it is said, /
    Some say. //
I say / it just
Begins to live
    That day. //

from *The Last Leaf*

OLIVER WENDELL HOLMES

I saw him once before, /
As he passed by the door, //
    And again
The pavement stones resound /
As he totters o'er the ground
    With his cane. //

They say that in his prime, /
Ere the pruning knife of Time
    Cut him down, /
Not a better man was found /
By the crier on his round
    Through the town. //

The safest instruction for the effective employment of verse cadence is to concentrate upon the meanings and feelings involved. If you will do so, the rhythmic pattern of sounds and silences will usually take care of itself.

With imagery, symbolism, figures of speech, sound devices, and the choice of inevitable words, a poet achieves the conciseness and communicative impact which distinguish poetry. Your recognition of these elements will enhance your capacity to interpret poetry.

STRUCTURE OF VERSE

While verse that is also poetry may involve any or all of the elements just listed, it is further characterized by *meter, rime,* and *stanzaic structure.* These features are also found in nonpoetic verse.

Meter. The form of rhythm called *meter* differs widely from one poem to another. It is the more or less regular recurrence of an identifiable pattern of stressed and unstressed syllables. Meter exists in four basic forms: iambic, trochaic, anapestic, and dactylic. However, these labels are not very significant, for they are often a matter of opinion. A metrical line can be divided into "feet." The iambic foot consists of a light beat followed by a heavy beat. The following stanza is iambic:

Thĕ cúr/fĕw tólls/ thĕ knéll/ ŏf pár/tĭng dáy,
Thĕ lów/ĭng hérd/ wĭnd slów/ly̆ o'ér/ thĕ léa,
Thĕ plów/măn hóme/wărd plóds/ hĭs wéa/ry̆ wáy,
Ănd léaves/ thĕ wórld/ tŏ dárk/nĕss ánd/ tŏ mé.

—THOMAS GRAY, *Elegy Written in a Country Churchyard*

In trochaic meter, the foot contains a heavy beat, followed by a light one:

Ónce ŭp/ón ă/míd-nĭght/ dréary̆,/ whíle Ĭ/ póndĕred,/ wéak ănd/ wéary̆,

—EDGAR ALLAN POE, *The Raven*

In anapestic meter, the foot contains three beats, two light and one heavy:

'Twăs thĕ níght/ bĕfŏre Chríst/măs, whĕn áll/ thrŏugh thĕ hóuse
Nŏt ă créa/tŭre wăs stír/rĭng, nŏt é/vĕn ă móuse;

—CLEMENT CLARKE MOORE, *A Visit from St. Nicholas*

In dactylic meter, the foot contains three beats, one heavy followed by two light beats:

Cánnŏn tŏ / ríght ŏf thĕm,
Cánnŏn tŏ / léft ŏf thĕm,
Cánnŏn ĭn / frónt ŏf thĕm
Vóllĕy'd ănd / thúndĕr'd̆;

—ALFRED, LORD TENNYSON,
The Charge of the Light Brigade

Rarely do any of these forms of meter exist within a poem in their pure form, without any irregularities. A line of good verse may well contain more than one type of metrical foot. Frequently, two types of feet, the spondee, containing two heavy beats, and the pyrrhic, containing two light beats, will appear. Do not be disturbed when you run across them; actually they provide interesting variety.

Unfortunately many young people in the public schools are being driven away from verse by an overzealous emphasis upon scansion. When students should be learning to find pleasure and inspiration in verse, they are being taught to mark the accented and unaccented syllables, to divide each line into poetic feet, to label both the feet and the lines, and to work out the rime scheme. As a result the schools retain their academic respectability, but many students learn to hate poetry. A technical knowledge of meter is not essential to the appreciation of verse. In fact, if our grade and high school teachers would forget meter entirely and simply help students to find in poems the meanings the authors intended, the works of the great poets might be more frequently read rather than relegated to the classroom and library shelves. The emphasis upon metrical scansion rather than upon the appreciation of meaning so misleads young students that nearly everyone who reads a poem aloud reads metrical beats instead of sense! Somehow people also get the impression that in reading a poem they should stop at the end of every poetic line. It is small wonder that the oral reading of verse is commonly intensely boring.

What, then, is the answer? How should one read a poem? Is not the meter important? These are some of the questions asked of the teacher of interpretative reading when he or she rails at the singsong reader. The answer is actually fairly simple: keep your mind on the purpose and meaning rather than the form of the poem. Emphasize primarily those words which carry the meaning rather than simply those upon which the metrical beats seem to fall. Unless a poet's primary purpose has been to convey rhythmic impressions as in Lindsay's "The Congo" in the sample recital at the end of this chapter, he wants you to read his poem with the sense uppermost in your mind. If you read meaning and feeling, you will find that, properly subordinated, the meter is an aid to communication, not a hindrance.

In reading most poems it is neither possible nor desirable to avoid the meter. For example, in reading Longfellow's "The Children's Hour" the accents of meaning consistently fall in the same places as the accents of meter. When you emphasize one, you also call attention to the other.

Between the dark and the daylight,
  When the night is beginning to lower,
Comes a pause in the day's occupations,
  That is known as the Children's Hour.

I hear in the chamber above me
  The patter of little feet,
The sound of a door that is opened,
  And voices soft and sweet.

Such regular meter does not require that all stressed syllables have exactly the same emphasis nor that all unstressed syllables be equal. An intelligent reading of "The Children's Hour" is characterized by the same attention to thought-centers, grouping, and pauses as in any other reading. In the first line, for example, *dark* and *daylight* are the most important words. The pause at the end of line one is properly shorter than the pause at the end of line two. In stanza two there is probably no appreciable pause after line one, and the pauses after lines two and three are approximately equal. The reader must learn to discriminate in the degree of emphasis and the lengths of pauses even in very regular verse.

In reading such a poem as Robert Frost's "Stopping by Woods on a Snowy Evening," if you confine your stresses entirely to the metrical beats and make them all approximately equal in importance, you communicate an absolute minimum of sense and destroy the beauty of this delicate, serene poem:

Whose woods these are I think I know.
His house is in the village though;
He will not see me stopping here
To watch his woods fill up with snow.

If instead of reading this poem in that manner you were to emphasize the most important words, subordinate the less important, discriminate among the degrees of emphasis and de-emphasis, group the words intelligently, and make the iambic meter the servant of the sense and feeling, you would communicate as the poet intended.

In the following version underlining is used to indicate words which might properly be emphasized. Perpendicular lines are used to indicate pauses: one line for a short pause, two for a longer pause, and three for an

STOPPING BY WOODS ON A SNOWY EVENING

ROBERT FROST

Whose woods these are I think I know. //
His house is in the village though; //
He will not see me stopping here /
To watch his woods fill up with snow. ///

My little horse must think it queer
To stop without a farmhouse near /
Between the woods and frozen lake /
The darkest evening of the year. //

He gives his harness bells a shake
To ask if there is some mistake, /
The only other sound's the sweep
Of easy wind and downy flake. ///

The woods are lovely, dark and deep, //
But I have promises to keep, /
And miles to go before I sleep, /
And miles to go/before I sleep.

even longer one. Read the poem aloud according to these suggestions. There are approximately twenty instances wherein sense emphasis and metrical scansion differ. Find as many of these as you can. For your assistance the metrical form has also been imposed upon the lines.

Do not fall into the "metrical rut." Concentrate upon the meanings and feelings involved. Enjoy poetry. Read it sensibly and with feeling, and you will read with rhythm, a rhythm far more meaningful and attractive to the listener than a "singsong."

Now to return to a statement made a few lines back: "keep your mind on the *purpose* rather than on the form of the poem." Having been emphasized, this principle must now be modified. A few poets have often and most poets have occasionally written lines or entire poems the purposes of which are dependent almost entirely on their form. Well-known examples are "The Bells" by Poe in Chapter 11, "Sante Fe Trail" by Lindsay, "The Congo" by Lindsay in the sample recital at the end of this chapter, and "The Song of the Chattahoochee" by Lanier. To read such poetry well you must emphasize the meter and other poetic sound devices, sometimes even to the exclusion of concern for word meanings. The problem is actually one of determining the degree to which sound values will contribute to the achievement of a poem's purpose. You must not feel that a verse is always read as if it were prose. You must remember that it should achieve its purpose: in some way it must communicate.

Rime. Traditional verse employs more or less regular rime. Because, in the following lines, the first ends in the same syllable as the third, the second the same as the fourth, the fifth the same as the seventh, and the sixth the same as the eighth, we say that the rime scheme is *a b a b c d c d*.

JENNY KISS'D ME

LEIGH HUNT

Jenny kiss'd me when we met,
    Jumping from the chair she sat in;
Time, you thief, who love to get
    Sweets into your list, put that in!
Say I'm weary, say I'm sad,
    Say that health and wealth have miss'd me,
Say I'm growing old, but add,
    Jenny kiss'd me.

The rime scheme in Leigh Hunt's little poem is quite simple, but much of our best literature employs a far more complicated and rigid rime scheme.

For example, the format of the English sonnet requires precisely fourteen rimed lines in the following scheme: *a b a b c d c d e f e f g g*. The beauty and the intricacy of the sonnet, involving the rime scheme and other standards of form, are best illustrated perhaps in the poems of Shakespeare. Notice that the following lines adhere exactly to the prescribed riming pattern. In doing so they contribute to the unity of the poem.

SONNET CXVI

Let me not to the marriage of true minds
Admit impediments. Love is not love
Which alters when it alteration finds,
Or bends with the remover to remove:
O, no! it is an ever-fixed mark,
That looks on tempests and is never shaken;
It is the star to every wandering bark,
Whose worth's unknown, although his height be taken.
Love's not Time's fool, though rosy lips and cheeks
Within his bending sickle's compass come;
Love alters not with his brief hours and weeks,
But bears it out even to the edge of doom.
    If this be error, and upon me prov'd,
    I never writ, nor no man ever lov'd.

From the sonnet with its involved rime scheme, we turn to verse which has no rime at all. Blank verse falls in this category, and it includes the plays of Shakespeare. Many modern poets write unrimed lines which are called free verse. Whitman, Masters, and Sandburg, all of whom are quoted extensively in this book, are examples.

Rime seems fundamentally to be a sound device. It produces a pleasant impression upon the ear. It contributes to the music of verse. It constitutes one of the reasons for calling verse an oral art. But rime is also a rhythmic device, for it involves a recurrence. For this reason, it is a part of the process of scansion and is frequently included in analyses of rhythmic structure.

Now, what use does the communicative oral reader make of rime? Certainly in the sonnet just quoted, he will not accentuate the rime. To do so would be to emphasize the form and to obscure the meaning. For example, the word *cheeks* in line 9 rimes with the word *weeks* in line 11. To force your listeners to recognize the rime would be to raise the pitch on the words in question, to increase the volume, or to pause afterwards. This would separate the subject of the clause in lines 9 and 10 from the verb and so destroy the sense.

The following well-known poem is frequently misread in exactly the same way. To see how the sense can be obscured by an emphasis upon rime, read the poem aloud, being careful to use a rising inflection on the last word in each line and to pause after that word. The result should illustrate what you should normally *not* do in the reading of verse.

THE TIGER

WILLIAM BLAKE

Tiger! Tiger; burning bright
In the forests of the night,
What immortal hand or eye
Could frame thy fearful symmetry?

In what distant deeps or skies
Burnt the fire of thine eyes?
On what wings dare he aspire?
What the hand dare seize the fire?

And what shoulder and what art
Could twist the sinews of thy heart?
And, when thy heart began to beat,
What dread hand and what dread feet?

What the hammer? What the chain?
In what furnace was thy brain?
What the anvil? What dread grasp
Dare its deadly terrors clasp?

When the stars threw down their spears,
And water'd heaven with their tears,
Did he smile his work to see?
Did he who made the lamb make thee?

Tiger! Tiger! burning bright
In the forests of the night,
What immortal hand or eye
Dare frame thy fearful symmetry?

Surely the author never intended that you should read the poem in this way. An overemphasis on rime, like an overemphasis on meter, tends to reduce the material to a set of nonsense syllables, rhythmic and perhaps pleasant to the ear but not communicative of sense. Thought-groups are broken. Proper thought-centers are replaced with false ones. The communicative role of reading is forgotten.

The really effective reader of verse, having worked diligently to understand the meaning and having disciplined himself to a maximum awareness of that meaning while reading, will give only as much emphasis to rime as the sense requires. He will subordinate the sound to the sense. He will phrase according to thought-groups and he will emphasize thought-centers. The flow of sound will frequently bridge the ends of lines. The analysis of "Stopping by Woods on a Snowy Evening" earlier in this chapter illustrates these principles of reading verse.

Only when the importance of the sound device of rime exceeds the importance of the ideas being communicated will the good reader emphasize riming words to the neglect of thought-centers. Effective reading of the verses of Ogden Nash frequently illustrates the exception to the general rule that sense must dominate.

Stanzaic structure. While prose employes the paragraph, verse uses the stanza. It is a section of one or more lines. Variety of stanzaic structure is almost limitless, for it involves not only the number of lines, but their meter and possibly their rime scheme as well. Critics speak of the following kinds of stanzas, to mention only a few: the one line; the couplet with two lines; the tercet with three; the quatrain with four; the cinquain with five; the sestet with six; the septet with seven; the octava rima with eight; the Spenserian stanza with nine lines of a prescribed form; etc. Actually the author may create whatever stanza form or forms he sees fit. A given poem may have more than one stanza form. The significant thing is that the author chooses the form he wishes to use. While it is nearly impossible to generalize about the significance of stanza form, it is often true that simple stanzaic structure best communicates simple content and more complicated structure is appropriate for complicated content. Limericks exemplify the first and sonnets the second. Emily Dickinson used simple stanzaic forms, and Eliot uses complicated ones.

IDENTITY OF FORM AND MEANING

Whatever may be the type of poetry or verse, the author's relationship to the meaning, and the techniques or the structure employed, these features and the meaning itself are one. The mode of expression and the meaning are one. Any really good poem or verse will demonstrate this fact, for example, the following lyric:

GOD'S WORLD

EDNA ST. VINCENT MILLAY

O world, I cannot hold thee close enough!
Thy winds, thy wide gray skies!
Thy mists that roll and rise!
Thy woods, this autumn day, that ache and sag
And all but cry with color! That gaunt crag
To crush! To lift the lean of that black bluff!
World, world, I cannot get thee close enough!
Long have I known a glory in it all
But never knew I this;
Here such a passion is
As stretcheth me apart. Lord, I do fear
Thou'st made the world too beautiful this year.
My soul is all but out of me—let fall
No burning leaf; prithee, let no bird call.

If you were to try to express the meaning of this poem in your own prose, you might say:

> World, I cannot get enough of you. Your winds, skies, mists, and woods in the fall are alive with color. For a long time I have found nature beautiful, but today, world, you are so beautiful that it hurts. Don't change anything.

This version is certainly inferior to the original: it has lost not only the form but much of the meaning too.

Read the following poem and then try to express the meaning in your own prose.

THE SECRET HEART

ROBERT P. TRISTRAM COFFIN

Across the years he could recall
His father one way best of all.

In the stillest hour of night
The boy awakened to a light.

Half in dreams, he saw his sire
With his great hands full of fire.

The man had struck a match to see
If his son slept peacefully.

He held his palms each side the spark
His love had kindled in the dark.

His two hands were curved apart
In the semblance of a heart.

He wore, it seemed to his small son,
A bare heart on his hidden one,

A heart that gave out such a glow
No son awake could bear to know.

It showed a look upon a face
Too tender for the day to trace.

One instant, it lit all about,
And then the secret heart went out.

But it shone long enough for one
To know that hands held up the sun.

Inevitably we find with good poetry or verse that to alter the form is to destroy the literature. Writing a paraphrase is helpful, but a good poem is really not translatable. You can no more reword it without losing a great deal than you can reproduce the perfection of one of Cicero's Latin orations when translating it into English. In poetry the meaning is one with the poem itself. You must master both if your oral interpretation is to do justice to the selection.

Summary

Certainly all suggestions about choosing material to read aloud, finding its meaning, and expressing and intensifying that meaning are applicable to the reading of poetry and verse. In this chapter, however, the following special suggestions for the effective oral interpretation of poetry and verse have been emphasized.

1. Generally speaking, read for others only those poems you feel you thoroughly understand and which you think your audience can understand.

2. Read poetry of recognized merit, the meaning of which is appropriate to our times.

3. Be sure that the form of the poem promotes communication of the meaning.

4. Strive for full personal identification with the meaning within the limits inherent in the poem.

5. As you read, be sure that the meaning dominates.

6. Be sure that the method of reading promotes communication in the fullest sense.

7. Avoid a singsong pattern.

8. Be sure that the audience response to the author's purpose is aided rather than hindered by the form he has employed.

A POETRY RECITAL ENTITLED "CORNFIELD POETS" [1]

Meandering through the prairie in central Illinois is a crooked creek called the Spoon River.[2] Most of the time it is only a little stream, and occasionally it diminishes to just a trickle: in the heat of summer it may disappear almost entirely. In the spring and fall, however, it often overflows its banks and floods pale yellow water and mud over hundreds of acres of rich cornfields. The land is fertile beyond compare, but we are concerned with the people of the valley. White people have lived here for over one hundred and fifty years. Much of the population is permanent: today the descendants of the early settlers still till the valley soil. In their devotion to their farms these people are much alike. They are alike in another way too, for they are generally characterized by a peculiar hate, or dislike at least. The object of that dislike is Edgar Lee Masters, American poet and lawyer who died March 5, 1950.

After reading from the poetry of Masters before a meeting of a men's service club, I met a visitor in the group who came up to tell this story.[3] He had landed in New York from his native Helsinki, Finland, only a few days before. Shortly after docking he went to a metropolitan bookstore and asked for a copy of *Spoon River Anthology* by Edgar Lee Masters. To his utter

[1] These footnotes are meant for guidance as a reader presents this lecture-recital. They are only suggestions, nothing more. The reader must make his own interpretation. He must obtain the necessary permissions from copyright owners whose names may be found among the acknowledgments at the beginning of the book.

[2] An introduction should give the audience an opportunity to get acquainted with the speaker as well as to prepare the way for the literature he is going to read. Be as personal, direct, and informal as you can. See Chapter 6.

[3] The purpose of this story is to emphasize the importance of Masters.

amazement, the bookseller replied that he had never heard of the book nor its author. The Finn explained that in his country Masters is considered a foremost American poet along with Poe and Whitman and that his book is readily available in Finnish.

It is this book I want to tell you about.[4] It is a collection of fictitious inscriptions from tombstones. They are fictitious in the sense that only one, to my knowledge, has ever been seen on a tombstone. They are not fictitious in another sense, for the people about whom they were written actually did live. They dwelt in the villages and countryside along the Spoon River. Herein lies the reason for the dislike people along the Spoon yet feel for Edgar Lee Masters. You see, Masters recorded the faults and foibles of his subjects as well as their virtues. Today the grandchildren still resent the frankness with which he treated the hopes, failures, and faults of their forebears. Sometimes he was kindly, but more often than not his penetrating insight was sharp and cruel. The bitter humor of this first inscription will show you what I mean.

DEACON TAYLOR

I [5] belonged to the church,
And to the party of prohibition;
And the villagers thought I died of eating watermelon.
In truth I had cirrhosis of the liver,
For every noon for thirty years,
I slipped behind the prescription partition
In Trainor's drug store
And poured a generous drink
From the bottle marked [6]
"Spiritus frumenti."

In contrast Masters wrote an inscription for Lincoln's childhood sweetheart, who also lived along the Spoon. This tribute is so gentle and beautiful that it has been placed over the grave of Anne Rutledge. We must digress for a moment to hear a story about this strange grave. At the age of nineteen Anne died in 1835 at New Salem. Her body was taken across the Sangamon River to a cemetery about seven miles away. There it lay for over fifty years until an enterprising promoter determined to start a new cemetery on a hill between what was left of New Salem and the up-and-

[4] Employ a strictly oral style: simple vocabulary and simple sentence structure.

[5] The manner of reading the first three lines is matter of fact, perhaps even a little sanctimonious. The rest is read with an air of cynical revelation of a secret.

[6] Pause significantly here, and then read the last line slowly and clearly in order that its point may not be missed.

coming town of Petersburg. In search of a way to give his project publicity, he crossed the river, traversed the miles, and dug into the almost forgotten grave of Anne Rutledge. Bringing back a few handfuls of dust and some pearl buttons, he buried them in his new cemetery and announced to the world that here lay the mortal remains of Lincoln's sweetheart. Since that day the great of many lands have stood over the dust and pearl buttons and entertained solemn thoughts of the Lincoln romance. While the story of how the grave came here may seem sordid, the majestic inscription on the marble monument surmounting the grave and enclosed with an iron fence is beautiful and inspiring.

ANNE RUTLEDGE[7]

Out of me unworthy and unknown
The vibrations of deathless music; [8]
"With malice toward none, with charity for all."
Out of me the forgiveness of millions toward millions [9]
And the beneficent face of a nation
Shining with justice and truth.
I [10] am Anne Rutledge who sleep beneath these weeds,
Beloved in life of Abraham Lincoln,
Wedded to him, not through union,
But through separation.
Bloom [11] forever, O Republic,
From the dust of my bosom!

In the same cemetery where one may see the inscription over the grave of Anne Rutledge, he may also come upon the two graves of Lucinda and Davis Masters, paternal grandparents of the poet. He has erected a simple stone for them, but in *Spoon River Anthology* he immortalized them as Lucinda and Davis Matlock. Here is the inscription he wrote for Lucinda. The towns mentioned in the poem are still to be visited in the country of the Spoon and Sangamon rivers. On the lips of his pioneer grandmother Masters has placed a challenge to "degenerate sons and daughters" of our own day.

[7] This is the most musical and has the most exalted content of all the epitaphs. Sustain the vowels and emphasize the musical quality.

[8] End this line with a slightly rising inflection and then a decided pause to call attention to Lincoln's quotation. Distinguish the quotation with a slightly different quality of voice and with special emphasis upon the thought-centers of "malice" and "charity."

[9] This three-line sentence should be read more emphatically than any part heretofore and should achieve a climax of intensity at the end.

[10] Try to employ a gentle touch in these four lines. Use a distinct pause at each comma.

[11] Emphasize the dedication expressed in the ending by using a fuller, more resonant voice and slower rate.

LUCINDA MATLOCK [12]

I went to the dances at Chandlerville,
And played snap-out at Winchester.[13]
One time we changed partners,
Driving home in the moonlight of middle June,
And then I found [14] Davis.
We were married and lived together for seventy years,[15]
Enjoying, working, raising the twelve children,[16]
Eight of whom we lost
Ere I had reached the age of sixty.
I [17] spun, I wove, I kept the house, I nursed the sick,
I made the garden, and for holiday
Rambled over the fields where sang the larks,
And by Spoon River gathering many a shell,
And many a flower and medicinal weed—
Shouting to the wooded hills, singing to the green valleys.[18]
At ninety-six I had lived enough, that is all,
And passed to a sweet repose.
What [19] is this I hear of sorrow and weariness,
Anger, discontent and drooping hopes?
Degenerate [20] sons and daughters,
Life is too strong for you— [21]
It takes life to love Life.

Carl Hamblin is also buried in Spoon River. He was the editor of the *Spoon River Clarion,* and through him Masters gave voice to his outraged social conscience. Hamblin too lived by some other name.

[12] It will help in reading Lucinda's epitaph to remember that a sweet and kindly old lady is speaking. Try to give the lines a quality of reminiscence by making the fullest possible use of imagery: there is great joy in remembering. Strive for an appearance of spontaneity.

[13] Find out all you can about place names and customs in order to make them real to you.

[14] This is the ideal place for a short but eloquent dramatic pause.

[15] Make the sound of the last two words long and tender, for they carry a wealth of living.

[16] Here you may use a hesitant pause, for it is not easy to relate tragedy.

[17] The next six lines are filled with generalized images and may be read a little more rapidly than the earlier ones.

[18] Make a long, pregnant pause in which you think the thought of the next two lines before you say them.

[19] Here Lucinda addresses herself more directly to the reader. It seems she is aware of the tiny frustrations each of us so often overemphasizes.

[20] Read this condemnation with more loudness than any other part of the poem.

[21] Use a long pause here and then repeat the moral of the poem quietly and distinctly. Be sure to pause after the first "life" and emphasize "takes" and "love" as the thought-centers.

CARL HAMBLIN

The [22] press of the Spoon River Clarion was wrecked,
And I was tarred and feathered,
For publishing this on the day the Anarchists were
Hanged in Chicago:
"I [23] saw [24] a beautiful woman with bandaged eyes
Standing on the steps of a marble temple.
Great multitudes passed in front of her,
Lifting their faces to her imploringly.
In her left [25] hand she held a sword.
She was brandishing [26] the sword,
Sometimes striking a child, again a laborer,
Again a slinking woman, again a lunatic.
In her right [27] hand she held a scale;
Into the scale pieces of gold were tossed
By those who dodged the strokes of the sword.
A man in a black gown read from a manuscript:
'She [28] is no respecter of persons.'
Then [29] a youth wearing a red cap
Leaped to her side and snatched away the bandage.
And [30] lo, the lashes had been eaten away
From the oozy eye-lids;
The eye-balls were seared with a milky mucus;
The madness of a dying soul
Was written on her face—
But the multitude saw why she wore the bandage." [31]

Using fictitious names gave the poet an opportunity sometimes to apply descriptive ones. Silas Dement must have been all that the name implies, but we think that he actually lived, and we know that the courthouse in this epitaph actually existed. Certainly Joliet, Illinois, is real too: it is the home of the state penitentiary. This inscription offers all the plot and excitement of a good short story, plus a typical O. Henry surprise ending.

[22] Use a forceful touch and a normal quality for the first four lines.

[23] This editorial was undoubtedly written under pressure of very intense feeling. Try to experience that feeling as you read.

[24] Do not neglect the imagery.

[25, 26, 27] Opportunities for restricted gesture!

[28] Use a very forceful touch. Perhaps you can reveal the cynicism of the editorial writer by showing it in your face.

[29] These two lines are exciting and must be read tensely and rapidly.

[30] These last six lines are designed to excite revulsion: read them slowly, emphatically, and point up the ugly thought-centers by lengthening the duration of the words.

[31] Hold the attention of your audience through an extended pause at the end of the poem: look into their faces.

SILAS DEMENT [32]

It [33] was moon-light, and the earth sparkled
With new-fallen frost.
It was midnight and not a soul was abroad.
Out of the chimney of the court-house
A grey-hound of smoke leapt and chased
The northwest wind.
I [34] carried a ladder to the landing of the stairs
And leaned it against the frame of the trap-door
In the ceiling of the portico,
And I crawled under the roof and amid the rafters
And flung among the seasoned timbers
A lighted handful of oil-soaked waste.
Then I came down and slunk away.
In [35] a little while the fire-bell rang—
Clang! Clang! Clang!
And the Spoon River ladder company
Came with a dozen buckets and began to pour water
On the glorious bon-fire, growing hotter,
Higher and brighter,[36] till the walls fell in,
And the limestone columns where Lincoln stood
Crashed like trees when the woodman fells them . . .
When [37] I came back from Joliet
There was a new court-house with a dome.
For [38] I was punished like all who destroy
The past for the sake of the future.

The epitaph for Stephen Spalding reminds us of Thomas Gray's romantic lines: "Full many a gem of purest ray serene the dark unfathomed caves of ocean bear." Spalding was a small town philosopher with all the

[32] With a rising inflection, raised eyebrows, and a smile you can reveal the significance of the man's name.

[33] Try to convey the furtive quality of the man by reading the first six lines rapidly as you "see" the scene before you. The lines may be almost whispered.

[34] The speaker is obsessed with his cleverness and reevals by his manner that he is anxious to tell the story.

[35] The following five and one-half lines are climactic, and you can show the incendiary's delight with eyes, a smile, and short, quick breaths as he speaks excitedly.

[36] Slow the pace and try to show the man's awe at the destruction.

[37] Here is an opportunity for you the reader to show that you are still at the helm. Insert rising inflections in this line, especially in "Joliet," to call attention to the irony.

[38] Here again you the reader may insert your special reactions to the story. Is not the last sentence both true in general and idiotic under these circumstances?

wisdom of a St. Francis and gave Masters another opportunity for social criticism.

STEPHEN SPALDING

Have [39] you considered, passer-by,
That all your laws and ethics
Are founded upon [40] "Thou shalt nots," [41]
And [42] are given for enforcement
The hateful handles of courts,
And of ostracisms, and of persecutions,
And of excommunications,
To crush into submission,
And to make into one image
The variable and fluid stuff of life?
And [43] that if any of these "Thou shalt nots,"
With their courts and ostracisms,
Were intended to support the great "Thou shalt"
Of "Love one another,"
That the intention failed through the hatred and strife
Of enforcing "Thou shalt nots"?
"Thou [44] shalt not make graven images"
Has [45] soaked the earth with blood.
"Love [46] one another" never made a wound,
Nor dimmed an eye with sorrow!

Above the village of Bernadotte on the banks of the river another philosopher used to sit and fish and think. He thought about Christian Dallman, a rich and prospering farmer, and Felix Schmidt, a little farmer. One had profited at the other's loss, and Schroeder the fisherman told the story on his tombstone, or rather Masters wrote it for the anthology.

[39] Speak out abruptly and forcefully as if you are calling out to stop a "passer-by."
[40] Dramatic pause.
[41] Should not you inflect this just the way you would the end of a question?
[42] These seven lines ought to be read quickly and with a forceful touch. The speaker is aggressive.
[43] Begin slowly, but quickly build to approximately the same rate and loudness used in the previous sentence. Be sure to make the quotations stand out by means of a slight pause both before and after. Notice that the quotations must be gently read.
[44] In keeping with the nature of a patriarchal god, read this line authoritatively, in a loud voice, and perhaps with a slightly pompous quality.
[45] Intimate and direct, with a sense of horror.
[46] Gentleness personified!

SCHROEDER THE FISHERMAN

I [47] sat on the bank above Bernadotte
And dropped crumbs in the water,
Just to see the minnows bump each other,
Until the strongest got the prize,
Or I went to my little pasture,
Where the peaceful swine were asleep in the wallow,
Or nosing each other lovingly,
And emptied a basket of yellow corn,
And watched them push and squeal and bite,
And trample each other to get the corn.
And [48] I saw how Christian Dallman's farm,
Of more than three thousand acres,
Swallowed the patch of Felix Schmidt,
As a bass will swallow a minnow.
And [49] I say if there's anything in man—
Spirit, or conscience, or breath of God
That makes him different from fishes or hogs,
I'd like to see it work!

In the days of Spoon River and indeed up to our own day, the question of man's origin has been the favorite of controversy and unhappily sometimes the downfall of our vaunted ideals of liberty and tolerance. Because she had the courage to bring truth as she saw it into the classroom, Catherine Ogg, teacher, was ousted from the Spoon River School.

CATHERINE OGG

"Tombstone" Johnson,[50] head of the school board,
Ashamed that he sprang from an egg,
And a wriggling sperm,

[47] The first ten lines may best be read as informally as possible.

[48] These four lines are intense by contrast with the first part. Use a great deal of intensity but restrain it to express anger and condemnation. Show the meaning in your face.

[49] Now the philosopher's verdict! Still intense but more quiet. See if you can show the speaker's cynicism as he recalls the exalted names for conscience: the very words are distasteful to him. The last two lines may amount to an almost explosive fury.

[50] See if you can express bitterness in Johnson's nickname. The first eight lines express a matter-of-fact displeasure in reminiscence. Be sure to get the cynical emphasis in the thought-centers.

But proud that man was created from dust,
Though dust is dirtier than eggs,
Ousted me from my place in the school
For showing a picture to the pupils
Of a child emerging from an egg shell,
And [51] telling them all the beauty and wonder
Of evolution that makes a mind
Out of an egg and sperm.
So [52] I retired and struggled along,
And starved a little, and brooded much
To the end of the farce!

Barn dances are still common in many parts of rural America, but in the old Spoon River times they constituted a major source of entertainment. Fiddler Jones provided the music for dancing at Little Grove not far from New Salem and many other spots near the Spoon. On his stone he defended himself against those who thought him a happy-go-lucky ne'er-do-well. On his lips Masters places the genuinely poetic expression of a man whose life was a failure by worldly standards but who would not, had he the chance, change the slightest feature of it. See if you can hear some of the brilliant sound images in the poem.

FIDDLER JONES

The earth keeps some vibration going
There in your heart, and that is you.
And if the people find you can fiddle,
Why, fiddle you must, for all your life.
What do you see, a harvest of clover?
Or a meadow to walk through to the river?
The wind's in the corn; you rub your hands
For beeves hereafter ready for market;
Or else you hear the rustle of skirts
Like the girls when dancing at Little Grove.
To Cooney Potter a pillar of dust
Or whirling leaves meant ruinous drouth;
They looked to me like Red-Head Sammy
Stepping it off, to "Toor-a-Loor."

[51] These three lines have none of the disillusionment of the earlier part: let your voice and face say "reverence" and "beauty." The pitch will probably be somewhat higher and the touch gentler.

[52] You can show the defeat and fatigue of the last lines by decreasing resonance, lower pitch, and a slow, halting rate.

How [53] could I till my forty acres
Not to speak of getting more,
With a medley of horns, bassoons and piccolos
Stirred in my brain by crows and robins
And the creak of a wind-mill—only these?
And [54] I never started to plow in my life
That some one did not stop in the road
And take me away to a dance or picnic.
I [55] ended up with forty acres;
I ended up with a broken fiddle—
And a broken laugh, and a thousand memories,
And [56] not a single regret.

Of all American poetry perhaps *Spoon River Anthology* is the best demonstration that poetry need not be just hearts and flowers. Masters wanted to speak out against the social sin of war, and so he chose Harry Wilmans, Spanish-American-War veteran who actually lived under some other name, and caused him to give voice to this epitaph. We can accept the story and the sentiment as genuine to the nth degree.

HARRY WILMANS

I [57] was just turned twenty-one,
And Henry Phipps, the Sunday-school superintendent,
Made a speech in Bindle's Opera House.
"The [58] honor of the flag must be upheld," he said,
"Whether it be assailed by a barbarous tribe of Tagalogs
Or the greatest power in Europe."
And [59] we cheered and cheered the speech and the flag he waved
As he spoke.
And [60] I went to the war in spite of my father,
And followed the flag till I saw it raised

[53] Can you sense that this old man is trying to justify his life? This five-line question is a pleading one, calling for approval.

[54] This sentence may be read with a flat, slow finality.

[55] These three lines bespeak the tragic conception of Jones that his neighbors must have shared. Use many downward inflections.

[56] Raise the pitch slightly and employ upward inflections together with appropriate facial expressions to make this line express the fiddler's satisfaction with his life.

[57] Perhaps you can express the disillusionment of the first three lines by using a near monotone and monorate.

[58] Cynicism of face, body, and voice!

[59] See if you can suggest cheers and waving in the way you say the words.

[60] This sentence ought to return to approximately the same rate and rhythm and tone as the first.

By our camp in a rice field near Manila,
And [61] all of us cheered and cheered it.
But there were flies and poisonous things;
And there was the deadly water,
And the cruel heat,
And the sickening, putrid food;
And the smell of the trench just back of the tents
Where the soldiers went to empty themselves;
And there were the whores who followed us, full of syphilis;
And beastly acts between ourselves or alone,
With bullying, hatred, degradation among us,
And days of loathing and nights of fear
To the hour of the charge through the steaming swamp,
Following [62] the flag,
Till [63] I fell with a scream, shot through the guts.
Now there's a flag over me in Spoon River!
A Flag! A flag!

Less than twenty miles from the valley of the Spoon is the little city of Galesburg, Illinois. Here Carl Sandburg once lived, and here his home may yet be seen. Sandburg is something of a rarity among writers, for he is "not without honor" in his own time and country. Now past the three-quarter-century mark, he has long since achieved pioneer status in the free verse movement. While perhaps not the free and outspoken writer at all times, as Masters is, he may be more the authentic artist. Being a poet of social criticism too, he seems most effective when dealing with deep-seated controversial problems.

Among his less well-known poems is this violent, uninhibited attack upon religious evangelists of the Billy Sunday variety. Although you may find it shocking, you must at the same time find it compelling and thought-provoking.

TO A CONTEMPORARY BUNKSHOOTER

You [64] come along . . . tearing your shirt . . . yelling about Jesus.
Where do you get that stuff?

[61] Fourteen lines of revulsion! Play up the images. Get empathy by expressing the revulsion with your body, primarily the face.

[62] Make the reading of this line and the word "flag" each time it appears in the following lines as intense as you can. Say it with an effort, a wrench.

[63] Brutal!

[64] These first three lines seem to require a very forceful touch, with a rather low pitch, and a hard, aggressive quality.

What do you know about [65] Jesus?

Jesus had a way of talking soft and outside of a few bankers and higher-ups among the conmen of Jerusalem everybody liked to have this Jesus around because he never made any fake passes and everything he said went and he helped the sick and gave the people hope.

You [66] come along squirting words at us, shaking your fist and calling us all damn fools so fierce the froth slobbers over your lips . . . always blabbing we're all going to hell straight off and you know all about it.

I've read Jesus' words. I know what he said. You don't throw any scare into me. I've got your number. I know how much you know about Jesus.

He never came near clean people or dirty people but they felt cleaner because he came along. It was your crowd of bankers and business men and lawyers hired the sluggers and murderers who put Jesus out of the running.

I say the same bunch backing you nailed the nails into the hands of this Jesus of Nazareth. He had lined up against him the same crooks and strong-arm men now lined up with you paying your way.

This Jesus was good to look at, smelled good, listened good. He threw out something fresh and beautiful from the skin of his body and the touch of his hands wherever he passed along.

You slimy bunkshooter, you put a smut on every human blossom in reach of your rotten breath belching about hell-fire and hiccupping about this Man who lived a clean life in Galilee.

Go [67] ahead and bust all the chairs you want to. Smash a whole wagon load of furniture at every performance. Turn sixty somersaults and stand on your nutty head. If it wasn't for the way you scare the women and kids I'd feel sorry for you and pass the hat.

I like to watch a good four-flusher work, but not when he starts people puking and calling for the doctors.

I like a man that's got nerve and can pull off a great original performance, but you—you're only a bug-house peddler of second-hand gospel—you're only shoving out a phoney imitation of the goods this Jesus wanted free as air and sunlight.

[65] Perhaps you should pause momentarily here, and certainly you should use a gentler touch, a higher pitch, and a more relaxed quality. The following six lines seem to call for this same gentleness.

[66] Aggressive again! Search for other places where your voice and manner will call attention to the contrast between Jesus and the "bunkshooter": there are many of them, and they are very important.

[67] You can catch the excitement of the "bunkshooter" at work if you will read at a fast, even rate.

You tell people living in shanties Jesus is going to fix it up all right with them by giving them mansions[68] in the skies after they're dead and the worms have eaten 'em.
You tell $6 a week department store girls all they need is Jesus; you take a steel trust wop, dead without having lived, gray and shrunken at forty years of age, and you tell him to look at Jesus on the cross and he'll be all right.
You tell poor people they don't need any more money on pay day and even if it's fierce to be out of a job, Jesus'll fix that up all right, all right—all they gotta do is take Jesus the way you say.
I'm telling you Jesus wouldn't stand for the stuff you're handing out. Jesus played it different. The bankers and lawyers of Jerusalem got their sluggers and murderers to go after Jesus just because Jesus wouldn't play their game. He didn't sit in with the big thieves.

I don't want a lot of gab from a bunkshooter in my religion.
I won't take my religion from any man who never works except with his mouth and never cherishes any memory except the face of the woman on the American silver dollar.
I ask you to come through and show me where you're pouring out the blood of your life.
I've[69] been to this suburb of Jerusalem they call Golgotha, where they nailed Him, and I know if the story is straight it was real blood ran from His hands and the nail-holes, and it was real blood spurted in red drops where the spear of the Roman soldier rammed in between the ribs of this Jesus of Nazareth.

From a relatively unknown product of Sandburg's pen we turn to his most famous poem, "Chicago." The strangest thing about "Chicago" is that whether the author is being thoroughly condemned or highly praised this poem is commonly quoted as evidence. Incidentally, it settled for all time the question of whether poetry must have "poetic" words and "poetic" subject matter. The slaughter pens of the Southside of Chicago and illicit behavior on State Street are not normal "poetic" content.

CHICAGO[70]

Hog Butcher for the World,
Tool Maker, Stacker of Wheat,

[68] Perhaps you can simulate the inflectional pattern of fluent evangelism here. Be sure you become abruptly direct with the word "after." The same contrast is used in the following two sentences also.

[69] The style of this last sentence seems to suggest an almost impromptu manner, as if these are deep convictions here voiced for the first time.

[70] To read this poem well, you must work out a whole series of vivid images. The object is to say the lines in a way consistent with the images.

Player with Railroads and the Nation's Freight Handler;
Stormy, husky, brawling,
City of the Big Shoulders:
They tell me you are wicked and I believe them,[71] for I have seen your painted women under the gas lamps luring the farm boys.
And they tell me you are crooked [72] and I answer: Yes, it is true I have seen the gunman kill and go free to kill again.
And they tell me you are brutal [73] and my reply is:
On the faces of women and children I have seen the marks of wanton hunger.
And [74] having answered so I turn once more to those who sneer at this my city, and I give them back the sneer and say to them:
Come [75] and show me another city with lifted head singing so proud to be alive and coarse and strong and cunning.
Flinging magnetic curses amid the toil of piling job on job, here is a tall bold slugger set vivid against the little soft cities;
Fierce as a dog with tongue lapping for action, cunning as a savage pitted against the wilderness,
Bareheaded,
Shoveling,
Wrecking,
Planning,
Building, breaking, rebuilding,
Under the smoke, dust all over his mouth, laughing with white teeth,
Under the terrible burden of destiny laughing as a young man laughs,
Laughing even as an ignorant fighter laughs who has never lost a battle,
Bragging and laughing that under his wrist is the pulse, and under his ribs the heart of the people,
Laughing!
Laughing the stormy, husky, brawling laughter of Youth, half-naked, sweating, proud to be Hog Butcher, Tool Maker, Stacker of Wheat, Player with Railroads and Freight Handler to the Nation.

As is typically the case with truly sensitive people, Carl Sandburg ponders the problem of modern war. He takes a powerful slap at the horrible, impersonal nature of war in this short and vivid bit of free verse.

[71] and [72] Each of these spots makes a contrast between ugly criticism and quiet, assured defense.

[73] Same as 71 and 72 contrasting ugly criticism and quiet, assured defense.

[74] Here is a sentence which may begin quietly and calmly but mounts to an intense challenge. Adjust your reading accordingly.

[75] The rest of the poem is confident and proud, the speaker glorying in his thoughts. Your images will remain the source of your vocal and visible variety.

BUTTONS

I [76] have been watching the war map slammed up for advertising in front of the newspaper office.
Buttons—red and yellow buttons—blue and black buttons—are shoved back and forth across the map.

A [77] laughing young man, sunny with freckles,
Climbs a ladder, yells a joke to somebody in the crowd
And then fixes a yellow button one inch west
And follows the yellow button with a black button one inch west.
(Ten [78] thousand men and boys twist on their bodies in a red soak along a river edge,
Gasping of wounds, calling for water, some rattling death in their throats.) [79]
Who [80] would guess what it cost to move two buttons one inch on the war map here in front of the newspaper office where the freckle-faced young man is laughing to us?

If you have ever been frustrated with the life you live, if you have ever longed for new and different settings, routines, and horizons, you will especially appreciate the story of "Mamie." Its tragedy is not unique.

MAMIE

Mamie beat her head against the bars of a little Indiana town and dreamed of romance and big things off somewhere the way the railroad trains all ran.[81]
She could see the smoke of the engines get lost down where the streaks of steel flashed in the sun, and when the newspapers came in on the morning mail she knew there was a big Chicago far off, where all the trains ran.[82]
She [83] got tired of the barber-shop boys and the post-office chatter and the

[76] Here are two long lines which are as nearly without emotion as lines can possibly be. The manner is that of an objective news report.

[77] The next four lines are characterized by the carefree attitude of the "laughing young man." Use a medium fast rate, a slightly higher than average pitch, and rising inflections.

[78] Contrast: slower rate, lower pitch, downward inflections, and perhaps a somewhat gentle touch.

[79] Increase loudness to a climax here.

[80] Tragedy: quiet and intense.

[81] Throw to the reader in one thrust the whole impact of Mamie's frustration by reading the first sentence as one thought-group.

[82] This is the first climax: pause.

[83] Emphasize the monotonous rhythm of the lines down through "herself."

church gossip and the old pieces the band played on the Fourth of July
 and Decoration Day,
And sobbed at her fate and beat her head against the bars and was going to
 kill herself [84]
When the thought came to her that if she was going to die she might as well
 die struggling for a clutch of romance among the streets of Chicago.[85]
She [86] has a job now at six dollars a week in the basement of the Boston Store
And even now she beats her head against the bars in the same old way and
 wonders if there is a bigger place the railroads run to from Chicago [87]
 where maybe there is
  romance
  and big things
  and real dreams
  that never go smash.

Last among the "Cornfield Poets" whom we are meeting now is Vachel Lindsay. Lincoln's Springfield is his city too. Indeed he is the favorite of Springfield, second only to Lincoln. There was something about his contagious enthusiasm and sincerity that fascinated his friends and arrests his readers.

We might call him the poet of the "three R's": rime, religion, and ragtime. He was poet, evangelist, and troubadour. He proved again and conclusively that poetry is fundamentally an oral art. His form is not new, for it is a revival of the old and illustrious ode—an oral form popular in the Middle Ages. Indeed he went about reading his poetry in much the same fashion as the medieval troubadour, exchanging his spoken verses for food and lodging.

The poetry has its faults: it has been, in fact, almost as widely condemned as praised. He was not always a careful artist but sometimes a sensationalist in both form and content. On the other hand, the virtues of his poetry are inescapable: the infectious and impulsive rhythm is often thought superior to that of anything else in the language. Furthermore, you may rest assured that whatever Lindsay says, it is deeply sincere.

His reading was characterized by an unlimited variety of both voice and manner. His voice encompassed an enormous range of pitch, quality, rate, and volume, and his action was confined only by the limits of the room in which he spoke. You might say that he employed a vaudeville form: one-third spoken, one-third sung, and one-third pantomime.

[84] Now make a contrast by using a pause, a gentler touch, and a slower rate.

[85] This seems to be the second climax: a long pause.

[86] Here is emotional depression in Mamie's return to her routine of frustration.

[87] You can interpret this as the third and last climax and read the last four short lines in a series of falling pitch steps.

"General William Booth Enters into Heaven," one of Lindsay's best-known poems, is a story of the Salvation Army. This is, of course, the organization characterized by black bonnets and caps, tambourines, cymbals, banjos, and drums, which has brought religion to the poorest, the lowest, and the most forsaken of society. Lindsay pays tribute, as any thoughtful man must, to the great spirit of evangelism characterized in General William Booth, founder of the Salvation Army. In the story he is an aged figure with sightless eyes and flowing beard leading a marching, motley crew into heaven. And heaven is in the form of a Middle Western county seat with its city square lorded over by the courthouse. There is gentle good humor in the story, but it is submerged in the poet's admiration for courageous evangelism. Be sure to give your imagination free rein as Lindsay vividly suggests the sight, sound, and rhythmic motion of Booth's fantastic horde marching into heaven.

GENERAL WILLIAM BOOTH ENTERS INTO HEAVEN[88]

(To be sung to the tune of "The Blood of the Lamb" with indicated instrument)

I

(*Bass drum beaten loudly.*)

Booth led boldly with his big bass drum—
(Are [89] you washed in the blood of the Lamb?)
The Saints smiled gravely and they said, "He's come."
(Are you washed in the blood of the Lamb?)
Walking [90] lepers followed, rank on rank,
Lurching bravoes from the ditches dank,
Drabs from the alleyways and drug fiends pale—
Minds still passion-ridden, soul powers frail:—
Vermin-eaten saints with moldy breath,
Unwashed legions with the ways of Death—
(Are you washed in the blood of the Lamb?)

[88] It is nearly impossible to tell you how to read the ragtime poetry of Lindsay. Throw your inhibitions away and give full expression to the insistent rhythm—nothing less than a chant will sometimes suffice. One caution: your listeners will find the rhythm more acceptable if you develop it slowly and do not begin in full swing.

[89] This frequent refrain is an aside and is almost sung, except in the last instance of the line, when the reader may choose to ask the question directly of the audience.

[90] Remember the imagery: it is abundant and essential. Assume the rhythm of tramping feet.

(*Banjos*)

Every [91] slum had sent its half a score
The round world over. (Booth had groaned for more.)
Every banner that the wide world flies
Bloomed with glory and transcendent dyes.
Big-voiced lasses made their banjos bang,
Tranced, fanatical, they shrieked and sang:—
"Are you washed in the blood of the Lamb?"
Hallelujah! It was queer to see
Bull-necked convicts with that land make free.
Loons with trumpets blew a blare, blare, blare
On, on upward thro' the golden air!
(Are you washed in the blood of the Lamb?) [92]

II

(*Bass drum slower and softer*)

Booth [93] died blind and still by Faith he trod,
Eyes still dazzled by the ways of God.
Booth led boldly, and he looked the chief
Eagle countenance in sharp relief,
Beard a-flying, air of high command
Unabated in that holy land.

(*Sweet flute music*)

Jesus [94] came from out the courthouse door,
Stretched his hands above the passing poor.
Booth saw not, but led his queer ones there
Round and round the mighty courthouse square.[95]
Yet in an instant all that blear review
Marched on spotless, clad in raiment new.
The lame were straightened, withered limbs uncurled
And blind eyes opened on a new, sweet world.

(*Bass drum louder*)

Drabs and vixens in a flash made whole!
Gone was the weasel head, the snout, the jowl!
Sages and sibyls now, and athletes clean,
Rulers of empires, and of forests green!

[91] The regular rhythm is relieved at places with lines like this. Lengthen the words.
[92] A climax of rate and intensity!
[93] More quiet and reverent.
[94] Even more reverent. Use a gentle touch.
[95] A climax of quiet intensity. The following lines express a kind of exaltation in the miracle. Rising inflections may help you to voice the wonder. Your face must show it too.

(*Grand chorus of all instruments. Tambourines to the foreground*)

The [96] hosts were sandaled, and their wings were fire!
(Are you washed in the blood of the Lamb?)
But [97] their noise played havoc with the angel choir.
(Are you washed in the blood of the Lamb?)
Oh,[98] shout Salvation! It was good to see
Kings and Princes by the Lamb set free.
The banjos rattled and the tambourines
Jing-jing-jingled in the hands of Queens.[99]

(*Reverently sung, no instruments*)

And [100] when Booth halted by the curb for prayer
He saw his Master thro' the flag-filled air.
Christ [101] came gently with a robe and crown
For Booth the soldier, while the throng knelt down.
He [102] saw King Jesus. They were face to face,[103]
And he knelt a-weeping in that holy place.
Are you washed in the blood of the Lamb? [104]

Now imagine that we are going to a ramshackle church somewhere in the deep South where an ignorant but eloquent minister is exhorting his audience. With a text from the classic *Uncle Tom's Cabin* he paints a surprisingly inviting picture of the "horrors" of hell.

*SIMON LEGREE ** A NEGRO SERMON*[105]

from *The Booker Washington Trilogy*

Legree's big house was white and green.
His cotton-fields were the best to be seen.
He had strong horses and opulent cattle,

[96] Now for the celebration, for real enthusiasm.

[97] See if you can read this line with gentle humor at the thought of the shouting army competing with the angel choir.

[98] Forceful.

[99] Another climax.

[100] This should be read in a voice and manner quite the opposite of the previous line. Sustain the vowels.

[101] Devout.

[102] Quite gentle.

[103] The last contrast: pause and read the last two lines quietly and reverently.

[104] If you have read well, your audience will want time to ponder the gospel invitation of the last line and then to return to you.

[105] This poem calls for a great degree of impersonation: in so far as you seem able to get audience acceptance, become the preacher. Use the chanting rhythm and a deep, full, resonant voice.

And bloodhounds bold, with chains that would rattle.
His garret was full of curious things:
Books of magic, bags of gold,
And rabbits' feet on long twine strings.
But [106] *he went down to the devil.*

Legree he sported a brass-buttoned coat,
A snake-skin necktie, a blood-red shirt.
Legree he had a beard like a goat,
And a thick hairy neck, and eyes like dirt.
His puffed-out cheeks were fish-belly white,
He had great long teeth, and an appetite.
He ate raw meat, 'most every meal,[107]
And rolled his eyes till the cat would squeal.
His fist [108] was an enormous size
To mash poor niggers that told him lies:
He was surely a witch-man in disguise.
But he went down to the devil.

He wore hip-boots, and would wade all day
To capture his slaves that had fled away.
But he went down to the devil.

He beat poor Uncle Tom to death
Who prayed for Legree with his last breath.
Then Uncle Tom to Eva flew,
To the high sanctoriums bright and new;
And Simon Legree stared up beneath,
And cracked his heels, and ground his teeth:
And went down to the devil.

He crossed the yard in the storm and gloom;
He went into his grand front room.
He said, "I killed him, and I don't care."
He kicked a hound, he gave a swear;
He tightened his belt, he took a lamp,[109]
Went down cellar to the webs and damp.
There in the middle of the mouldy floor

[106] This refrain is always heavy and ominous.

[107] This previous part has provided an opportunity to achieve a very rapid rate. Then, at this spot change to a slow, drawn-out one. Use your eyes.

[108] Use generous visible action here and at just about every opportunity.

[109] About here the story can become quite eerie, not unlike a child's ghost story.

He heaved up a slab, he found a door—
And went down to the devil.

His lamp blew out, but his eyes burned bright.
Simon Legree stepped down all night—
Down, down to the devil.

Simon Legree he reached the place,
He saw one half of the human race,
He saw the Devil on a wide green throne,
Gnawing the meat from a big ham-bone,
And he said to Mister Devil:
"I [110] see that you have much to eat—
A red ham-bone is surely sweet.
I see that you have lion's feet;
I see your frame is fat and fine,
I see you drink your poison wine—
Blood and burning turpentine."

And the Devil said to Simon Legree:
    "I [111] like your style, so wicked and free.
    Come sit and share my throne with me,
    And let us bark and revel."

[112]And there they sit and gnash their teeth,
And each one wears a hop-vine wreath.
They are matching pennies and shooting craps,
They are playing poker and taking naps.
And old Legree is fat and fine:
He eats the fire, he drinks the wine—
Blood and burning turpentine—
    Down,[113] *down with the devil.*
        Down, down with the devil.
            Down, down with the devil.

Lest you think him superficial, we must hasten to say that Lindsay was more than an advocate of ragtime, no matter how successful he was in that respect. With an amazing lack of discrimination he exalts a thousand

[110] Try to use a voice which bespeaks the cocky, insolent conceit of Simon.

[111] Perhaps the Devil would beam on Simon, almost laugh his approval.

[112] Now the preacher returns from the narrative proper to address himself to his audience and describe the "horrors" of hell.

[113] See if you can read these three refrains in a pattern of falling pitch steps and a decreasing rate.

heroes and expounds a thousand causes, but none more enthusiastically nor with more apparent sincerity than the cause of peace and human brotherhood. "Sew the Flags Together" is as significant and as appealing as it was forty years ago. It was addressed then to the young people and might well be heard by today's youth.

SEW THE FLAGS TOGETHER

(Written for William Stanley Braithwaite's
Victory Anthology issued at once, after
Armistice Day, November, 1918)

Great wave of youth, ere you be spent,
Sweep over every monument
Of caste, smash every high imperial wall
That stands against the new World State,
And overwhelm each ravening hate,
And heal, and make blood-brothers of us all.
Nor let your clamor cease
Till ballots conquer guns.
Drum on for the world's peace. . . .
Sew the flags together.
Do not tear them down.

The following two poems are considered by many the best of Lindsay. The first of the two is not remarkable so much for its form, although that form is appropriate and musical, but rather for its profound thought. It is an expression of a philosophy of life which was close to the poet's heart. Look for the three symbols he uses: dew for beauty, rain for physical sustenance, and moonlight for rest.

A NET TO SNARE THE MOONLIGHT

(What the Man of Faith Said) [114]

The dew, the rain and moonlight
All prove our Father's mind.
The dew, the rain and moonlight
Descend to bless mankind.

Come, let us see that all men
Have land to catch the rain,

[114] This poem is marked with an ethereal quality which calls for delicacy of treatment.

Have grass to snare the spheres of dew,
And fields spread for the grain.

Yea, we would give to each poor man
Ripe wheat and poppies red,—
A peaceful place at evening
With the stars just overhead:

A net to snare the moonlight,
A sod spread to the sun,
A place of toil by daytime,
Of dreams when toil is done.

Last and best is "The Congo," which is an amazingly successful attempt to incorporate in English the insistent, savage beat of aboriginal music and the spirit of the African jungle. Seeing young Negroes dancing and singing in an old warehouse somewhere in America, the poet conjures up their ancestors as they beat out the same rhythm on the banks of the Congo River. He incorporates into words the climactic sound and action of the drums and dance. There is one symbol you should be aware of before hearing "The Congo." The mad elephant, which no man can stop or escape, is said to represent death to the primitive African as surely as a skull and crossbones mean death to us.

from THE CONGO

A STUDY OF THE NEGRO RACE [115]

Fat black bucks in a wine-barrel room,
Barrel-house kings, with feet unstable,
Sagged and reeled and pounded on the table, *A deep rolling bass.*
Pounded on the table,
Beat an empty barrel with the handle of a broom,
Hard as they were able,
Boom, boom, BOOM,
With a silk umbrella and the handle of a broom,
Boomlay, boomlay, boomlay, BOOM.[116]
THEN I had religion, THEN I had a vision.
I could not turn from their revel in derision.
THEN [117] I SAW THE CONGO, CREEPING *More deliberate. Solemnly chanted.*
THROUGH THE BLACK,

[115] The techniques of reading this poem are much like those suggested for "General William Booth Enters into Heaven." We shall make only a few comments, for this is much too complex for brief printed analysis. Notice Lindsay's marginal notes.

[116] Climax.

[117] Full, deep, resonant voice in a slow and sustained rhythm. Draw out the vowels.

CUTTING THROUGH THE FOREST WITH A
GOLDEN TRACK.
Then [118] along that river bank
A thousand miles
Tattooed cannibals danced in files;
Then [119] I heard the boom of the blood-lust song
And [120] a thigh-bone beating on a tin-pan gong.
And "BLOOD" [121] screamed the whistles and the fifes
of the warriors,
"BLOOD" screamed the skull-faced, lean witchdoctors,
"Whirl [122] ye the deadly voo-doo rattle,
Harry the uplands,
Steal all the cattle,
Rattle-rattle, rattle-rattle,
Bing.[123]
Boomlay, boomlay, boomlay, BOOM,"
A [124] roaring, epic, rag-time tune
From the mouth of the Congo
To the Mountains of the Moon.
Death [125] is an Elephant,
Torch-eyed and horrible,
Foam-flanked and terrible.
BOOM, steal the pygmies,
BOOM, kill the Arabs,
BOOM, kill the white men,
HOO,[126] HOO, HOO.
Listen to the yell of Leopold's ghost
Burning in Hell for his hand-maimed host.
Hear [127] how the demons chuckle and yell
Cutting his hands off, down in Hell.
Listen [128] to the creepy proclamation,
Blown through the lairs of the forest-nation,
Blown past the white-ants' hill of clay,

A rapidly piling climax of speed and racket.

With a philosophic pause.

Shrilly and with a heavily accented metre.

Like the wind in the chimney.

[118] Here are three lines of short quick vocal strokes.

[119] Much slower.

[120] Faster.

[121] Pitch this cry as high as you can, and the next one too.

[122] Lindsay read these four lines in a nassal voice and at a rapid rate.

[123] He read "Bing" with a very high and resonant nasality so that it sounded metallic.

[124] Conversational, very little resonance, most of the tones confined to the mouth.

[125] Six lines without a falter in the rhythm.

[126] A high pitched, song-like call.

[127] Let the demoniac sound and fury mount through "Hell" in the next line: climax again.

[128] Begin this line in the quiet and eerie voice suggestive of fear and let it increase in intensity through four lines.

Blown past the marsh where the butter-flies play:—
"Be [129] careful what you do,
Or Mumbo-Jumbo, God of the Congo,
And all of the other
Gods of the Congo,
Mumbo-Jumbo will hoo-doo you,
Mumbo-Jumbo will hoo-doo you,
Mumbo-Jumbo will hoo-doo you."

All the "o" sounds very golden. Heavy accents very heavy. Light accents very light. Last line whispered.

Suggested Readings

Eastman, Max. *The Enjoyment of Poetry—with Anthology.* New York: Scribner, 1951.

Engle, Paul. "The Source of Poetry," *College English* (March 1940), pp. 471–80.

Gwynn, Frederick L., Ralph W. Condee, and Arthur O. Lewis, Jr. *The Case for Poetry.* Englewood Cliffs, N.J.: Prentice-Hall, 1954.

Lee, Charlotte I. *Oral Interpretation.* (Second edition) Boston: Houghton Mifflin, 1959, Part Four, "The Interpretation of Poetry."

Lowrey, Sara, and Gertrude E. Johnson. *Interpretative Reading.* (Revised edition) New York: Appleton-Century-Crofts, 1953, Chapter V, "Structure in Interpretative Reading."

Parrish, Wayland Maxfield. *Reading Aloud.* (3rd edition) New York: Ronald Press, 1953, Chapter VII, "Verse," Chapter IX, "Poetry."

Rosenthal, M. L., and A. J. M. Smith. *Exploring Poetry.* New York: Macmillan, 1955.

Stageberg, N. C., and W. L. Anderson. *Poetry As Experience.* New York: American Book, 1952.

Wood, Clement. *Poets' Handbook.* New York: World, 1940.

[129] This quotation is meant to be a native chant and can grow in rate and volume through the next to the last line, after which it can subside in a slow whisper. It is a mixture of trochaic and iambic feet, regular and insistent.

15

SUGGESTIONS ON THE INTERPRETATIVE READING OF DRAMA

Most of us enjoy plays as they unfold on stage, radio, television, or film, but comparatively few persons enjoy reading a play from a book. Play reading requires a greater imaginative effort than story reading. Whereas the story writer or novelist *tells* a story, the dramatist *presents* it, in dialogue form, without much descriptive, expository, or analytical embellishment. As readers of dramatic literature we must apply our imaginations to the words of the characters and the author's brief stage directions and permit the characters to enact their story on an imaginary stage within ourselves. We must actively visualize the play rather than passively permit a writer to tell it to us. In short, we must be creative. Thus, the reading of a play requires more time and effort than most persons are willing to give during their recreational hours.

We might well ask, then: Why read plays? The reason is simply stated by John Gassner, in the volume *The Wonderful World of Books:* "Some of the greatest minds and spirits have expressed themselves in plays." This critic and scholar points out that the best-known writers in English, French, German, and Scandinavian are the dramatists: Shakespeare, Shaw, T. S. Eliot, O'Neill, Molière, Goethe, Schiller, and Ibsen, to name only a few. Not only have the greatest minds spoken to us in drama, but some of man's best thoughts, finest expressions of feeling, and most brilliant imaginative characters appear in drama.

The next question to answer is: Why read plays to other persons? There are many good reasons. First, plays are written to be spoken and to be heard; they are intended to receive audible and visible communicative treatment rather than to lie inert as mere symbols upon the printed page. Second, plays have a definite audience appeal. Good plays come to us tested by an audience. Given an adequate presentation, they obtain favorable responses. Third, plays are—and there seems to be no other way of saying this!—plays are *dramatic*. They are concise, concrete, and suspenseful. They possess colorful characters and interest-holding conflicts and situations. Fourth, the greatest plays contain the greatest of man's poetry. It is in this fine combination of poetry and drama that we recognize the supremacy of Shakespeare. Fifth, the oral interpreter can "produce" a play upon the imaginative stages of his listeners' minds without having to use the trappings of the physical stage. Instead of being burdened with scenery, costume, make-up, properties, and lighting, he needs only a manuscript, himself, and an audience. We do not say that drama should be read aloud rather than acted; we do contend that it is excellent for interpretative reading as well as for the theatre. Furthermore, many persons who are unable to see plays enacted in the theatre will enjoy hearing them read well aloud. Sixth, practice in the interpretative reading of plays is the best possible training for the student actor. Of course, he should learn to read all kinds of literary materials, but experience in reading dramatic lines will enable him to deal more effectively with them on the stage.

The basic techniques for the reading of drama are largely the same as those for reading other forms of literature; however, the reading of drama does require much skill and technical preparation not discussed elsewhere in this text. The following suggestions should prove helpful:

SELECTING THE DRAMATIC SCENE

Select scenes from plays which are strong in plot, character, mood, thought, and/or language, for these are aspects which the oral reader can handle with some degree of efficiency. Dialogue which advances the plot is interesting to listen to. Character and mood are elements which can be developed as easily by the reader as by the actor. Plays which communicate considerable thought make excellent material for the oral reader, and those which are rich in language, particularly poetry, cannot be surpassed as literature for oral communication.

You should avoid selecting plays which are highly dependent on physical activity and/or the visible trappings of the stage, such as costumes, properties, or scenery. It should be evident that the reader has a difficult time trying to suggest much action, although he can suggest a minimal amount. Of course, you should never waste your efforts trying to read a play which cannot really be appreciated except when aided by the stage technician's visible and audible effects. Spectacles, costume dramas, and period pieces do not make good material for the reader.

Two other suggestions concerning the selection of dramatic materials should be heeded. Simplify your task immeasurably by selecting scenes in which only one, two, or three characters appear, for it is quite difficult for the reader to handle more than this number, even though good readers often do manage it. Read good plays rather than those insignificant ones produced on many high school stages. Hundreds of good plays are available. Do not waste your time and the audience's time with a poor play.

STUDYING THE PLAY

Dramatic structure is among the most difficult of literary forms for the writer to master, and it is not simple for the student to study. Of particular significance is a study of organization: the development of dramatic action in acts and scenes. An essential element of drama is conflict—increasing tensions which create climaxes. Not only does the play as a whole have a major climax, or turning point, but also each act and each scene within the act has a climax. You should prepare to build this climax in your reading and also be aware of the relationship of the scene you are reading to the play as a whole.

Mood is another major consideration in drama. Every good dramatic scene has a predominant mood and undoubtedly also subtle changes in mood wrought by the relationships of the characters.

Probably most important in the understanding of a play is an understanding of the characters. Fortunately, several avenues are available for the study of characterization: what the characters say and do, what other characters say about them, what the author says in his play directions, and what literary and theatre critics say in their reviews of the play.

Too many amateurs wish to read or act a play without conducting a thorough study of the play, which is laziness or willful ignorance, or both.

ADAPTING THE SCENE FOR READING

As a reader of dramatic literature you will almost certainly be faced with the necessity for cutting the selection. Nonessential, confusing, or unnecessarily time-consuming material will have to be pruned from the play script. Easiest to cut are the author's play directions. Anything essential in them will usually be presented to the audience in an introduction or in transitions between scenes. (We must admit that a few dramatists—Shaw, for example—have written play directions of literary quality, worth reading aloud, but these are rather rare.) Other items fairly easy to omit are lines which are meaningful only to the entire play and meaningless in a short scene prepared for oral reading. Similarly, lines and even characters which do not advance the scene or are likely to confuse the listener can be deleted. One should be careful, however, not to distort the playwright's intentions or impair the action of the play. Each cut should have a sound reason behind it, and the final product should be consistent with the purpose of the original play. Although the beginner usually feels that the cutting of a single line constitutes a butchery of the play, limitations in time, space, and activity often require the interpretative reader to cut the dramatic scene for reading to an audience.

SUGGESTING THE DRAMA

You will recall that in Chapter 1 we said that the short aesthetic distance of the usual reading situation forces the reader to suggest rather than to portray in order to be most effective. The reading of dramatic scenes offers a great temptation to the reader to forget the powers of imaginative suggestion and to try to *show* the characters to the audience. Of course, dramatic literature does permit a relatively high degree of impersonative treatment, with more pronounced audible and visible characterization than is suitable with other materials. The reader should consider himself a purveyor of *interior* rather than *exterior* drama. He should be an effective reporter of a dramatic scene he sees in his "mind's eye."

This means that the reader will never turn a profile to the audience to make one character appear to talk to another character on the platform. The audience would then logically expect to see the other character also on the platform. Instead, the reader uses the technique, previously described in Chapter 13, of directing each character's lines over the heads of the audience in one specific direction: Character A, slightly to the left of the center of the back wall of the room; Character B, slightly to the right, and so on. Sometimes, readers will choose not to separate the characters in this way and will direct all characters straight down the middle of the room. They are sometimes successful readers but they assume an additional burden of suggesting each character vividly in other ways, audible and visible. The point is: the simple technique of separating characters works for most readers of drama.

SUGGESTING CHARACTER

The chief problem of the interpretative reader of drama is usually the suggestion of character. Unlike the actor, who has plenty of time with no distractions, the reader must be able to suggest two or more characters instantly, switching back from one character to another, and without the assistance of make-up, costumes, gross pantomime, or scenic effects. He does this through much practice and the ability to switch his concentration instantaneously. His techniques are: characteristic body and facial tone, slight suggestive action and facial expression, characteristic voice quality, pitch key, pitch pattern, rate of speaking, rhythm of speaking, use of pauses and duration, degree of loudness, and use of touch. To handle these well requires a skill just as great, and probably greater, than that of the actor. We think you can easily see why training in interpretative reading should be good for aspiring actors.

A common pitfall of the reader of drama is to seize upon some distinctive visual or vocal characteristic and to depend on it alone to communicate a character rather than to develop a deep interior conception of the character and to suggest the character in depth. The result is a stereotype, or stock character—a flat cardboard figure—rather than a rounded, breathing being. Of course, sometimes good dramatists will create stock characters purposely (witness the gangsters in *Mrs. McThing*), but most characters in good plays have three dimensions instead of two. Any reader who treats Brady in *Inherit the Wind* as merely a stereotyped political windbag will fail to suggest the intended tragedy of his breakdown in the courtroom. We cannot feel sorry for a piece of cardboard. The reader, as well as the actor, must make his characters human.

INTERACTION OF CHARACTERS

Characters in plays, like persons in actual life, not only speak to each other, they also listen to each other: one may react to another while he is speaking. Whereas the poor reader of drama merely speaks lines, the effective reader reads dialogue in such a way as to suggest that each character reacts to the other's words. This reaction comes fleetingly, just as the character begins to speak, reacting to the previous line. This must be planned, practiced, and then strongly experienced during the reading. It is easy for one actor to react to another actor; it is much harder for the interpretative reader to suggest multiple characters reacting to each other.

KEEPING IT MOVING

A dramatic scene must *move,* not bog down. Actors learn to pick up the cues by starting to speak as the last word of the preceding line is uttered. Similarly, the interpretative reader must also pick up cues quickly or the scene will drag. The reader who has to look back at his script for every line can hardly be effective. Therefore, you will have to know your drama script well. Study thoroughly and practice much.

MULTIPLE READING

In recent years readers have experimented a great deal with multiple reading of literature: two or more readers functioning together. This has resulted in many forms of presentation, called by a variety of names. In the reading of plays by several readers, the form is commonly called Readers' Theatre. Within the compass of this term, there are also many forms of presentation, reflecting the originality of those participating. Such experimentation often results in effective reading productions of all forms of literature.

There are really no rules for multiple reading performances. Most persons who try Readers' Theatre eventually subscribe to the notion that the techniques of interpretative reading rather than those of acting are appropriate. Thus, readers still suggest, rather than portray, characters, even though they now face a stronger temptation to portray because they are usually reading only one character at a time, instead of two or more, and because other readers are present reading the lines of other characters. Participants in such productions should be on guard against too strong an identification with the character and also the tendency to "play to" the other readers instead of reading to an audience.

The world of multiple reading is wide open, awaiting exploration. Perhaps you will wish to team up with another member of your class and try some form of it for a classroom exercise.

A READING PROGRAM OF A SCENE FROM *TIGER AT THE GATES* [1]

As World War II began in Europe, the French playwright, Jean Giraudoux, wrote a new version of the events leading to the Trojan War, in which he compared war to a tiger lurking at the gates. No matter how hard man tries (and sometimes he does not try very hard), he cannot keep the tiger out: war is inevitable. The play, translated into English by Christopher Fry and titled *Tiger at the Gates,* contains many memorable characters in brilliantly conceived scenes. One of the most interesting scenes is the one in which Hector, son of King Priam, who is trying to avert war with the Greeks, attempts to convince Helen to leave her lover, Paris, and return to her Greek husband, Menelaus.

Hector is a sensitive, peace-loving, modern soldier in ancient armor. Helen, traditionally the ultimate in feminine seductiveness, seems in this play to be a mixture of the beautiful-but-dumb and the beautiful-and-intelligent woman.

HECTOR. Is Greece a beautiful country? [2]

HELEN. Paris found it ravishing.[3]

HECTOR. I meant is Greece itself beautiful, apart from Helen? [4]

HELEN. How very charming of you.[5]

HECTOR. I was simply wondering what it is really like.[6]

HELEN. Well, there are quite a great many kings, and a great many goats, dotted about on marble.[7]

~~HECTOR. If the kings are in gold, and the goats angora, that would look pretty well when the sun was rising.~~

~~HELEN. I don't get up very early.~~

~~HECTOR. And a great many gods as well, I believe? Paris tells me the sky is crawling with them; he tells me you can see the legs of goddesses hanging down from the clouds.~~

[1] This program is intended only for purposes of illustration and instruction. Its inclusion in this textbook gives no one the right to read it publicly without permission from Samuel French, Inc. (25 West 45th Street, New York 36, New York).

[2] Hector is merely starting a conversation.

[3] Helen begins to play with Hector, immediately, with her reference to her own beauty and power over men. A pause before "ravishing" and a good deal of attention to the meaning of the word could help to make the line quite effective.

[4] Is Hector gracious, patronizing, or sarcastic? It makes a great deal of difference in how the line is read.

[5] The meaning of "charming" depends on Hector's specific meaning in the preceding line, for Helen is reacting to Hector's words.

[6] Are the sparks flying already?

[7] Helen continues to play with Hector.

~~HELEN. Paris always goes about with his nose in the air. He may have seen them.~~

~~HECTOR. But you haven't?~~

~~HELEN. I am not gifted that way. I will look out for them when I go back there again.~~[8]

HECTOR. You were telling Paris you would never be going back there.

HELEN. He asked me to tell him so. I adore doing what Paris wants me to do.[9]

HECTOR. I see. Is that also true of what you said about Menelaus? Do you not, after all, hate him? [10]

HELEN. Why should I hate him?

HECTOR. For the one reason which might certainly make for hate. You have seen too much of him.

HELEN. Menelaus? Oh, no! I have never seen Menelaus. On the contrary.[11]

HECTOR. You have never seen your husband? [12]

HELEN. There are some things, and certain people, that stand out in bright colours for me. They are the ones I can see. I believe in them. I have never been able to see Menelaus.[13]

~~HECTOR. Though I suppose he must have come very close to you sometimes.~~

~~HELEN. I have been able to touch him. But I can't honestly tell you I saw him.~~

~~HECTOR. They say he never left your side.~~

~~HELEN. Apparently. I must have walked across him a great many times without knowing it.~~[14]

HECTOR. Whereas you have seen Paris.[15]

HELEN. Vividly; in the clearest outline against the sky and the sun.[16]

HECTOR. Does he still stand out as vividly as he did? Look down there: leaning against the rampart.[17]

HELEN. Are you sure that's Paris, down there? [18]

HECTOR. He is waiting for you.

[8] These lines are cut because they do not significantly advance the scene. In order to condense a scene to fit time limits, the reader cuts nonessential material, while taking care not to distort the author's purpose.

[9] Is Helen teasing Hector, or could she already be a bit bored with Paris?

[10] Hector asks a leading question with all the finesse of a trial lawyer.

[11] Helen seems casual in this reply, but she has a subtle meaning for "seen."

[12] Hector knows she has seen him. He is not shocked, surprised, or confused. Rather, he is making a sarcastic statement, not asking a question.

[13] Now, Helen puts the full meaning into "see Menelaus."

[14] These lines are cut for the same reason as the previous cutting.

[15] "Paris" receives the emphasis of contrast with "Menelaus."

[16] Helen continues to play with words. Her excessive gusto reveals her insincerity.

[17] Hector senses that she has lost her enthusiasm for Paris.

[18] Mockingly?

~~HELEN. Good gracious! He's not nearly as clear as usual!~~

~~HECTOR. And yet the wall is freshly whitewashed. Look again: there he is in profile.~~[19]

HELEN. It's odd how people waiting for you stand out far less clearly than people you are waiting for.[20]

HECTOR. Are you sure that Paris loves you? [21]

HELEN. I don't like knowing about other people's feelings. There is nothing more embarrassing. Just as when you play cards and you see your opponent's hand. You are sure to lose.

HECTOR. What about yourself? Do you love him?

HELEN. I don't much like knowing my own feelings either.

HECTOR. But, listen: when you make love with Paris, when he sleeps in your arms, when you are circled round with Paris, overwhelmed with Paris, haven't you any thoughts about it? [22]

HELEN. My part is over. I leave any thinking to the universe. It does it much better than I do.[23]

HECTOR. Have there been many others, before Paris? [24]

HELEN. Some.[25]

HECTOR. And there will be others after him, wouldn't you say, as long as they stand out in clear relief against the sky, or the wall, or the white sheets on the bed? It is just as I thought it was. You don't love Paris particularly, Helen; you love men.[26]

HELEN. I don't dislike them. They're as pleasant as soap and a sponge and warm water; you feel cleansed and refreshed by them.[27]

~~HECTOR. Cassandra! Cassandra!~~

~~CASSANDRA (entering). What do you want?~~ [28]

HECTOR. ~~Cassandra,~~ Helen [you are] going back this evening with the Greek ambassador.

HELEN. I? What makes you think so?

HECTOR. Weren't you telling me that you didn't love Paris particularly?

HELEN. That was your interpretation. Still, if you like.[29]

[19] A small pruning of the script.

[20] Which "you" and which "for" receive the major emphasis of the sentence? Again, she is being clever.

[21] What is the important word?

[22] Hector is boring in on his cross-examination.

[23] An extreme effort to be casual.

[24] Hector is becoming ruthless.

[25] She admits no more than is necessary.

[26] Nasty. Hector builds one climax at the end of the first sentence and an even bigger one at the end of the speech.

[27] Helen answers very quickly and gets a laugh from the audience. Then, she pauses and philosophizes, again.

[28] This cut and the redirection of the next speech enable us to eliminate a character who is not vital to this scene.

[29] On which word would extended duration be most effective?

HECTOR. I quote my authority. You have the same liking for men as you have for a cake of soap.

HELEN. Yes; or pumice stone perhaps is better. What about it? [30]

HECTOR. Well, then, you're not going to hesitate in your choice between going back to Greece, which you don't mind, and a catastrophe as terrible as war?

HELEN. You don't understand me at all, Hector. Of course I'm not hesitating. It would be very easy to say 'I will do this or that, so that this can happen or that can happen.' You've discovered my weakness and you are overjoyed. The man who discovers a woman's weakness is like the huntsman in the heat of the day who finds a cool spring. He wallows in it. But you mustn't think, because you have convinced me, you've convinced the future, too. Merely by making children behave as you want them to, you don't alter the course of destiny.

HECTOR. I don't follow your Greek shades and subtleties.

HELEN. It's not a question of shades and subtleties. It's no less than a question of monsters and pyramids.[31]

HECTOR. Do you choose to leave here, yes or no? [32]

HELEN. Don't bully me. I choose what happens in the way I choose men, or anything else. I choose whatever is not indefinite and vague. I choose what I see.[33]

HECTOR. I know, you said that: what you see in the brightest colours. And you don't see yourself returning to Menelaus in a few days' time? [34]

HELEN. No. It's very difficult.[35]

HECTOR. We could no doubt persuade your husband to dress with great brilliance for your return.[36]

HELEN. All the purple dye from all the murex shells in the sea wouldn't make him visible to me.[37]

HECTOR. Here you have a rival, Cassandra. Helen can read the future, too.

HELEN. No, I can't read the future. But when I imagine the future some of the pictures I see are coloured, and some are dull and drab. And up to now it has always been the coloured scenes which have happened in the end.[38]

[30] Her manner must infuriate Hector by this time.

[31] Another cut, merely to shorten the scene. It is regrettable that good lines must be sacrificed, but this is inevitable.

[32] Almost a violent outburst. Hector's intellectualism is nearly lost in his exasperation.

[33] Helen blasts back at him, losing her composure, momentarily. Then, she speaks emphatically.

[34] Very sarcastic on the first sentence. The last sentence gets back to the argument.

[35] A pause before "difficult" emphasizes the inadequacy of the word.

[36] The sarcasm now becomes almost playful.

[37] Very dramatic manner.

[38] Pruning, as before.

HECTOR. We are going to give you back to the Greeks at high noon, on the blinding sand, between the violet sea and the ochre-coloured wall. We shall all be in golden armour with red skirts; and my sisters, dressed in green and standing between my white stallion and Priam's black mare, will return you to the Greek ambassador, over whose silver helmet I can imagine tall purple plumes. You see that, I think? [39]

HELEN. No, none of it. It is all quite sombre.

HECTOR. You are mocking me, aren't you? [40]

HELEN. Why should I mock you? Very well, then. Let us go, if you like! Let us go and get ready to return me to the Greeks. We shall see what happens.[41]

~~HECTOR. Do you realize how you insult humanity, or is it unconscious?~~

~~HELEN. I don't know what you mean.~~[42]

HECTOR., You realize that your coloured picture-book is holding the world up to ridicule? While we are all battling and making sacrifices to bring about a time we can call our own, there are you, looking at your pictures which nothing in all eternity can alter. What's wrong? Which one has made you stop and stare at it with those blind eyes? I don't doubt it's the one where you are standing here on the ramparts, watching the battle going on below. Is it the battle you see?

HELEN. Yes.[43]

HECTOR. And the city is in ruins or burning, isn't that so?

HELEN. Yes. It's a vivid red.

HECTOR. And what about Paris? You are seeing his body dragged behind a chariot?

HELEN. Oh, do you think that is Paris? I see what looks like a flash of sunlight rolling in the dust. A diamond sparkling on his hand. Yes, it is! Often I don't recognize faces, but I always recognize the jewelry. It's his ring, I'm quite certain.[44]

HECTOR. Exactly. Do I dare to ask you about Andromache, and myself, the scene of Andromache and Hector? You are looking at us. Don't deny it. How do you see us? Happy, grown old, bathed in light? [45]

HELEN. I am not trying to see it.[46]

[39] This is Hector's big speech, emphasizing all the colors. Climax is reached in the last sentence. Hector is probably visibly tired when he asks the question at the end.

[40] Helen's obstinacy has finally got the best of him.

[41] A sudden reversal: an "All right, I'll prove it!" manner.

[42] More pruning.

[43] She pretends to see something she really does not see.

[44] Helen is apparently becoming entangled in Hector's net.

[45] A fast rate. He is boring in.

[46] She balks at playing the game further.

HECTOR. The scene of Andromache weeping over the body of Hector, does that shine clearer?

HELEN. You seem to know. But sometimes I see things shining, brilliantly shining, and they never happen. No one is infallible.[47]

HECTOR. You needn't go on. I understand. There is a son between the weeping mother and the father stretched on the ground? [48]

HELEN. Yes. He is playing with his father's tangled hair. He is a sweet boy.[49]

HECTOR. And these scenes are there in your eyes, down in the depths of them. Could I see them there? [50]

HELEN. I don't know. Look.[51]

HECTOR. Nothing. Nothing except the ashes of all those fires, the gold and the emerald in dust. How innocent it is, this crystal where the future is waiting. But there should be tears bathing it, and where are they? Would you cry, Helen, if you were going to be killed? [52]

HELEN. I don't know. But I should scream. And I feel I shall scream if you go on at me like this, Hector. I am going to scream.[53]

HECTOR. You will leave for Greece this evening, Helen, otherwise I shall kill you.[54]

HELEN. But I want to leave! I'm prepared to leave. All that I'm trying to tell is that I simply can't manage to distinguish the ship that is going to carry me there. Nothing is shining in the least, ~~neither the metal on the mast, nor the ring in the captain's nose, nor the cabin-boy's eyes, nor anything.~~[55]

HECTOR. You will go back on a grey sea under a grey sun. But we must have peace.

HELEN. I cannot see peace.

~~HECTOR. Ask Cassandra to make her appear for you. Cassandra is a sorceress. She can summon up shapes and spirits.~~

~~A MESSENGER (entering). Hector, Priam is asking for you. The priests are opposed to our shutting the Gates of War. They say the gods will consider it an insult.~~

~~HECTOR. It is curious how the gods can never speak for themselves in these difficult matters.~~

[47] The emptiness of her answer proves she sees nothing.

[48] Hector is revealing his *own* visions of the future.

[49] Embellishing a scene she does not see.

[50] A climax of tension.

[51] "Look" must convey a tremendous amount of meaning, possibly: "Look for yourself, Hector. So many men have found something in my eyes."

[52] A long pause before "Nothing." A slow rate during the second sentence. His manner changes abruptly with "But there should be tears. . . ." He ends with a hint of the threat to come.

[53] Near panic.

[54] Strong, virile, commanding.

[55] Helen begins to break. The cutting was also made in the professional acting edition of the play.

~~MESSENGER. They have spoken for themselves. A thunderbolt has fallen on the temple, several men have been killed, the entrails of the victims have been consulted, and they are unanimously against Helen's return to Greece.~~

~~HECTOR. I would give a good deal to be able to consult the entrails of the priests . . . . I'll follow you.~~

~~(The MESSENGER goes)~~ [56]

Well, now, Helen, do we agree about this?

HELEN. Yes.[57]

HECTOR. From now on you will say what I tell you to say? You will do what I tell you to do?

HELEN. Yes.

HECTOR. ~~Do you hear this, Cassandra?~~ Listen to this solid wall of negation which says Yes! They have all given in to me. Paris has given in to me, Priam has given in to me, Helen has given in to me. And yet I can't help feeling that in each of these apparent victories I have been defeated. You set out, thinking you are going to have to wrestle with giants; you brace yourself to conquer them, and you find yourself wrestling with something inflexible reflected in a woman's eye. ~~You have said yes beautifully, Helen, and you're brimful of a stubborn determination to defy me!~~ [58]

A SUGGESTED LIST OF PLAYWRIGHTS FOR ORAL INTERPRETATION

Aeschylus
Anderson, Maxwell
Anouilh, Jean
Aristophanes
Barrie, James M.
Brecht, Bertolt
Capote, Truman
Capek, Karel
Chayefsky, Paddy
Chekhov, Anton
Eliot, T. S.
Euripides
Fry, Christopher
Galsworthy, John
Giraudoux, Jean
Green, Paul
Hart, Moss, and George S. Kaufman
Hellman, Lillian
Howard, Sidney
Ibsen, Henrik
Inge, William
Ionesco, Eugène

[56] These lines are essential to the play as a whole but not to this scene as a psychological unit.

[57] Helen's meanings for this and the following "Yes" may be far from simple. A short word with complex meanings is among the most difficult of lines to interpret. The final sentence of Hector's last speech in this scene may give a clue.

[58] Hector realizes he has won an intellectual fray, but that fate has ruled him the loser in his struggle for peace. His last sentence is cut because it points ahead to additional dialogue and dramatic action. The previous sentence provides a potent ending to this scene.

Lorca, Federico García
Lindsay, Howard, and Russel Crouse
MacLeish, Archibald
Marlowe, Christopher
Miller, Arthur
Molière
Nash, N. Richard
O'Casey, Sean
Odets, Clifford
O'Neill, Eugene
Saroyan, William
Sartre, Jean-Paul
Shakespeare, William
Shaw, George Bernard
Sheridan, Richard Brinsley
Sherwood, Robert
Sophocles
Strindberg, August
Synge, John Millington
Van Druten, John
Wilde, Oscar
Wilder, Thornton
Williams, Tennessee

Suggested Readings

Bacon, Wallace A., and Robert S. Breen. *Literature as Experience.* New York: McGraw-Hill, 1959, pp. 251–71.

Cobin, Martin. *Theory and Technique of Interpretation.* Englewood Cliffs, N.J.: Prentice-Hall, 1959, pp. 204–17.

Crocker, Lionel, and Louis M. Eich. *Oral Reading.* (2nd edition) Englewood Cliffs, N.J.: Prentice-Hall, 1955, Chapter X, "The Public Recital."

Grimes, Wilma H., and Alethea Smith Mattingly. *Interpretation: Writer, Reader, Audience.* Belmont, Cal.: Wadsworth, 1961, Chapter VII, "Drama."

Lee, Charlotte I. *Oral Interpretation.* (2nd edition) Boston: Houghton Mifflin, 1959, Part Three, "The Interpretation of Drama."

Parrish, Wayland Maxfield. *Reading Aloud.* (3rd edition) Ronald Press, 1953, Chapter XII, "Impersonation."

INDEX OF AUTHORS AND TITLES

INDEX OF TOPICS